FROMMER'S

COMPREHENSIVE TRAVEL GUIDE

Philadelphia

8th Edition

by Jay Golan

MACMILLAN • USA

About the Author

Jay Golan has been writing about travel in Europe, Asia, and the United States since college. Educated at Harvard, Oxford, and Columbia universities, he has worked for major cultural institutions in Boston and New York for over a decade, most recently on the Carnegie Hall centennial celebration. He and his young family live in New York City and frequently visit relatives and friends in Philadelphia.

MACMILLAN TRAVEL
A Simon & Schuster Macmillan Company
1633 Broadway
New York, NY 10019

ISBN 0-02-860051-7

ISSN 0899-3211

Design by Michele Laseau
Maps by Geografix Inc.

Special Sales

Bulk purchases (10+ copies) of Frommer's Travel Guides are available to corporations at special discounts. The Special Sales Department can produce custom editions to be used as premiums and/or for sales promotions to suit individual needs. Existing editions can be produced with custom cover imprints such as corporate logos. For more information write to: Special Sales, Simon & Schuster 1230 Avenue of the Americas, New York, NY 10020.
Manufactured in the United States of America

Contents

List of Maps

What the Symbols Mean

Frommer's Favorites Hotels, restaurants, attractions, and entertainments you should not miss.

Super-Special Values Really exceptional values.

In Hotel and Other Listings

The following symbols refer to the standard amenities available in all rooms:

A/C   air conditioning
MINIBAR   refrigerator stocked with beverages and snacks
TEL   telephone
TV   television

The following abbreviations are used for credit cards:

AE   American Express
CB   Carte Blanche
DC   Diners Club
DISC   Discover
ER   enRoute
JCB   Card
MC   MasterCard
V   Visa

Trip Planning with This Guide
USE THE FOLLOWING FEATURES:

What Things Cost   To help you plan your daily budget

Calendar of Events   To plan for or avoid

Suggested Itineraries   For seeing the city

What's Special About Checklist   a summary of the city's highlights

Easy-to-Read Maps   Walking tours, city sights, hotel and restaurant locations

Fast Facts   All the essentials at a glance: climate, currency, embassies, emergencies, information, safety, taxes, tipping, and more

Frommer's Smart Traveler Tips   Hints on how to secure the best value for your money

Invitation to the Reader

In researching this book, I have come across many wonderful establishments, the best of which I have included here. I am sure that many of you will also come across appealing hotels, inns, restaurants, guesthouses, shops, and attractions. Please don't keep them to yourself. Share your experiences, especially if you want to comment on places that have been included in this edition that have changed for the worse. You can address your letters to:

Jay Golan
Frommer's Philadelphia 8th Edition
c/o Macmillan Travel
15 Columbus Circle
New York, NY 10023

A Disclaimer

Readers are advised that prices fluctuate in the course of time, and travel information changes under the impact of the varied and volatile factors that influence the travel industry. Neither the author nor the publisher can be held responsible for the experiences of readers while traveling. Readers are invited to write to the publisher with ideas, comments, and suggestions for future editions.

Safety Advisory

Whenever you're traveling in an unfamiliar city or country, stay alert. Be aware of your immediate surroundings. Wear a moneybelt and keep a close eye on your possessions. Be particularly careful with cameras, purses, and wallets, all favorite targets of thieves and pickpockets.

1

Introducing Philadelphia

OLD HISTORY AND NEW EXCITEMENT—THESE ARE PHILADELPHIA TODAY. When you scratch the surface of William Penn's "Greene countrie town," you find a wealth of pleasures and pastimes.

Try these descriptions on for size: Philadelphia is the largest colonial district in the country, with dozens of treasures plus Independence National Historical Park. It boasts the most historic square mile in America, where the United States was conceived, declared, and ratified—and you can see the Liberty Bell to prove it. It offers some of the best dining values and several of the finest restaurants in America. It's a stroller's paradise of restored Georgian and Federal structures that are integrated with smart shops and contemporary row-house courts to create a working urban environment. Philadelphia is a center of professional and amateur sports, with over 7,000 acres of parkland within the city limits. And it's a city filled with art, crafts, and music for every taste, with boulevards made for street fairs and parades all year long.

Between postwar urban-renewal efforts and sprucing up for America's bicentennial in 1976, the Constitution's bicentennial in 1987, and the brand-new 1993 Pennsylvania Convention Center (10th largest in the nation), Philadelphia turned itself into an ideal vacation city. From row-house boutiques to the Second Continental Congress's favorite tavern, from an Ivy League campus to street artists and musicians, from gleaming skyscrapers to Italian marketplaces, Philadelphia is a city of gentle and easy living.

Even geographically, Philadelphia sits pretty. Some 60 miles inland, it's the country's busiest freshwater port, controlling the Delaware Valley. It's a natural stopping place between New York and Washington, D.C., with easy access by rail and road. And the casinos and beaches of Atlantic City, the revolutionary war sites of Valley Forge and Brandywine, Pennsylvania Dutch Country, and the great Du Pont family mansions all lie about an hour away. In fact, 38% of the nation's population is within a $4^1/_2$-hour drive from the city.

Economically, Philadelphia's a great deal too. A 1994 study of corporate travel showed that the city's average daily cost of lodging and meals—$132.50—was 51% of New York's, 68% of Washington's, and 78% of Boston's. Family-style travel is even more of a bargain.

1   Culture, History & Background

Geography/People

Philadelphia occupies a tongue of land at the confluence of the Delaware River—one of the largest U.S. rivers feeding into the Atlantic—and the Schuylkill River. The original settlement, and the heart of Center City today, is the band about five miles north that didn't dwindle into marshland in the 1600s. Since then, of course, the city has drained and used the entire tongue to the south and has exploded into the northeast and northwest.

The city and its region are flat and fertile ground. Philadelphia has traditionally looked south, to shipping and manufacturing along

3

What's Special About Philadelphia

Architectural Highlights
- Independence Hall (1732), with its classic, quiet magnificence.
- The Liberty Bell, always visible and always visited.
- The newly restored Fisher Fine Arts Library (1890), with gargoyles designed by Frank Furness on the University of Pennsylvania's campus.
- Christ Church (1744), at 2nd and Market, with its Palladian altar window—the wonder of the 1740s.
- Logan Square fountain, brilliantly landscaped.

Museums
- The Philadelphia Museum of Art and the Barnes Foundation.

Streets/Neighborhoods
- Society Hill and Independence National Historical Park, a square-mile chronicle of U.S. birth pangs.
- Boathouse Row, where the toy-village boathouses along the Schuylkill River twinkle every night.
- Olde City, with a working stone drinking fountain for horses.
- Head House Square, a covered market for provisions and crafts since the 1740s.
- South Philadelphia, the home of "pasta with red sauce."

Events/Festivals
- The Mummer's Parade, on New Year's Day.
- The Welcome America! celebration, just before July 4, with outdoor events of all types.

For the Kids
- The Zoo, the Please Touch Museum, and the rejuvenated Franklin Institute (see Chapter 7, "Cool for Kids").

Shopping
- Shops at Liberty Place, a gleaming new urban mall.
- Franklin Mills, off I-95, the world's largest outlet and entertainment center.

Natural Spectacles
- Along the Schuylkill River behind the Philadelphia Museum of Art, a springtime burst of thousands of azaleas and rhododendrons.
- Fairmount Park, 4,000 acres of greenery.

After Dark
- The world-famous Philadelphia Orchestra.

Literary Shrine
- The Rosenbach Museum, featuring original manuscript of *Ulysses* and first editions of Herman Melville.

Introducing Philadelphia Culture, History & Background

the Delaware, and west, to produce being brought across the Schuylkill from inland Pennsylvania. In the 19th century, the city improved on nature's fortunes through extensive canals and rail links that made it central to hundreds of miles of coal and oil fields, timberlands, and farms.

The waves of settlement and immigration witnessed by the area now known as Philadelphia are fascinating, starting with the Delaware or Lenape branch of the Algonquian Indians, who were found by the first European settlers from Sweden in the 1640s. Unusual tolerance, personified by Quakers, led to two separate strains of immigrants between this period and 1800. One was made up of entire European families of almost every sort—English, Scottish, Sephardic Jews, and German (*Deutsch* in German—whence the term Pennsylvania "Dutch")—who often made the decision to immigrate based on promises of cheap farmland. The other included thousands of London-based craftsmen, servants, and sailors who wanted to dwell in America's premier city.

After 1800, immigration was a push-pull thing; English commoners fled the industrialization of their countryside in the 1820s, Irish escaped from the 1840s potato famine, and waves of Germans and other central Europeans sought peace and stability throughout the 1870s. From the 1880s to the 1920s, Russians and Jews from eastern Europe, Italians, and free blacks from the American South all migrated in record numbers to the city. In recent years, Asian and Hispanic inflows have balanced the suburban outflow of descendants of earlier immigrants, creating a more multicultural Philadelphia than ever before. The classic pattern of these groups has been to stake out a section of the city as "home turf" in the first generation—South Philadelphia for Italians, South Street for Russian Jews, and North Philadelphia for blacks—and to move away from that section in later generations.

These various influences have shaped the modern city. To cite just one example, the Mummer's Parade mixes an English country-fair tradition with music of the black South of a century ago. The Philadelphia experience has not always been happy, however. The city has suffered from riots, protests, and bigotry along racial, religious, and economic lines. These have been most pronounced in times of economic distress.

Dateline

- **1644** William Penn born.
- **1682** The 300-ton *Welcome,* with William Penn aboard, lands at New Castle (Delaware). Penn rows up to the tongue of

➤

History/Politics

Although Philadelphia may conjure up thoughts of William Penn and the revolutionary period in the minds of most Americans, it was in fact a tiny group of Swedish settlers who first established a foothold here in the 1640s. (You can see models of the two ships that brought them over in the Gloria Dei Church.)

COLONIAL PHILADELPHIA   Where does William Penn fit in? Well, his father

Mid-Atlantic States

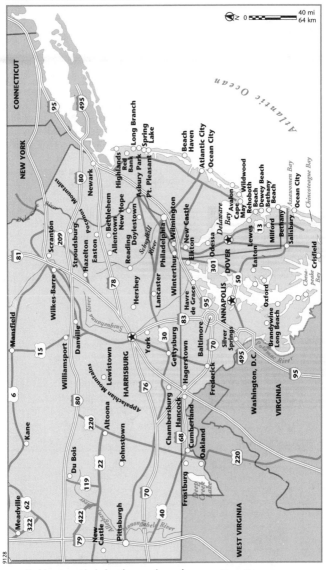

had been an admiral and a courtier under Charles II of England. The king was in debt to Admiral Penn, who died in 1670, and the younger Penn asked to collect the debt through a land grant on the west bank of the Delaware River, a grant that would eventually be named Pennsylvania, or "Penn's forest." At the time, Penn was in prison. His Quaker religion, anti-Anglican church attitudes, and contempt for

Dateline

land between the Delaware and Schuylkill rivers and names the area Philadelphia.

■ **1701** Penn leaves Philadelphia for the last time.

➤

Dateline

- 1718 William Penn dies in England.
- 1723 Sixteen-year-old Benjamin Franklin arrives by boat from Boston.
- 1745 Trim arcades of the Second Street Market, between Pine and Lombard streets, built to house market stalls.
- 1748 First Philadelphia Assembly, an annual ball that in the 1990s still represents "making it" in social circles.
- 1749 First theater company in the colonies opens.
- 1752 Franklin performs his kite-flying experiment, proving that lightning is a form of electricity, in an open field that's now the location of St. Stephen's Episcopal Church at 10th and Ludlow streets.
- 1755 Franklin and others open America's first hospital at 8th and Spruce streets.
- 1765 Mass protests on news of English Parliament's passage of the Stamp Act, with boycotts of imports and office "strikes."
- 1774 First Continental Congress held in the State House (now Independence Hall).

➤

authority had gotten him expelled from Oxford and arrested for conspiracy and "tumultuous assembling" numerous times. The chance for him to set up a utopia in the New World, based on Quaker principles, was too good to pass up. Since Swedish farmers owned most of the lower Delaware frontage, he decided to settle upriver, where the Schuylkill met the Delaware. The name he chose was Philadelphia—the City of Brotherly Love.

In 1982 Philadelphia celebrated its 300th anniversary, and—incredibly—Penn's original city plan still adequately described the Center City, down to the public parks and the site for City Hall. Because of London's terrible 1666 fire, exacerbated by narrow streets and semidetached wooden buildings, the founder figured that broad avenues and city blocks arranged in a grid were the safest answer here. As he intended to treat Native Americans and fellow settlers equally, he planned no city walls or neighborhood borders. Front Street, naturally, faced the Delaware, as it still does, and parallel streets were numbered until 24th Street and the Schuylkill. Streets running east to west were named after trees and plants (Sassafras became Race Street, for the horse-and-buggy contests run along it). To attract prospective investors, Penn promised bonus land grants in the "Liberties" (outlying countryside) to anyone who bought a city lot; he took one of the largest for himself, now Pennsbury Manor (26 miles north of town). Colonies were in the business of attracting settlers in those days, and Penn had to wear a variety of hats—those of financier, politician, religious leader, salesman, and manufacturer.

Homes and public buildings filled in the map, but slowly—that's why all the colonial row houses of Society Hill and Elfreth's Alley (continuously inhabited since the 1690s) are so near the Delaware docks. When he wrote the Declaration of Independence in 1776, almost a century later, Thomas Jefferson could still say of his boardinghouse on 7th and Market that it was away from the city noise and dirt! The city spread west to Broad Street even later, around 1800. Philadelphia grew along the river and not west as Penn had planned. Southwark, to the south, and the Northern Liberties, to the north, housed the less affluent, including most of the rougher sailors and their taverns set up in unofficial alleys. These were Philadelphia's first slums—unpaved, without public services, and populated by those without enough property or money to satisfy voting requirements.

Although Philadelphia had been founded after Boston and New York, manufacturing, financial services, excellent docking facilities, and fine Pennsylvania farm produce soon propelled it to the first city of the colonies—the largest English-speaking city in the British Empire except for London. Some 82 ships docked in 1682, in a cove that Dock Street has filled in and along docks at Front Street up to Vine. By 1770 the figure was 880 ships along 66 wharves.

Despite its urban problems, colonial Philadelphia was a thriving city in virtually every way, boasting public hospitals and streetlights; cultural institutions and newspapers; stately Georgian architecture and Chippendale furniture; imported tea and cloth; and, above all, commerce. William Penn put the stamp of his rough genius on the young city. However, the next generation turned away from his vision of brotherly love geographically, politically, and religiously, re-creating the institutions they had known in English towns. But in the third and fourth generations men like James Logan, the first Biddles, and David Rittenhouse proved even more influential in determining a distinct Philadelphia style—genial, cooperative, and relaxed, though without the later Main Line inbred gentility. Alexander Graydon, a journalist, wrote in 1811, "of all the cities in the world, Philadelphia was for its size, perhaps, one of the most peaceable and unwarlike."

Dateline

- **1776** Declaration of Independence debated and adopted on July 2.
- **1777** General Howe, moving up from Maryland, takes Germantown on October 4 and occupies Philadelphia soon after; members of the Continental Congress, with the Liberty Bell, flee to Lancaster.
- **1778** British troops abandon Philadelphia in June to advance on New York City.
- **1780** Pennsylvania becomes the first state to abolish slavery, calling for general emancipation by 1827.
- **1782** Bank of North America opens on the corner of Chestnut and Third streets
- **1787** Constitutional Convention meets in the State House.
- **1790–1800** Philadelphia is the capital of the United States.
- **1799** Private bathing becomes a fashion. Elizabeth Drinker writes, "I bore it better than expected, not having been wet all over once in my life."
- **1805** First permanent bridge spans ➤

Dateline

the Schuylkill,
connecting the city
to Pennsylvania's
rich farmlands.
- 1812–15 English
blockade of
international trade
shuts down
Philadelphia
shipping, though its
Navy Yard outfits
most of U.S. Navy.
- 1820s Transforma-
tion of the seaport
city into America's
first major
industrial city.
- 1832 Railroad to
Germantown built.
- 1844 Riots over rail
laying through
Kensington for the
Trenton route.
- 1840s Anti-
Catholic (Irish)
riots; troops guard
churches against
"Know-Nothing"
bigots.
- 1854 Consolidation
Act expands
Philadelphia
tremendously,
creating a city of
154 square miles.
- 1857–61 Bank
panic, stagnation,
and depression
burden city until
Civil War.
- 1860 First baseball
game played in
Philadelphia.
- 1861 Civil War
begins. City elite,
made wealthy
through Southern
trade, are against
the war, despite
strong popular
antislavery
sentiment.

➤

One man will always be linked with
Philadelphia—multitalented, insatiably
curious Benjamin Franklin. Franklin had
an impulse to set things right, whether it be
stoves, spectacles, or states. It sometimes
seems that his hand appears in every aspect
of the city worth exploring! The colonial
homes with the four-hand brass plaques
were protected by his fire-insurance company; the post office at 3rd and Market
streets was his grandson's printing shop; the
Free Library of Philadelphia, the University
of Philadelphia, Pennsylvania Hospital at
8th and Spruce streets, and the American
Philosophical Society all were begun
through Franklin's inspiration. He was an
inventor, a printer, a statesman, a scientist,
and a diplomat—an all-around genius.

**FROM REVOLUTION TO CIVIL
WAR** Like most important Philadelphians, Franklin considered himself a loyal
British subject until well into the 1770s,
though he and the other colonists were increasingly subject to what they considered
capricious English policy. Philadelphia
lacked the radicalism of New England, but
after Lexington and Concord and the meeting of the First and Second Continental
Congresses, whose delegates were housed all
over Philadelphia, tremendous political
debate erupted. William Allen said, "We are
to be England's Milch Cow, but if they are
not prudent . . . we shall turn dry upon their
hands." The moderates—wealthy citizens
with friends and relatives in England—held
out as long as they could. But with the April
1776 decision in Independence Hall to
consider drafting a declaration of independence, revolutionary fervor became
unstoppable.

"These are the times that try men's
souls," wrote Thomas Paine in *The Crisis*—
and they certainly were for Philadelphians,
with so much to lose in a war with Britain.
Thomas Jefferson and John Adams talked
over the situation with George Washington, Robert Morris, and other delegates at
City Tavern by night and at Carpenter's
Hall and Independence Hall by day. On

July 2, their declaration was passed by the general Congress; on July 6, it was read to a crowd of 8,000, who tumultuously approved.

Your visit to Independence National Historical Park will fill you in on the Revolution's effect on the City of Brotherly Love. Of the major colonial cities, Philadelphia had the fewest defenses. The war came to the city itself because British troops occupied patriot homes during the harsh winter of 1777 to 1778. Woodford, a country mansion in what is now Fairmount Park, hosted many Tory balls, while Washington's troops drilled and shivered at Valley Forge. Washington's attempt to crack the British line at Germantown ended in a confused retreat. The city later greatly benefited from the British departure and the Peace of Paris (1783), which ended the war.

Problems with the new federal government brought a Constitutional Convention to Philadelphia in 1787. This body crafted the Constitution the United States still follows. It's hard to say whether Philadelphia had an effect on the beautifully and strongly worded sessions that fostered both the Declaration of Independence and the Constitution, but its native tolerance and acuity must have stood the young country in good stead.

In the years between the ratification of the Constitution and the Civil War, Philadelphia prospered. For 10 of these years, 1790 to 1800, the U.S. government operated here, while the District of Columbia was still marshland. George Washington lived in an Executive Mansion where the Liberty Bell is now; the Supreme Court met in Old City Hall; Congress met in Congress Hall; and everybody met at City Tavern for balls and festivals.

In general the quality of life was high, despite a disastrous 1793 yellow fever epidemic. The legacies of Benjamin Franklin flourished, from printing and publishing to fire-insurance companies (you can still visit the period headquarters of the Contributionship and the Mutual Assur-

Dateline

- **1862** Philadelphia is an armed camp with tremendous demand for locomotives, uniforms, and supplies manufactured here.
- **1863** Battle of Gettysburg in July saves city from Confederate attack but brings loss of thousands of local troops.
- **1865** Antiblack riots culminate in an ordinance forbidding blacks to ride in the horsecars; Jim Crow laws persist until the 1870s. Lincoln's body lies in state in Independence Hall on its way to burial in Illinois.
- **1860–90** Rise of the saloon (6,000 by 1887) as a focus of German and Irish immigrant society.
- **1866–72** Chestnut Street bridge spurs the quick development of West Philadelphia; University of Pennsylvania moves there in 1872.
- **1874** Groundbreaking on July 4 for both City Hall and the Centennial Exhibition in Fairmount Park.
- **1876** President Grant and the emperor of Brazil open the Centennial Exhibition; 38 nations and 39

➤

Dateline

states and territories
are represented.
First public demon-
stration of the
telephone and other
wonders of the age.

- **1878** First use of
electric lighting for
houses and offices;
first Bell telephone
exchange at 400
Chestnut St.
- **1884** Mayor King
appoints the city's
first African-
American police
officer.
- **1890** Drexel
University founded
at 32nd and
Chestnut streets.
- **1892** First trolley
car, on Catharine
and Bainbridge
streets.
- **1893** Reading
Terminal built for
Reading Railroad.
- **1894** Cobblestones
replaced by asphalt
on Broad Street.
- **1899** First motor
car arrives in
Philadelphia,
brought from
France by a local
merchant.
- **1900** More people
own houses in
Philadelphia than in
any other city in the
world; a middle-
class house with
seven rooms rents
for $15 per month.
City's population is
over 1.25 million,
with 25% foreign
born.
- **1901** First
Mummer's Parade
marches up Broad
Street on New

➤

ance Company). The resources of the
Library Company became available to the
public, and both men and women received
"modern" educations—that is, with more
emphasis on accounting and less on classics.
The 1834 Free School Act established a
democratic public school system, but such
private academies as Germantown Friends
School and Friends Select are still going
strong today. The Walnut Street Theater,
founded in 1809, is the oldest American
theater still in constant use, and the Musical Fund Hall at 808 Locust St. (now
apartments) hosted operas, symphony orchestras, and chamber ensembles. The 1805
Pennsylvania Academy of Fine Arts, now at
Broad and Cherry streets, taught such
painters as Washington Allston and the
younger Peales. Charles Willson Peale, the
eccentric patriarch, set up the first American museum in the Long Hall of Independence Hall; its exhibits included a portrait
gallery and the first lifelike arrangements of
full-size stuffed animals.

It makes sense that Philadelphia retained
the federal charter to mint money, build
ships, and produce weapons even after the
capital moved to Washington. The transportation revolution that made America's
growth possible was fueled by the city's
shipyards, ironworks, and locomotive
works. Philadelphia vied with Baltimore
and New York City for transport routes to
agricultural production inland. New York
eventually won out as a shipper, thanks to
its natural harbor and the Erie Canal. Philadelphia, however, was the hands-down
winner in becoming America's premier
manufacturing city, and it ranked even with
New York in finance. The need to harness
Philadelphia's neighborhoods better for
large-scale enterprises, in fact, led to the
1854 incorporation of outlying suburbs
into one 154-square-mile city.

During the Civil War, Philadelphia's
manufacturers weren't above supplying
both Yankees and Confederates with guns
and rail equipment. Fortunately for the city,
the Southern offensive met with bloody
defeat at Gettysburg, not far away. With the

end of the Civil War in 1865, port activity rebounded, as Southern cotton was spun and shipped from city textile looms. Philadelphia became the natural site for the first world's fair held on American soil: the Centennial Exposition. It's hard to imagine the excitement that filled Fairmount Park, with 200 pavilions and displays. There's a scale model in Memorial Hall, one of the few surviving structures in the park; it gives a good idea of how seriously the United States took this show of power and prestige. University City in West Philadelphia saw the establishment of campuses for Drexel University and the University of Pennsylvania, and public transport lines connected all the neighborhoods of the city.

20TH-CENTURY PHILADELPHIA

In the 20th century Philadelphia's fortunes have been checkered. While port and petroleum-refining operations bolstered its position as an industrial center until the 1980s, manufacturing in general has moved out of the city and the region. As industry has moved out, the city has tried to develop a tax base around service businesses. Tourism has become a major revenue source, and public and private efforts coordinate to create the relaxed but efficient attitude you'll find all over Center City. Major corporate headquarters in Philadelphia now include SmithKline Beecham (pharmaceuticals); ARA Services (food and hospitality); CoreStates, Meridian, and Mellon banks; and CIGNA (insurance).

Politically, the city in 1900 was controlled by a small core of moderate Republican bosses, most with old-Philadelphia pedigrees. Immigrant populations united behind President Franklin D. Roosevelt to swing the city Democratic in the 1930s, and in the name of unions and the liberal state, they grew their own form of abuses of government. The period 1949 to 1962, under mayors Joseph Clark (later a U.S. senator) and Richardson Dilworth, was the height of "good government" reform. It was succeeded in the 1970s by the controversial "law-and-order" administration of Frank

Dateline

Year's Day. It's taken from English traditions but quickly becomes a city institution. Wanamaker's department store and Bellevue Hotel open.

■ **1908** Shibe Park, home of baseball's American League Athletics, opens.

■ **1910** First airplane flight from New York City to Philadelphia.

■ **1913** Woman suffrage marches. President Wilson dedicates restored Congress Hall.

■ **1917–18** Philadelphia is a beehive of activity in World War I, with the world's largest ship-construction plant.

■ **1922** Palatial movie houses open on Market and Chestnut streets.

■ **1922–26** Delaware River Bridge connects Philadelphia and New Jersey; ferry trade persists until the 1950s.

■ **1924** "The City Beautiful" movement, exemplified by Benjamin Franklin Parkway, designed along French lines.

■ **1926** Sesquicentennial Exposition on site of present-day Veterans Stadium;

➤

Dateline

highlights are Jack Dempsey–Gene Tunney prizefight, movie "talkies," and electric refrigerator.

- **1928** Philadelphia Museum of Art opens.
- **1929–37** Great Depression in the United States; Democratic party strength in popular vote replaces traditional Republicanism in Philadelphia.
- **1934** With repeal of Prohibition, establishment of state liquor stores (as opposed to those privately owned). Opening of 30th Street Station, the city's main railroad terminus.
- **1936** Special June Mummer's Parade entertains Democratic Party National Convention.
- **1944** Due to World War II labor shortages, black workers make substantial gains, despite union opposition.
- **1946** First computer, ENIAC, developed at University of Pennsylvania for the U.S. Army.
- **1950** Restoration and renovation of Society Hill begins.
- **1951** National Park Service establishes Independence National Historical Park.

➤

Rizzo, who rose to fame as the police commissioner who tried to control the anti-Vietnam War and racial disturbances of the 1960s. Ironically, one of Rizzo's successors, Wilson Goode, is linked to the highly criticized leveling of a city block in West Philadelphia in order to protect public safety.

In terms of urban homeowners—an area in which Philadelphia led the world for decades—there have been good reasons for successful citizens to leave for pleasanter suburban areas. The urban-renewal projects at Society Hill, the commercial developments at Penn Center, the boom period of expansion along the Parkway, and the establishment of Independence National Historical Park have combated the migration somewhat. The city boomed during a splendid bicentennial celebration of the 1787 drafting and signing of the U.S. Constitution.

The early 1990s have brought mixed fortunes to Philadelphia. Many of the problems that plague urban centers throughout America—homelessness, drugs, crime, and inadequate resources for public services—have hit Center City. The city was technically bankrupt in 1990, and the planned 1995 closing of the Philadelphia Navy Yard will hit hard.

The administration of Ed Rendell (1993–) has taken tremendous steps to reform waste in city government through selective privatization of services, more forceful collection of revenues (watch those parking violations!), and rooting out wasteful labor practices. Rendell is also instilling a rejuvenated sense of community through tireless cheerleading, keeping business in town, and personal attention to major strategic areas like tourism and the arts.

TODAY & TOMORROW   The opening of the $522 million Pennsylvania Convention Center in June 1993, only minutes from both historic and business districts, has tremendous implications for the city and its tourists. The Train Shed, Grand Hall, permanent art exhibition, and Ballroom are all breathtakingly beautiful, and Reading Terminal will be its showcase entrance from Market Street by 1995. The hundreds of conventions, millions of visitors, and billions of dollars projected in meeting revenues over the next decade will keep the restaurants, hotels, sights, and entertainments we recommend afloat, after some lean years. There's already more nightlife and sidewalk safety.

Pennsylvania Convention Center dollars also tie into great infrastructure improvements. A dark blue "Direction Philadelphia" signage program, clear and coherent, can guide you on and off a reconstructed expressway system, now connecting I-95 and I-76 (along the two rivers), with plenty of easy entrances and exits. The airport is undergoing a $1-billion capital improvement, with new terminals, a new hotel connected to Terminal B, and new runways. 30th Street Station, the nation's second busiest Amtrak stop, has completed a $100-million restoration, with a new bakery, charcuterie, and rejuvenated services like bookstores.

Hot areas in town have radiated out from the city core. The northwest quadrant of Center City is undisputably the corporate entertainment center. The Delaware River waterfront's piers and warehouses have been transformed into frenetic pleasure domes: bars, clubs, sports palaces, and beach resorts, complete with a pleasant water taxi linking them every 20 minutes. On the other side, the once blue-collar terraced streets of Manayunk along the Schuylkill River host high to funky fashion, cuisine, and shopping, along with a new farmer's market.

And speaking about cash near water, it is very likely that by 1996, Philadelphia voters will approve of riverboat gambling on the Delaware, with expected docking sites from South Philadelphia to just north of the Ben Franklin Bridge. Philosophical or cultural questions aside, legal gambling would pump many millions into city coffers annually.

No one can ignore that Philadelphia

Dateline

- **1954** Philadelphia International Airport (domestic flights since 1940) dedicated.
- **1958** Pennsylvania Railroad merges with New York Central.
- **1950s** Pop singing stars like Fabian, Frankie Avalon, and Chubby Checker emerge from Philadelphia neighborhoods.
- **1960** Dr. John Gibbons invents heart-lung machine at Jefferson Medical Center.
- **1964, 1967** Racial disturbances, said to have been aggravated by Police Commissioner Frank Rizzo, who would serve as mayor from 1972 to 1980.
- **1964** Society Hill Towers, symbolic of old and new in the neighborhood, constructed to design of I. M. Pei.
- **1974** Chestnut Street urban mall project built; seen as a failure by 1980.
- **1975** Philadelphia Flyers win National Hockey League's Stanley Cup.
- **1976** Liberty Bell moved from Congress Hall to the new Independence Mall; America's bicentennial celebrated.

➤

Dateline

- **1980** Phillies win their first World Series championship.
- **1982** Philadelphia's 300th anniversary celebration. Tall ships line Penn's Landing.
- **1984–92** Administration of Wilson Goode, Philadelphia's first black mayor, tainted by the 1985 MOVE bombing of a city block in West Philadelphia in the name of law and order.
- **1987** Bicentennial of U.S. Constitution celebrated at Independence Hall.
- **1993** Pennsylvania Convention Center opened with celebration and speech by Pres. Bill Clinton.

has finally entered the age of the super-skyscraper with One Liberty Place, the energetic and gracious 945-foot spire. The 150,000-square-foot Shops at Liberty Place are the true flagships of city merchandising, after a decade of retrenchment in such institutions as Wanamaker's and Bonwit Teller. Other megaliths planned or completed are the 58-story Two Liberty Place, the 54-story One Mellon Center at 18th and Market streets, 1919 Market St., the Bell Atlantic Building, and a second tower at Commerce Square. What all these projects have done, however, is leave the fabled Rittenhouse Square area, especially Chestnut Street, looking a bit seedy by comparison, and these locations must redevelop to maintain their cachet.

The arts are finally attracting major projects and investment, particularly along South Broad Street, where the city is trying hard to establish a safe, convenient core zone of the performing arts. The Philadelphia Orchestra is building a new home for itself along this "Avenue of the Arts" at Spruce Street, leaving the Academy of Music free to book traveling orchestras and the like. The Wilma Theater, the new Pennsylvania Ballet's home, and the new Arts Bank at South Street are also on the boards. In May 1996, the Philadelphia International Arts Festival will transform the city into one huge showcase for world premieres in opera, dance, and music. Meanwhile, the Philadelphia Museum of Art has completed a broad gallery renovation and anticipates a blockbuster 1996 Cézanne show. The Philadelphia Zoo has new exhibits and two rare white lions.

In sports, look for the Phillies to continue their winning ways and for the 1996 All-Star Game. The John F. Kennedy Stadium has been demolished, and a new Spectrum II will house the 76ers and Flyers in luxury. The old Spectrum will host more concerts, truck pulls, and one-of-a-kind events.

Famous Philadelphians

Richard Allen   (1760–1831) Born enslaved to a Pennsylvania attorney general, he became an itinerant Methodist preacher and eventually the founder and first bishop of the original African Methodist Episcopal Church, still at 419 S. 6th St.

Marian Anderson   (b. 1902) A noted contralto, she began her career in the Union Baptist Church Choir and broke operatic racial barriers throughout America. In 1955 she both made her Metropolitan Opera debut and served as a U.S. delegate to the United Nations.

Nicholas Biddle   (1786–1844) Born of old Philadelphia stock, he was a scholar and literary figure until the War of 1812 drew him into a directorship of the Second Bank of the United States. Thanks to his hard work and talent, he became president of the Second Bank from 1823 to 1839, resigning after the controversy with President Andrew Jackson over the bank's right to a national charter. His home in Andalusia is still an attraction.

Mary Cassatt   (1845–1926) An impressionist painter from an old Philadelphia family (her brother, president of the Pennsylvania Railroad, lived on the current site of the Rittenhouse Hotel), she lived in Paris from 1874 on. A protégée of Degas, Cassatt is noted for figures of washerwomen and domestic scenes in pastels, oils, and especially etchings.

John Coltrane   (1926–67) A jazz musician and composer who spent his adolescence in North Philly practicing at the AME Zion Church at 12th and Oxford streets, he joined the Miles Davis Quintet in 1955. He later struck out on his own, with African and Indian-influenced, highly cerebral and arpeggioed jazz.

Bill Cosby   (b. 1937) An entertainer, a comedian, an actor, and an author born in Germantown, he has a B.A. from Temple. After winning several Emmys, he ended eight years on the hugely popular "Cosby Show" in 1992.

Thomas Eakins   (1844–1916) He was the quintessential painter and teacher and was generally considered, with Winslow Homer, to be a leading American artist of the 19th century. Eakins spent his life in Philadelphia, except for study trips to Europe, rising from student to teacher.

His work emphasizes the human figure and the dignity of common things; his *Clinic of Dr. Gross* (1875) is a well-known masterpiece.

W. C. Fields   (1880–1946) He ran away from home at 11 to perfect his vaudeville skills, then moved on to the theater, the Ziegfeld Follies, and the movies. His best-known film roles were in *The Bank Dick* (1940) and as Mr. Micawber in *David Copperfield* (1935).

IMPRESSIONS

I have never observed such a wealth of taverns and drinking establishments as are in Philadelphia. . . . There is hardly a street without several and hardly a man here who does not fancy one his second home.
—Thomas Jefferson, Letter to a Virginia friend, 1790

The question eagerly put to me by every one in Philadelphia is, 'Don't you think the city greatly improved?' They seem to me to confound augmentation with improvement. It always was a fine city, since I first knew it; and it is very greatly augmented.
—William Cobbett, *A Year's Residence in the United States of America*, 1817–19

Philadelphia Area

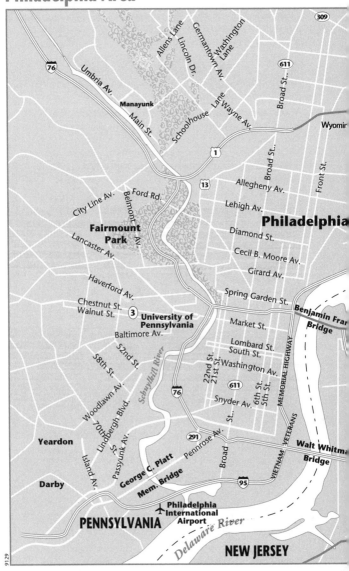

Benjamin Franklin (1706–90) He was a ubiquitous talent as a statesman, a printer, a citizen, a scientist, and an inventor. There probably wouldn't have been a United States without him; he shepherded American interests at home and abroad for 60 years.

The Kelly Family Patriarch John Kelly (1889–1960) championed the rise of the Irish by becoming an Olympic rowing medalist, the

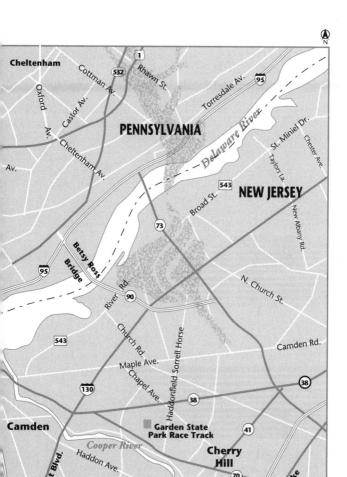

Democratic party chairman from 1934 to 1941, and a multimillion-aire construction contractor. His son Jack also won an Olympic rowing medal, and his daughter Grace (1929–80) rose to stardom in theater and films (such as *Rear Window* and *The Country Girl*, both 1954) before marrying Prince Rainier of Monaco.

Patti LaBelle   (b. 1944) Born Patricia Louise Holte, she began with the Bluebelles and has sung and acted solo since 1977. Her 1986 album "Winner in You" went platinum, and her film roles include *A Soldier's Story* (1985).

Eugene Ormandy   (1899–1981) Born in Hungary, he led the Philadelphia Orchestra for over 40 legendary years, giving its string and brass sections an instantly recognizable sheen and richness. He was a pioneer in orchestral recordings.

Charles Willson Peale   (1741–1827) A portrait painter and naturalist, he moved to Philadelphia in 1776, just in time to establish a career painting official portraits of the U.S. founders. An accomplished collector with 16 children, he also established the first American museum in Independence Hall. He helped found the Pennsylvania Academy of Fine Arts in 1805.

Teddy Pendergrass   (b. 1950) A singer with a romantic, rich bass, he recorded many hits, including "If You Don't Know Me By Now." He now lives and works out of suburban Bala Cynwyd.

William Penn   (1644–1718) The founder of Philadelphia, Penn had a nature in many ways combining doses of peevishness and idealism that led to his personal tragedies. (See the description in this chapter.)

Benjamin Rush   (1745–1813) The most influential doctor and public-health figure in the colonies and the young United States, he signed the Declaration of Independence and also promoted Thomas Paine to agitate for American independence. His theory of treatment by purging blood proved disastrous during the 1793 yellow fever epidemic, yet his clinical analyses set standards for American medicine.

IMPRESSIONS

It is a handsome city, but distractingly regular. After walking about it for an hour or two, I felt that I would have given the world for a crooked street. The collar of my coat appeared to stiffen, and the brim of my hat to expand, beneath its Quakery influence. My hair shrunk into a sleek short crop, my hands folded themselves upon my breast of their own calm accord, and thoughts of taking lodgings in Mark Lane over against the Market Place, and of making a large fortune by speculations in corn, came over me involuntarily.
—Charles Dickens, *American Notes,* 1842

The vast extent of the streets of small, low, yet snug-looking houses. . . .Philadelphia must contain in comfort the largest number of small householders of any city in the world.
—London *Times* Reporter William Bussell, *My Diary North and South,* 1850

2 Recommended Books & Films

Books

HISTORY

It is impossible to read about the transition from the colonies to the United States and the first 50 years of independence without learning about Philadelphia. Carl Bridenbaugh's *Rebels and Gentlemen* (Oxford University Press, 1965) is a good summary of events leading up to independence. Catherine Drinker Bowen's *Miracle at Philadelphia* (Atlantic-Little, Brown, 1960) is a vivid retelling of the 1787 Constitutional Convention.

E. Digby Baltzell's *Puritan Boston and Quaker Philadelphia* (Free Press, 1980) is a thoughtful and amusing comparison between these two preeminent colonial cities, explaining why their histories turned out so differently—in particular, why the emphasis placed on keeping a civil society dampened outstanding individual achievements in Philadelphia. Baltzell's first classic effort here was *Philadelphia Gentlemen: The Making of a National Upper Class* (Free Press, 1958).

W. E. B. Du Bois's *The Philadelphia Negro* (University of Pennsylvania Press, 1899) is a classic analysis of racism and its social effects in the North since the Civil War.

Edwin Wolf II's *Philadelphia: Portrait of an American City* (Stackpole Books, 1975) is one of the more engaging recent histories, with beautiful and appropriate illustrations. The building of the Benjamin Franklin Parkway, a swath like the Champs Elysées in the midst of a colonial grid, is covered in David Bruce Brownlee's *Building the City Beautiful* (Philadelphia Museum of Art catalog, 1989).

Philadelphia in the Mayor Rizzo years is covered in Conrad Weiler's *Philadelphia: Neighborhood, Authority and the Urban Crisis* (Praeger, 1974). Of the three books on the MOVE tragedy, try Charles Bowser's *Let the Bunker Burn* (Camino Books, 1989).

THE ARTS

There is a surfeit of material on Philadelphia's architecture; try *Philadelphia Architecture* (MIT Press, 1984), which goes into environmental issues as well, or George B. Tatum's *Penn's Great Town* (University of Pennsylvania Press, 1981) for a survey of historic houses. Roslyn Brenner's *Philadelphia's Outdoor Art: A Walking Tour* (Camino Books, 1987) has a makeshift text but contains good

IMPRESSIONS

Of all goodly villages, the very goodliest, probably, in the world; the very largest, and flattest, and smoothest. . . . The absence of the note of the perpetual perpendicular, the New York, the Chicago note, . . . seemed to symbolize exactly the principle of indefinite level extension and to offer, refreshingly, a challenge . . . to absolute centrifugal motion.

—Henry James, *The American Scene,* 1905

photography. *Center City Philadelphia: The Elements of Style* (University of Pennsylvania Press, 1984) examines artistic works involving views of Philadelphia.

Fredric Miller has put together two superb photographic histories of the city: *Still Philadelphia,* covering 1890 to 1940, and *Philadelphia Stories,* covering 1920 to 1960—both published by Temple University Press. Robert Llewellyn has also assembled a sensitive book of contemporary photographs called *Philadelphia* (Thomasson-Grant, 1986).

FICTION, TRAVEL & BIOGRAPHY

FICTION   Try Pete Dexter's *God's Pocket* (Warner Books, 1990) for a gritty contemporary look at the city by a former newspaper reporter turned big-league novelist and scriptwriter. Donald Zochert's *Murder in the Hellfire Club* (Holt, Rinehart & Winston, 1978) is an amusing historical mystery, with colonists framed in London of the 1770s and Ben Franklin on hand to solve the case.

TRAVEL   If you find old guidebooks fascinating, consult *Magee's Illustrated Guide* for the 1876 city or the *Federal Writer's Project Guide to Philadelphia* (1937; Scholar Press, reprint 1978). Witty and perceptive is Christopher Morley (1890–1957), the Haverford-born author of *Kitty Foyle* and recent subject of a Rosenbach Museum show; a selection from his *Travels in Philadelphia* has been published as *Christopher Morley's Philadelphia* (Fordham University Press, 1990). *Bicentennial City: Walking Tours of Historic Philadelphia* (Pyne Press, 1974), by John Francis Marion, is fine, although it's definitely dated and presupposes a real "inside" knowledge of the city's history and personages.

BIOGRAPHY   John Lukacs's *Philadelphia: Patricians & Philistines 1900–1950* (Farrar, Straus & Giroux, 1981) is a charming, slightly offbeat collection of profiles of seven colorful figures who flourished during this period and have faded into obscurity since. The book opens and concludes with wonderful ruminations on what made Philadelphia so different—its geniality and datedness.

One of those chronicled by Lukacs, Albert C. Barnes of the legendary Barnes Foundation and its Renoirs, is further examined in Howard Greenfield's *The Devil and Dr. Barnes: A Portrait of an American Art Collector* (Viking, 1987).

The Kelly family—John, Jack, and Grace—receives a hagiographic and slightly dated treatment in John McCallum's *That Kelly Family* (A.S. Barnes, 1957). Another "immigrant-made-good" story, although more measured, is the biography of former Mayor Frank Rizzo, Joseph Daughen's *The Cop Who Would Be King* (Little, Brown, 1977).

FOR KIDS

Robert Lawson's classic *Ben and Me* (Houghton Mifflin, 1939) tells of Ben Franklin's career from a mouse's point of view. Katherine Milhous's *Through These Arches: The Story of Independence Hall*

(Lippincott, 1965) is illustrated and engaging. For younger readers there's Elvajeen Hall's *Today in Old Philadelphia* (Children's Press, 1975), combining historic buildings and sights with daily life. John Loeper's *The House on Spruce Street* (Atheneum, 1984) concentrates on Philadelphia history during the restoring of a grand old Society Hill house.

Elizabeth Gray Vining's *The Taken Girl* (Viking, 1972) is a lovely story of an orphan girl taken on as a helper in the 1840s Quaker household of John Greenleaf Whittier and how she becomes involved in the antislavery movement. In Susan Lee's *The Fall of the Quaker City* (Children's Press, 1975), a Quaker family must decide whether to support the American Revolution.

FILMS

Philadelphia (1993), winner of two Oscars—Tom Hanks as best actor, Bruce Springsteen for best song—will remain in film history as the first major release on the AIDS crisis. This story of a dying lawyer who sues his former firm for wrongful termination was shot by Jonathan Demme all over town, from City Hall to Famous Deli.

The classic *The Philadelphia Story* (1940), adapted from a play by Philip Barry, involves Katharine Hepburn as a headstrong Philadelphia socialite who learns to find love with her first husband (Cary Grant) on the eve of her wedding to a very proper second husband. But not a frame was shot in Philadelphia itself.

Intervening films include Sylvester Stallone's *Rocky* (1976), in which the young Kensington (*not* South Philadelphia) boxer searching for a future jogs through the Italian Market and up the Philadelphia Museum of Art's steps; *Blow Out* (1981), in which John Travolta plays a sound technician who hears mysterious noises when a presidential candidate's car runs off a Wissahickon Creek bridge; *Trading Places* (1983), a prince-and-the-pauper comedy about Eddie Murphy and Dan Aykroyd, set throughout Center City's banks and clubs; and *Witness* (1985), with Harrison Ford as a Philadelphia detective forced to go undercover in Amish country.

2

Planning a Trip to Philadelphia

THIS CHAPTER IS DEVOTED TO THE WHERE, WHEN, AND HOW OF YOUR TRIP—the advance-planning issues required to get it together and take it on the road.

After deciding where to go, most people have two fundamental questions: What will it cost? and How do I get there? This chapter will answer both questions and also resolve other important questions, such as when to go, what insurance coverage is necessary, and where to obtain more information about Philadelphia for special needs.

1   Information & Money

INFORMATION   The **Philadelphia Visitors Center,** 16th Street and John F. Kennedy Boulevard, Philadelphia, PA 19102 (☎ **215/636-1666** or toll free **800/537-7676**), should be your first resource. They offer a wealth of publications, from seasonal calendars of events to maps; knowledgeable volunteers staff their phones. If you obtain nothing else, request the "Official Visitors Guide," an annual compendium. Guest Informant, a company that places upscale city guides in hotel rooms, has developed **"Quick Guide,"** a 60-page publication that provides the basics and is issued every four months. It's dropped in lobbies all over town, but you can write or call for a copy at 1700 Walnut St., Suite 518-9, Philadelphia, PA 19103 (☎ **215/546-5155**).

MONEY   Except for truly deluxe experiences, you will find moderate prices in Philadelphia: less than those in New York and on a par with or slightly above those in Washington, D.C. Expenses for a family of four staying in a hotel, with meals in restaurants and a healthy dose of sightseeing in Independence Park (all free) and museums, should run about $200 per day.

Minimal cash is required, since credit cards are accepted universally and automatic-teller machines linked to national networks are strewn around tourist destinations and increasingly within hotels. To get more specific information on the **Cirrus** network, call toll free **800/424-7787;** for the **Plus** system, call toll free **800/843-7587.** The three major traveler's check agencies are **American Express** (☎ toll free **800/221-7282**); **BankAmerica** (☎ toll free **800/227-3460**); and **VISA** (☎ toll free **800/227-6811**).

2   When to Go

Philadelphia has four distinct seasons with temperatures ranging from the 90s (F) in summer to the 30s (F) in winter, although below-zero (F) temperatures normally hit only one out of every four winters. Summers tend to be humid, so pack lightweight, comfortable clothes in light colors if you plan to be in the sun. In the fall, the weather becomes drier; heavier cottons, light knits, and wools are the best bet, with a sweater or jacket for the evening. Winter wear requires more

What Things Cost in Philadelphia	U.S. $
Taxi from the airport to Center City	25.00
Airport train to Center City (cash on board)	5.00
Local telephone call	.25
Double at Ritz-Carlton Philadelphia (deluxe)	205.00
Double at Doubletree Hotel Philadelphia (expensive)	145.00
Double at Holiday Inn–Independence Mall (moderate)	113.00
Double at Comfort Inn at Penn's Landing (budget)	85.00
Two-course lunch for one at The Garden (expensive)	18.00
Two-course lunch for one at the Food Court at Liberty Place (budget)	7.00
Three-course dinner for one at Dilullo Centro (expensive)	45.00
Three-course dinner at Circa (moderate)	27.00
Three-course dinner at Marabella's (inexpensive)	18.00
Bottle of beer	2.75
Coca-Cola	1.50
Cup of coffee	1.50
Roll of ASA 100 Kodacolor film, 36 exposures	5.00
Admission to Philadelphia Museum of Art	6.00
Movie ticket	7.50
Concert ticket at the Academy of Music	12.00–45.00

layers with heavier wools. Spring is variable; count on comfortable breezes and keep a jacket on hand.

Average Temperatures and Precipitation in Philadelphia

	High °F	Low °F	Precipitation in Days
Jan	40	26	11
Feb	41	26	9
Mar	50	33	11
Apr	62	43	11
May	73	53	11
June	81	63	10
July	95	68	9
Aug	95	66	9
Sept	80	60	8
Oct	66	49	8
Nov	54	39	10
Dec	43	29	10

Philadelphia Calendar of Events

For more details, contact the **Convention and Visitors Bureau,** 1515 John F. Kennedy Blvd., Philadelphia, PA 19102 (☎ **215/636-1666**).

January

⭐ Mummer's Parade

Starting in late morning and lasting most of the day, 30,000 spangled strutters march with feathers and banjos in a celebration that must have been pagan in origin. If you go to the Mummer's Museum, the gaudiness and elaborateness of the costumes won't amaze you quite so much. But the music (everyone ends up humming "Oh, Dem Golden Slippers" sooner or later) and gaiety will have you entranced.

Where: Broad Street, from South Philadelphia up to City Hall. (There's talk of reversing the direction or winding up at the new Convention Center.) **When:** January 1; the following Saturday in case of poor weather. **How:** Just line up on Broad Street, dressed for winter. If you want reserved seats, they're available from early December at the Convention and Visitors Bureau for $2. Call **215/336-3050** for details.

- **Benjamin Franklin's Birthday,** The Franklin Institute. Call **215/448-1200** for details. Midmonth Sunday.

February

- **Chinese New Year.** You can enjoy dragons and fireworks at 11th and Arch streets, traditional 10-course banquets, or a visit to the Chinese Cultural Center at 125 N. 10th Street. Call **215/923-6767** for details. Between late January and midmonth.
- **Black History Month.** The Afro-American Museum, 7th and Arch streets, offers a full complement of exhibitions, lectures, and music. Call **215/574-0380** for details. All month long.
- **George Washington's Birthday.** Valley Forge Historical Park holds a Cherries Jubilee weekend. Call **215/783-7700** for details. Third Sunday and Monday.
- **Peco Energy Presidential Jazz Weekend.** More than 90 events are held around-the-clock, from concerts to screenings and meals. Call **215/636-1666** for details. Presidents' Day weekend.
- **Comcast U.S. Indoor Tennis Championships.** This event features some of the world's best players. At the Spectrum. Call **215/947-2530** for particulars. Third weekend.

March

- **Philadelphia Flower and Garden Show,** at the Civic Center, 34th Street and Civic Center Boulevard in 1995, but will move to the Convention Center in 1996. It's the largest in the country, with acres of gardens and rustic settings. There are usually tickets at the door, but the Pennsylvania Horticultural Society at 325 Walnut St. sells them in advance. Call **215/625-8250** for information. First half of month in 1995, and probably late February thereafter.

★ The Book and the Cook Festival

For the past decade, Philadelphia has combined the love of reading and eating into this festival. For five days, eminent food critics, cookbook authors, and restaurateurs are invited to plan dream meals with participating city restaurants. If you're a "foodie," you know that the chance to stroll through Reading Terminal Market with Alice Waters, or to dine on what she turns up, is not to be declined. The festival has recently expanded into food samplings and wine and beer tastings.
Where: All over town. **When:** Usually the third week in March. **How: Call 215/686-3662** for a schedule and to make a reservation.

- **St. Patrick's Day Parade.** The parade starts at noon on 20th Street and the Parkway. Call the Visitors Bureau for details. The Irish Pub at 2007 Walnut St. will be packed. March 17.

April

- **Philadelphia Antiques Show.** Started in 1961, this is probably the finest in the nation, with 57 major English and American exhibitors in 1994. 103rd Engineers Armory, 33rd and Market Streets. Call **215/387-3500** for information. First weekend.
- **American Music Theater Festival.** In its 12th year in 1995, this festival offers premieres of music-theater works by major American artists, ranging from traditional Broadway-bound musicals to avant-garde works. Call **215/893-1570** for information. Through June.
- **Easter Sunday.** This day brings fashion shows and music to Rittenhouse Square. The Easter Bunny usually makes an appearance at Wanamaker's and the Gallery. Call **215/686-2876** for details.
- **Spring Tour of Fairmount Park.** The dogwoods and cherry trees along both sides of the Schuylkill are in blossom. Trolleybuses make a special run along Wissahickon Creek, a lovely woodland minutes away from Center City. Call **215/636-1666** for details. Last Sunday (or first in May).

May

- **Philadelphia Open House.** These tours give you a rare chance to see Germantown, Society Hill, and University

City mansions. Call **215/928-1188** for information. Late
April to early May.

- **Rittenhouse Square Flower Market.** This has been an
annual event since 1914. Plants, flowers, baked goodies,
and lemon sticks are some of the irresistibles for sale.
Call **215/525-7182** for details. Third Thursday.
Also, the azaleas behind the Museum of Art literally stop
traffic with their brilliance—there are over 2,000 azaleas
and rhododendrons exhibiting their finery.

- **Mozart on the Square.** Also around Rittenhouse Square,
this festival brings about 20 chamber performances of good
younger talent to town. Performances cost $5 to $15; for
information contact P.O. Box 237, Merion Station, PA
19006 (☎ **215/668-1799**). All month.

- **International Theater Festival for Children.** Another
new tradition, this takes place on or near the University
of Pennsylvania campus, based at 3680 Walnut St.
Call **215/898-6791** for programs and prices. Last week
of month.

- **Israel Independence Day.** This holiday brings a Center
City parade and daylong Israeli bazaar to the Parkway.
Call **215/922-7222** for details. Sunday in mid-May.

- **Jambalaya Jam.** This was cooked up as a way for
Philadelphia to pay homage to New Orleans and to use
its own waterfront better. It's based at the Great Plaza at
Penn's Landing, and the best of Dixieland and zydeco and
Cajun and Creole cuisine are in full force. In recent years,
Dr. John and the Preservation Hall Jazz Band have been in
attendance. Call **215/636-1666** for particulars. Late May.

- **Devon Horse Show,** Route 30, Devon. This event outside
Philadelphia includes jumping competitions and carriage
races and a great country fair, with plenty of food stalls
under cheerful awnings. General admission $6. Call
610/964-0550 for details. End of month.

- **Dad Vail Regatta.** This is one of the largest collegiate
rowing events in the country. You can picnic on East River
Drive near Strawberry Mansion. Call **215/542-7844** for
details. Second weekend.

June

- **Rittenhouse Square Fine Arts Annual.** Philadelphia
moves outdoors with this event, in which hundreds of
professional and student artworks go on sale. Call
215/634-5060 for details. First two weeks.

- **Head House Square.** Local craftspeople, food vendors,
and street artists set up shop on Saturday from noon to
midnight, Sunday from noon to 6pm. Throughout
summer.

- **Elfreth's Alley Days.** The row-house dwellers, many in
colonial costumes, open up their homes for inspection and

admiration. Reenactments of colonial crafts; troops are also present. First weekend. Call **574-0560** for details.

- **CoreStates Pro Cycling Championships.** The 156-mile-long course of this country's premier 1-day cycling event starts and finishes on the Parkway. First weekend.
- **Betsy Ross House.** Flag Day festivities are held here. June 14.
- **Mellon Jazz Festival.** A top-drawer collection of artists are featured in the Mann Music Center and the Academy of Music. Second or third week.
- **Bloomsday.** The Irish Pub at 2007 Walnut St. celebrates the 24-hour time span of James Joyce's novel, *Ulysses.* June 16.

July

⭐ **Welcome America!**

The whole town turns out for this festival to celebrate America's birthday with fountains, theater, free entertainment, and assorted pageantry.
Where: Principal locations are the terrace by the Philadelphia Museum of Art, City Hall (to dive into the world's largest hoagie), and Independence Mall. **When:** Week before July 4. The Fourth of July brings special ceremonies to Independence Square, including a reading of the Declaration of Independence, a presentation of the prestigious Freedom Medal, and a parade. There's also a Schuylkill regatta on the Fourth. **How:** Call **215/636-1666** for information. Note that in 1996, the festival will stretch until July 9, when Veterans Stadium will host the major league baseball All-Star Game.

- **Philadelphia Orchestra Summer Concerts,** Mann Music Center in Fairmount Park. The concerts are free on Monday, Wednesday, and Thursday through August. Also, there are pop concerts at low prices at Robin Hood Dell East and dance at Art Museum Terrace.

August

- **Philadelphia Folk Festival,** Suburban Poole Farm, Schwenksville. This festival has a national reputation and brings major crowds. Call **215/242-0150** for details. Late month.
- **Pennsylvania Dutch Festival.** Reading Terminal Market venue for quilts, music, food, crafts, and such. Daily throughout the first week.

September

- **Fairmount Park Festival.** This festival includes the Harvest Show at Memorial Hall and parades of varying themes down the Parkway almost every weekend. Through November. Call **685-0052** for details.

- **Philadelphia Distance Run.** One of the nation's premier tests, it's a half-marathon through Center City and Fairmount Park. In town, it's bigger than the November marathon and gets plenty of national running figures. Call **215/665-8500** if you wish to join the field of 7,500. Usually the third Sunday.

October

- **Columbus Day Parade.** Parkway. Also look for South Philadelphia fairs. Second Monday.

⭐ **Super Sunday**

Think of a party for an entire city—that's Super Sunday, held on the Parkway from Logan Circle to the Museum of Art. There are clowns, jugglers, mimes, rides, craft vendors, and a flea market. The museums and academies along the Parkway have sponsored this since 1970, rain or shine, and most have reduced admissions and special events. This is one day when parking on the grass won't get you a ticket. **Where:** Benjamin Franklin Parkway. **When:** Third Sunday. **How:** Call **215/665-1050** for information.

November

- **Philadelphia Marathon.** The finish line is at Independence Hall. Sunday at midmonth.
- **Virginia Slims Women's Tennis Championships.** Spectrum. Call **215/568-4444** for details. Second week.
- **Thanksgiving Day Parade.** This parade features cartoon characters, bands, floats, and Santa Claus. Fourth Thursday.

December

- **Holiday Activities Around Town.** It's not surprising that Christmas occasions lots of activities in Center City, beginning with the tree lighting in City Hall courtyard. The Gallery at Market East, "A Christmas Carol" at Strawbridge and Clothier, a Colonial Christmas Village at Market Place East, and Wanamaker's all host elaborate extravaganzas, with organs and choruses. The Society Hill and Germantown Christmas walking tours are lovely, with the same leafy decorations as Fairmount Park. All month long.
- **Christmas Tours of Fairmount Park and Germantown.** Colonial mansions sparkle with wreaths, holly, and fruit arrangements donated by local garden clubs. Call **215/787-5449** or **215/848-1777** for details. From midmonth.
- **Private Lights.** For an unusual Christmas experience, visit the 2700 block of South Colorado Street, south of Oregon Avenue, between 17th and 18th streets. The sight of some

40 houses bathed in interconnected strands of holiday lights is not to be believed. All month long.

- **Lucia Fest,** Old Swedes' Church. It sounds Italian, but the Lucia Fest is a Swedish pageant held by candlelight. First weekend.
- **Nutcracker Ballet.** The Pennsylvania Ballet performs Tchaikovsky's classic at the Academy of Music. Call **215/551-7014** for details. Most of month.
- **New Year's Eve.** Fireworks are held at the Great Plaza of Penn's Landing. December 31.

3 Tips for the Disabled, Seniors, Singles, Families & Students

FOR THE DISABLED   Philadelphia is accessible to the disabled in favorite tourist areas. Even though many streets in Society Hill and bordering Independence National Historical Park have uneven brick sidewalks and Dock Street itself is paved with rough cobblestones, all curbs are well-cut at intersections. The same is true for Chestnut Street, the parkway, and the University of Pennsylvania campus. Virtually all theaters and stadiums accommodate wheelchairs. Call ahead to plan routes. To aid the hearing impaired, the Academy of Music provides free infrared headsets for concerts; the Annenberg Center rents them for $2.

A national resource, the **Travel Information Service** at Moss Rehabilitation Hospital, will provide telephone information at **215/456-9603.**

For basic information, contact the **Mayor's Commission on People with Disabilities,** Room 143, City Hall, Philadelphia, PA 19107 (☎ **215/686-2798**). SEPTA publishes a special "Transit Guide for the Disabled"; you can request it from **SEPTA Special Services,** 130 S. 9th St., Philadelphia, PA 19107 (☎ **215/580-7365**). The most popular bus routes are accessible; the subway is not.

The Free Library of Philadelphia runs a **Library for the Blind and Physically Handicapped,** very conveniently located at 919 Walnut St. (☎ 925-3213); it's open Monday to Friday from 9am to 5pm. It adjoins the **Associated Services for the Blind,** which offers transcriptions into braille for a fee.

If you travel with Amtrak or Greyhound/Trailways, be aware that on the former you can receive a 25% discount and a special seat with advance notification (☎ toll free **800/523-6590**) and on the latter a free seat for a companion (☎ toll free **800/345-3109**).

FOR SENIORS   Seniors should bring some form of photo ID because many city attractions grant special discounts, especially during weekdays. Some hotels, too, will shift their rates, particularly on weekends. The Convention and Visitors Bureau publishes "Seniors on the Go," which lists dozens of specific benefits around town—from flat taxi fares to museum admissions; write ahead or pick it up at the Visitors Center. They'll also give you a "Ben's Pass for Senior Citizens," good for a calendar year.

If you haven't already done so, think about joining the **American Association of Retired Persons (AARP),** 1909 K St. NW, Washington, DC 20049 (☎ **202/872-4700**). Their Purchase Privilege Program unlocks an incredible chest of discounts.

Many seniors prefer places with convenient local transportation between sites, and Philadelphia is wonderful in this regard. Seniors might consider the SEPTA DayPass ($5), available at the Visitors Center at 16th Street and John F. Kennedy Boulevard, which offers unlimited on-off rides; or the Ben Frankline, which goes from Society Hill up to the Art Museum and Zoo (50¢ per ride).

You can pick up a **Golden Age Passport** at Independence National Historical Park if you are 62 or over. Since this park is free, it won't matter there, but the passport provides free admission to all parks, monuments, and recreation areas operated by the National Park Service.

Some of the educational programs run by **Elderhostel** are in the Philadelphia area. You must be over 60 (and your spouse or companion over 50) to participate. The cost of the program itself averages $350 per person; for information contact them at 75 Federal St., third floor, Boston, MA 02110 (☎ **617/426-7788**).

FOR SINGLES   The main problem for single travelers can be meeting other people. There is, of course, the bar scene (see Chapter 10). You might consider signing up for one of the many tours through parts of Independence National Historical Park at their Visitors Center or join tours of Fairmount Park and other city areas at the Visitors Center at 16th Street and John F. Kennedy Boulevard. The Friday Philadelphia *Inquirer* "Weekend" section lists many other participatory events. Urban mall spaces like Liberty Place and the bookstore Borders attract a friendly clientele. You might also consider staying in a smaller hotel, such as Independence Park Inn, or in a hotel with a health club.

FOR FAMILIES   Planning is essential for success here in Philadelphia—I know from personal experience! If your kids are old enough to appreciate the destination, let them read something ahead of time; for a brief list of literature for children see "Recommended Books & Films" in Chapter 1.

Airlines and Amtrak both let children under two travel free and offer discounts for children and/or families. Once you arrive, children under 12 (in some cases 18) can stay free in the same room as their parents in virtually all Philadelphia hotels. Be sure to reserve cribs and playpens if needed in advance. Restaurants all over the country are increasingly aware of the need to provide the basics, and "Cool for Kids" in Chapter 6 will cover some favorites.

The best current resource for family travel in Philadelphia is *Metrokids,* a bimonthly newspaper available at the Visitors Center at 16th Street and John F. Kennedy Boulevard. It lists all special cultural attractions geared to families, along with theme issues on factory tours, the Camden aquarium, and the like. Call **215/735-7035** with specific questions.

FOR STUDENTS   It's not well known, but there probably are more colleges and universities in and around Philadelphia than any other city in the country. So accredited students will find a warm reception from area vendors and sites. With an **International Student Identity Card (ISIC),** available to any full-time high-school or university student, you are entitled to special discounts on cultural sites, accommodations, car rentals, and more. Contact your own campus or the **Council on International Educational Exchange (CIEE),** 205 East 42nd St., New York, NY 10017 (☎ **212/661-1414**). While in Philadelphia, students might head for the **University of Pennsylvania,** 34th and Walnut streets (☎ **898-5000**); **Temple University,** Broad Street and Montgomery Avenue (☎ **787-8561**); or **International House,** 3701 Chestnut St. (☎ **387-5125**). All publish free papers listing lectures, performances, films, and social events.

4 Getting There

By Plane

All flights into and from Philadelphia use **Philadelphia International Airport** (☎ **215/492-3181**), at the southwest corner of the city. There are flights to more than 100 cities in the United States and more than 1,000 arrivals and departures daily.

THE MAJOR AIRLINES

You can check flight schedules and make reservations on the following domestic airlines. **American Airlines** (☎ **215/365-4000** or toll free **800/433-7300**); **American Eagle** (☎ toll-free **800/433-7300**); **Continental Airlines** (☎ toll free **800/525-0280**); **Delta Air Lines** (☎ **215/667-7720** or toll free **800/221-1212**); **Midway Airlines** (☎ toll free **800/446-4392**); **Midwest Express** (☎ toll-free **800/452-2022**; **Northwest Airlines** (☎ toll free **800/225-2525** domestic, **800/447-4747** international); **TWA** (☎ **215/923-2000**, or toll free **800/221-2000** domestic, **800/892-4141** international); **United Airlines** (☎ **215/568-2800** or toll free **800/241-6522**); and **USAir** and **USAir Express** (☎ toll free **800/428-4322**).

International carriers include **Air Jamaica** (☎ toll free **800/523-5585**); **British Airways** (☎ toll free **800/633-3942**) and **Swissair** (☎ toll free **800/221-4750**).

AIRFARES

Airfares these days shift quickly, depending on the date and day of week, advance reservations, prepayment, nonstop or transfer status, competition for the flight among carriers, and length of stay, just for starters. If this sounds confusing, that's why it's imperative to shop around or have a friendly travel agent do so for you.

The various price classes on flights range from first class—the most expensive—through business class to economy—which carries no special restrictions. The cheapest direct-flight option usually is the **APEX (Advance Purchase Excursion)** fare, which typically is valid from 7 to 60 days and must be purchased at least 14 to 21 days in advance. Any round-trip fare will be lower still if it includes a Saturday-night stay.

There's always less demand, and consequently greater seat availability and lower prices, for off-peak hours of travel, especially after 7pm. Monday, Thursday, and Friday are the heaviest travel days. Holidays generally are the worst times of year to travel.

The two domestic airlines that use Philadelphia International Airport as a hub are Midway Airlines and USAir, so look for competitive fares from cities in which they both have stops.

Shuttle service up and down the East Coast can be high-priced, and flights from the Southwest are limited. International rates are best to and from Mexico, London, and Jamaica and some other Caribbean islands.

There aren't too many superbudget options to and from Philadelphia by air. Because of the vagaries of routing, domestic airlines may make it cheaper to fly via larger New York or Atlanta hubs, with a switch onto a plane that is stopping in Philadelphia on its way to another destination. Bucket shops, or ticket consolidators, may be able to deliver a rate lower than anything advertised by the airlines; try **Council Charter,** 205 E. 42nd St., New York, NY 10017 (☎ **212/661-0311** or **800/800-8222**), a longtime charter operator.

Frommer's Smart Traveler: Airfares

1. Shop all airlines that fly to Philadelphia.

2. Ask for the lowest fare, not just a discount fare, and be prepared to transfer midroute.

3. Keep calling the airline to check fares. As a departure date draws nearer, more seats are sold at lower prices, so keep checking if you can cope with the uncertainty.

4. Ask about senior-citizen discounts (usually 10%).

5. Check reputable bucket shops for last-minute discount fares that are even cheaper than advertised fares.

6. Look for special promotions offered by major carriers trying to protect hubs or gain a foothold in the Philadelphia market.

By Train

Philadelphia is a major Amtrak stop. It's on the Boston–Washington, D.C., northeast corridor, which has extensions south, west to Pittsburgh and Chicago, and east to Atlantic City. The Amtrak terminal is Penn (30th Street) Station, about 15 blocks from City Hall. Regular service from New York City takes 85 minutes; Metroliner service is 15 minutes faster. Philadelphia is 5 hours from Boston and 100 minutes from Washington, D.C., by Metroliner (☎ toll free **800/USA-RAIL**).

SEPTA commuter trains also connect 30th Street Station and several Center City stations to Trenton, N.J., to the northeast, Harrisburg to the west, and directly to airport terminals to the south.

These are sample round-trip fares on Amtrak: New York City to Philadelphia, $64 regular, $52 excursion (not valid Friday from noon to 7pm); Washington to Philadelphia, $70 regular, $54 excursion (no time restrictions); and one train daily to or from Chicago, $128 to $242.

Keep in mind that Philadelphia trips can be much cheaper if you take **Transport of New Jersey (TNJ)** commuter trains out of Penn Station in New York City or Newark to Trenton, then switch across the platform to a Philadelphia-bound SEPTA commuter train that makes several Center City stops before heading out to Chestnut Hill. Total one-way cost is $17; ☎ **215/569-3752**.

By Bus

Peter Pan/Trailways, the chief U.S. intercity operator, operates a great new office and terminal on 11th Street between Filbert and Arch streets, right across from the Convention Center (☎ **215/931-4000** or toll-free **800/343-9999**). Bus travel is definitely cheaper than train travel, but it's generally slower and more cramped. Depending on advance purchase and length of stay, a round-trip ticket to or from New York City is $22.95 for the 120-minute trip. The same condition to Washington, D.C., produces a fare of $24.95. Transport of New Jersey (TNJ) (☎ **215/569-3752**) also operates buses out of Philadelphia, with terminals at Camden, Atlantic City, and other nearby destinations.

By Car

Philadelphia is better served than ever before by a series of interstate highways that circle or pass through the city. I-95 whizzes by the southern and eastern side of the city. The Pennsylvania Turnpike (I-276) is just north of the city, but I-76 splits off and snakes along the Schuylkill River into town. A branch, I-676, leads to adjacent Camden, N.J., via the Ben Franklin Bridge over the Delaware. I-276 and I-76 are connected with I-95 by I-476 (the "Blue Route") about 15 miles west of the city. Philadelphia is some 300 miles (six or so hours) from Boston, 100 miles (two hours) from New York City, 135 miles (three hours) from Washington, D.C., and 450 miles (nine hours) from Montreal. Tolls between either New York City or Washington come to about $10.

3

For Foreign Visitors

THE ENTIRE WORLD KNOWS AMERICAN POP ENTERTAINMENT AND CULTURE—but a first visit to the United States will quickly bring you into contact with different and complex life-styles. Philadelphia, as a first destination, is slightly easier to take than most other cities, especially if you have been to or live in London; after all, the city was the second city of the British Empire for 100 years. Nevertheless, you will encounter many uniquely American situations.

1 Preparing for Your Trip

Any American city can be a bit bewildering for a foreign tourist on first arrival, even a city that has accepted as many immigrants throughout its history as Philadelphia. The City of Brotherly Love wants to make the foreigner feel at home, so it has set up an **International Visitors Center** at 1600 Arch St., Philadelphia, PA 19103 (☎ **215/686-4471**). This center offers special services to visitors from overseas.

Entry Requirements

DOCUMENT REGULATIONS   Canadian citizens may enter the United States without visas; they need only proof of residence. Citizens of the U.K., New Zealand, Japan, and most western European countries traveling on valid national (or EC) passports may not need visas for holiday or business travel in the United States of 90 days or less if they hold round-trip or return tickets and if they enter the United States on an airline or cruise line that participates in the visa waiver program.

Note: Citizens of these visa-exempt countries who first enter the United States may then visit Mexico, Canada, Bermuda, and/or the Caribbean islands and then reenter the United States, by any mode of transportation, without needing a visa. Further information is available from any U.S. embassy or consulate.

Citizens of countries other than those above, including citizens of Australia, must have two documents: a valid **passport,** with an expiration date at least six months later than the scheduled end of the visit to the United States; and a **tourist visa,** available without charge from the nearest U.S. consulate. The traveler must submit a completed visa application form (either in person or by mail) with a $1^{1}/_{2}$-inch square photo and demonstrate binding ties to a residence abroad. If applying in person you will generally receive your visa at once or within 24 hours at most; try to avoid the summer rush from June to August. If applying by mail, enclose a large self-addressed stamped envelope and expect an average wait of two weeks. Visa application forms are available at airline offices or from travel agents as well as from U.S. consulates. The U.S. tourist visa (visa B-2) is theoretically valid for a year and for any number of entries, but the U.S. consulate that issues the tourist visa will determine whether you will be issued a multiple- or single-entry visa and any restrictions regarding the length of your stay.

MEDICAL REQUIREMENTS   No inoculations are needed to enter the United States unless you are coming from areas known to be suffering from epidemics, especially of cholera or yellow fever.

If you have a disease requiring treatment with medications containing narcotics or drugs requiring a syringe carry a valid, signed prescription from your physician.

Travel Insurance—Baggage, Health & Accident

All insurance is voluntary in the United States. Given the very high cost of U.S. medical care, however, I strongly advise every traveler to arrange for appropriate coverage before setting out. There are specialized insurance companies that will, for a relatively low premium, cover loss or theft of baggage; trip-cancellation costs; guarantee of bail in case of arrest; sickness or injury costs (medical, surgical, and hospital); and costs of an accident, repatriation, or death. Insurance packages (for example, Europ Assistance, 252 High St., Croydon, Surrey CR0 1NF, England; ☎ **01/680-1234**) are sold by automobile clubs at attractive rates, as well as by banks and travel agencies.

---

2   Getting To & Around the United States

Travelers from overseas can take advantage of the **APEX (Advance Purchase Excursion) fares** offered by major U.S. and European carriers. Aside from these, attractive values are offered by **Icelandair** on flights from Luxembourg to New York or Orlando and by **Virgin Atlantic Airways** from London to New York–Newark or Miami.

Some large airlines (for example, TWA, American Airlines, Northwest, United, and Delta) offer transatlantic and transpacific travelers special discount tickets under the name **Visit USA,** allowing travel between U.S. destinations at minimum rates. They are not on sale in the United States. This system is the best, easiest, and fastest way to see the United States at low cost. You should obtain information well in advance from your travel agent or the office of the relevant airline, since conditions attached to these discount tickets can change at any time.

International visitors can also buy a **USA Railpass,** good for 15 or 30 days of unlimited travel on Amtrak. The pass is available through many foreign-travel agents. Prices in 1994 for a 15-day pass are $208 off-peak, $308 peak; a 30-day pass costs $309 off-peak, $389 peak. (With a foreign passport, you can also buy passes at some Amtrak offices in the United States, including locations in San Francisco, Los Angeles, Chicago, New York, Miami, Boston, and Washington, D.C.) Reservations are generally required and should be made for each part of your trip as early as possible.

Visitors should also be aware of the limitations of long-distance rail travel in the United States. With a few notable exceptions (for instance, the Northeast Corridor line between Boston and Washington, D.C.), service and convenience are rarely up to European standards. Thus, cross-country train travel should be approached with caution.

The cheapest way to travel the United States is by **bus.** Greyhound, a nationwide bus line, offers an **Ameripass** for unlimited travel for 7 days (for $250), 15 days (for $350), and 30 days (for $450). Bus travel in the United States can be both slow and uncomfortable, so this option is not for everyone.

For information on transportation to Philadelphia from elsewhere in the United States, see "Getting There" in Chapter 2.

Fast Facts: For the Foreign Traveler

Automobile Organizations   Auto clubs can supply maps; recommended routes; guidebooks; accident and bail-bond insurance; and, most important, emergency road service. The leader, with some 850 offices and 28 million members, is the **American Automobile Association (AAA),** with national headquarters at 1000 AAA Dr., Heathrow, FL 32745 (☎ toll-free **800/336-4357**). The AAA can provide you with an **international driving permit** validating your foreign license. The local office is **Keystone AAA,** 2040 Market St., Philadelphia, PA 19103 (☎ **215/864-5000**). Local emergency road service is **569-4411.**

Auto Rentals   To rent a car, you will need a major credit card. Minimum driver age is usually 21, and you'll need a valid driver's license.

The majors are **Hertz** (☎ toll free **800/654-3131**), **Avis** (☎ toll free **800/831-2847**), **National** (☎ toll free **800/328-4567**), **Budget** (☎ toll free **800/527-0700**), and **Alamo** (☎ toll free **800/327-9633**). Also check smaller local companies and car dealers like **Sheehy Ford** (☎ **698-7000**).

Business Hours   Public and private **offices** are usually open Monday through Friday from 9am to 5pm.

Banking hours are generally Monday through Friday from 9am to 3pm, in some cases Friday until 6pm and Saturday morning.

Post offices are open Monday through Friday from 8am to 5:30 or 6pm, Saturday from 8am to noon.

Store hours are Monday through Saturday from 9 or 10am to 5:30 or 6pm, though often on Wednesday until 9pm in Philadelphia. Most shopping centers, drugstores, and supermarkets are open Monday through Saturday from 9am to 9pm, with some open 24 hours a day.

Climate   See "When to Go" in Chapter 2.

Currency   The U.S. monetary system has a decimal base—one **dollar** ($1) = 100 **cents** (100¢).

The commonest **bills** (all mostly green, all the same size) are the $1 ("a buck"), $5, $10, and $20 denominations. There are also $2 (seldom encountered), $50, and $100 bills (the latter two are not welcome when paying for small purchases).

There are six denominations of **coins:** 1¢ (one cent, a penny); 5¢ (nickel); 10¢ (dime); 25¢ (quarter); 50¢ (half dollar); and the rare $1 piece.

Traveler's checks denominated in U.S. dollars are readily accepted at hotels, motels, restaurants, and large stores. The best place to change traveler's checks is at a bank. Do not bring traveler's checks denominated in other currencies.

The payment method most widely used is the **credit card**—VISA (BarclayCard in Britain), MasterCard (EuroCard in Europe, Access in Britain, Chargex in Canada), American Express, Discover Card, Diners Club, and Carte Blanche. You can save yourself trouble by using "plastic money," rather than cash or traveler's checks, in most hotels, motels, restaurants, and retail stores. A growing number of food and liquor stores now accept credit cards. A credit card can serve as a deposit when renting a car; as proof of identity (often carrying more weight than a passport); or as a "cash card," enabling you to draw money from automatic-teller machines and at banks.

Currency Exchange   For major foreign currencies, the following Philadelphia institutions in Center City provide exchange service: American Express Travel Service, 2 Penn Center Plaza (☎ **587-2342** or **587-2343**); Continental Bank, 1201 Chestnut St. (☎ **564-7188**); Thomas Cook Currency Services, Inc., 1800 John F. Kennedy Blvd. (☎ **563-5544**); CoreStates Philadelphia National Bank, 5th and Market streets (☎ **629-4402**); First Fidelity Bank, Broad and Walnut streets (☎ **985-7068**); Mellon Bank, Broad and Chestnut streets (☎ **553-2145**); Meridian Bank, 1700 Arch St. (☎ **854-3549**); and PNC National Bank, Broad and Chestnut streets (☎ **585-5000**).

Customs and Immigration   Every adult visitor may bring in, free of duty: 1 liter of wine or hard liquor; 200 cigarettes or 100 cigars (but *no* cigars from Cuba) or 3 pounds (1.35kg) of smoking tobacco; and $100 worth of gifts. These exemptions are offered to travelers who spend at least 72 hours in the United States and who have not claimed them within the preceding six months. It is forbidden to bring into the country foodstuffs like cheese, fruit, cooked meats, and canned goods and plants (vegetables, seeds, tropical plants, and so on). Foreign tourists may bring in or take out up to $10,000 in U.S. or foreign currency with no formalities; larger sums must be declared to Customs on entering and leaving.

The visitor arriving by air, no matter what the port of entry—New York, Boston, Miami, Honolulu, Los Angeles, or the rest—should cultivate patience and resignation before setting foot on U.S. soil. The U.S. Customs and Immigration services are among the slowest and most suspicious on earth. You should plan on a minimum allowance of two to three hours' delay for connections between international and domestic flights.

In contrast, for the traveler arriving by car or by rail from Canada, the border-crossing formalities have been streamlined to the vanishing point. And for the traveler by air from Canada, Bermuda, and some points in the Caribbean, you can go through Customs and Immigration at the point of *departure,* which is much quicker and less painful.

Drinking Laws   You must be 21 or older to consume alcohol in public. In Philadelphia, establishments may serve alcoholic beverages from 9am to 2am (private clubs may serve to 4am). Liquor purchasing in Pennsylvania is quite restricted (see Chapter 9).

Electric Current   U.S. wall outlets give power at 110 to 120 volts, 60 cycles, compared to 220 to 240 volts, 50 cycles, in most of Europe. In addition to a 110-volt converter, small appliances of non-American manufacture, such as hair dryers and shavers, will require a plug adapter with two flat, parallel pins.

Embassies/Consulates   All embassies are located in Washington, D.C., as it's the nation's capital, and many consulates are located there as well. Among the embassies are those for **Australia,** 1601 Massachusetts Ave. NW, Washington, DC 20036 (☎ **202/797-3000**); **Canada,** 501 Pennsylvania Ave. NW (☎ **202/682-1740**); **France,** 4101 Reservoir Rd. NW 20007 (☎ **202/944-6000**); **Germany,** 4645 Reservoir Rd. (☎ **202/298-4000**); **Netherlands,** 4200 Linnean Ave. NW (☎ **202/244-5300**); **United Kingdom,** 3100 Massachusetts Ave. NW, Washington, D.C. 20008 (☎ **202/462-1340**). You can obtain the telephone numbers of other embassies and consulates by calling "information" in Washington (dial **202/555-1212**).

Emergencies   In all major cities (including Philadelphia) you can call the police, an ambulance, or the fire brigade through the single emergency telephone number **911.** Another useful way of reporting an emergency is to call the telephone-company operator by dialing **0** (zero, *not* the letter "O"). Outside major cities, call the county sheriff or the fire brigade at the number you will find in the local telephone book.

If you encounter such travelers' problems as sickness, accident, or lost or stolen baggage, it will pay you to call the **Travelers Aid Society** at **546-0571** or **386-0845**. It's an organization that specializes in helping distressed travelers, whether American or foreign.

For medical emergencies at Philadelphia International Airport, call **365-5350**.

Gasoline [Petrol]   One U.S. gallon equals 3.75 liters, while 1.2 U.S. gallons equals one imperial gallon. You'll notice several grades (and price levels) of gasoline at most gas stations. And you'll also notice that their names change from company to company. The unleaded grades with the highest octane are the most expensive, but most rental cars take the least expensive "regular" unleaded. Leaded gasoline is rarely used anymore.

Holidays   On the following national legal holidays, banks, government offices, post offices, and many stores, restaurants, and museums are closed.

January 1 (New Year's Day)
Third Monday in January (Martin Luther King Day)
Third Monday in February (Presidents Day, marking Washington's and Lincoln's birthdays)
Last Monday in May (Memorial Day)
July 4 (Independence Day)
First Monday in September (Labor Day)
Second Monday in October (Columbus Day)
November 11 (Veterans Day/Armistice Day)
Fourth Thursday in November (Thanksgiving Day)
December 25 (Christmas)

The Tuesday following the first Monday in November is Election Day. It is a legal holiday in presidential-election years (1996).

Legal Aid   The foreign tourist will probably never become involved with the American legal system. If you are cited for a minor infraction (for example, of the highway code, such as speeding), never try to pay the fine directly to a police officer; you may wind up arrested on the much more serious charge of attempted bribery. Pay fines by mail or directly to the clerk of a court. If you're accused of a more serious offense, it is wise to say and do nothing before consulting a lawyer. Under U.S. law, an arrested person is allowed one telephone call to a party of his or her choice. Call your embassy or consulate.

Mail   Generally found at major road or street intersections, mailboxes are blue with a red-and-white stripe and carry the inscription "U.S. MAIL." If your mail is addressed to a U.S. destination, don't forget to add the five-figure postal code or ZIP code after the two-letter abbreviation of the state to which the mail is addressed (CA for California, MA for Massachusetts, NY for New York, PA for Pennsylvania, and so on). 1994 rates are 19¢ for domestic postcards, 29¢ for domestic letters.

Philadelphia's **main post offices** are located at 9th and Market streets and across from Penn Station at 30th Street.

Newspapers/Magazines   National newspapers include the *New York Times, USA Today,* and the *Wall Street Journal.* There are also several national news weeklies including *Newsweek, Time,* and *U.S. News & World Report.* For information on local Philadelphia periodicals, see "Newspapers/Magazines" in "Fast Facts: Philadelphia," in Chapter 4.

Radio/Television   Audiovisual media, with three coast-to-coast networks—ABC, CBS, and NBC—joined in recent years by the Public Broadcasting System (PBS) and the Fox Broadcasting Network and the cable network CNN, play a major part in American life. In big cities like Philadelphia, televiewers have a choice of about a dozen channels, most transmitting 24 hours a day, without counting the pay-TV channels showing movies or sports events. All options are indicated on your hotel TV. You'll also find a wide choice of local radio stations.

Safety   Whenever you're traveling in an unfamiliar city, stay alert. Be aware of your immediate surroundings. Wear a money belt—or, better yet, check valuables in a safety-deposit box at your hotel. Keep a close eye on your possessions and be sure to keep them in sight when you're seated in a restaurant, theater, or other public place. Don't leave valuables in your car—even in the trunk. While driving a car, be extremely cautious when unlocking doors or leaving your car for any reason. Every city has its criminals. It's your responsibility to be aware and be alert even in the most heavily touristed areas.

Taxes   In the United States there is no VAT (value-added tax) at the national level. Every state, and each city in it, can levy its own local tax on purchases, including hotel and restaurant checks, airline tickets, and the like. It is automatically added to the price of certain services, such as public transportation, cab fares, phone calls, and gasoline. It varies from 4% to 10%, depending on the state and city, so when you are making major purchases such as photographic equipment, clothing, or high-fidelity components, it can be a significant part of the cost. Philadelphia's sales tax is 7%, except for clothing.

Each locality can levy its own separate tax on hotel occupancy. Since this tax is in addition to any general sales tax, taken together these two taxes can add a considerable amount to the cost of your accommodations. In Philadelphia, in addition to your hotel rate, you pay 7% sales tax plus a 5% surcharge.

Telephone/Telegraph/Telex   You will find **pay phones** an integral part of the American landscape. They are almost everywhere—at street corners; in bars, restaurants, public buildings, stores, and service stations; along highways; and on and on. Telephones are provided by private corporations, which perhaps explains the high standard of service. In Philadelphia local calls cost 25¢.

Generally, hotel surcharges on long-distance and local calls are astronomical. These are best avoided by using a public phone, calling collect, or using a telephone charge card.

For **long-distance** or **international calls,** stock up with a supply of quarters; the pay phone will instruct you when, and in what quantity, you should put them into the slot. For direct overseas calls, first dial 011, followed by the country code and then by the city code and the number of the person you wish to call. For calls to Canada and long-distance calls in the United States, dial 1 followed by the area code and number.

For **reversed-charge** or **collect calls,** and for **person-to-person calls,** dial 0 (zero, *not* the letter "O") followed by the area code and number you want; an operator will then come on the line, and you should specify that you are calling collect or person-to-person or both. If your operator-assisted call is international, ask for the overseas operator.

For local **directory assistance** ("information"), dial 411; for **long-distance information,** dial 1, then the appropriate area code and **555-1212**.

Like the telephone system, **telegraph** and **telex** services are provided by private corporations, such as ITT, MCI, and above all, Western Union, the most important. You can bring your telegram in to the nearest Western Union office (Philadelphia alone has over 75) or dictate it over the phone (a toll-free call, **800/325-6000**). You can also telegraph money or have it telegraphed to you very quickly over the Western Union system.

Telephone Directory   See "White and Yellow Pages," below.

Time   The conterminous United States is divided into four **time zones** (six, if Alaska and Hawaii are included). From east to west, these are: eastern standard time (EST), central standard time (CST), mountain standard time (MST), Pacific standard time (PST), Alaska standard time (AST), and Hawaii standard time (HST). For example, noon in New York City (EST) is 11am in Chicago (CST), 10am in Denver (MST), 9am in Los Angeles (PST), 8am in Anchorage (AST), and 7am in Honolulu (HST). Philadelphia is on EST.

Daylight saving time (DST) is in effect from the first Sunday in April through the last Saturday in October (actually, the change is made at 2am on Sunday) except in Arizona, Hawaii, part of Indiana, and Puerto Rico. Daylight saving time moves the clock one hour ahead of standard time.

Tipping   This is part of the American way of life, on the principle that you must pay for any service received. Bartenders should receive 10% to 15%; bellhops, 50¢ per bag; cab drivers, 15% of the fare; chambermaids, $1 a day; waiters, 15% to 20% of the check.

White and Yellow Pages   There are two basic kinds of telephone directories. The general directory is the so-called **White Pages,** in which private and business subscribers are listed in alphabetical order. The inside front cover lists emergency numbers for police, fire, and ambulance as well as other vital numbers (the Coast Guard, poison-control center, crime-victims hotline, and so on). The first few pages include community service numbers and a guide to long-distance and international calling, complete with country codes and area codes. A thin **Blue Pages** in the back of the White Pages book lists federal, state, and local government offices.

The second basic directory, the **Yellow Pages,** lists local services, businesses, and industries by type of activity, with an index at the back.

4

Getting to Know Philadelphia

THIS CHAPTER SETS OUT TO ANSWER ALL YOUR TRAVEL QUESTIONS, FURNISH-
ing you with all the practical information that you'll need during your
stay in Philadelphia to handle any and every experience—from the
city layout and transportation to emergencies to business hours.

1 Orientation

Arriving

BY PLANE

Philadelphia International Airport (☎ **215/492-3181**), in the
southwest part of the city, has become one of the country's busiest
in the last 10 years. Under a $315-million improvement plan, the
new international Terminal A (Dilworth Terminal) and additional
garages have been built; a new runway and general facelift are still in
progress.

The airport is laid out with a central corridor connecting the five
basic depots. Terminal B is the place to catch taxis, buses, and hotel
limousines. The areas with the most amenities are between Terminals B and C and between Terminals D and E.

If you're driving to the airport, long-term parking is available for
$14 per day at the Terminals C and D garages or $6 per day for regular
long-term parking. The **Guest Quarters/Days Inn** complex on Island Avenue has an enclosed, 24-hour security Park-and-Fly
with a shuttle bus; parking there costs $6 per day, and the lot is 8
minutes from terminals. You might also try **Flying Carport**
(☎ **215/492-2161**), an airport valet service where you drop off your
car and are taken to the airport by van.

A taxi from the airport to Center City takes about 25 minutes and
costs upward of $25 plus tip. If you're interested in airport limou-
sines (actually, some are vans), several connect with area destinations.
Expect a rate of $70 for a sedan or $81 for a stretch limo (both include tip) to nonhotel addresses at Center City; $81 and $119, respectively, to Valley Forge; and $115 and $145, respectively, plus
tip and tolls, to Atlantic City. Try **Airport-Limelight**
(☎ **215/342-5557**; fax **215/347-7121**), **Carey Limousine**
(☎ **215/492-8402**), or **Philadelphia Airport Shuttle, Inc.**
(☎ **215/969-1818**).

A high-speed rail link with direct service between the airport and
Center City was opened in 1985. The trains run daily every 30 minutes from 5:30am to 11:25pm. They leave the airport at 10 and 40
minutes past the hour. Trains to the airport depart from Market East
(and a Convention Center connection), Suburban Station at 16th
Street, and 30th Street Station. The 35-minute trip costs adults $6
if they buy their tickets on board, $5 if they prepurchase; children's
fares are $3 and $2.50, respectively, and the family fare is $15.

BY TRAIN

All Northeast Corridor **Amtrak** trains stop at the 30th Street Station (☎ **215/824-1600** or toll free **800/872-7245**), a gloriously

clean and well-lit terminal just across the Schuylkill River in West Philadelphia. It now handles more than 3.2 million passengers per year, second only to New York City's Penn Station, and more trains are on the way, thanks to the renewed Atlantic City rail link. From 30th Street Station, catch one of the commuter trains for a free shuttle into Suburban Station at 16th Street and John F. Kennedy Boulevard. This station serves Harrisburg and West Chester and connects to the other commuter lines at the Market Street East Station, at 10th and Market streets. Remember, you can also pick up the rail link direct to the airport. If you want to leave a car in the adjoining lots, the rate is $14 per day.

BY BUS

Greyhound (☎ 215/931-4075) and Peter Pan/Trailways (☎ 215/413-3420) opened a new 24-hour concrete structure in summer 1987. It's behind the Gallery, an urban mall, and less than a block from the new Pennsylvania Convention Center at 10th and Filbert streets. Filbert, one block north of Market Street, is a commuter-rail stop and very well situated for the new Convention Center. Peter Pan/Trailways carries people, while Greyhound handles freight.

BY CAR

Most of Philadelphia's sights and sounds are in Center City, the band stretching between the Delaware and Schuylkill rivers at the thinnest point. I-95 snakes along the eastern side of Center City, along the Delaware River, while the Schuylkill Expressway, I-76, follows a route along the western side (mostly just over the Schuylkill River). Here are directions to City Hall, in the very center of town, from various directions:

From the Northeast and Eastern Canada

JERSEY TURNPIKE SOUTHBOUND EXIT 6   Take the Pennsylvania Turnpike westbound to the first exit, Exit 29, and change to U.S. 13 southbound. Follow the signs a short distance to I-95 southbound and enter at Exit 22, heading south. Exit for Center City at I-676 (Vine Street Expressway) westbound to 15th Street, then turn left and travel southbound two blocks.

NEW JERSEY TURNPIKE EXIT 4   Take N.J. 73 northbound to N.J. 38 westbound, then change to U.S. 30 westbound (the signage is abominable) and follow it over the Ben Franklin Bridge ($2 this way, but free eastbound) to I-676. Go south on 6th Street to Walnut Street (historic district will be on the left), turn right, and travel westbound to 15th Street.

From Southeastern Pennsylvania, Delaware, and Maryland

FROM I-95 NORTHBOUND   Just past Philadelphia International Airport, take Pa. 291 toward Center City, Philadelphia. Cross the George C. Platt Memorial Bridge and turn left onto 26th Street, then follow 26th Street directly onto I-76 (Schuylkill Expressway) westbound to Exit 39 (30th Street Station). Go one block to Market

Street and turn right. Go east on Market Street to City Hall, which will be in front of you.

FROM THE PENNSYLVANIA TURNPIKE [I-76]   Take Exit 24 to I-76 (Schuylkill Expressway) eastbound to I-676 (Vine Street Expressway). Take I-676 eastbound to 15th Street, turn right, and proceed southbound two blocks.

Tourist Information

The **Philadelphia Convention and Visitors Bureau,** 1515 John F. Kennedy Blvd., Philadelphia, PA 19102 (☎ **215/636-1666**), is one of the very best in America. It looks like a shiny layer.cake between Suburban Station and City Hall, and its reception desk is staffed by enthusiastic and knowledgeable volunteers. You can pick up coupons for reduced admissions to many museums and attractions, too, as well as free aids for the blind and disabled. They parcel out free tickets to the New Year's Day Mummers Parade and to the Mann Music Center for summer concerts in the park and they also sell such tickets as the SEPTA DayPass ($5) and "A Gift of Gardens" for 14 regional sites ($7.95). Some floor space has been devoted to a city gift shop.

The bureau is open daily from 9am to 5pm (except Christmas Day) and until 6pm on summer weekdays. If you think ahead, call toll free **800/537-7676** to get material on all the special promotions of the season. In summer, if you show up at noon, there's usually outdoor entertainment on the adjoining plaza, which anchors one end of the Benjamin Franklin Parkway (known simply as "the Parkway").

City Layout

Unlike Boston, Philadelphia has no colonial cowpaths that were turned into streets. If you can count and remember the names of trees, you'll know exactly where you are in the Center City grid. For the overview, go to (or pretend you're at) the top of **City Hall,** that overiced wedding cake in the very center of things, at the intersection of Broad and Market streets. Admission is free, and it's open daily from 9am to 4:30pm (see Chapter 7). **Broad Street** runs four miles south, where the Delaware and Schuylkill flow together, and eight miles north—all perfectly straight. The other major north-south streets are numbered (the opposite of those in New York City). Except for a few two-way exceptions, traffic on even-numbered streets heads south and on odd-numbered streets, north. **Front Street** (should be 1st Street), once at the Delaware's edge off to the right, and neighboring **2nd Street** were the major thoroughfares in colonial times. In-between streets are named. The major east-west streets in Philadelphia's Center City run from Spring Garden Street to the north to South Street. You'll spend much of your time between Arch and Pine streets, especially south of Chestnut Street. Addresses on these streets add 100 for every block away from the axis of Market (north-south) or Front Street (east-west); 1534 Chestnut St. is between 15th and 16th streets, and 610 S. 5th St. is between six and seven blocks south of Market.

The colonial city, now **Independence National Historical Park** and reconstructed row houses, grew up along the Delaware north and south of **Market Street,** extending west to 6th Street by 1776. The 19th century saw the development of the western quadrants (including most museums and cultural centers) and suburbs in every direction. The city blocks planned by William Penn included five parks spaced between the two rivers. Four parks have been named for local notables (including George Washington, who headed the federal government here in the 1790s), and the fifth supports City Hall. A broad northwest boulevard, dividing the grid like a slice of Paris, ends in the majestic arms of the Philadelphia Museum of Art. The entire quadrant west and north of City Hall has been the site of intensive development of hotels, office buildings, and apartment houses.

Just beyond, the Schuylkill separates Philadelphia from West Philadelphia from 24th Street to about 30th Street—if you're looking for an address in this area, ask which side it's on. **Fairmount Park** lines both sides of the Schuylkill for miles above the museum.

For descriptions of Philadelphia neighborhoods, see under "More Attractions" in Chapter 7.

2 Getting Around

By Public Transportation

SEPTA (Southeastern Pennsylvania Transportation Authority) operates a complicated and extensive network of trolleys, buses, commuter trains, and subways. In the past 10 years the capital budget for new equipment has increased from $20 million to $120 million; new cars gleam on the Broad Street line.

Fares for any SEPTA route are $1.50, with 40¢ more for a transfer, and *exact change or tokens are required.* Anyone can purchase a 5-pack for $5.25 or a 10-pack for $10.50. Seniors pay nothing and the disabled pay half-fare during off-peak hours. Certain buses and trolleys run 24 hours a day. The $5 DayPass is good for all buses, subways, and one ride on the Airport loop; a weekly TransPass, good from Monday to the next Sunday, is $16.

An **Information center** (open Monday to Friday from 7am to 6pm, also on Saturday in summer) in the underground arcade at 15th and Market streets will give you free timetables and routes for individual lines (take the down escalator across the street from City Hall and turn right). The official street and transit map, which puts the entire picture together, costs $1.50 and is available here or at newsstands. If you have questions about how to reach a specific destination, call SEPTA headquarters at **215/580-7800** between 6am and midnight—but expect to wait.

SUBWAY-SURFACE LINE

This "local" connects City Hall and 30th Street Station, stopping at 19th and 22nd streets along the way. West of the Amtrak station, it branches out, moving aboveground to the north and south.

RAPID TRANSIT

In Center City, these fast cars speed under Broad Street and Market Street, intersecting under City Hall. The Broad Street line now connects directly to Pattison Avenue and Philadelphia sporting events to the south. The Market Street line stops at 2nd, 5th, 8th, 11th, 13th (Convention Center), 15th, and 30th Street stations and stretches to the west and northeast. Both run all night, but residents suggest caution during late-hour use.

PATCO

This commuter rail line (☎ **215/922-4600**) begins at Walnut and Locust streets around Broad Street, connects with rapid transit at 8th and Market, and crosses the Ben Franklin Bridge to Camden. To get to the Aquarium, get off at Broadway to transfer to the New Jersey Transit's Aqualink Shuttle. Transfers connect to the Jersey shore from Lindenwold.

BUS

Even though there are dozens of routes, you'll often find yourself on the **Chestnut Street Transitway,** a stretch of Chestnut between 17th and 6th streets open only to buses and taxis. Bus no. 42 swoops along Chestnut from West Philadelphia to 2nd at all hours. Route 76, the **Ben FrankLine,** is a subsidized tourism deal at 50¢; it connects Society Hill at 3rd and Chestnut streets to the Parkway all the way to the Museum of Art and the Zoo; it operates every 10 minutes weekdays, every 20 minutes weekends. The first trip from 3rd Street is at 9am, and the last pick up at the Museum of Art is at 6:11pm. Market Street serves several bus routes; the **Mid-City loop** ($1.50, with a 40¢ transfer to another bus) goes up Market and down Chestnut between 5th and 17th streets. Route 32 goes up Broad Street and the Parkway and through Fairmount Park to Andorra; the full trip is 15 miles. New double buses now swivel through many major routes.

TROLLEY

There are no more "true" city trolleys like in Boston or San Francisco. A privately operated **Penn's Landing Trolley** chugs along Christopher Columbus Boulevard (formerly Delaware Avenue) between the Benjamin Franklin Bridge and Fitzwater Street; you can board at Dock Street or Spruce Street. Fare is $1.50 for adults, 75¢ for children, and the trolley runs Thursday through Sunday from 11am to dusk in the summer.

Replicas of 1930s open-air trolleys operate as 39-seat buses run by **American Trolley Bus** (☎ **333-0320**) and **Old Town Trolley** (☎ **928-8687**), with guides who point out all the high spots. Admission ranges from $6 to $14, depending on length of tour and family size. Pick-up spots include Liberty Bell Pavilion, Independence Park Visitors Center, and the Franklin Institute.

TRAIN

The Philadelphia area is served by one of the great commuter-rail networks in America. Chestnut Hill, a wealthy enclave of fine shops and restaurants, can be reached from both Suburban Station at 16th Street and John F. Kennedy Boulevard and Reading Terminal at 12th and Market streets, now connected themselves by the new rail link. The famous term "Main Line" refers, in fact, to the old Pennsylvania Railroad line from Suburban (now Penn Center) Station to Harrisburg. What in the suburbs would interest the tourist? Merion is home to the great Barnes Foundation art collection and the Buten Museum of Wedgwood. Bryn Mawr, Haverford, Swarthmore, and Villanova are sites of noted colleges. Devon hosts a great horse and country fair. One-way fares for all destinations are under $5, and you can buy tickets at station counters or vending machines.

By Other Transportation

TAXI

Philadelphia's notorious shortage of taxis is improving, with about 1,400 currently licensed. Under 1991 legislation, gypsy cabs have been outlawed in return for increasing taxi medallions. Cabbies must pass stringent tests for city knowledge and maintain clean vehicles. Fares are currently $1.50 for the first one-seventh mile and 20¢ for each additional one-seventh of a mile or minute of stasis. Tips are expected, naturally.

If you need to call for a cab while in the city, the three largest outfits are **Olde City Taxi** (☎ 338-0838), **United Cab** (☎ 238-9500), and **Quaker City** (☎ 728-8000).

CAR

Philadelphia's streets were once considered so wide that there was room for market stalls in the divides. Unfortunately, that was 200 years ago. So on Center City streets there's little room for parked or moving cars. You might try the streets below Chestnut. Locust, Spruce, and Pine are often the best. Be forewarned that—except for lower Market Street, the Parkway, Vine Street, and Broad Street—*all streets are one-way.* Convention and Visitors Bureau at the foot of the Parkway offers a Center City traffic map. Traffic around City Hall follows a counterclockwise pattern, but traffic lights seem to follow none. Try not to get caught vehicle bound during rush hours.

Since Philadelphia's so walkable, it is easier to leave your car while you tour. Many hotels offer free or reduced-rate parking to registered guests.

Heaven forbid that you should need an emergency car repair, but if you do, try **Center City Auto Care,** 901 N. Broad St. (☎ 763-8328), or **Mina Motors,** Broad and Fitzwater streets (☎ 735-2749), for same-day service. **Keystone AAA** is at 2040 Market St., Philadelphia, PA 19103 (☎ 864-5000).

RENTALS   Philadelphia has no shortage of cars and very good rental rates as a consequence. For example, you can pick up a weekend sedan from **Avis** (☎ toll free **800/331-1212**) for $35 per day, with unlimited mileage, at one of their lots: 2000 Arch St. (☎ **563-8976**), 30th Street Station (☎ **386-6426**), or under Independence Place at 6th and Locust streets (☎ **928-1082**). Avis and all other major renters maintain offices at the airport. These include **Budget** (☎ **492-9442** at the airport, **557-0808** at 21st and Market, or toll free **800/527-0700**); **Dollar** (☎ **365-1605** at the airport or toll free **800/562-7850**); and **Hertz** (☎ toll free **800/654-3131** to all locations). **Ambassador** now has an office at the Sheraton Society Hill, 2nd and Dock streets (☎ toll free **800/637-8946**).

PARKING   Call the **Philadelphia Parking Authority** (☎ **563-7670** or **977-7275**) for current information.

Garage rates are fairly similar: Outside of hotels, no place exceeds $22 per day, with typical charges of $3.50 per hour and $10 for an evening out.

Parking can be found for **Independence Park** at 125 S. 2nd St. (Sansom Street is the cross street); Independence Mall Garage, 41 N. 6th St.; Spruce Street between 5th and 6th streets (private lot); and Head House Square, 2nd and Lombard streets (city meters). **Convention Center Area** parking includes Kinney Chinatown at 11th and Race streets (private garage); Kinney underneath the Gallery II mall at 11th and Arch streets; the Autopark beside the Gallery mall at 10th and Filbert streets; or the garage underneath the adjoining Marriott at Arch and 13th Streets. **City Hall Area** parking is underneath Wanamaker's, between Market and Chestnut streets at 13th Street (private garage on Doubletree Street); Hotel, Broad, and Spruce streets (private garage); and Kennedy Plaza, 15th Street, and John F. Kennedy Boulevard (underground city garage; enter on Arch, one block north of the plaza).

BICYCLE

Plaisted Hall, the former bicycle and boat rental facility, on 1 Boat House Row, behind the Museum of Art on the banks of the Schuylkill, burned down in 1993, but may be reconstructed by 1996 and back in business. In Center City, try Via Bicycle at 1134 Pine St. (☎ **627-3370**); rate is $8 per hour, plus deposit. Since anyone who enjoys cycling would love the outlying countryside, note that you can also rent bicycles in Lumberville, eight miles north of New Hope on the Delaware (☎ **215/297-5388**), and in Lancaster, the heart of Amish farmland (☎ **717/684-7226**).

Fast Facts: Philadelphia

Area Code   Philadelphia's telephone area code is **215.** As of 1994, Bucks County and half of Montgomery County will keep 215 also, but Delaware, Chester, and half of Montgomery will have switched to **610.**

Airport   See "Orientation," in this chapter.

American Express   AmEx, at 16th Street and John F. Kennedy Boulevard (☎ **587/2342**) or the airport (☎ **492-4200**) can handle currency exchanges, wiring money, and card services such as extension of credit.

Babysitters   Rocking Horse Child Care Center at the Curtis Center, Walnut and 6th streets (☎ **592-8257**), can accommodate children almost any age under 6. Hourly care is available for $6 per hour for those under 2, for $5 per hour for ages 3 to 6. Comparable is **Call-A-Granni, Inc.,** 1133 E. Barringer St. (☎ **924-8723**). Many hotels provide bonded sitters as well.

Business Hours   Banks are generally open Monday through Thursday from 10am to 3pm, Friday until 6pm, with some open on Saturday from 9am to noon as well. Banks charge less commission and offer better exchange rates than hotels or restaurants. Most **bars** and **restaurants** serve food until 10 or 10:30pm (some Chinatown places stay open until 3am), and social bars are open Friday and Saturday until 1 or 2am. **Offices** are open strictly Monday through Friday from 9am to 5pm. **Stores** are open daily from 9am to 5pm, and most Center City locations keep the doors ajar later on Wednesday evening. Olde City, South Street, and Head House Square are the most active late-night districts. Some SEPTA routes run all night, but the frequency of buses and trolleys drops dramatically after 6pm.

Car Rentals   See "Getting Around," in this chapter.

Climate   See "When to Go," in Chapter 2.

Courier Services   Federal Express (☎ **923-3085**) and **UPS** (☎ **463-7300**), of course, reach almost everywhere in the United States overnight, and they have many drop-off points and offices throughout Center City. For service within the city, try **Heaven Sent,** 60 N. 2nd St. (☎ **923-0929**). They will pick up from major hotels and promise same-day service to New York and Washington. For what it's worth, I've gotten cheap and excellent service using **Amtrak Package Express** (30th Street Station; ☎ **895-7111**) and local pick up. **American Eagle,** 1810 Callowhill St. (☎ **569-3300**), goes all around the city with similar dispatch.

Dentist   Call **925-6050** in a dental emergency.

Doctor   Call the Philadelphia County Medical Society at **563-5343**. You can always dial **911** in an emergency. Every hospital in town has an emergency ward.

Drugstores   I've searched all over for a 24-hour pharmacy. An alert correspondent tells of a 24-hour **CVS** at 6501 Harbison Ave. (☎ **333-4300**), but this is miles from Center City. The **Medical Tower Pharmacy,** 255 S. 17th St. (☎ **545-3525**), is open until 9pm Monday to Friday and 6pm Saturday. During regular hours, try **Barclay Pharmacy,** 18th and Spruce streets (☎ **735-1410**), and **Green Drugs,** 5th and South streets (☎ **922-7440**).

Emergencies   In an extreme emergency, telephone **911.** In case of accidental **poisoning,** call **386-2100.** For **police,** call **231-3131;** for **fire and rescue,** call **922-6000.** Ambulance and emergency transportation can be summoned through **Care & Emergency, Inc.** (☎ **877-5900**), or **SEPTA Paratransit** (☎ **574-2780**).

Eyeglasses   Snyder Opticians at 251 S. 17th St. (☎ **735-5656**) is not open late, but it does do on-site repairs. **Contact Lens Neun** at 255 S. 17th St., sixth floor (☎ **545-7355**), promises same-day replacement.

Hairdressers/Barbers   Pierre and Carlo, who enjoy a fine reputation with both sexes, are at **Downstairs at the Bellevue** (☎ **790-9910**). Two other good salons are **Oggi,** 1702 Locust St. (☎ **735-0707**), and **Thunder,** 110 S. 19th St. (☎ **563-2665**). **Pileggi on the Square,** 717 Walnut St. (☎ **627-0565**), has a reputation for great service and competence. Telephone for hours. Many Center City hotels have their own concessions as well.

Hospitals   Medical care in Philadelphia is excellent. Major hospitals include Children's Hospital, 34th St. and Civic Center Boulevard (☎ **590-1000**); Graduate Hospital, 1800 Lombard St. (☎ **893-2000**); Hahnemann, Broad and Vine streets (☎ **762-7000**); University of Pennsylvania Hospital, 3400 Spruce St. (☎ **662-4000**); Pennsylvania Hospital, 8th and Spruce streets (☎ **829-3000**); and Thomas Jefferson, 11th and Walnut streets (☎ **955-6000**).

Information   See "Tourist Information," earlier in this chapter.

Laundry/Dry Cleaning   Many of the better hotels in town can perform this service for you. Moderate accommodations listed in Chapter 5 often have their own basement washers and dryers. For dry cleaning in a pinch, try **Ye Olde Cleanery,** 23 S. 19th St. (☎ **567-9933**), or **Nu-Way Cleaners** at 520 S. 5th St. (☎ **923-6108**).

Libraries   The jewel of the public system is the **Central Free Library** at 19th and Vine streets (☎ **686-5322;** see Chapter 7 for a description). Another central oft-used collection is the **City Institute Branch** at 19th and Locust streets (☎ **735-9137**).

Liquor Laws   There are some inconvenient things about Philadelphia's Quaker roots. One is the government monopoly on package liquor sales. You, or any tavernkeeper or restaurateur, can buy liquor only in state stores. Usually open Monday through Wednesday from 9am to 5pm, Thursday through Saturday until 9pm, these carry what they carry—period. The selection has improved greatly in the past decade. You cannot get chilled beer or champagne—just what's on the shelf. (Try a delicatessen or licensed supermarket for the bubbles.) See Chapter 9 for some state stores. Minimum drinking age is 21.

Lost Property   If you lose something on a SEPTA train or subway, try the stationmaster's office in Suburban Station.

Mail Information   The main **post office** at 2970 Market St. (☎ **596-5577**), just across the Schuylkill and next to 30th Street station, is always open; the number of its 24-hour window is **895-8989**. The post office on the subway concourse at 2 Penn Center, 15th Street and John F. Kennedy Boulevard, is open Monday through Friday from 7am to 6pm, Saturday from 9am to noon. Wanamaker's department store contains a post office that's open Monday through Saturday from 10am to 6pm. The Blue Pages (government offices) of the phone directory contain a complete list.

Newspapers/Magazines   Philadelphia has two main print journals, both now owned by the same firm. The *Inquirer* is the "highbrow" paper, with a string of recent Pulitzer Prizes, and you'll probably want to look at the Friday "Weekend" supplement for listings and prices of entertainment as well as special events and tours. The *Daily News* is more close-to-home Philadelphia material. Free tabloid weeklies with surprisingly good articles and listings include *The City Paper* and *Welcomat;* you'll find them at record and book stores and on street-corner boxes. For the most complete selection of journals and newspapers, try **Avril 50,** 3406 Sansom St. (☎ **222-6108**) in University City, with lots of international fripperies such as cigarettes and candies as well. The Society Hill equivalent is **Popi,** 526 S. 4th St. (☎ **922-4119**), and 116 S. 20th St. (☎ **557-8282**), near Rittenhouse Square.

Photographic Needs   For emergency camera repair, film purchase, or one-hour processing, you might try **Photo Cine Shop,** 129 S. 18th St. (☎ **567-7410**), near Rittenhouse Square. **The Camera Shop** and **Jack's Cameras** have branches all over Center City. **Happy Photo,** at 8th and Chestnut streets (☎ **922-4422**) and 1600 John F. Kennedy Blvd. (☎ **977-2945**), offers 24-hour developing.

Police   The emergency telephone number is **911.**

Post Office   See "Mail Information," above.

Radio   There's intense competition among more than 60 stations, so the following programming emphasis is subject to change: all news, KYW (1060 AM); album-oriented rock, WMMR (93.3 FM); classic rock, WYSP (94.1 FM); oldies, WOGL (98.1 FM); soft rock, WIOQ (102.1 FM); country, WCZN (1590 AM) and WXTU (92.5 FM); ethnic urban orientation, WUSL (98.9 FM), WDAS (1480 AM), and WHAT (1340 AM); classical music, WFLN (95.7 FM) and National Public Radio, WHYY (91.0 FM) and WXPN (88.5 FM).

Religious Services   The following are some of Philadelphia's places of worship. **Baptist:** 711 S. 12th St. (☎ **922-6691**). **Episcopal:** Church of the Holy Trinity, Walnut Street and Rittenhouse Square (founded 1859; ☎ **567-1267**); St. Clement's, 20th and

Cherry streets (1856; ☎ **563-1876**); **Jewish:** Mikveh Israel, 44 N. 4th St. (1976; ☎ **922-5446**); Israel, 1610 Spruce St. (☎ **545-3290**); Society Hill, 418 Spruce St. (1830; ☎ **922-6590**). **Lutheran:** University Church, 3637 Chestnut St. (☎ **387-2885**). **Methodist:** St. George's, 324 New St. near Vine (1767; ☎ **825-7788**).**Presbyterian:** Tenth Presbyterian, 17th and Spruce streets (1854; ☎ **735-6210**); Old Pine Street, 412 Pine St. (☎ **925-8051**). **Roman Catholic:** 936 Market St. (☎ **587-3520**); Cathedral of Saints Peter and Paul, 18th Street at the Parkway (1864; ☎ **561-1313**). **Society of Friends (Quaker):** Free Meetinghouse, 5th and Arch streets (1783; ☎ **923-6777**); **Unitarian:** First Unitarian, 2121 Chestnut St. (1886; ☎ **563-3980**). The Yellow Pages list other places of worship.

Restrooms   Public restrooms can be found at 30th Street Station; the Independence National Historical Park Visitors Center; and at major shopping complexes like Liberty Place, the Bourse, the Gallery, and Downstairs at the Bellevue. You can usually use hotel lobby and restaurant facilities.

Safety   Philadelphia exhibits many preconditions of crime: It's large and populous, suffering from overall job losses in the last decade and a widening gap between haves and have-nots. You won't see too much of this underside if you concentrate on major tourist destinations, but stay alert and be aware of your immediate surroundings. Keep a close eye on your possessions. If you are planning to explore Philadelphia in unusual neighborhoods, at unusual hours, or in a style that makes you conspicuous, be especially careful. Center City has recently responded to visible signs of urban distress, including tourist crime, with a combination of police staffing and specially identified "Community Ambassadors," so incidents are rare under normal circumstances.

Shoe Repairs   Try **Capa's,** 1015 Chestnut St. (☎ **923-0990**), **Benjamin's Shoe & Handbag Repair,** 9th and Sansom streets (☎ **625-0444**), or **Superior Shoe Repair,** 138 S. 15th St. (☎ **972-9680**).

Taxes   Hotel-room charges incur a 7% state tax and a 5% city surcharge. There is a 7% on restaurant meals and on general sales (clothing is tax free).

Taxis   See "Getting Around," in this chapter.

Television   Network affiliates include Channel 3 (NBC), KYW; Channel 6 (ABC), WPVI; Channel 10 (CBS), WCAU; Channel 12 (PBS), WHYY; and Channel 29 (FOX), WTXF. Most hotels have cable with offerings like Home Box Office, CNN, ESPN, and Disney.

Tipping   Aim for 15% in restaurants, 15 to 20% for taxis, and $1 per bag for porters. See also "Tipping" in "Fast Facts: For the Foreign Traveler," in Chapter 3.

Transit Info   If you have questions about how to reach a specific destination, call **SEPTA** headquarters at **215/574-7800**—but expect to wait.

3 Networks & Resources

For Gay Men & Lesbians

Center City is used to, and tolerant of, homosexual populations, and the rectangle bordered by 9th and 18th streets and by Walnut and South streets is filled with gay social services, restaurants, bookstores, and clubs.

A Bookstore   With a diverse stock, **Giovanni's Room,** 345 S. 12th St., Philadelphia, PA 19107 (☎ **923-2960**), is a national resource for publications produced by and for gays and lesbians, as well as for feminist and progressive literature.

Counseling   A national **Gay/Lesbian Crisisline** (☎ toll free **800/767-4297**) can provide instant medical or legal counseling and local support listings as well. The **Gay Switchboard** (open daily from 7 to 10pm) is at **546-7100**; the **Lesbian Hotline** is at **222-5110**.

Information   For meetings, classes, gallery exhibitions, and social events, consult **Penguin Place,** 201 S. Camac St. (☎ **723-2220**).

Political/Community Organizations   To report antigay violence or discrimination, call the **Philadelphia Lesbian and Gay Task Force Hotline** at **563-4581**. **ACT UP/Philadelphia** meets on Monday; call **731-1844**.

Publications   *Philadelphia Gay News* is widely available, and *Au Courant* is slightly less so. Both are weeklies.

For Women

A Bookstore   The aforementioned **Giovanni's Room** is also a center for feminist books, recordings, and periodicals.

Crisis Centers/Clinics   For serious problems, call **Women Against Abuse** (☎ **386-7777**) or **Women Organized Against Rape** (☎ **985-3333**). The **Blackwell Center for Women,** 1124 Walnut St. (☎ **923-7577**), can direct you to health clinics.

Information   The **Women's Switchboard** is at **829-1976**.

Political/Community Organizations   The **National Organization of Women** local office is at 1218 Chestnut St. (**922-6040**). **Women's Alliance for Job Equity** is at 1422 Chestnut St., Suite 1100 (☎ **561-1873**). The **Penn Women's Center** (☎ **898-8611**), at the University of Pennsylvania, is quite active during the academic year.

A Publication   *Labyrinth* is available free at Giovanni's Room and some newsstands.

For Seniors

Information   The Philadelphia corporation for the Aging runs a **Senior Hotline** at **765-9040**. Most services are offered for Philadelphians rather than for tourists, however.

Political/Community Action   The **Action Alliance of Senior Citizens** is at 1211 Chestnut St. (☎ **564-1622**).

5

Philadelphia Accommodations

A CENTURY AGO PHILADELPHIA WAS FULL OF INNS, HOSTELRIES, AND European-style hotels for all pocketbooks and tastes. The names and faces are different today, but the situation is again the same, after decades of less than top quality or quantity in lodgings. Philadelphia, as part of its new reliance on tourism, has begun paying serious attention to the comfort of guests, and it shows.

In 1995–96, Philadelphia hotels will start to recover from the slump of the early 1990s, thanks to the dozens of conventions being booked by the new Pennsylvania Convention Center. The adjoining Philadelphia Convention Center Marriott, slated to open in early 1995, even with 1,200 rooms (the largest in the state), can't soak up all this demand, so look for increased occupancy in Center City's other 5,600 hotel rooms. Price increases will be minimal in 1995–96, but you'll have to look a little harder for discounts and promotions by hotels—especially luxury and near luxury. Concentrate on those great weekend packages around town, and check out the increased bed-and-breakfast and smaller inn listings below for a cheaper, fresh alternative.

Geographically, look to hotels in the Rittenhouse Square area for larger, more individualized prewar spaces. Corporate activity in the northeast quadrant between City Hall and the Philadelphia Museum of Art has produced sleek 1980s hotels, with a lesser surge of smaller hotels in or near historic Society Hill. Outside Center City, West Philadelphia is only a bus ride away and rates are a bit cheaper.

Philadelphia has an additional 8,000 hotel beds within a 20-mile circumference out of town. This includes a full complement of airport hotels 20 minutes away, many of them recently opened in response to the growth of the airport itself. Two fine hotels sit atop a bluff near I-76 that overlooks the downtown skyline. Roosevelt Boulevard hides some smaller properties, about 20 minutes out of town.

Outlying countries are full of lovely old inns like the 1740 House in Bucks County; see Chapter 11 for listings as you go. The **Visitors Center,** 16th Street and John F. Kennedy Boulevard, Philadelphia, PA 19102 (☎ **215/636-1666**), can help with any questions.

RATES   Hotel prices in Philadelphia are markedly lower than those in New York City or Washington, D.C. Recommendations are divided here into five categories: **very expensive** ($190 to $290 per night, double occupancy), **expensive** ($140 to $190), **moderate** ($80 to $140), **inexpensive** ($60 to $80), and **budget** (under $60). All rooms have private baths unless otherwise indicated, and you can count on a state tax of 7% plus a city surcharge of 5%. You are strongly advised to bargain for lower rates, because there is keen competition to boost occupancy rates. Also, be sure to inquire about garaging a car or arrangements for children if you are going to bring either with you.

BED & BREAKFAST AGENCIES   It's natural that the Philadelphia area should have several excellent bed-and-breakfast operations.

Bed & Breakfast of Philadelphia, 1530 Locust St., Philadelphia, PA 19102 (☎ **215/735-1917**), was started in 1980. One of the owners runs a host home, so they're very close to travelers' needs. B&B of Philadelphia has about 135 homes, 40 in Center City and the remainder in New Jersey, Delaware, and surrounding Pennsylvania countries. The agency has assembled a group of interesting, warm hosts, including linguists, gourmet cooks, and therapists; several keep kosher kitchens. Most are not in stay-at-home situations. Philadelphia accommodations include a contemporary loft with a spectacular view of the Delaware River, a converted factory in Society Hill with a three-story winding staircase, and a town house tucked in an alley seconds from Rittenhouse Square. In greener pastures, you could pick from a certified 1810 farmhouse with original fireplaces, and a nonworking gristmill in Chester Country—the bedroom's in the former granary.

B&B of Philadelphia's prices range from $35 to $65 per night for a single person, $35 to $110 for a couple. Many at lower prices have shared baths, and children are a point to discuss. The agency will select a compatible lodging for you or allow you to choose from their directory for $5. American Express, VISA, and MasterCard are accepted for last-minute reservations.

Bed and Breakfast Traveler (☎ **215/687-3565**) lists more than 35 personally inspected accommodations throughout the area. Rates similar to those above apply, and major credit cards are accepted. Janice Archbold at **Guesthouses,** Box 2137, West Chester, PA 19380 ☎ **610/692-4575**), has more than 200 host situations lined up, not only in Philadelphia but also throughout the Mid-Atlantic region. Most buildings are architecturally or historically significant, and rates average $100 and up. Finally, **All About Town–B&B in Philadelphia,** P.O. Box 562, Valley Forge, PA 19481 (☎ **215/783-7838** or toll-free **800/344-0123** for reservations 9am to 9pm; fax 610/783-7783), is a no-fee reservation service with 130 town-and-country choices from Main Line, Bucks County, Lancaster County, and West Chester. Singles start at $35 per night, and doubles at $50, with a $5 surcharge for one night's lodging.

1 Historic Area

Very Expensive

Omni Hotel at Independence Park, 4th and Chestnut Sts., Philadelphia, PA 19106. ☎ **215/925-0000** or toll free **800/843-6664**. Fax 215/925-1263. 141 rms, 9 suites. A/C MINIBAR TV TEL
Rates: $195–$260 single or double. Weekend rates available from $135 double per night. Children free in parents' room. AE, CB, DC, MC, V.
Parking: $12.50 self-parking, $18.50 valet parking.

This small, polished hotel has a tremendous location in the middle of Independence National Historical Park, three blocks south of Ben Franklin Bridge (Chestnut Street runs one-way east, so approach from 6th Street). All rooms have Independence Park views, and horse-drawn carriages clip-clop past the valet parking drop off and an elegant glass-and-steel canopy. The $25-million hotel was opened in October 1990, and its prices reflect the new, almost-luxury ambience. The lobby is classic—with current newspapers, huge vases of flowers, and a bar featuring a piano or a jazz trio nightly.

Each room is cheery—with plants and original pastels of city views—and state of the art—with plastic coded room key, voice mail, VCR, two telephones, and fax- and computer-compatible jacks. All rooms have individual temperature controls, windows that open, and closets with three different kinds of hangers. Rooms for nonsmokers are available. The staff here is noteworthy for its quality and park knowledge.

Dining/Entertainment: The second-floor Azalea is one of Philadelphia's top restaurants; chef Aliza Green has created imaginative treatments of American regional dishes. Typical are cold roast chicken with quince mayonnaise and spicy fried oysters and sirloin with mustard seed and fresh herbs. The restaurant is open for breakfast, lunch (main courses for $8.50 to $13.75), brunch, and dinner (main courses for $13.50 to $23). Hearty (not English) afternoon tea is served in the lobby lounge, which also features a piano trio most nights.

Services: 24-hour room service, concierge, valet parking. Complimentary van to Center City stops, weekdays 7am to 7pm.

Facilities: Indoor lap pool (no lifeguard) available daily 7am to 11pm; whirlpool and sauna adjoining, with Stairmaster and exercise area; Ritz 5 movie theater tucked into the back corner.

Sheraton Society Hill, 1 Dock St., Philadelphia, PA 19106.
☎ **215/238-6000** or toll free **800/325-3535.** Fax 215/922-2709. 365 rms, 17 suites. A/C MINIBAR TV TEL

Rates: $165–$190 single, depending on view; double occupancy $25 extra. Weekend packages available from $103–$136 double per night. Children under 17 free in parents' room. AE, DC, MC, V. **Parking:** $11.

Located three blocks from Head House Square and four blocks from Independence Hall, the 1986 Sheraton Society Hill nestles among the tree-lined cobblestone streets of this historic district. Set on a triangular 2 1/2-acre site between Dock and South Front streets, the building was designed in keeping with the area's Flemish Bond architecture. Its skylit, four-story atrium is entered via a circular courtyard with a splashing fountain. To the right waits a sitting/cocktail area with comfortable chintz country sofas.

The guest rooms—on the long, low second, third, and fourth floors (the only Delaware River views are from the latter)—are a bit smaller than you'd expect; half have one king-size bed, and the others have two double beds. The furnishings of each are top-quality Drexel Heritage mahogany, with four lamps, two-post headboards, an upholstered loveseat and chair, and glass-and-brass coffee tables. In each bath, dark marble tops the vanity and Martex bathrobes are provided. All rooms have remote-control cable TVs (Spectravision, with pay-per-view movies at $8.50 each). The decor is gender neutral, with American art prints.

Dining/Entertainment: Hadleys, a moderately priced restaurant, features creative seasonal menus and health-conscious main dishes. The Courtyard has piano music for a cappuccino/dessert bar nightly and light fare throughout the day and evening.

Services: 24-hour room service, free shuttle van to Center City, concierge on duty daily from 6am to 11pm.

Facilities: Superior meeting facilities; fourth-floor indoor pool (open daily from 6am to 10pm), whirlpool, and small health club with trainers; third-floor sauna.

Moderate

⭐ **Best Western Independence Park Inn,** 235 Chestnut St., Philadelphia, PA 19106. ☎ **215/922-4443** or toll free **800/624-2988.** Fax 215/922-4487. 36 rms. A/C TV TEL

Rates (including breakfast and afternoon tea): $120–$155 single; $130–$165 double. Weekend packages from $99. 15% AAA discount. AE, DC, MC, V. **Parking:** $9 at nearby enclosed garage.

This top choice for bed-and-breakfast-style accommodations has a great location, two blocks from Independence Hall. It's a handsome 1856 former dry-goods store with renovated rooms, developed by a Philadelphian, Richard Trevlyn; it is now a Best Western franchise.

The eight floors of guest rooms have four different color schemes; you'll find armoires, lathed bedposts, and lots of illumination, with an overhead light at each entrance foyer and four standing lamps in each room. The baths have big beveled mirrors, dropped ceilings, and soap dishes that are at both bath and shower heights. Although all the windows are triple casement and double glazed, specify an interior room if you're sensitive to noise from the traffic on Chestnut Street. A third bed can be wheeled into your room for a child, at no additional charge.

Dining: The Independence Park has no restaurant. However, it serves a very passable continental breakfast in a glass-enclosed garden courtyard, with the Dickens Inn (see Chapter 6) supplying a complimentary afternoon tea. Special discount coupons to nearby restaurants are available at the desk.

Holiday Inn–Independence Mall, 4th and Arch Sts., Philadelphia, PA 19106. ☎ **215/923-8660** or toll free **800/843-2355.** Fax 215/829-1796. 364 rms. A/C TV TEL **Transportation:** Airport limousine stops here.

Rates: $113 standard with double bed; $130 room with king-size bed. Weekend packages from $98. Extra person $10 (up to four in a room). Children 18 and under free in parents' room. AE, DC, MC, V. **Parking:** $10.

This Holiday Inn, set back from the street, is absolutely the closest you're going to sleep to the Liberty Bell; just turn the corner and you're at the pavilion that houses it. The continued renovation of the bedrooms and public spaces and the addition of a concierge have given it a "superior" rating within the Holiday Inn organization. All rooms have individual climate control.

Dining: You might consider the buffet lunch served in the renovated Benjamin's, done in handsome salmon and blue, or the less expensive Café Plain and Fancy.

Facilities: Washer/dryers; roof top outdoor pool; game room; and children's programs in the summer.

Penn's View Inn, Front and Market Sts., Philadelphia, PA 19106.
☎ **215/922-7600** or toll free **800/331-7634.** Fax 215/922-7642. 28 rms. A/C TV TEL

Rates (including continental breakfast): $132 single or double. Weekend rate is $99 per room; a package at $229 includes 2 nights, champagne upon arrival, and Panorama restaurant dinner. AE, DC, MC, V. Guarantee requested on reservation. **Parking:** $6 at adjacent lot.

Tucked behind the Market Street ramp to I-95 in a renovated 1836 shipping warehouse, this inn is small and exquisite, with a European flair. It was developed by the Sena family, who started La Famiglia 150 yards south (see Chapter 6 for details) and have grown a small neighborhood empire. When you enter you'll feel like you're in a private club.

The decor is floral and rich; the basic question is traffic noise, but the rooms are well-insulated, with large framed mirrors, armoires, and efficient bath fixtures. The ceilings have been dropped for modern vents. A third bed can be wheeled into your room for $15.

Dining: Ristorante Panorama offers excellent contemporary Italian cuisine at moderate prices. The 120 different wines served by the glass attract a connoisseur clientele.

Thomas Bond House, 129 S. 2nd St., Philadelphia, PA 19106.
☎ **215/923-8523** or toll free **800/845-2663.** Fax 215/923-8504. 12 rms, 2 suites. A/C TV TEL

Rates (including breakfast and afternoon wine and cheese): $80–$150 single or double. Weekends bring full, hot breakfasts. MC, V. **Parking:** $9 at adjacent lot.

This 1769 Georgian row house sitting almost directly across from the back of Independence Park is owned by the federal government, which kept the shell and gutted the interior. It's run by John and Peggy Poth, who have turned the guest rooms into cheerful, comfortable colonial-style accommodations. Guests now enter through the former side entrance, encountering a basic cream-and-blue color scheme, with map illustrations and secretary desks. The charming parlor has pink sofas and a replica Chippendale double chair, while the breakfast room has four tables for four. All rooms are individually decorated and feature private baths and period furnishings. Fresh-baked cookies are brought with turndown service. The hotel is named after the first occupant, the doctor who cofounded Pennsylvania Hospital with Benjamin Franklin.

Philadelphia Accommodations

PENNSYLVANIA

Harrisburg ★

Philadelphia ●

Bank Street Hostel **21**
Best Western
  Independence Park Inn **20**
Comfort Inn at
  Penn's Landing **16**
Doubletree Hotel
  Philadelphia **14**
Embassy Suites Center City **5**

Four Seasons Hotel **4**
Holiday Inn–Center City **8**
Holiday Inn–
  Independence Mall **17**
Hotel Atop the Bellevue **13**
Kormansuites Hotel and
  Conference Center **2**
The Latham **10**

Inexpensive

$ **Comfort Inn at Penn's Landing,** 100 N. Columbus Blvd.
(formerly Delaware Ave.), Philadelphia, PA 19106.
☎ **215/627-7900** or toll free **800/228-5150.** Fax 215/238-0809.
185 rms, 9 suites. A/C MINIBAR TV TEL

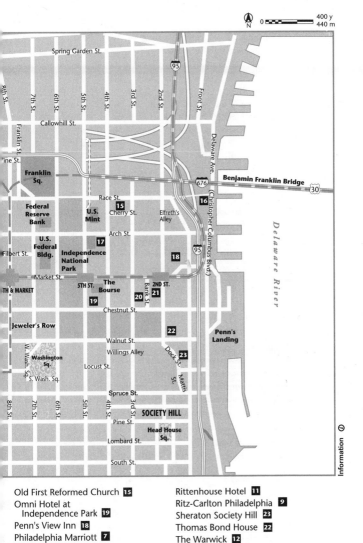

Map legend:

Old First Reformed Church **15**	Rittenhouse Hotel **11**
Omni Hotel at Independence Park **19**	Ritz-Carlton Philadelphia **9**
Penn's View Inn **18**	Sheraton Society Hill **23**
Philadelphia Marriott **7**	Thomas Bond House **22**
Ramada Inn–Center City **1**	The Warwick **12**
Ramada Suites **6**	Wyndham Franklin Plaza Hotel **3**

Rates (including continental breakfast): $75 single, $85 double. Weekend packages from $60 per night. Children under 18 free in parents' room. AE, DC, MC, V. **Parking:** Free in adjacent lot.

One of Philadelphia's newest hotels, Comfort Inn at Penn's Landing is the area's only waterfront hotel as well, nestled into a corner of Old City between I-95 and the Delaware River, three blocks from the northbound ramp off the expressway. A shuttle van to Center City stops here, and the crosstown subway line is two blocks away.

A basic steel skeleton hung with blue-and-white concrete panels, Comfort Inn has been built to airport-area noise specifications, with insulated windows and other features to lessen the din of traffic. The eastern views of the river are stupendous. There's a coin laundry on the second floor, and half the rooms are designated for nonsmokers.

Comfort Inn has no restaurant, but a complimentary continental breakfast—cold or microwavable food—is served in the cocktail lounge. Its fitness room stocks weights, treadmills, and bicycle machines.

Budget

Bank Street Hostel, 32 S. Bank St. (between 2nd and 3rd Sts. and Market and Chestnut Sts.), Philadelphia, PA 19106.
☎ **215/922-0222** or toll-free **800/392-4678.** 60 bunk-bed places (shared bath). **Directions:** 3 blocks east from 5th and Market SEPTA station.
Rates: $14, plus $2 a night for bedsheets. No credit cards. Check in before 10am or after 4:30pm. **Parking:** $8–$10 per day at nearby garages.
Open: All year.

David Herskowitz opened up this 140-year old former factory and its two neighbors in 1992 to those who want Spartan accommodations on a budget, without wanting a flophouse. It works quite well, in a very convenient part of town. The dormitory-style rooms are spread over four floors of the complex, which also includes a pool table and lounge with large-screen TV. Baths are shared in clean dorm-style areas. Groups are welcome.

Old First Reformed Church, 4th and Race Sts., Philadelphia, PA 19106. ☎ **215/922-4566.** 20 hostel mattresses (shared baths).
Rates (including continental breakfast): $11 singles aged 18–26 only. Check in between 5–10pm; maximum stay 3 nights. **Parking:** $8 per day at garage on 5th Street between Market and Chestnut. **Open:** July–Aug.

This church has responded to the major lack of Center City student accommodations by making its basement social hall available.

Showers and security for valuables are available. There's a midnight curfew, after which the church doors are locked. Built in 1837, the church is situated one block east and two north of the 5th and Market streets SEPTA station.

2   Center City

Very Expensive

The Four Seasons Hotel, One Logan Square, Philadelphia, PA 19103. ☎ **215/963-1500** or toll free **800/332-3442.** Fax 215/963-9506. 371 rms, 9 suites. A/C MINIBAR TV TEL

Rates: From $240 single; from $270 double; Four Seasons minisuites from $290; suites from $320. Weekend packages from $170 per night. AE, DC, MC, V. **Parking:** $21 weekdays, $15 weekends, valet.

The Four Seasons, one of the two best hotels in Philadelphia, is a member of a distinguished luxury chain that includes New York's Pierre, the Four Seasons in Dallas and Washington, and London's Inn on the Park. Its luxury is spare, refined, and understated.

Built in 1983, The Four Seasons is an eight-story curlicue on Logan Square. It's separated from the "partner" CIGNA headquarters, in complementary stone, not by a wall but by a fountain and landscaped courtyard that opens as a café in summer. The hotel has landscaped the Logan Circle gardens as well.

As you're waved into the porte cochere on 18th Street, your first view is of enormous masses of flowers, with stepped-stone levels, water, and honeyed woods stretching far into the distance. The lounge and promenade serve as foyers to the dining and meeting facilities and are paneled in a rare white mahogany.

The guest rooms mix Federal-period furniture with richer, more Victorian color schemes. There is a very direct American elegance in each room: the desk, settee, armoire, and wing chair/ottoman combinations are top-quality Henredon. All the rooms have large windows or private verandas boasting marvelous views of Logan Circle or the interior courtyard. Also featured are free HBO, digital clock-radios, lockable closets, and two telephones.

Dining/Entertainment: The Four Seasons restaurants regularly collect raves from local reviewers. The Fountain Restaurant, serving

---

Frommer's Smart Traveler: Hotels

1. Relatively few smart hotel patrons end up paying the listed "rack rates." Between corporate rates, AARP memberships, and affiliations with credit cards, frequent-flyer programs, and car-rental clubs, you should be able to find a stated policy for a 5% to 15% discount. The Philadelphia Convention and Visitors Bureau is a clearinghouse for discount coupons from several hotels (often the Holiday Inns and Comfort Inn) offered seasonally.

2. Ask about summer discounts. All city hotels—even the most expensive in a tourist destination such as Philadelphia—offer dramatic discounts.

3. Most hotels offer big discounts or package rates on weekends (Friday to Sunday night). If you're staying on a weekend, always ask about these.

4. Consider the bed-and-breakfast alternatives.

5. Before selecting a hotel, always ask about parking charges. These can range from complimentary to $22 per night in Center City.

all three meals, continues the low-key elegance of the hotel by combining luxury (150 seats in wide, comfortable armchairs) with intimacy. Natural light streams over tapestries, fresh flowers, and walnut paneling.

The Swann Lounge, closer to the lobby corridor, has marble-top tables and a colorful, civilized look out of a Maurice Prendergast sketch. It's open for an extensive lunch, afternoon tea, early evening cocktails, and dessert and drinks until midnight. As summer visitors can't help noticing, the Courtyard Café bubbles with light refreshments.

Services: Concierge, 24-hour room service, complimentary overnight shoeshine, terry-cloth robes, and town-car service within Center City.

Facilities: Besides European spa weekends, the basement health center includes a heated pool (large enough for laps), a superheated whirlpool, Universal machines, exercycles, and exercise mats—all spotlessly maintained. The pool area, in particular, is a beautifully designed setting of greenery, granite, and geraniums. The full-service hair salon right next door to the spa's reception room is open 7:30am to 6pm; the small sundries shop off to the left of the lobby is open 7am to 7pm.

Hotel Atop the Bellevue, Broad and Walnut Sts., or 1415 Chancellor Court (between Walnut and Locust Sts.), Philadelphia, PA 19102. ☎ **215/893-1776** or toll free **800/222-0939.** Fax 215/893-9868. 170 rms. A/C MINIBAR TV TEL

Rates: $215 standard room; $235 deluxe room; $265 executive room. Weekend rates (an extraordinary $120) often available. AE, DC, MC, V.
Parking: $13 per day at connected garage.

The "grande dame of Broad Street" was the most opulent hotel in the country when it first opened in 1904, and it was fully renovated in 1989. A notch below the Four Seasons, Rittenhouse, or Ritz-Carlton, it's still a grand experience in a great location, and the value is substantial.

The luxury hotel is now managed by former officers of Cunard, Inc., which ran Hotel Atop the Bellevue from 1989 until 1993. The ground floor houses internationally renowned retailers like Tiffany & Co. and Polo/Ralph Lauren, while the lower level was recently renovated into a gourmet food court, featuring quick and easy gourmet fare and take-out from Bookbinder's and others. A separate elevator lifts you to the 19th-floor registration area and foyer for the hotel restaurants.

The rooms, occupying floors 12 through 17, are as large as ever, and all slightly different, with a green-and-white decor and wall moldings reproduced from the 1904 designs. The make-over has added to each room extralarge goose-down pillows, three separate two-line phones adaptable for a computer modem, a VCR to supplement the TV/radio, a large bed, a writing desk, a round table, and four upholstered chairs. Closets have built-in tie racks and automatic lighting. The baths are dated but have amenities like hair dryers, TVs, and illuminated close-up mirrors.

Dining/Entertainment: Founders Dining Room, the signature 19th-floor restaurant recently voted one of the top 50 restaurants in the nation by *Conde Nast Traveler,* has two spectacular semicircular windows draped with dramatic swags of brown and cream. It serves dinner Mondays through Saturdays, 5:30 to 10:30pm, and Sundays, 5:30pm to 8:30pm; other meals include breakfast and lunch on Saturdays and Sunday brunch. The 80 seats are spaciously arranged, with candlelit tables, pink napery, wide armchairs, and modern scrollwork. There is dinner dancing to a trio weekend evenings and quiet live music Sundays through Thursdays. Service is classic French.

The Library Lounge is quiet and a bit precious. With a copy of a Gilbert Stuart full-length portrait and a collection of books by and about Philadelphians, the lounge is open all day but serves from 11am to 1am. The Ethel Barrymore Room serves afternoon tea and a view of the Philadelphia skyline Wednesday through Saturday from 3 to 5pm.

On the 12th floor is the equally impressive Conservatory, at the base of a dramatic 80-foot atrium carved out of the original hotel. It has a wonderful, whimsical café ambience, with trellises, oval cloud mural, porch swings, and two-story palms. It serves a generous breakfast buffet and lunch buffet on weekdays.

Services: 24-hour room service, concierge, complimentary glass of champagne or hot drink on arrival, full-day child-care facility at the Sporting Club.

Facilities: A fourth-floor skywalk from the hotel at the ballroom level leads directly to the garage on the other side of Chancellor Court. It also goes to the Sporting Club, a Michael Graves–designed facility that boggles the eye with 93,000 square feet of health space, including half-mile jogging track; a four-lane, 25-meter junior Olympic pool; and corridors of squash and racquetball courts. The club is open daily from 6:30am to 10pm and is available only to members and hotel guests.

⭐ **Rittenhouse Hotel,** 210 W. Rittenhouse Sq. Philadelphia, PA 19103. ☎ **215/546-9000** or toll free **800/635-1042.** Fax 215/732-3364. 98 rms. A/C MINIBAR TV TEL

Rates: From $200 single; from $225 double. Weekend rates from $140. Packages including health club, dinners, and other amenities are usually available. AE, DC, MC, V. **Parking:** $21.

Among Philadelphia's luxury hotels, the Rittenhouse has the fewest and largest rooms, the most satisfying views, and the more homegrown Philadelphia feel. Built in 1989, it's a jagged concrete-and-glass high rise off the western edge of Philadelphia's most distinguished public square. The lobby is truly magnificent, with inlaid marble floors and a series of frosted-glass chandeliers and sconces. This and The Four Seasons (see above) are AAA's only 5 Diamond Award winners in the state.

The Rittenhouse Hotel has 98 guest rooms on floors five through nine; the other floors contain condominium residences. The rooms have bay windows, reinforced walls between rooms, and solid-wood doors. All have great views: The park is wonderfully green nine months of the year, but the western view of the Schuylkill and the Parkway is even more dramatic. The decor in some rooms is primarily dark woods set against greens and purples, with wing chairs. Other rooms have peony-patterned moldings, squares of white pine, and canopy beds. Armoires contain the TVs and VCRs, with spirited renderings of city scenes by local artists on the walls.

Dining/Entertainment: Executive chef James Coleman oversees the cuisine in the hotel's two restaurants and two lounges. The restaurants occupy the second floor and overlook the park. The "star" is 210, serving lunch and dinner (closed Sunday). Physically, it's a stunning contemporary study in black and white. Tree Tops is a sun-filled café that has surprisingly moderate prices for midday sandwiches and superb dinners. Breakfast is also served. The Boathouse Row Bar is the nicest imaginable Ralph Lauren–type re-creation of an authentic boathouse, with an entire rowing scull mounted overhead; however, it does get rowdy in the evening.

Completing the picture is the ground-floor Cassatt Tea Room and Lounge. The site was the original town house of the painter Mary Cassatt's brother, and the Rittenhouse has adorned an ingenious trellised private garden triangle with three drypoints by this American master.

Services: 24-hour room service, two Clef d'Or concierges, turn-down service with written weather report for the morrow and radio tuned to soft classical music, twice-daily room cleaning. Many cooking classes and/or lunch events are held for children.

Facilities: The third floor is split between Nan Duskin (the city's toniest retailer) and Toppers Spa, a fitness club with a five-lane

Frommer's Cool for Kids: Hotels

Embassy Suites Center City   (p. 73) There's an innovative play area designed by the Please Touch Museum, with hand puppets, CD-ROM interactive "edugames," and more—perfect for kids two to nine.

The Four Seasons Hotel   (p. 66) The Saturday Lunch Club is a three-course meal for $21.50 designed for and presented to kids; it's featured on the first Saturday of the month.

Rittenhouse Hotel   (p. 69) It intermittently offers children's cooking classes taught by Rena Coyle and also features some Saturday theme lunches for kids and their parents.

Sheraton Inn Northeast   (p. 84) This hotel makes a special attempt to cater to families with its staffed pool and game room. It offers weekend packages with the nearby Sesame Place.

Sheraton Society Hill   (p. 61) There's a special children's check-in to the right of the lobby as well as concierge treatment with free snacks, the use of the game room, and so on.

indoor pool, a sun deck, and an exercise-machine and aerobics room. The floor above is devoted to an executive business center, with fax machines and typists on call. Philadelphia National Bank maintains a personal service branch and ATM in the building.

⭐ **The Ritz-Carlton Philadelphia,** 17th and Chestnut Sts. at Liberty Place, Philadelphia, PA 19103. ☎ **215/563-1600** or toll free **800/241-3333.** Fax 215/564-9559. 290 rms, 17 suites. A/C MINIBAR TV TEL

Rates: $205–$245 single or double; $285 Ritz-Carlton Club. Weekend rates from $149. Packages include valet parking and fitness center. AE, DC, MC, V. **Parking:** $17.50 self-parking, $22 valet.

If The Four Seasons is luxury with a 20th-century slant and the Rittenhouse captures the 19th century, then The Ritz-Carlton claims the 18th century. Opened in 1990 as part of Liberty Place, the past decade's most exciting effort to reclaim the preeminence of "downtown," the hotel is a superb blend of luxury amenities and service, steps away from the best in urban life.

A small porte cochere and a ground-floor lobby on 17th Street lead to a series of smaller, almost residential rooms that contain the front and concierge desks, the dining areas, and the elevators on the second floor.

The guest rooms feature bedside walnut tables, desks, beds with spindle-top headboards (with four pillows!), and Wedgwood or Sandwich glass lamps. Large walnut armoires house the TVs, clothing drawers, and minibars. The color schemes are muted, and all rooms are provided with two phone lines and fax- or computer-capable lines. The modern baths are outfitted with black-and-white tiles, silverplate fixtures, Miroir Brot (magnifying mirrors), and lots of toiletries. The service is simply impeccable, as a result of fanatical training.

Dining/Entertainment: Three distinctive locations combine uncompromising cuisine with gracious service and ambience. (See also Chapter 6.) The Dining Room is decorated in American Federal and concentrates on contemporary continental under the hand of chef Troy Thompson, late of the 5-star 5-Diamond Ritz-Carlton in Buckhead, Atlanta. On the other side of the lounge fireplace, the mahogany-paneled and period-furnished Grill and Grill Bar have quickly become "Best of Philly" winners, with daily lunches and dinners of steaks, chops, and fish specialties. The Lobby Lounge has expanded its offerings to a continental breakfast, a formal tea, and hors d'oeuvres and desserts, with a constantly crackling fireplace. Classical and jazz music accompanies afternoon and evening service.

Services: 24-hour room service, 24-hour concierge, turndown service, complimentary morning newspapers, transport to and from airport, car-rental arrangements, very frequent weekend or month-long festivals in connection with museum exhibitions or city theme events. These include a January to April Wine Festival, a February film weekend, and wine seminar in September.

Facilities: There are a small exercise and sauna facility, superb business meeting rooms, and the like, but the most impressive extra is the internal connection to the 70 Shops at Liberty Place (see Chapter 9), a very successful urban mall built around a Crystal Palace–like rotunda. The shops include The Coach Store, J. Crew, Godiva, Crabtree & Evelyn, Handblock, and Brentano's.

Expensive

Doubletree Hotel Philadelphia, Broad St. at Locust St., Philadelphia, PA 19107. ☎ **215/893-1600** or toll free **800/222-8733.** Fax 215/893-1663. 427 rms. A/C TV TEL

Rates: $140–$170 single or double; $185–$200 deluxe. Weekday special rates from $99. Weekend package $79+ per night available for up to four family members staying in one room. AE, DC, MC, V. **Parking:** $13 in adjoining garage for self-parking, $17 for valet.

In 1993, Sprint Hospitality Group took this property over and switched its management to Doubletree Hotels. Although the location is no longer ideal for business travelers, it is prime for tourists, and the weekend packages are quite affordable.

You'll probably enter through the corridor connecting the lobby to the garage on the block's southern side. The motor entrances ingeniously keep traffic flows separate for three floors of meeting facilities. During registration, take a good look at the four-story atrium: A web of steel struts finished in black enamel supports a diagonal sheet of glass panes, sloping down to a glass wall at street level. Decor features classic browns and whites, sky-blue tapestries, and Degas-style murals alluding to the orchestral and ballet life at the Academy of Music across the street.

The guest rooms, all completely renovated in the last two years, each have two views of town because of the sawtooth design. Obviously, the higher floors afford the better views; the views of the Delaware River (eastern) or City Hall (northeast corner) are the most popular. Ten rooms, next to the elevators on certain floors, are designed for the disabled.

Dining: The Café Académie, an informal 220-seat restaurant and lounge, continues the glossy atrium connection and is due for renovation by 1995. If you dine here (breakfast, lunch, and dinner served), ask for one of the tables overlooking the action outside. The decor is colonial-meets-California. The Lobby Bar, also being renovated, serves until midnight.

Services: Green boxes of great chocolate-chip cookies are delivered to your room on arrival. Quick breakfasts are guaranteed. A guest services desk is staffed 16 hours daily. Budget will deliver rental cars to the hotel door.

Facilities: The fifth-floor Racquet and Health Club is free to all guests. You can tan, steam, swim in an indoor pool, sun, whirlpool, or work out on CAM II exercise machines, Lifesteps, or Schwinn Airdynes. Two racquetball courts can be reserved for $10 per hour, with no equipment charge. A small jogging track circles a huge oak-planked deck, and summer brings many hotel parties and parade views.

Embassy Suites Center City, 1776 Benjamin Franklin Pkwy. at Logan Square, Philadelphia, PA 19103. ☎ **215/561-1776** or toll free **800/362-2779.** Fax 215/963-0122. 288 suites. A/C TV TEL

Rates: $169 single; $184 double, with full complimentary breakfast. Weekend packages from $119. AE, DC, MC, V. **Parking:** $15.50 weekdays, $10 weekends in underground garage.

The big cylinder of marble and glass on the Parkway at 18th Street looks dated, but Bell Atlantic Properties (corporate headquarters are next door) and Embassy Suites have put $10 million into a 1993 refurbishment and it works quite well within their "room plus kitchen plus living room area" format.

The hotel has an interesting set of strengths and weaknesses. It was designed in the 1960s as luxury apartments radiating out from a central core—the Kelly family had the last penthouse here—but the quality of views varies widely, and the basic shape is weirdly disorienting. It's evident that the elevators and porte cochere weren't equipped to handle this volume. On the other hand, amenities such as the full breakfast at TGI Friday's (the connected restaurant), fitness room, nightly managers' reception, and Please Touch Too room for the kids all exceed expectations.

The suites themselves have a sleek severity, with black matte and putty surfaces for TV stands and a spare walnut inset bedroom armoire. The kitchenette eschews oven and dishwasher, but includes microwave, under-the-counter refrigerator, and coffee maker; dishes and silver are provided upon request. An especially nice 48-inch round table with four chairs overlooks the small balcony terraces with sliding doors. Baths have large Italian marble tiles, plush white towels, and hair dryers. With two double beds, the bedrooms don't have a lot of extra room. HVAC is customized to the room.

Dining/Entertainment: TGI Friday's, which has a "more is more" pub atmosphere, is open until 1am daily, connected on two levels, and used for hotel breakfasts. The lobby lounge hosts happy hour.

Services: Valet parking; toiletries available at front desk upon request.

Facilities: The second-floor fitness center has Nordic Trak, Stairmasters, rowing machine, and unisex sauna. The adjoining Please Touch Too room for children two to nine is great, with a "store," interlocking foam tiles, hand puppets, and programmed "edugames" on PCs.

 KormanSuites Hotel and Conference Center, 2001 Hamilton St. (just off the Parkway), Philadelphia, PA 19130. ☎ **215/569-7300.** Fax 215/569-0584. 170 rms, 12 Grand Club suites. A/C TV TEL

Rates (including continental breakfast): $139–$159 single; $149–$189 double; one-bedroom suite $169; two-bedroom suite $189. Weekend packages from $89 double per night. Children free in parents' room. AE, DC, MC, V. **Parking:** Free.

The amenities and the location of this hotel make it an excellent value at rack rates; the weekend packages make it outstanding. You'll recognize it by the bright neon scribble near its roof north of Logan Circle, visible from anywhere south.

KormanSuites is really a grand hotel, but it's in separate pieces. A 28-story tower is connected by a marble-and-mahogany lobby and a glass-enclosed corridor to KormanSuites' restaurant and lush Japanese sculpture garden and pool.

The standard rooms are unbelievably spacious, and a corridor contains a microwave, a minibar, and a coffee maker. The suites add full kitchens with dishwashers, stoves, coffee makers, and telephones. Each "living" area has a full dining table for four, a TV, a full couch, and three double closets. Each bedroom features a queen-size bed and another TV (in suites, with built-in VCR), and the adjoining bath has a stacked washer/dryer. The views are great: to the north, highlights of 19th-century manufacturing and churches; to the south, 20th-century Center City. In short, you could live here with a family very happily for the price of a single room.

Dining: Catalina, the hotel restaurant, succeeds as a neighborhood favorite for moderate California-style mixtures of East Coast and West Coast. Hotel guests are offered complimentary continental breakfasts from 6 to 10am.

Services: Complimentary shuttle van running hourly through Center City to Independence Park, concierge, 24-hour message center, and garage attendants.

Facilities: Outdoor pool, Jacuzzi, two tennis and platform tennis courts, high-tech spa and fitness center, full-service hair salon, ATM on-site.

The Latham, 135 S. 17th St. at Walnut St., Philadelphia, PA 19103. ☎ **215/563-7474** or toll free **800/528-4261**. Fax 215/563-4034. 140 rms, 3 suites. A/C MINIBAR TV TEL

Rates: $130 standard single; $145 double; $165–$180 superior with king-size bed; $325+ suite. Basic weekend package $99 double per night (breakfast and parking included); other packages $129+ double per night (with more amenities). One or two children free in parents' room. AE, DC, MC, V. **Parking:** $14 in nearby lot.

The Latham brings to mind a small, superbly run Swiss hostelry, with its charm, congeniality, and small attentions. The Latham was an apartment house until about 20 years ago.

On weekday mornings the lobby, a high-ceilinged salon with terrazzo highlights, is filled with refreshed executives who look as though the Latham truly is their home away from home. Dealings with the reception area are quick and professional, and newsstand and lobby phones discreetly nestle in one corner. The Latham does no convention business.

The guest rooms, renovated from 1988 to 1990, are not huge or lavish but perfectly proportioned and done in burgundy or light green. Each minibar combines a digital drink dispenser (with totals registered automatically at the cashier's) with space for storing your own supplies. Louis XIV–style writing tables, modern upholstered armchairs, and contemporary prints mix the taste of different eras harmoniously. The bathrooms feature Princess phones, embossed soaps, and Bic disposable razors. Full-wall mirrors, large marblelike basins, and oversize towels accentuate the white-toned interiors. **Note:** The weekend packages are great bargains.

Dining: Michel's has gotten raves since its 1993 opening for its highly stylized variations of continental dishes.

Services: Concierge, turndown service with Godiva chocolate mints, valet parking.

Facilities: Free access to nearby fitness club with indoor pool; complimentary HBO, CNN, and ESPN.

Philadelphia Marriott, 12th and Market Sts., Philadelphia, PA 19107. ☎ **215/972-6700** or toll free **800/228-9290.** Fax 215/972-6704. 1,200 rms. A/C TV TEL

Rates: Not yet set at press time; anticipate $195 single, $215 double, but also look for lower introductory rates. Weekend specials $110+ per night. AE, DC, MC, V. **Parking:** $10–$12, valet only.

After more than a decade's planning and construction, the Marriott chain is opening the biggest hotel in Pennsylvania in January 1995, linked by an elevated covered walkway to the Reading Terminal Shed of the Convention Center. The major auto entrance of the hotel itself will be on Filbert Street (two ways between Market and Arch streets), with an equally grand pedestrian entrance adjoining Champions Sports Bar and retail on Market Street. The lobby is sliced up into a five-story atrium, enlivened by a 10,000-square-foot water sculpture, a lobby bar, and a gourmet coffee shop. Setbacks and terraces will provide plenty of natural light and views from the hotel rooms in floors 6 through 23. The decor and furnishings are traditional Marriott: dark woods, maroon and green drapes and bedspreads, a TV armoire, club chair and ottoman, round table plus a separate desk. Baths have heavy chrome fixtures and tuck sinks and counters in the corners for more dressing room–type space.

Dining/Entertainment: J. W. Steakhouse overlooks the lobby atrium and Market Street; K. T.'s American Grille serves casual meals all day long, and a continental sidewalk café fronts 12th Street. There are also three lounges.

Services: All possible corporate and some luxury services. Concierge floor.

Facilities: Complimentary seventh-floor health club with indoor lap pool, whirlpool, aerobics/fitness room, locker rooms, and wet and dry saunas. Direct internal connection to SEPTA subways and airport train.

Wyndham Franklin Plaza Hotel, 17th and Race Sts., Philadelphia, PA 19103. ☎ **215/448-2000** or toll free **800/996-3426.** Fax 215/448-2864. 758 rms, 36 suites. A/C MINIBAR TV TEL

Rates: $155 single; $175 double; $195–$215 deluxe. Weekend package $89 for 1 night, with a second night at 50%. Also, a $99 package includes parking and next-day brunch. Group rates negotiable. Children

18 and under free in parents' room. AE, DC, MC, V. **Parking:** $13, self; $17, valet.

The Wyndham is a convention hotel in a city that is finally filling it through a real convention center seven blocks away. Nevertheless, it's been functioning as a convenient meeting center and urban resort just off I-676 (two blocks north of Suburban Station) since the late 1970s, with four restaurants, a health club, a swimming pool, a clever and breathtaking lobby, and rooftop dancing.

The complex uses a full city block. The lobby, lounge, and three restaurants are beautifully integrated under a dramatic 70-foot glass roof.

Two thirds of the guest rooms have a pair of double beds. All are done in pleasant pastel shades and have such near-deluxe features as floor-to-ceiling mirrors, TVs with AM/FM radios, and upholstered chrome chairs. Request a west view above the 19th floor to get an unobstructed peek at the Parkway, although be forewarned that the cathedral bells below ring hourly from 7am.

Dining/Entertainment: Horizons—open Monday to Friday from 5pm to 11pm, Saturday and Sunday until 1am—is a swanky rooftop affair, with pin lights and mirrors. The Terrace is a coffee shop and serves excellent fare daily from 7am to 11pm. Between Friends, the flagship, features French tableside service in opulent surroundings of oil portraits, banks of flowers, and mirrored angle piers. Dinner will cost about $40 per person; lunch is also served. A small atrium with an enclosed sidewalk café connects to the SmithKline building; the café is open daily from 7am to 3pm.

Services: Room service, travel service.

Facilities: The third-floor Clark's Uptown offers an indoor swimming pool (21 by 45 feet), a sauna, and a track—all free to hotel guests. An all-day fee of $10 gets you racquetball (three courts), squash (three courts), outdoor handball (three courts), and tennis (two courts). Around the latter is a one-eighth-mile jogging track. A sun deck, a whirlpool, a Nautilus machine, a snackbar, and superb locker and exercise facilities round out the picture.

Moderate

Holiday Inn–Center City, 18th and Market Sts., Philadelphia, PA 19103. ☎ **215/561-7500** or toll free **800/465-4329.** Fax 215/561-4484. 445 rms, 72 suites. A/C TV TEL
Rates: $130 single; $138 double; $150 suite. Weekend rates from $69. Children under 18 free in parents' room. AE, DC, MC, V. **Parking:** $11.

The Holiday Inn was the only hotel to open in Philadelphia in the 1970s, and it underwent a 1993 $9.5-million refurbishment after Holiday Inn Worldwide bought it back from the local franchiser. It's very popular with conventioneers and relocating executives, but hotel policy is to leave at least 40% of the 445 rooms free for tourists. For solid accommodations with no real surprises, slightly above normal Holiday Inn criteria, this is an excellent choice.

The lobby, which dispenses coffee all day and looks like a club library in the evening, combines bowls of apples, plush armchairs, and entrances from both 18th Street and the garage. The glass marquee canopy on Market Street is new as of 1994. Above lobby level, a parking garage and meeting halls occupy the next 6 floors, and rooms and several suites fill the next 17.

By Philadelphia standards, the inn's guest rooms are large, each holding two firm double beds or king and pullout sofa, a Formica desk or table, and cheerful quilted bedspreads. The redone furnishings include color TVs, digital clock radios, deep carpeting, drapes, and 1876 *Harper's* magazine prints of the city's Centennial Exposition. Baths are slightly shabby. Two floors are devoted to Executive Level suites, offering upgraded decor and complimentary breakfast.

Dining: The hotel restaurant, an English pub called Elephant & Castle, serves largely continental fare 6:30am to 11pm.

Facilities: The outdoor pool perched atop the garage extension's roof (open daily from 10am to 9pm in summer) is free to guests, who can also use a weight room with rowing and Nautilus machines.

The Warwick, 17th and Locust Sts., Philadelphia, PA 19103.
☎ **215/735-6000** or toll free **800/523-4210.** Fax 215/790-7766. 180 rms, 20 suites. A/C MINIBAR TV TEL

Rates: $125 single with one queen-size bed; $150 double with two beds; suites from $185. Package rates available from $109. AE, DC, MC, V. **Parking:** $13.75 self-parking in adjacent garage, $16.75 valet.

If you wanted to live in a luxurious older apartment building you'd head for The Warwick. Most recently renovated over 1991–94, 200 rooms are rented or belong to condo owners, while 200 rooms and suites are the hotel's.

The Warwick's lobby mixes the old and the new: Many of the 1926 friezes and mantels have been reworked and repainted, while gleaming contemporary ensembles stretch themselves on Persian carpets. The mirrored pilasters may edge toward garishness, but the wall braziers and broad-leafed plants ensure a warm, splendid atmosphere.

The guest rooms are basically done in English country, with hand-milled sandalwood soap, bedside clock radios, and complimentary HBO on the armoire-mounted TVs. They're used by many meeting groups.

Dining: Mia's, with white tablecloths and dark-wood paneling, offers cuisine at moderate prices. It's open for mostly Italian breakfasts, lunches, and dinners. Capriccio's is a wonderful Italian-style espresso bar and sweetshop.

Services: Concierge (Betty George is one of the best in town), room service, overnight complimentary shoeshine.

Inexpensive

The Barclay, 237 S. 18th St., Philadelphia, PA 19103.
☎ **215/545-0300** or toll free **800/421-6662.** Fax 215/545-2896. 240 rms. A/C TV TEL

Rates: Official rates $135–$175 single; $155–$175 double; minisuites from $180, but deep discounts are virtually always in effect. Weekend packages from $75 double per night on Fri–Sat. AE, DC, MC, V. **Parking:** $16 in nearby lot.

The Barclay, a quiet hostelry on Rittenhouse Square East since 1929, used to be the host of celebrities ranging from Katharine Hepburn to the Grateful Dead and the residence of such local luminaries as Eugene Ormandy. The lobby, a long thin arcade of glass and ivory, and the hotel restaurant have long been local sentimental favorites.

However, the Barclay is having a tough time since the opening of the Rittenhouse across the square; it was put up for sale in 1989, but there are still no takers. So look for deep discounts: summer of 1994 brought a "loss-leader" single or double rate of $55, including continental breakfast, seven days a week—but also don't expect the best in the way of new TVs, electronics, or speedy service.

Dining/Entertainment: One restaurant, Le Beau Lieu. Jazz piano in hotel lounge.

Services: Concierge, room service.

Ramada Inn Center City, 501 N. 22nd St., Philadelphia, PA 19130. ☎ **215/568-8300** or toll free **800/272-6232.** Fax 557-0259. 181 rms, 4 suites. A/C TV TEL

Rates: $55 single; $75 double. Children under 18 free in parents' room. Weekend packages from $63 for two. AE, CD, MC, V. **Parking:** Free.

This hotel joined the Ramada system in late 1991, after previous stints as a Quality Inn. While rates are low, readers have complained about room conditions and ambience—so be forewarned.

The Ramada Inn–Center City is an easy 10-block distance from all three major train stations and a short loop off the Schuylkill Expressway. Under the porte cochere you'll find three wings of rooms off a central hub. They face the Parkway and the gardens of the Rodin Museum. There are a swimming pool and parking around and even under the facility, since part of the Ramada Inn is raised on concrete piers.

Dining: Red Lion Diner.

Facilities: Swimming pool, free parking, convenience store across Hamilton Street.

★ $ **Ramada Suites Historic Downtown Suites,** 1010 Race St., Philadelphia, PA 19107. ☎ **215/922-1730** or toll free **800/272-6232.** Fax 215/922-6258. 92 suites. A/C MINIBAR TV TEL

Rates (including continental breakfast): $79–$99, depending on suite size, single or double. Each additional person $10. AE, DC, MC, V. **Parking:** Free, validated (overnight) in garage next door.

You'll find spacious and reasonable accommodations at the new Ramada Suites Historic Downtown Suites in the heart of Philadelphia's Chinatown—and around the corner from the new Convention Center. It's a property purchased at a low price and then properly renovated for high hotel occupancy.

The building itself, from the 1880s, is handsome dark-red brick with lots of terra-cotta tiling and wide arches. For many years a bentwood furniture factory, it retains 13-foot ceilings, solid floors, and wood cross beams. You'll enter the inn through large double Chinese doors flanked by Ming lions. The reception desk and site of continental breakfast is to the right. Check in is set a bit late, at 3pm, but your bags can be left with reception.

Ramada Suites Downtown offers a couple special advantages for families. There's a very clean and well-stocked Chinese market directly across the street, and Reading Terminal Market is within two blocks. (No hotel restaurant, however.)

3 University City

Moderate

$ Penn Tower Hotel, Civic Center Blvd. at 34th St., Philadelphia, PA 19104. ☎ **215/387-8333** or toll free **800/356-7366.** Fax 215/386-8306. 175 rms, 7 suites. A/C TV TEL **Transportation:** Limo service to and from the airport.

Rates: $85–$115 single; $85–$125 double. A 25% discount for relatives of patients in University and Children's hospitals. Weekend packages start at $85 per couple per night. AE, DC, MC, V. **Parking:** $10.

Penn Tower is a greatly improved version of a former Hilton, built with a direct skywalk to University Hospital and within steps of the University of Pennsylvania, 30th Street Station, the Civic Center, and Drexel University. The University of Pennsylvania bought it in 1986. The hotel part of the tower comprises floors 11 through 20 (lower floors are used by the university as medical offices), as well as an enclosed garage and ground-floor restaurants and shops.

You'll have to get used to spirited displays of red and blue, the Penn colors, and a long lobby corridor of rough-textured concrete that leads to the reception desk. Florist and sundries shops are on the right, and I.D.E.A.S., a lounge, is on the left. Also on the left is an escalator that leads to second-floor meeting areas. Those handsome chairs and rugs were picked up for a song from the Bellevue Hotel in 1986.

Dining/Entertainment: I.D.E.A.S. is the lobby cocktail lounge. P. T.'s, a casual restaurant-coffee shop, serves breakfast, lunch, and dinner.

Services: Complimentary van service to Independence Park/historic district.

Facilities: Penn Tower is fully accessible to the disabled. It offers complimentary guest passes to Penn's nearby Hutchinson Health Complex for its track and rowing machines and makes tennis reservations at courts one block away.

Sheraton University City, 36th and Chestnut Sts., Philadelphia, PA 19104. ☎ **215/387-8000** or toll free **800/325-3535.** Fax 215/387-7920. 377 rms. A/C TV TEL

Rates: $89–$125 single; $89–$135 double; $195+ suites. Extra person $10. Children under 12 free in parents' room. Weekend and package rates from $89–$118 per night. AE, DC, MC, V. **Parking:** $8.

A favorite with business and academic visitors, located west of the Schuylkill River, this cheerful, moderately priced hotel is close to Center City via public transport or car. Though privately owned, this Sheraton offers the same comfort standard of any Sheraton—a little nicer, in fact, because the building (14 years old) is totally renovated. Also, there's a fine view of the university and the Philadelphia sky-line (the Civic Center is only four blocks away).

You'll enter the inn through a spacious Spanish-tiled lobby with access to the parking garage, located on the first 5 floors. The remaining 15 floors hold guest rooms with the same basic decor of floral-print bedspreads and curtains, dark-blue or gold carpeting, and beige wallpaper. The accoutrements include white molded-plastic chairs, octagonal coffee tables, and low-slung Mediterranean dressers with TVs and AM/FM radio consoles built in. The beds are extremely firm.

Dining/Entertainment: In the hotel are Smart Alex restaurant, a deli, and a cocktail lounge.

Facilities: Small outdoor pool open in summer, ice and soft drinks available on every other floor.

Inexpensive

Gables, 4520 Chester Ave. (at S. 46th St.), Philadelphia, PA 19104.
☎ **215/662-1921.** 8 rms. A/C TV

Rates: $50 (shared bath) or $70 (private bath) single; $60–$80 double, full breakfast included. AE, DC, MC, V. **Parking:** Free on-site.

This 1889 Victorian mansion was one of West Philadelphia's first and finest, and it has been reclaimed from boardinghouse status in the last five years. The location is about eight blocks west of the University of Pennsylvania's main campus and five blocks south of South Street, but it's right at the SEPTA trolley line stop into Center City and five minutes from 30th Street Station or 15 min-utes from the airport. For visiting academics, parents of University of Pennsylvania students, prospective applicants, and relaxed tour-ists, it's an excellent value choice.

Donald Caskey and Warren Cederholm are outfitting eight "formal" areas including sitting rooms, breakfast room, library, and wraparound porch, as well as four private bath and four shared bath bedrooms on the top two floors. All have gorgeous inlaid wood floors, and three have charming corner turrets; closets, armoires, lamps, and desks also fit the period. Home-baked muffins, breads, fresh fruit, and casseroles fill out breakfasts.

Budget

International House, 3701 Chestnut St., Philadelphia, PA 19104.
☎ **215/387-5125.** Fax 215/895-6535 379 rms (most with shared bath). A/C

Rates: 57 single; $69 double (private bath). Refundable deposit fee equal to 1 night's stay required on registration. No children allowed. MC, V. **Parking:** Many lots are nearby.

This is a tremendous value, but it depends on who you are, since International House is not a formal hotel but a residence during the academic year for U.S. and foreign students and academics. Some (under 100) rooms for academically affiliated transients are generally available year-round, more in summer. Related facilities and programs include a low-cost International Bazaar shop; many coffee hours, concerts, and films at the student center, all at nominal costs; a full-service restaurant and bar, and a travel agent. To get here, you can take bus 21 on Walnut Street from Center City.

Most guest rooms will resemble your college single; doubles are rarely available. Tough blue carpeting covers all floors, and the lighting is adequate, with two lamps and a vanity lamp above the mirror. The walls are solid and acoustically dead. Linen and towels are in the rooms, but soap and cups are your own responsibility. There are plenty of sparkling-clean showers, sinks, and bathrooms on each floor and a 24-hour security staff.

Facilities: Lounges with pay phones on each floor, student center for residents and guests with stream of cultural and social events, coin-operated laundry.

University City Guest Houses, P.O. Box 28612, 2933 Morris Rd., Philadelphia, PA 19151. ☎ **215/387-3731.** A/C TEL
Rates: $25–$75 single or double. Children allowed in some situations. Traveler's checks accepted but no credit cards.

This is basically a neighborhood collection of bed-and-breakfasts, most within walking distance of the University of Pennsylvania and University Hospital. Most hosts are academically affiliated. Parking is provided at most places.

4   Near the Airport

By the end of 1995, a new 419-room **Philadelphia Airport Terminal Hotel** connected to Terminal B will be open, but no further information was available at press time.

Expensive

Guest Quarters Suite Hotel, 4101 Island Ave., Philadelphia, PA 19153. ☎ **215/365-6600** or toll free **800/424-2900.**
Fax 215/492-9858. 251 rms. A/C MINIBAR TV TEL **Transportation:** Free shuttle from the airport.
Rates (including buffet breakfast): $155 single or double; look for seasonal specials as low as $119. Weekend package from $89. Children under 12 stay free in parents' room. AE, DC, MC, V. **Parking:** Complimentary to guests; $6 per day for nonguests.

For first-class prices you get deluxe suites of beautifully furnished bedrooms and living rooms that encircle dramatic multistory atriums containing restaurant and lounge seating. The occupancy rates are among the highest in town. The standard rooms have recently been made deep green and mauve, with a king-size bed, round dining room table for four, armoire concealing a TV with remote control, convertible sofa bed, and telephone with speaker. Minimal airport noise. HVAC controls are located near the wet bar, small refrigerator, and marble-topped vanity and bath.

Dining/Entertainment: The Terrace Lounge offers fairly lavish complimentary hors d'oeuvres and low drink prices Friday to Sunday from 5 to 7pm. At the Atrium Lounge and Café, underneath palms and ficus trees, the favorites include a delicious shellfish-and-mushroom bisque or samplings from the mesquite grill, served with stir-fried vegetables.

Services: *USA Today* delivered to door; complimentary coffee machines; Ambassador car rental in lobby.

Facilities: Complimentary indoor pool, whirlpool, sauna, and steam bath.

Philadelphia Airport Marriott Hotel, 4509 Island Ave., Philadelphia, PA 19153. ☎ **215/365-4150** or toll free **800/228-9290.** Fax 215/365-3875. 331 rms. A/C MINIBAR TV TEL

Rates: $126–$139, single or double. Weekend rate $73 single or double. AE, DC, MC, V. **Parking:** Free.

The Philadelphia Airport Marriott is removed from flight patterns, features a lobby and cocktail lounge built around a lushly planted indoor pool, and offers serious dining possibilities. Like all airport hostelries, business travelers predominate during the week, and reservations would be desirable. The guest rooms, all renovated in 1993, are classically American—spacious, comfortable, and anonymously elegant. All TV controls can be handled from the night table. The barrel chairs and sofa bed, in tan and deep brown, show unusual understanding of human contours.

Dining/Entertainment: Harper's, a turn-of-the-century bistro, has a salad bar and prime ribs ($8.95 lunch buffet). Sigi's fits the bill as a cocktail lounge with a DJ. Pride of place belongs to Chardonnay's, one of Philadelphia's best wine-by-the-glass restaurants (open for dinner Monday to Saturday from 6 to 10pm).

Services: Free cable with HBO, ESPN, and CNN; complimentary daily newspaper.

Facilities: Indoor pool, whirlpool, health club (open daily 6am to 11pm), sauna.

Radisson Hotel Philadelphia Airport, 500 Stevens Dr., Philadelphia, PA 19113. ☎ **215/521-5900** or toll free **800/333-3333.** Fax 215/521-4362. 350 rms, 52 suites. A/C TV TEL

Rates: $119 single; $129 double. Lower weekend packages available. AE, DC, MC, V. **Parking:** Free.

Opened in March 1991, the Radisson is trading on its spanking new looks, sleek 12-story glass atrium, and corporate clout even while rates have declined to match the competition. The design is ingenious; with northward balcony views of Center City expanded by a second enclosed atrium, overlooking a pool and health club. The guest rooms have two phones (one a speakerphone), and the materials are mostly veneers and hollow core. To get here, drivers should take Route 291, one mile west of the airport, and follow the signs over a winding road.

Dining/Entertainment: The Atrium Lounge (open to 1am) has a triangle of bar seats around postmodern pyramids. Trophies sports bar (open to 2am) is a 1960s-style room with jukeboxes and the like. Hampton Grille, a trendy coffee shop, serves breakfast, lunch, and dinner.

Services: Courtesy vans to and from airport, room service.

Facilities: Indoor pool, health club, game rooms.

Moderate/Inexpensive/Budget Options

Hotel chain options are very well represented at this level, including: **Holiday Inn Philadelphia Stadium,** 10th Street and Packer Avenue, Philadelphia, PA 19148 (☎ **215/755-9500** or toll free **800/424-0291**), which charges $100 to $110 for standard rates and as low as $49 for specials; **Airport Ramada Inn,** 76 Industrial Hwy., Essington, PA 19029 (☎ **610/521-9600** or toll free **800/228-2828**), with rates of $79 single, $84 double, $67 weekends; **Days Inn,** 4101 Island Ave. (between I-95 and Pa. 291), Philadelphia, PA 19153 (☎ **215/492-0400** or toll free **800/325-2525**), charging $99 single, $109 double, $89 weekends; **Comfort Inn Airport,** 53 Industrial Hwy., Essington, PA 19029 (☎ **610/521-9800** or toll free **800/228-5150**), with rates of $73 single, $79 double, and $57 weekends; and **Red Roof Inn,** 49 Industrial Hwy., Essington, PA 19029 (☎ **610/521-5090** or toll free **800/843-7663**), with rates of $51 single, $61 double.

5   City Line & Northeast

City Line Avenue (U.S. 1) just off the Schuylkill Expressway has become a vital part of the Philadelphia scene, with major retail stores like Saks Fifth Avenue and Lord & Taylor anchoring booming malls.

Expensive

Adam's Mark Philadelphia, City Ave. and Monument Rd., Philadelphia, PA 19131. ☎ **215/581-5000** or toll free **800/444-2326.** Fax 215/581-5069. 515 rms, 9 suites. A/C TV TEL **Rates:** $145 single; $157 double; from $157 executive room. Getaway weekend package $89+ per night. AE, DC, MC, V. **Parking:** Free in front lots or rear-connected garage; $5 valet.

The Adam's Mark looks like an airport control tower, but there's also an extensive brick complex of connected restaurants and function rooms.

The hotel is a bit ungainly in size—80% of business is convention, since the lower levels contain 50,000 square feet of meeting space—but makes up for it in friendly service, good value, and individual touches. From customized plastic Safe-keys and clear elevator signage, to the six nonsmoking floors (out of 23) and recently replaced individual HVAC units, constant attention is at work. The

1992 renovation brought dark-green checks, beige carpets, firm new beds, and Spectravision and remote controls for the TVs. Each room maintains solid-core doors, two armchairs, and round wood table and wall-length drapes. Baths, done the year before, have new counters and resurfaced tubs.

Dining/Entertainment: The Adam's Mark's food and beverage operation really shines. The gardenlike Appleby's is several notches above your average coffee shop, with "all you can eat" meals, 30-foot ziggurat skylights, and local antiques. Lines start forming early at the Marker, an improbable re-creation of French château orangerie, paneled English library, and western ranch that's somehow relaxing. It seats 150 on three levels, and evenings bring French tableside service. Quincy's, with some of the city's best hors d'oeuvres complimentary to 7pm, offers backgammon, dancing to 1940s-style bands nightly, and so forth in a decor of old copper and wood. There's no cover Monday through Thursday, $10 on Friday and Saturday (open from 8pm to 2am). Players, a sports bar, serves until 2am.

Services: Budget car rental in lobby; Barclay unisex hair salon; Squires travel service; extensive sundries shop.

Facilities: The excellent health-club operation, open 7am to 10pm, includes indoor and outdoor pools with sunken whirlpool in a comfortable, high-ceilinged room. Two racquetball courts rent for $10 for a 45-minute session. Stairmasters, treadmills, Lifecycles, a rowing machine, and eight-station Nautilus and sauna round out the area.

Moderate/Inexpensive/Budget Options

Thoroughly comfortable lodgings at representatives of national chains dot this area, including: **Holiday Inn City Line,** 4100 Presidential Blvd. (City Line Avenue at I-76), Philadelphia, PA 19131 (☎ **215/477-0200** or toll free **800/465-4329**), charging $105 single, $115 double; **Sheraton Inn Northeast,** 9461 Roosevelt Blvd. (U.S. 1 at Grand Avenue), Philadelphia, PA 19114 (☎ **215/671-9600** or toll free **800/800-325-3535**), with rates of $75 single, $85 double, or $69 weekend, with Sesame Place packages at $116; and the **Best Western Philadelphia Northeast,** 11580 Roosevelt Blvd., Philadelphia, PA 19116 (☎ **215/464-9500** or toll free **800/528-1234**), charging $80 single, $85 double.

A Youth Hostel

Chamounix Hostel Mansion, West Fairmount Park, Philadelphia, PA 19131. ☎ **215/878-3676** or toll free **800/379-0017.**

Directions: Take I-76 (Schuylkill Expressway) to Exit 33, City Line Ave., turn right (south) on City Ave. to Belmont Ave., left on Belmont to first traffic light at Ford Rd., left on Ford, through stone tunnel to stop sign, then a left onto Chamounix Dr. and follow to the end. **Bus:** Take SEPTA route 38 from John F. Kennedy Blvd. near City Hall to Ford and Cranston Sts. (a 30-minute ride), then walk under the overpass and left onto Chamounix Dr. to the end.

Rates: $10 AYH members; $13 nonmembers; $2 sheet charge. Maximum 3-day stay. Traveler's checks, MC, V. **Closed:** Dec 15–Jan 15.

The oldest building offering accommodations in town, this renovated 1802 Quaker farmhouse is also the cheapest. Chamounix Mansion is a Federal-style edifice constructed as a country retreat at what is now the upper end of Fairmount Park. About 20 years ago the only thing about to cross the threshold was the wrecker's ball, but then it was converted into a youth hostel. It has 6 dormitory rooms for 44 people, with limited family arrangements, and another 37 spots in a fully renovated adjoining carriage house. Write or call ahead for reservations, since the hostel is often 90% booked in summer by groups of boat crews or foreign students.

You can check in daily between 4:30 and midnight and show an American Youth Hostel card or IYHF card for member rates. Check out is from 8 to 11am. Call AYH directly at **215/925-6004** for information on hostel trips in the area.

6

Philadelphia Dining

A RESTAURANT RENAISSANCE CAPTURED PHILADELPHIA'S IMAGINATION IN THE 1970s and 1980s. New spots opened constantly, with distinctive menus, superb service, and cozy surroundings. The 1990s legacy? In the 1994 *Condé Nast Traveler*'s readers poll, the city had seven restaurants placed among America's top 50—including #1, Le Bec-Fin, and #2, The Fountain at The Four Seasons Hotel. Below them are literally dozens of young entrepreneurs turned on to excellent gourmet fare, combining tastes from around the world. The line between special-occasion restaurants and more casual, moderately priced, everyday bistros has blurred to the advantage of both.

Unfortunately, this chapter cannot include many of the more renowned Main Line and other suburban restaurants. If you're heading out that way, many volunteers staffing the desk at the **Convention and Visitors Bureau,** 16th Street and Kennedy Boulevard (☎ **568-1666**), hail from those parts and have crackerjack knowledge.

Dining Notes

Dining in Philadelphia is an excellent value! Compared to places in New York, the average quality and attention in Philadelphia restaurants set a higher standard, and the prices fall between one-third and one-half less, particularly in the upper reaches. This chapter will categorize **very expensive** restaurants as those charging $40 or more per person for dinner without wine; **expensive** as $30 to $40 per person; **moderate** as $20 to $30; **inexpensive** as $10 to $20; and **budget** as under $10. These are only rough guidelines, however, since many luxury restaurants also include lower-priced choices. The cost of wine can be a considerable expense—restaurants usually double the state store prices. You might call ahead to ask about bringing your own.

Meal tax is 7%, and standard tipping is 15% (the latter is occasionally included on the tab). For most restaurants I have given only summer hours; you can expect plenty of 9pm (as opposed to 10pm) closings in other seasons.

It's always a good idea to make reservations—they're a necessity for the posher spots, especially on the weekend. Ask about validated parking nearby too.

What do Philadelphians wear to dine? Pants (not jeans) on women are accepted everywhere, and a man with a jacket but without tie has almost universal success. A sweater could substitute for the sports jacket in most budget and moderate restaurants.

1 Historic Area

Very Expensive

Old Original Bookbinder's, 125 Walnut St. ☎ **925-7027.**

Cuisine: SEAFOOD/AMERICA. **Reservations:** Recommended.
Prices: Appetizers $4.95–$12.95; main courses $17.95–$40.95; lunch $5.95–$24.95. AE, DC, MC, V.

Open: Lunch Mon–Fri noon–2:45pm; dinner Mon–Fri 2:45–10pm, Sat noon–10pm; Sept–June, Sun 3–9pm; July–Aug Sun 3–10pm.

If dining at an institution is your predilection, head for this place. Sam Bookbinder opened this seafood restaurant in 1865; his wife announced lunch by ringing a bell. The restaurant acquired status as the *only* place to dine in town for decades. The family sold to the Taxins, now operating it for the third generation, in the 1930s and moved to 15th Street (see Bookbinder's Seafood House in Section 2, "Center City," below).

Over the years this Bookbinder's has expanded to encompass almost the entire block across from the Sheraton Society Hill. Just past two cigar-store Indian sentries, to the left of the ship's wheel, Bookbinder's Gift Shop sells city memorabilia along with pies and cans of the most popular soups—snapper with sherry, New England clam chowder, and Manhattan clam chowder. To the right the rooms stretch on and on—three bars and seven dining rooms that are served by 185 staff members.

Bookbinder's is most renowned for lobsters, which it transports live from Maine in tanks. The less-expensive baked imperial crabmeat with pimientos, a touch of Worcestershire, and green peppers is beyond reproach. The dinner menu is huge: all sizes and kinds of shellfish and fish, steaks, and veal. Their shortcake, strawberry cheesecake, and apple-walnut pie have all won gastronomic awards. The wine list, fairly standard, offers plenty of domestic vintages for under $15.

Frommer's Smart Traveler: Restaurants

1. By eating the same fare for luncheon that you would eat for dinner—and if you're on vacation, why not?—you'll save from 20% to 30%. Put another way, you can sample the best restaurants in town at lunch but pay a fraction of the dinner prices.
2. Philadelphia has some great inexpensive ethnic restaurants, particularly Greek, Italian, and Chinese.
3. To save time and money, picnic or grab a sandwich at a takeout spot or a food court like Liberty Place or the Bourse.
4. Watch your liquor intake with meals: Individual drinks can add a lot to the tab.
5. Some Philadelphia restaurants have adopted the pleasant French custom of a prix-fixe menu, which usually includes three courses for 30% less than à la carte prices. The portions are generally a bit smaller, however.
6. Many smaller hotels and bed-and-breakfasts have discount arrangements with fine neighboring restaurants. Don't accept or reject these without checking a little first, however.

Expensive

The Chart House, 555 S. Columbus Blvd. (formerly Delaware Ave.) at Penn's Landing. ☎ **625-8383.**

Cuisine: SEAFOOD. **Reservations:** Recommended.

Prices: Appetizers $4.95–$8.95; main courses $15.95–$34.95. Sun brunch $16–$18. Children's menu available. AE, DC, MC, V.

Open: Dinner Mon–Thurs 4–11pm, Fri 5pm–midnight, Sat 4pm–midnight, Sun 4–10pm; brunch Sun 10:30am–2pm.

The busiest restaurant in all Philadelphia has to be The Chart House, a convention center right on the Delaware River. You may not love everything about it—expect a spirited crowd and frequent birthday celebrations—but the Chart House chain has a track record for reasonably priced dinners, with soup, fresh molasses or sourdough bread, and an unlimited salad bar included. All seats have spectacular views, and the service will make you wish you had had camp counselors that enthusiastic.

Start with New England clam chowder, of course, or raw oysters. The unlimited salad bar is $12.95 by itself—with over 50 components such as beets, cherry tomatoes, fresh fruit, and hearts of palm—or free with main course such as prime rib or a steak of halibut, tuna, or other fish. The desserts are very sweet: mud pie, turtle pie, or an ice-cream sundae built on a crust of chocolate cookies.

 La Famiglia, 8 S. Front St. ☎ **922-2803.**

Cuisine: ITALIAN. **Reservations:** Required.

Prices: Appetizers $5.95–$8.95; main courses $16–$28. AE, CB, DC, MC, V.

Open: Lunch Tues–Fri noon–2pm; dinner Tues–Fri 5:30–9:30pm, Sat 5:30–10pm, Sun 4:30–9pm **Closed:** Mon.

The name La Famiglia should tip you off that this place is a refined Italian restaurant—and in this case it refers to both the proprietors and the clientele. In the 1980s La Famiglia was chosen one of the 25 best Italian restaurants in the country by *Bon Appetit* magazine. The Neapolitan Sena family (parents and three children) aim for elegant dining, service, and presentation; their success here has spawned Penn's View Inn and its Ristorante Panorama (see below).

This restaurant seats 60 in a private, warm setting of hand-hammered Venetian chandeliers and majolica tiles. Recordings of arias give some of the best aural accompaniment in the city. Downstairs by the restrooms, you can see the privy excavations and 1680s foundations.

The chefs at La Famiglia make most of their own pasta, so you might concentrate on such dishes as gnocchi al pesto, which adds walnuts and pecorino cheese to the noodles. There's a choice of five or six vegetables with meals, and the marinated string beans and zucchini with pepper have never failed to please. For dessert, try a *mille foglie,* the Italian version of the napoleon, or the profiteroles in chocolate sauce. People often remain here well after the closing hour, lingering over Sambuca.

Moderate

 Chef Theodore, 1100 S. Columbus Blvd. (formerly Delaware Ave.) at Washington Ave. ☎ **271-6800.**
Cuisine: GREEK. **Reservations:** Recommended.
Prices: Appetizers $4.25–$9.95; main courses $9.95–$15.95. AE, CB, DC, MC, V.
Open: Tues–Sat 4–11pm, Sun 1–10pm.

The best Greek restaurant along South Street migrated to the waterfront in 1989, to a Delaware Avenue (locals will never honor the official 1993 street name switch to Columbus Boulevard) shopping center near the multiplex Riverfront cinemas (it's not practical to get there unless you have a car). While the decor is unassumingly white and the ambience is casual, the quality of the food is unusually good. Start with the enormous *mezze* (a combination platter of standards like baba, tarama, and octopus) or with the sausage or dry goat's milk cheese; both are flamed at your table. You can sample from more combination platters for a main course or stick with the salmon with roasted potatoes or the shrimp casserole. The service is unobtrusive and wine prices reasonable.

City Tavern, 2nd and Walnut Sts.
Cuisine: AMERICAN. **Reservations:** Recommended
Prices: Undetermined (see below).
Open: Undetermined (see below).

If the hunger to relive those good old 1780s overcomes you in Independence Park, there's at least one authentic restaurant that will let you use that newfangled credit card to pay for colonial fare: City Tavern—the same tavern that members of the Constitutional Convention used as coffee shop, ballroom, and club some 200 years ago. The U.S. government now owns the building, which is operated by a concessionaire, Walter Staib.

However, as we went to press, City Tavern was undergoing major changes in decor, menu, and pricing. Chef Derek Banks plans duck sausage, rabbit with potato dumplings, and turkey hash. You'll pass it, for sure; let us know if other readers should patronize it!

 The Dickens Inn, 421 S. 2nd St. ☎ **928-9307.**
Cuisine: BRITISH/CONTINENTAL. **Reservations:** Recommended.
Prices: Appetizers $5.25–$7.25; main courses $13.50–$21.50; lunch $4.95–$7.95. AE, CD, DC, MC, V.
Open: Lunch, daily 11:30am—3pm, dinner Mon–Sat 5:30–10pm, Sun 3–9pm; brunch Sun 11:30am–3pm.

This three-story Federal town house on Head House Square has proved to have real staying power since it has survived with crumbling New Market behind it. The key elements here are atmosphere and friendly service. Opened in 1980 by the owners of the famous Dickens Inn by the Tower of London, the American version re-creates an English pub and restaurant (19th-century London is all over the walls and tables) that serves fine country-house cuisine.

Paneling lines the walls, and wooden tables, exposed beams, and frosted-glass lamps mix at every turn with lithographs of scenes from Dickens novels and framed Dickensiana. Don't miss the cupboard of Blue Willow.

The main courses are extremely generous, tasty, and attractive, served on large speckled crockery. Traditional beef Wellington and prime rib with Yorkshire pudding are offered along with lighter dishes. The seafood choices displayed on a cart raw for your choice include bay scallops poached with basil, tomatoes, and muscadet. All main courses are served with a platter of steamed fresh vegetables. To finish, select a dessert from the Dickens Inn's own bakery, rolled in on a trilevel wooden cart, or sample the English Stilton cheese with fresh fruit.

Lunch is a less ambitious affair, with Cornish pasty (traditional pastry filled with lamb, carrots, and potatoes and flavored with fresh herbs), shepherd's pie, trout filet, and a wild-mushroom-and-vegetable crêpe. A traditional homemade soup is offered daily.

There are four bars, with 14 English imported beers. The skylit tavern room, with one of the best happy hours in town, was chosen by *Esquire* magazine to be one of the top 100 bars in America.

⭐ **Dinardo's Famous Crabs,** 312 Race St. ☎ 925-5115.
💲 **Cuisine:** SEAFOOD. **Reservations:** Required for six or more.
Prices: Appetizers $2.95–$6.95; crabs $2 each; other main courses $9.95–$19.95; lunch $3.95–$7.95. AE, CB, DC, MC, V.
Open: Mon–Thurs 11am–11pm, Fri–Sat 11am–midnight, Sun 4–9pm.

Dinardo's Famous Crabs springs to mind as the best moderately priced spot in the area around the Betsy Ross House and Elfreth's Alley. The door nearest 3rd Street is the real entrance.

Dinardo's expanded to the City of Brotherly Love only because too many Philadelphians were trekking to the original Wilmington locale. It's still a tight family operation: Only William Dinardo and his son mix the crab seasonings.

Dinardo's has two unique factors—the site and the prices. The building at 312 Race St. was an inn for Tory soldiers in 1776, in the oldest part of town, and later it served as a prison for Confederate soldiers. Three ground-floor dining rooms were recently reclaimed from mid-20th-century disrepair. The well-lighted chambers have subtly striped wallpaper, huge crab specimens, various net buoys, and simple Formica tables.

Prime live catches from Texas and Louisiana are flown up north daily. Experienced hands dredge the crabs with the house seasoning of 24 spices and pack heavy-gauge steel hampers with them. Then the crabs are steamed, not boiled (this keeps the seasoning on), for 25 minutes. All crabs are served on plastic platters, with nutcrackers and red sauce. If you're not in a crabby mood, there are at least 30 other succulent items, from raw-bar oysters to seafood platters.

Downey's Pub, northwest corner of Front and South Sts.
☎ 629-9500.
Cuisine: IRISH. **Reservations:** Recommended.

Prices: Appetizers $3.25–$5.75; main courses $6–$19; lunch $8–$11. AE, DC, MC, V.

Open: Lunch Mon–Fri 11:30am–3pm; dinner Mon–Fri 4:30–10:45pm, Sat 4:30pm–12:30am, Sun 4:30–9:45pm; brunch Sat–Sun 11:30am–3pm.

About 250 years ago Front Street from Race to Fitzwater streets was a jumble of docks, shops, and public houses that reminded English and Irish seamen of home. Downey's Pub has succumbed to such modern blandishments as electricity and daily quiche, but it's still a place any Irishman or -woman would be proud to frequent. Much of the ground floor was lifted from a Dublin bank built in 1903; the upstairs is from a pub in Cork City.

Downey's obviously started off less "lace curtain" than it is now, since the downstairs walls are covered by yellowing shellacked newspapers. The current urbane, comfortable layer throws in brass rails, coat stands, and framed Victorian prints. In summer, café tables grace both the South Street and the river patios. Upstairs, which added a wraparound deck in 1993, is tonier still, with Beerbohm caricatures, skylights, and beveled mirrors on beautiful wood paneling. Don't miss the details here, such as the Irish coins nailed to the portal and the tin-sheet-plate ceiling. The staff, in white shirts and Limerick-green bow ties, is gracious and lively.

Lunch and dinner retain some Irish dishes with American fillips, but are balanced by Italian and lighter fare. The soups are strong here—the potato soup and the lobster bisque use thick milk and have plenty of body. Crab cakes are Downey's most popular item, and roast beef and turkey are carved on your order. The fish of the day, done any way you like, is served with a fresh vegetable.

Live music is a staple of Downey's, both at the weekend brunches and in the upstairs Piano Bar on Friday and Saturday from 8pm to 1am.

La Grolla Bar and Trattoria, 782 S. 2nd St. ☎ 627-7701.

Cuisine: ITALIAN. **Reservations:** Required for Sun lunch.
Prices: Appetizers $4.95–$8.95; main courses $12.95–$26.95. AE, DC, MC, V.
Open: Dinner only, Mon–Thurs 5–10pm, Fri–Sat 5pm–midnight.

Just when you think the gentrified area south of South Street is about to run into South Philadelphia's corner stores and artificial stone facades, La Grolla spreads its bright-orange awning amid an enticing fragrance of garlic, spices, and stock. As of 1991, a relaxed Piedmontese restaurant was turned into a bar and trattoria, but rotund and expansive Giovanni Massaglia and Mamma Bertina still preside over casalinga pasta and unusual dishes. There's plenty of on-street parking nearby.

La Grolla (Italian for "cup of friendship") is narrow and fairly small, and you'll probably want to head straight to the intimate back room. Waiters in white shirts and black bow ties will not let you order before explaining all the dishes—the more Piedmontese ones are quite unusual.

You might start with the cannelloni stuffed with veal sausage and topped with a tomato bechamel or a tarragon seasoning. The salads are on the small side but fresh. No pasta is offered as main course, but there are always several venison dishes, for which the place is especially known. The side helpings of vegetables are seasonal, and winter brings braised fennel bulbs and a sweet fried polenta cake. The wine list is on the expensive side, with few choices under $20.

The desserts are especially good and unusual. The *torta di mele* is actually not a tart but a cold custard pie with apples, cocoa, and cinnamon. If pastry's what you want, try the *sfogliatelle*, a custard underneath a napoleon that's beribboned with fresh whipped cream.

⭐ **Jeannine's Bistro,** 10 S. Front St. ☎ **925-2928.**
Cuisine: FRENCH BISTRO. **Reservations:** Recommended.
Prices: Appetizers $3.95–$6.95; main courses $9.95–$17.95. AE, MC, V.
Open: Tues–Fri noon–2pm, Tues–Sat 6–10pm. **Closed:** Sun–Mon.

In 1991, the popular classic French restaurant downstairs decided to open a bistro, with cut-down dishes. Lunch is served downstairs, with dinner and entertainment upstairs. Owner Jeanne Mermet herself makes a vocal appearance on Fridays to augment the guitar-and-violin duo that plays most nights. The chef, Todd Davies, has credentials from Aureole and the River Café in Manhattan.

The dining room is charming, with floral-print wallpaper and tablecloths, burgundy pillows, and candlelight. Watch the climb, though. The menu selections include braised pork, grilled fish, and poultry. The desserts are most like what restaurant diners get downstairs, with white-chocolate mousse and the like.

Judy's Cafe, 3rd and Bainbridge Sts. ☎ **928-1968.**
Cuisine: AMERICAN. **Reservations:** Recommended for parties of four or more.
Prices: Appetizers $2.95–$6.95; main courses $13–$22. AE, DC, MC, V.
Open: Dinner only, Mon–Thurs 6–10pm, Fri–Sat 6–11pm, Sun 5–9:30pm.

An agreeable bistro outgrowing its countercultural beginnings, Judy's is one of the finest examples of the South Street renaissance. The place opened in 1976, with Judy and Eileen as co-owners. Judy left soon after, but the locale retains a neighborhood feeling, though it's not really a family place. The regulars banter with the waiters, who dine here on their nights off, and the service at the well-stocked bar may depend on how you strike the person behind it. Jonathan Demme, director of the film *Philadelphia,* ate here throughout film production.

Judy's two rooms are simply furnished: Photo-realist canvases co-exist with a quizzical neon strip embracing the wall behind the bar. There's nothing quizzical about the cuisine, however. The menu changes with the season, but the quality is high.

The main courses are eclectic. A Monday through Thursday special includes your choice of stir-fried duck, lamb stew, or the catch of the day with soup and coffee. Whatever seafood's on the menu will undoubtedly be fresh. The very, very chocolate cake could deserve a third *very;* for those not hooked on fudge, the carrot cake's moist and scrumptious. *Note:* Local papers often advertise 2-for-1 weeknight specials.

Meiji-en, upstairs at Pier 19, on the Delaware River at Callowhill St. ☎ **592-7100.**

Cuisine: JAPANESE. **Reservations:** Recommended.
Prices: Appetizers $4–$10; main courses $14–$28. AE, CB, DC, MC, V.
Open: Dinner Mon–Thurs 5–9:30pm, Fri–Sat 5–11pm, Sun 5–9pm; brunch Sun 10:30am–2:30pm.

Meiji-en opened in 1988 as a huge harbinger of the waterfront development needed to support a 600-seat restaurant. The restaurant now enjoys high volume and offers consistent quality. Meiji-en falls somewhere between an indoor tennis court and a Japanese theme park; everyone from a romantic couple to a huge family can take pleasure in a visit.

Be sure to call ahead to request a water view and don't be deterred by the slightly forbidding Delaware Avenue approach, four blocks north of the Benjamin Franklin Bridge. Valet parking nearby is $6.

You'll almost need a floor plan to plot your course because there are separate areas for sushi, tempura, teppanyaki (or stove top at table), and regular table seating (the latter two are river views to the east), as well as a bar with live jazz on Friday and Saturday. Everything is scrupulously clean, and the service is impeccable. The decor features lots of hanging rice-paper globes, blond-wood screens and seats, and comfortable black-and-red cushions.

Many of Meiji-en's dishes have the same basic ingredients—filets of fish and chicken—done with different preparations, from being boiled to being quick grilled to being diced in gyoza dumplings. Many dishes are marked as especially health conscious. Among the appetizers I recommend the shrimp shumai (light rice dumplings served in a bamboo steaming tray, with dipping sauce) and the fried eggplant boats with chicken. The teppanyaki dishes are cheapest and most fun; your group will sit around horseshoe-shaped tables of granite-and-steel stove tops while you're served seared meat and greens. If you're ordering regular service, expect fish steaks or marbled beef that are beautifully presented. The Sunday jazz brunch has an opulent $18.95 buffet.

Philadelphia Fish & Company, 207 Chestnut St. ☎ **625-8605.**

Cuisine: SEAFOOD/AMERICAN. **Reservations:** Recommended.
Prices: Appetizers $2.95–$6.95; main courses $10.95–$19.95. AE, MC, V.
Open: Lunch Mon–Fri 11:30am–4pm, Sat noon–3pm; dinner Mon–Thurs 4–10pm, Fri–Sat 4pm–midnight, Sun 3–10pm.

It's inevitable that you'll pass Philadelphia Fish & Company, given its location next to Independence National Historical Park sites and outdoor patio dining, weather permitting. I can confirm that it's okay to enter, since the restaurant offers a quite modern selection of fish and preparations new to Philadelphia, with premium freshness. For example, you'll encounter lots of grilling over mesquite: yellowfin tuna, salmon, and rock cod, with increasing use of Asian spices, soys, and sesame oil. The $6.95 executive lunch is a great deal: a cup of soup, the fish special, green salad, and beverage. The wine list, skewed toward white wines, is very reasonable for Philadelphia, with good quality. Late night here can get noisy amid the windsor chairs and soft lighting.

★ **Ristorante Panorama,** Front and Market Sts. ☎ **922-7800.**

$ **Cuisine:** ITALIAN. **Reservations:** Recommended.

Prices: Appetizers $4.95–$7.95; main courses $8.95–$17.95. AE, CB, DC, MC, V.

Open: Daily noon–midnight. Dinner service 5:30–10pm Sun–Thurs, 5:30–11pm Fri–Sat.

Although the Ristorante Panorama is on the waterfront, its view is a colorful mural of the Italian countryside. The cuisine is a wonderful, choice list of lighter Italian dishes. Pasta, salads, and fish predominate, with a few veal and beef favorites. The bread is served without butter but with a tiny bowl of pesto. Favorite appetizers are the fantasy platter of grilled vegetables, beautifully arranged, and the croquettes of shrimp and lamb served on a bed of arugula. The fish are usually grilled and lightly seasoned with garlic and tomatoes. The tiramisu, with its triple-creme mascarpone cheese drizzled with chocolate, needs either an espresso or a dessert wine as an accompaniment.

Panorama is also one of the city's best new wine bars, with 120 (not all Italian) wines served in 3- or 5-ounce glasses from a Cruvinet system to a sophisticated, lively crowd. In fact, diners can take a "map" of their selections, with space for notes and ratings.

Inexpensive

Los Amigos, 50 S. 2nd St. ☎ **922-7061.**

Cuisine: MEXICAN. **Reservations:** Not accepted.

Prices: Appetizers $2.95—$5.50; main courses $8–$13; combination plates $8–$11. Dinner minimum $5 per person. AE, DC, MC, V.

Open: Mon–Thurs 11:30am–11:30pm, Fri–Sat 11:30am–1am, Sun 1–10pm. Bar open Mon–Sat until 2am.

Unassuming, piquant touches encourage your eye to wander around Los Amigos's arcade of brick and stucco. You might expect sombreros and silver-plate photographs, but not the clay wall niches, the inset bricks, and the inactive bell.

One of the combination plates makes a satisfying light meal and a sampler in Mexican cooking as well. Chile rellenos, one of Los Amigos's best items, are chile peppers stuffed with a cheese mixture, thoroughly cooked in batter (not just dipped in it for a quick fry), then served with tomato sauce and a dollop of sour cream. The chile taste never overwhelms. I also like the chicken *budin azteca,* a chicken and sausage casserole with tortilla layers. One or two nontortilla dishes, such as arroz con pollo (chicken with rice), sneak onto the menu. The refried pinto beans have a finely puréed smokiness, although the rice seems overbaked. For dessert, the flan is smooth in a light caramel sauce and the sopaipillas come with honey and powdered sugar on their fried dough. Exotic coffees and Mexican beer are available, as is a limited selection of wines and pitchers of margaritas.

Brasil's, 112 Chestnut St. ☎ 413-1700.

Cuisine: BRAZILIAN. **Reservations:** Recommended.
Prices: Appetizers $3–$8; main courses $7–$13. AE, DC, MC, V.
Open: Sun–Fri 5pm–11pm, Sat 5pm–midnight.

This warm new bistro in the heart of the historic district has gotten positive press for all-you-can-eat feijoada Sundays and churrasco Tuesdays. The former is the Brazilian national stew of black beans, sausage, seafood, and orange garnish; the latter a spicy grilled beef. There are plenty of more standard meat and poultry offerings, along with live entertainment on weekends.

Thai Palace, 117 South St. ☎ 925-2764.

Cuisine: THAI. **Reservations:** Recommended.
Prices: Appetizers $4–$6; main courses $7–$13. AE, DC, MC, V.
Open: Dinner only, daily 5:30–10pm.

This long-standing Thai location has a new lease on life as Thai Palace, boasting all the sweet and hot pastes and spices you'd expect. It isn't much to look at—white, clean, and spare—so start right in on the satay, a highly spiced and marinated meat kebab. For something hot that doesn't sear the taste buds, try the chicken *ka prow* (chicken with fried hot pepper) done in an unusual basil-and-lemongrass sauce. The desserts here are not their strong points; perhaps dessert doesn't flourish in cultures accustomed to single-pot communal meals. BYOB.

Walt's King of the Crabs, 804–806 S. 2nd St. ☎ 339-9124.

Cuisine: SEAFOOD. **Reservations:** Not accepted.
Prices: Appetizers $2.95–4.95; main courses $7.95–$12.95. No credit cards.
Open: Mon–Sat 11am–12:30am; Sun 2–10pm.

Walt's makes no bones (or shells?) about the house specialty, and this little, unpretentious storefront hangout has acquired a fanatical following. Owner Ted Zalewski is an extremely nice, beefy Queen Villager who cares about serving lots of people well. Unless your taste includes both bizarre ocean-scene murals and Patti Page records, ignore the decor and dig in.

The platters include truly tasty coleslaw and french-fried potatoes. The deviled crab comes in a great minced patty, fried but never greasy. At last hearing, chicken lobsters were offered for $9.50 each. The house specialty features two jumbo shrimp stuffed with crabmeat. Draft beer costs $1 a glass or $6 a pitcher. Take-out costs 25¢ extra. You'd be advised to call ahead to find out about waiting time, because the lines in summer and on weekends are fierce.

Budget

★ **Jim's Steaks**, 400 South St. ☎ **928-1911.**

Cuisine: AMERICAN. **Reservations:** Not accepted.

$ **Prices:** Lunch and main courses $3.50–$4.95. No credit cards.

Open: Mon–Thurs 10am–1am, Fri–Sat 10am–3am, Sun noon–10pm.

Philadelphia cheesesteak is nationally known. The best practitioner of the fine art of hoagiedom in this area is Jim's Steaks in Queen Village; they also do the mightiest steak sandwiches in town.

Jim's has a certain art deco charm, with a black-and-white enamel exterior and tile interior, plus omnipresent chrome. But most of the ground floor is taken up by the counters, containers, and ovens, although there is a counter with bar stools along the opposite wall. Take-out is highly recommended in clement weather.

Proper hoagie construction can be debated endlessly, but Jim's treatment of the Italian hoagie with prosciutto ($3.95) is a benchmark. A fresh Italian roll is slit before your eyes and layers of sliced salami, provolone, and prosciutto (Italian ham) are laid over the open faces. You choose your condiment: mayonnaise or oil and vinegar. Salad fixings—lettuce, tomatoes, and green peppers, with options on onion and hot peppers—come next, with more seasoning at the end. The result is not subtle but pungent, filling, and delicious. The steak submarines are less succulent than in the past but also cheaper at $3.25 (melted cheese additional). Beer and soft drinks are sold in cans and bottles.

2   Center City

Very Expensive

★ **Le Bec-Fin**, 1523 Walnut St. ☎ **567-1000.**

Cuisine: FRENCH. **Reservations:** Required—a week ahead for weeknights, months ahead for Fri–Sat.

Prices: Prix-fixe lunch $32; prix-fixe dinner $94. AE, DC, MC, V.

Open: Lunch Mon–Fri seatings at 11:30am and 1:30pm; dinner seatings at 6 and 9pm Mon–Thurs, 6 and 9:30pm Fri–Sat. Bar Lyonnais downstairs serves food and drink until midnight.

There's no doubt that Le Bec-Fin is the best in Philadelphia and certainly one of the top 10 in the country. Patron Georges Perrier hails from Lyon, France's gastronomic capital, and commands the respect of restaurateurs on two continents for his culinary accomplishments.

Le Bec-Fin looks exactly as it's supposed to—elegant and comfortable, with apricot (this may be changed to deep red by 1995) silk covering acoustic panels. A portrait of one of Perrier's ancestors, a Russian émigré, peers benignly from the 18th century. Mirrors in back of wall brackets and candlelight add to the warm lighting—seeing your food can only enhance your meal. The table settings include bountiful bouquets; Christofle silver; and the same china—an 18th-century Limoges pattern—Paul Bocuse uses in his Lyon restaurant. In addition to the main dining room, the Blue Room (seating 25) may be reserved for private parties. As review after review has noted, it is virtually impossible not to enjoy yourself here, even before your meal begins.

With leisurely timing, an evening at Le Bec-Fin waltzes through hors d'oeuvres, a fish course, a main course, a salad, cheese, a dessert, and coffee with petits fours. Since most of the menu changes seasonally—and your special orders are welcome as well—dishes listed are illustrative. A roast lobster in a butter sauce infused with black truffles is unbelievably flavorful. The terrine of three fish contains a layer of turbot mousse, then a layer of salmon mousse, then one of sole mousse, each with its own dressing; the total effect, with shallots, couldn't be more subtle. The escargots au champagne are renowned as a first course, as the garlic butter also includes a touch of chartreuse and hazelnuts.

The main dishes give you the opportunity to try some rarities—pheasant, venison, and pigeon. The last (stuffed with goose liver, leeks, and mushrooms) comes in a truffle sauce. So does the mouthwatering dish of four filets of venison, covered by a thick milk-mustard sauce. The desserts become grand opera, with trays, tables, and ice cream and sherbets (in the little aluminum canisters they were churned in) zooming from guest to guest. With the addition of pastry chef Bobby Bennett—who just placed fifth in a worldwide World Cup of Pastry—the desserts tray looks and tastes like Dante's Paradiso, especially the 18-inch-high Mont Blanc with sides of sheet chocolate. The finest coffee in the city, served in Villeroy & Boch flowered china, makes those petits fours you really don't need easier to take. Cigars, cordials, liqueurs, and marcs and other fortified spirits gild the lily.

The wine list starts at around $35 per bottle and rises astronomically.

In 1991 M. Perrier opened the basement ★ **Le Bar Lyonnais** for more affordable snacking and champagne toasts. Open until midnight, it has only four tables and bar stools, but trompe l'oeil pilasters and paisley wallpaper expand its effect. Expect to spend about $10 a nibble and $7 for a glass of house wine. The later it gets, the more likely dishes from upstairs are to arrive—and M. Perrier himself, for that matter.

Expensive

Bookbinder's Seafood House, 215 S. 15th St. ☎ **545-1137.**

> **Cuisine:** SEAFOOD. **Reservations:** Recommended for Fri lunch and for dinner.
>
> **Prices:** Appetizers $3.95–$10.95; main course $14.95–$28.95; lunch $3.95–$12.95. Occasional prix fixe dinners from $25. AE, CB, DC, MC, V.
>
> **Open:** Mon–Fri 11:30am–10pm, Sat 4–11pm, Sun 3–10pm. Dinner served from 3pm.

A trip to Philadelphia once automatically meant a seafood meal at Old Original Bookbinder's (see "Historic Area," above). But even before the 1970s restaurant renaissance, the third generation of Book-binders moved downtown and set up shop at Bookbinder's Seafood House. Now fourth-generation Richard presides over 400 seats spread over two floors.

The Old Original trades off its worldwide fame, age, and location near the Delaware; the 15th Street Booky's is less self-congratulatory and has its own solid clientele. The high ceilings give plenty of room for the mounted fish, nautical chandeliers, oak paneling, and captain's chairs. The heavy wood tables hold goblets of croutons for chowder.

You might start with the famous snapper soup laced with sherry. All the seafood but the smoked fish comes from Chesapeake Bay trawling—the smelts get especially high marks for freshness. You can get that basket of clams you've been pining for, a large box of Chincoteague oysters, or lobsters from $19.95. The mussels in red sauce are probably the best known among Philadelphians. To adapt to modern tastes, more sauces are being served on the side and new imports, such as mako shark, have been added.

★ **Ciboulette,** 200 S. Broad St. ☎ **790-1244.**

Cuisine: FRENCH. **Reservations:** Strongly recommended.
Prices: Appetizers $6–$14; main courses $22–$35; prix-fixe lunch $21 (three course) or $29 (four course); prix-fixe dinner $45 (four course) and $60 (five course). AE, DC, MC, V.
Open: Lunch 11:30am–2:30pm Mon–Fri; dinner Mon–Sat 5:30–10:30pm, Sun 5–9pm.

Ciboulette, French for "chives," is upward mobility in action. Bruce Lim, born in Singapore and trained in Paris and across town at The Four Seasons, opened up his inventive application of southern French cooking principles and Asian touches at a small row house in 1988. In 1993, he moved to the palatial digs vacated by Pierre Deux at the Bellevue, turning out meals applauded by *Esquire* and *Travel/ Holiday* for their elegance and service.

You'll enter a suite of 19th-century bourgeois baroque rooms with ornate fireplaces, plaster ceiling lozenges, and gilt-framed ormolu mirrors. The food, from a selective menu, is wonderful, and has followed the decor in enhanced classic French grandeur, with virtually all organic meat and poultry, vegetables, and herbs. A sweetbread appetizer sautées them in a mustard demiglaze, garnished with snow peas. Look for tender, seared slices of squab or duck, in reductions of unusual sauces, or sea bass steamed in olive oil with organic artichokes and fennel. Desserts like lemon galette and crème brûlée are flawless. I particularly recommend the tasting prix-fixe menus; they give excellent value and afford you some explorations off the regular menu with items like a vegetarian Wellington with truffles.

★ **Dilullo Centro,** 1407 Locust St. ☎ **546-2000.**

Cuisine: ITALIAN. **Reservations:** Strongly recommended.
Prices: Antipasto $6–$9; main courses $16–$25; lunch $10–$16. AE, CB, DC, MC, V.

Open: Lunch Mon–Fri 11:30am–1:30pm; dinner Mon–Sat 5:30–10pm. Dilullo's Fox Chase: Dinner Mon–Thurs 5:30–10pm, Fri–Sat 5:30–10pm, Sun 4:30–9pm.

Philadelphia residents know that the best choice in town for sophisticated, exquisite Italian cuisine is Dilullo's, either right across from the Academy of Music in a renovated theater or in the original Fox Chase suburban location. Dilullo Centro lacks the original's booth with grandmothers making fresh filled pastas, but it is even more spectacular, with at least $750,000 invested in such opulent and slightly decadent items as a huge copper antipasto cart, enlarged copies of impressionist and expressionist works, a series of booths separated by etched glass, ebonied wood, and wrought-metal armchairs. In fact, this kind of product is especially threatened by the curtailment of business expense accounts, but go while you can.

Begin a meal with an antipasto—sautéed buffalo-milk mozzarella slices, marinated pepperoni, sun-dried tomatoes, and the like on a single plate or a single seafood terrine or mousse. Italian meals of this quality demand a small first course of pasta; followed by a second of fish, meat, or poultry with vegetables; and finally optional fruit, sweets, and coffee. For a real splurge, the tagliatelle with black mushrooms is smoky and wild yet smooth. Main courses include thin-sliced fresh monkfish in lemon sauce and three slices of veal loin sautéed, then baked after a slow marinade in rosemary and garlic. If you order a grilled dish, be aware that many Americans perceive the Italian style as underdone. The vegetables are strictly seasonal, and the all-Italian wine list ranges from $22 (Orvieto, Corvo) to $48 (Gattinara).

Naturally, you'll want to finish with an espresso, which comes in a silver pot, and some dessert. Dilullo's produces its own gelato, with ground fruits or beans and a splash of spirits.

Friday Saturday Sunday, 261 S. 21st St. (between Locust and Spruce Sts.) ☎ **546-4232.**

Cuisine: CONTINENTAL. **Reservations:** Accepted.
Prices: Appetizers $5–$6.50; main courses $12.50–$19.50. AE, CB, DC, MC, V.
Open: Lunch Mon–Fri 11:30am–2:30pm; dinner Mon–Sat 5:30–10:30pm, Sun 5–10pm.

There's a lot to be said for a restaurant that installed a window on Rittenhouse Street for the kitchen staff. Friday Saturday Sunday is a romantic survivor of the early restaurant renaissance that has adapted to the times, offering informality, abundant personal attention, and a relaxed confidence in cuisine. Chef Aliza Green of Azalea recently upgraded ingredients and found better suppliers for the 1990s.

Friday Saturday Sunday is classy but unostentatious: The cutlery and china don't match, flowers are rare, and the menu is a wall-mounted slate board with inscriptions in several Day-Glo colors. But these touches of bohemia are eclectic or vestigial, since the interiors are darkly handsome. Pin lights frame a row of rectangular mirrors set in wood paneling, and fabric flecked with gold swathes the upstairs ceiling (downstairs, it's striped). An aquarium bubbles behind a cosmopolitan holding bar. Dress is anywhere from jeans to suits, and the service is vigilant but hands-off.

Try the fairly spicy Thai green salad with chicken breast, served over a marinade of soy, honey, and sesame. Or sample the colorful Szechuan salad with sweet red peppers and wok-fried beef slivers. The portions (both first and second courses) are well laden, so you're advised to split an appetizer and even a dessert between two. If you have any taste at all for duck, the double-baked and mildly curried half duck is excellent. The wine card lists about 30 vintages. The desserts change often.

⭐ **The Garden,** 1617 Spruce St., near Rittenhouse Square.
☎ **546-4455.**

Cuisine: CONTINENTAL. **Reservations:** Recommended.
Prices: Appetizers $5–$10; main courses $14.95–$24.95; lunch $9.95–$19.95. AE, CB, DC, MC, V.
Open: Lunch Mon–Fri 11:30am–1:45pm; appetizers Mon–Fri 2:30–5:30pm; dinner Mon–Sat 5:30–10pm. **Closed:** Sat–Sun in July–Aug.

The Garden keeps sprouting up. Although it's 20 years old, Kathleen Mulhern's place captures the city's sense of style—taste without ornateness—better than any other spot I know. The tables and bar are antiques, set off by the many 19th-century prints of fruit and animals. In this former music academy, the oyster bar on the left was renovated in 1993, but it will keep the liquor. The three softly lit dining areas—Swan Room, with wooden decoys; Print Room, a floral back parlor; and the Main Room, a former concert hall with practice rooms—can become noisy when crowded; fortunately, the great outdoors is only paces away, weather permitting. Thanks to five tons of soil and gravel brought in each spring, the gaily bedecked back garden is a fragrant and spectacularly quiet enclave, making it the preferable dining locale, either for candlelit evenings or for sun-shaded luncheons. Potted flowers vie with the yellow umbrellas for brightness. **Note:** Garden now offers valet parking and reduced rates in a nearby garage.

The house's favorite appetizer, a raw filet of beef (carpaccio) sliced very thinly is more typical of dinner than lunch, which leans more toward seafood, poultry, and salads. Spinach gnocchi made by "Aunt Diddy" is feather light with a sweet Gorgonzola sauce. All main courses include vegetables. Four or five dishes—featuring grilled salmon, oysters, and delicate Dover sole—can be ordered as delicious light main courses. The French chocolate cake has been called the best dessert in Philadelphia by *Food & Wine* magazine, and the chocolate sampler plate is frighteningly good.

⭐ **Jack's Firehouse,** 2130 Fairmount Ave. ☎ **232-9000.**
Cuisine: CONTEMPORARY AMERICAN. **Reservations:** Recommended.
Prices: Appetizers $4.95–$11.95; main courses $16.95–$22.95; prix-fixe menus $45 and $52. Bar service available; sandwiches from $6.95. AE, DC, MC, V.

Open: Mon–Sat 11:30am–10:30pm; Sun brunch 11am–3pm. Bar open nightly until 2am.

In many ways this is one of the most imaginative, and one of the most hotly debated, restaurants now operating in Philadelphia. Chef Jack McDavid, after raves for Reading Terminal's Down Home Diner (inside) and Reading Terminal Restaurant at 12th and Filbert streets has taken a turn-of-the-century firehouse and incorporated contemporary (and rotating) art by Philadelphia artists, a beautiful rowing shell, and a glass-and-walnut island bar. It's warm and homey, but the cuisine features dramatic juxtapositions of American ingredients and flavors, with special emphasis on the rare, the nearly lost varietal, and the inheritances of immigrant cultures. The game is outstanding, and McDavid's dressing and preparation of gopher, bear, bison, and beaver tail (to name a few) make this a national pilgrimage of sorts. The historical steeping in many dishes, such as Pennsylvania shad and bacon, is impeccable, and McDavid is fanatical on organic ingredients.

A typical menu starts with a basket of buttermilk muffins. It then presents main courses like suckling pig with a thin and slightly sweet sauce, garnished with lettuce and Granny Smith tempura; shrimp with fennel in a lime-pepper sauce; and three thick medallions of venison in a succulent berry-and-meat stock, served with haricots and baby carrots and a red-bean-and-wild-rice mélange. The desserts could be a smooth peanut-butter-and-chocolate cake or sweet pecan pie.

The same stretching of boundaries goes for the extensive all-American wine list, ranging from $16 to $90 per bottle. Several microbreweries, such as Stoudt's of Pennsylvania, are represented with quality beer, on tap and in bottles.

To save a bundle, try a simple meal of the black-eyed pea soup, the cornmeal crêpe, or a hearty sandwich for under $20 with your drink.

Morton's of Chicago, One Logan Square (19th and Cherry Sts.) ☎ 557-0724.

Cuisine: STEAK. **Reservations:** Accepted for 5:30–7pm only.

Prices: Appetizers $6.95–$9.95; main courses $18–$32. AE, CB, DC, MC, V.

Open: Lunch Mon–Sat 11:30am–2:30pm; dinner Mon–Thurs 5:30pm–11pm, Fri–Sat 5:30pm–11:30pm, Sun 5–10pm.

Looking for sirloin? Morton's of Chicago has become a staple both for business lunches near Logan Square and for celebratory evenings. Don't kid yourself about the specialty—the double-cut filets, sirloins, and T-bones come in aged, well-marbled tender masses. The house porterhouse weighs in at 24 ounces; if you wish, the waiter will bring your cut of meat or fish raw to your table for precooking inspection. The cauliflower soup also is touted, and the Sicilian veal chop with garlic bread crumbs is a "hometown" hit. If you must branch out farther, sample the crab cocktail or the smoked salmon served on dark bread with horseradish cream, capers, and onions.

Morton's looks as sedate as you'd expect, with glass panels between the tables and booths and dim lighting that makes the brass glow. The art deco bar has a wall lined with wine bottles. Expect to pay $25 for lunch and at least $35 for dinner. **Note:** Jacket and tie required.

Striped Bass, 1500 Walnut St. ☎ **732-4444.**

Cuisine: SEAFOOD. **Reservations:** Almost essential.

Prices: Appetizers $6.50–$9; main courses $15–28; lunch $8–$18. AE, DC, MC, V.

Open: Lunch Mon–Fri 11:30am–2:30pm; dinner Mon–Sat 5–11pm.

This long-awaited 1994 creation of Neil Stein, formerly of The Fish Market, has an absolutely spectacular setting in a former brokerage office. In terms of ambience and setting, the 16-foot steel sculpture of a leaping bass poised over the exhibition kitchen sets the tone. With rows of plateaued banquettes, warm lighting, and carpeted floors to soak up all the din bouncing off marble walls, you'll experience a rare and exotic sense of theater. The cuisine promises creative, simple preparations of seafood, with the emphasis on fresh herbs and clean flavors. At press time, it's still a promise: timing problems meant some dishes were arriving cool, and flavors weren't yet harmonious. By 1995, these difficulties should be solved. A mostly domestic wine list starts at $22.

Moderate

 Circa, 1518 Walnut St. ☎ **545-6800.**

Cuisine: AMERICAN/MEDITERRANEAN. **Reservations:** Recommended.

Prices: Appetizers $3–$6; main courses $8–$16; lunch $6–$10. AE, MC, V.

Open: Lunch Mon–Fri 11:30am–2:30pm; dinner Mon–Thurs 4:30–10pm, Fri–Sat 4:30–11pm. Dancing Thurs–Sat 10:30pm–2:20am, Labor Day to Memorial Day.

This 1994 labor of love is one of Philadelphia's hottest spots: it's got great food on a great restaurant block, it combines dinner with a sophisticated dance club, it's magnificent and yet engaging and comfortable, and it's cheaper than you think it's going to be. Owners Philippe Daouphars and David Mantelmacher took their club success at Xero on South Street into Center City, where they teamed up with thoughtful chef Albert Paris for Mediterranean cuisine with a twist up and westward.

The former bank building provides Circa with great beaux arts columns and windows along the east wall's long bar, opening up to a square, pleasant room upstairs—and also original steel and brass vault fittings downstairs. Chef Paris likes flavorful food—you'll find choices like duck ravioli, goat cheese, and sun-dried cherries or roast shrimp with spinach and pine nuts—but has cleverly chosen dishes that won't suffer from a complicated trip upstairs. Sauces, vegetables, and starches are expected to complement main meals, and every dish is a "signature": its ingredients are unique on the menu. Wines, from $18, are well chosen.

Circa is not a club, but at 10:30 on Thursdays, Fridays, and Saturdays, the ground floor and mezzanine become a club with a jammed dance floor. The sound is excellent, and the lines go around the block.

Cutter's Grand Cafe and Bar, in the Commerce Square building on Market St. at 20th St. ☎ **851-6262.**

Cuisine: AMERICAN. **Reservations:** Recommended.
Prices: Appetizers $5–$9; main courses $12–$20. AE, DC, MC, V.
Open: Lunch Mon–Fri 11:30am–2:30pm; dinner Mon–Thurs 5–10pm, Fri–Sat 5–11pm, Sun 5–9pm.

This place has all the things you'd expect of a restaurant in a big, spanking-new, impressive skyscraper—modern, cool lighting and a huge bar (120 seats) for singles. There aren't too many competitors for this type of urban bistro. But it's also an impeccable, convenient, 180-seat restaurant that's surprisingly warm for a romantic dinner, given that you're in white-collar clothes and paying white-collar prices.

The bar has become noted for its huge selection, with the bottles stacked vertically so that bartenders scamper up and down like gymnasts. Look for highly polished surfaces in wood and stone, glass lampshades, and floor-to-ceiling murals in leafy hues. Fortunately the high ceilings soak up much of the din.

Seafood (the corporate owner is based in Seattle) and pasta—from yakisoba buckwheat noodles to fettuccine—are what's notable here. The biggest single item is the filet of salmon (flown in fresh daily) grilled over mesquite wood. Pasta comes with seafood also—the fettuccine with scallops, for example—and such touches as toasted hazelnuts. Pizza, lamb chops, game, and steaks fill out the extensive menu, with delicious flat bread to nibble while you wait. The desserts are as good as you'd expect: lots of chocolate and a wonderful crème brûlée and bread pudding. The validated parking is complimentary after 5pm.

Ruth's Chris Steak House, 260 S. Broad St. ☎ **790-1515.**

Cuisine: STEAK. **Reservations:** Recommended.
Prices: Appetizers $3.50–$8.95; main courses $13.95–$22.95; lunch $8.50–$13.95. AE, MC, V.
Open: Mon–Fri 11:30am–11:30pm, Sat 5–11:30pm, Sun 5–10:30pm.

Ruth's Chris Steak House, just south of the Academy of Music, has gotten rave reviews since 1989. Ruth's Chris serves only U.S. prime beef that's custom aged, never frozen and rushed to Philadelphia by the New Orleans distributor for the chain. The rib-eye steak in particular is presented lovingly, almost ritually, in a quiet and respectful setting, and garnishes are almost nonexistent. The portions are so large that you might want to skip the side dishes, although Ruth's Chris touts potatoes done nine ways. Several fish and chicken choices also are available. The desserts, mostly southern recipes with lots of sugar and nuts, average $5.

★ **Sansom Street Oyster House,** 1516 Sansom St.
☎ 567-7683.

$ **Cuisine:** SEAFOOD. **Reservations:** Not accepted.
Prices: Appetizers $3.50–$6.50; main courses $10.75–$18; lunch $4.25–$10.75. Four-course prix-fixe dinner $16. AE, DC, MC, V.
Open: Lunch Mon–Sat 11am–3pm; dinner Mon–Sat 3–10pm.

Chef David Mink knows oysters from every angle—where they come from, how their flavors differ, and how to prepare them. The Sansom Street Oyster House, located on one of Philadelphia's most colorful shopping blocks, is where David puts his acumen into action. In 1989, he added the Samuel Adams Brew House upstairs, the first brew pub in town, with two ales and porter on tap.

The ambience is that of a traditional seafood parlor, with such 20th-century concessions as a tiled floor (instead of sawdust) and plywood paneling. The blackboards listing the daily specials perch beside an endless collection of antique oyster plates and nautical lithographs.

You'll probably want an appetizer of several different types of oysters: metallic belons; cooler, meatier Long Island half-shells; and larger, fishier box oysters. You can judge a similar rivalry between cherrystone and littleneck clams for yourself. All are opened right at the raw bar. For dinner, most people choose one of the specials— local shad or tilefish, for instance. The homemade bread pudding is the most reliable dessert. The liquor prices are moderate and draft Samuel Adams beer is $2.25.

Susanna Foo, 1512 Walnut St. ☎ **545-2666.**

Cuisine: CHINESE. **Reservations:** Recommended for dinner.
Prices: Appetizers $4–$9; main courses $15–$24; lunch $9–$16. AE, MC, V.
Open: Lunch Mon–Fri 11:30am–2:30pm; dinner Mon–Thurs 5–10pm, Fri–Sat 5–11pm.

Susanna Foo has been touted in *Gourmet* and *Esquire* magazines and just about everywhere else as one of the best blends of Asian and Western cuisines in this country. A fall 1993 redecoration incorporated her collection of Chinese art and textiles, a new kitchen, and a second-floor café.

The cuisine is the main thing, so expect to pay first-class prices. Appetizers feature such delicacies as curried chicken ravioli with grilled eggplant, slightly crispy but not oily. Noodle dishes, salads, and main courses similarly combine East and West: water chestnuts and radicchio, smoked duck and endive, grilled chicken with Thai lemongrass sauce, and spicy shrimp and pear curry. Ms. Foo does include French caramelizing of certain dishes but not any butter-based sauces or roux; the Asian technique is to sear small amounts of ingredients, combining them just before service. The wine list, designed to complement these dishes, specializes in French and Californian white wines. Desserts such as the ginger creme with strawberries and the hazelnut meringue are light and delicate.

A long-awaited dim-sum café and bar was opened upstairs at Susanna Foo's in 1993. In this cuisine, diners graze from up to 30 choices of tidbit platters. These are exquisite, from pork-stuffed jalapeños and lamb wantons to tiny spring rolls.

Inexpensive

 Dock Street Brewing Company, Two Logan Square (corner of 18th and Cherry Sts.). ☎ **496-0413.**

Cuisine: INTERNATIONAL. **Reservations:** Required for six or more. **Prices:** Appetizers $4–$8; main courses $6–$14; lunch $4–$9. Fresh-brewed tap beer $2.50–$3.50 per glass. AE, CB, DC, DISC, MC, V. **Open:** Mon–Thurs 11am–midnight, Fri–Sat 11am–2am, Sun noon–11pm.

This brew pub is just right for the 1990s: relaxed, with a definite hook in the spotless on-premises microbrewery. Jeffrey Ware saw a market niche for a brewery that could operate in combination with a popular restaurant, since other "normal" microbrewery costs wouldn't apply. You can take a tour, but at any time six or more fresh beers, ales, stouts, and porters will be on tap; sample the subtle distinctions in hops, yeast, temperature and length of fermentation, and filtration. The 200-seat restaurant features a 40-foot bar, a paneled billiard room to the rear, spacious banquettes, and high ceilings (it's ironic that this place is located in a brand-new corporate granite skyscraper!). **Note:** Dock Street brewery products are served only at the bar.

Main dishes range in price from $6 to $14. The lunch menu offers soups, several fresh salads, and pub-style sandwiches, including a grilled vegetable pita with black-bean hummus. Dinner main courses include maple-chipotle barbecued salmon, hand-carved roast beef, traditional English fish-and-chips with malt vinegar and house-made tartar, and a Stilton blue cheese tart in whole-wheat crust with apples and leeks.

Marabella's, 1420 Locust St. ☎ **545-1845.** Also at Benjamin Franklin Pkwy. at 17th St. ☎ **981-5555.**

Cuisine: INTERNATIONAL. **Reservations:** Not accepted for dinner. **Prices:** Appetizers $2.95; main courses $7.95–$14.95; lunch $3–$6. AE, DC, MC, V. **Open:** Mon–Thurs 11:30am–11pm, Fri–Sat 11:30am–midnight, Sun 3–11pm.

Are you looking for a trendy trattoria that offers pastas, pizza, sandwiches, and grilled seafood, all with contemporary flair? That's Marabella's, a restaurant that is not only fun and chic but also reasonably priced. Marabella's offers the same menu at lunch and dinner, with almost every item under $12. Both locations are convenient for families and posttheater dining:

Before you order, your waiter will bring you bread and roasted peppers—hard to resist. The appetizers range from such old favorites as mussels in red or white sauce, fried mozzarella, and antipasto to a more unusual platter of fish and shellfish in sauce, something like a seafood stew. The roasted garlic cloves to be spread on the delicious bread are another pleasure. The wine list boasts a good selection of inexpensive California and Italian wines.

For a main course, try a contemporary dish such as tortellini with goat cheese, sun-dried tomatoes, and olives. The old standards, spaghetti and meatballs and lasagne with meat sauce, are very well done here; the pasta is homemade, and the sauces are carefully seasoned. If you want to go with pizza instead, the version with goat cheese, sun-dried tomatoes, and black olives is very popular. The desserts are gelati, ricotta cheesecake, burned-sugar custard, and a chocolate concoction called "original sin" (don't ask).

Mezzanotte, 1701 Green St. ☎ **765-2777.**

Cuisine: ITALIAN. **Reservations:** Recommended.

Prices: Appetizers $3.95–$5.95; main courses $7–$14. AE, DC, MC, V.

Open: Sun–Thurs 11:30 am–11pm, Fri–Sat 11:30am–midnight. Bar open until 2am.

Mezzanotte, six blocks north of the Wyndham Plaza and north of Logan Circle, features a quirky combination of contemporary Italian American food at moderate prices. Mezzanotte is most known for its individualized pizzas: a thin crust (a combination of white and whole wheat) topped with various combinations, including caramelized onions, walnuts, and Gorgonzola. Many of the recipes are taken from Spago's in Los Angeles or Greens in San Francisco—you get the idea. Other recipes include frittatas—thicker Italian versions of omelets—special pastas, and fish with herbs. The wine list is short and affordable.

Rib-It, 1709 Walnut St. ☎ **568-1555.**

Cuisine: AMERICAN/RIBS. **Reservations:** Not accepted.

Prices: Appetizers $2.95–$5.95; main courses $6.95–$14.95. AE, DC, MC, V.

Open: Lunch Mon–Sat 11:30am–3pm; dinner daily 4:30–10pm. Early bird special Mon–Fri 3:30–5:30pm, Sun noon–4pm. Bar Mon–Sat until 2am, Sun 12:30–10pm.

Rib-It does a lot of casual, off-the-street trade and gives wonderful value for ribs, an onion loaf, or a quick drink. Rib-It has a relaxed sense of comfort, featuring an old tin ceiling with cone moldings and soft lighting that sets a subdued, but not unpleasant, tone. Swirling stained glass, much from the old Waldorf-Astoria in New York, decorates the bar and all the windows.

Vernon Hill, Rib-It's young entrepreneur, won't reveal exactly what's in the western barbecue, but it's brushed on the baby-back ribs ($14.95 at dinner, $8.95 at lunch) for a lean, smoky taste. The portions are quite large, to say the least. An appetizer called Wonder Wings dishes up over a pound of barbecued chicken wings, and it's known to make a meal for two. Whatever you order, don't leave without trying the onion-ring loaf, which consists of true onion rings pressed into a bread mold. The drinks average $3, with draft beer $1.50 per mug. If you get hungry between lunch and dinner, try the early bird special, a full dinner for $6.

Samuel Adams Brew House, 1516 Sansom St., 2nd floor.
☎ **563-2326.**
   Cuisine: PUB. **Reservations:** Not required.
   Prices: Appetizers $3.50–$5.95; main courses $6–$13.50. AE, DC, MC, V.
   Open: Lunch Mon–Sat 11am–4pm; dinner Mon–Thurs 4–11pm, Sat–Sun 4pm–midnight.

The Samuel Adams is a traditional, no-smoking English-style brew pub with an American twist—a microbrewery. While you sit at the handsome hand-carved English bar, you can watch as three varieties of beer are made. In addition to best bitter, amber ale, and porter, they offer seasonal specials like Spring Boch. The menu features such English favorites as fish-and-chips and grilled sausage, plus such Americanisms as burgers, crab cakes, and ribs.

Budget

Charlie's Water Wheel, downstairs at 1526 Sansom St.
☎ **563-4155.**
   Cuisine: DELI/ROMANIAN. **Reservations:** Not accepted.
   Prices: Sandwiches/main courses $6.95. No credit cards.
   Open: Lunch only, Mon–Sat 11am–4pm.

Charlie Rechnitz is a Romanian circus all in himself, and the Water Wheel is best known for the massive quantity of freebies—pickles, fried mushrooms, and meatballs—available with any order. The steaks, sandwiches, and cheesesteaks here are popular with the pin-striped set. Charlie dispenses apples and bananas at the cashier's desk, along with a steady stream of dialogue.

Diner on the Square, 19th and Spruce Sts. ☎ **735-5787.**
   Cuisine: AMERICAN. **Reservations:** Not necessary.
   Prices: Sandwiches $3.25–$4.95; main courses $6–$8.
   Open: 24 hrs.

Say that you're strolling around Rittenhouse Square and have an urge for the type of square meal you'd associate with a roadside restaurant. A dressed-up place like that is waiting for you at Peter Bruhn's Diner on the Square. Don't let its pink neon fool you; it has booths at which burgers, hash browns, and the best milk shakes in Philadelphia make their cheerful appearances—for about $5 per person. The Diner also branches out as a deli, with a whitefish platter and delicious omelets, and offers some fancier cuisine, such as a chicken-breast sandwich. The lunch and Sunday-brunch crowds can be fierce, so try to beat the rush.

Rex Pizza, 20 S. 18th St. ☎ **564-2374.**
   Cuisine: ITALIAN. **Reservations:** Not accepted.

Prices: Pizza $3.75–$7.25; hoagies from $3.55. No credit cards.
Open: Mon–Sat 11am–1am.

For those self-indulgent moments when you need a large pepperoni pizza or a tuna hero, one of the most convenient—and surprisingly good—spots is Rex Pizza. They do a fine, nongreasy, thick-crust whole pizza for about $5.95 and a full-scale submarine sandwich for $3.95. Even when they're busy, your wait will rarely exceed 10 minutes.

3 South Philadelphia

South Philly—literally square miles of basic row houses in straight lines between Bainbridge Street and the sports stadiums—is the best place on earth for one particular cuisine: adaptations of the dishes of south and central Italy to American ingredients and meal sizes. What makes South Philly interesting is that this "American cousin" is frozen sometime between 1920 and 1990, and you can always tell unmistakably by the decor, menu, and music what decade a particular restaurant is frozen in. So I've selected the best on their own terms.

Expensive

Aglio, 937 E. Passyunk Ave. ☎ **336-8008.**

   Cuisine: ITALIAN. **Reservations:** Recommended.
   Prices: Appetizers $5–10; main courses $13–$24. AE, DC, MC, V.
   Open: Dinner 5:30–11pm daily. **Closed:** Sun–Mon in summer.

Aglio—"garlic"—denotes the use of roasted garlic as a spread on the wheat bread distributed at this 1993 new-style Italian bistro. It also says something about owner Frank Audino's desire to get close to natural and unusual ingredients like sorrel, barley, brown rice, and risotto. Neighborhood regulars are applauding its elegance, the flavored gnocchi made on premises, and the freshness of the sauces.

Osteria Romana, 935 Ellsworth St. ☎ **271-9191.**

   Cuisine: ITALIAN. **Reservations:** Recommended.
   Prices: Appetizers $4.50–$12; main courses $14.50–$26. AE, DC, MC, V.
   Open: Dinner Tues–Thurs 5:30–10:30pm, Fri–Sat 5:30–11pm, Sun 5–9:30pm. **Closed:** Mon.

This 1981 Roman import just missed the top 50 in the national *Conde Nast Traveler* reader survey of the best restaurants in America. The DiMarcos (Ivana is Roman born and will run the kitchen until she finds satisfactory help—which, by her standards, may take forever) get rave reviews for simple, unpretentious specialties like pasta, osso buco, and saltimbocca.

You start off with a basket of *bruschetta*—olive-oil brushed toast with fresh tomatoes. If you've never had an honest minestrone, this might be the place and time. The tomato stock is light and sweet, and the vegetables retain body and flavor. As a first course, the pastas are uniformly excellent—thick, tubular, and gently resilient. If you're used to American pasta sauces, these may seem a bit dry and meager, but startlingly fresh.

The best meat dish (and the most expensive) is a grilled steak that tastes like it just came off a charcoal fire; while crispy outside, it retains tenderness within. All main courses come with a seasonal vegetable, such as asparagus with crushed garlic and lemon. The DiMarcos have been working on expanding the dessert tray; if it has a sort of custard torte covered with fresh fruit, jump at it.

The Saloon, 750 S. 7th St. ☎ **627-1811.**

Cuisine: CONTINENTAL. **Reservations:** Virtually required.
Prices: Appetizers $5–$16; main courses $14–$34. AE.
Open: Lunch Tues–Fri 11:30am–2pm; dinner Mon–Thurs 5–10:30pm, Fri–Sat 5–11:30am.

The Santore family has tended here since the late 1960s, and the tastes of the time have again rolled around to the freshness and quality of their cuisine, which deserves its rare top rating from *Philadelphia Magazine.* The decor is solid wood paneling, soft, uplit sconces, and antiques and Tiffany lamps amid a second floor which above one excellent bar and surrounded by a second with an old National cash register.

The Saloon has a long menu, and many specials add to it. The Santores like standards like clams casino and crabmeat salads, but also serve sautéed radicchio with shiitake mushrooms and superb salads. The heavy artillery is the 25-ounce porterhouse steak with greens and roasted potatoes and the lightly breaded veal slices with sweet and hot peppers. The wines are expensive, and the desserts high cholesterol and exquisite, thanks to the pastry chef on board.

Moderate

 Victor's Cafe, 1303 Dickinson St. ☎ **468-3040.**

Cuisine: ITALIAN. **Reservations:** Recommended. **Directions:** Follow Broad St. south to Dickinson, then walk 2 blocks east.
Prices: Antipasti and appetizers $4.25–$6.95; main courses $12.75–$19.75. AE, CB, DC.
Open: Dinner Tues–Thurs 5–11pm, Fri–Sat 4:30pm–12:30am, Sun 4–9:30pm.

Victor's is a South Philly shrine to opera, with waiters who deliver arias along with hearty Italian classics. Started in the 1930s by John Di Stefano, who covered the walls with photos of Toscanini, local Mario Lanza, and the like, the family still plays over 70,000 78s and hires the best voices they can find. The food has come in for some quizzical comments recently, though; best to stick to basics like the cannelloni Don Carlos, with its two enormous shells filled with beef and veal and covered in marinara.

Budget

$ Marra's, 1734 E. Passyunk Ave. (between Morris and Moore Sts.) ☎ **463-9249.**

Cuisine: ITALIAN. **Reservations:** Not necessary.
Prices: Main courses $5–$12. Basic pizza $5.75 small, $7 large. No credit cards.
Open: Tues–Thurs 11:30am–11pm, Fri–Sat 11:30am–12am, Sun 2pm–11pm. **Closed:** Monday.

No list of eateries would be complete without a pizzeria, and Marra's wins the "Best Pizza" award hands down. It's in the heart of South Philadelphia, and the brick ovens give these thin-crust versions a real Italian smokiness. Marra's is noted for its homemade lasagne, its tomato sauce, and its squid on Friday.

⭐ **Ralph's,** 760 S. 9th St. ☎ **627-6011.**

Cuisine: ITALIAN. **Reservations:** Recommended.
Prices: Antipasti and appetizers $5.50–$7.50; pasta $8; main courses $9–$15. No credit cards.
Open: Lunch and dinner Sun–Thurs noon–9:45pm, Fri–Sat noon–10:45pm.

This two-story restaurant a few blocks above the Italian Market is the epitome of the "red gravy" style: unpretentious, comfortable, reasonable, owned by the same family for decades. The baked lasagne and spaghetti with sausage have fans all over the city, and the extensive menu features veal and chicken in particular. The service is friendly and attentive.

💲 **Strolli's,** 1528 Dickinson St. ☎ **336-3390.**

Cuisine: ITALIAN. **Reservations:** Essential. **Directions:** Follow Broad St. south to Dickinson, then walk 2 blocks west.
Prices: Antipasti and appetizers $1.50–$3; pasta $3; main courses $5–$8. No credit cards.
Open: Lunch Mon–Sat 11:30am–1:30pm; dinner Mon–Sat 5–10pm, Sun 4–9pm.

With all those Italians in South Philly, you'd figure on an extremely inexpensive, wholesome, family restaurant in the middle of a neighborhood, right? Right—and the place is Strolli's. It used to look like a burned-out storefront at the corner of Mole Street—now there's a sign and an identifiable side door. Implacable, pipe-puffing John Strolli presides over two plain rooms, with plywood paneling and bare plaster enlivened by an ancient cigarette machine and a life preserver dedicated to Strolli's wife, Carmela. Music emanates from a corner radio. You'll make your own atmosphere, and any description of the size, taste, or pricing of the dishes won't be believed.

You'll want to start with an antipasto; a medium-size one is fully 10 inches long and 4 inches high, so the large would suit three fine. All seafood platters come with tomato, lettuce, and coleslaw—would you believe a scallop-crammed plate for $5.50? The veal-cutlet platter is an extraordinary piece of sautéed red veal. While you're making reservations, you might ask for the special stuffed shells—they're legendary.

⭐💲 **The Triangle Tavern,** at the intersection of Passyunk Ave. and 10th and Reed Sts. ☎ **467-8683.**

Cuisine: ITALIAN. **Reservations:** Recommended.

Prices: Main courses $6–$10. No credit cards.
Open: Lunch Mon–Sat 11am–2pm; dinner Mon–Sat 4pm–midnight, Sun 3pm–midnight.

Inexpensive, heaping dishes of homemade pasta and bowls of mussels are served here amid the Fraletta's 60-year-old steamy atmosphere of good humor. You'll enter through the neighborhood bar, complete with large-screen TV; keep pushing toward the back. Nothing costs more than $10, and most items are closer to $6: chicken cacciatore, gnocchi, and spaghetti in white clam sauce. The mussels in red sauce are famous. On Friday and Saturday nights, look for plenty of audience participation in helping the steady guitar trio along with old favorites. Be prepared to wait for a table.

4   University City (West Philadelphia)

Moderate

Palladium, 3601 Locust Walk. ☎ 387-3463.
> **Cuisine:** CONTINENTAL. **Reservations:** Recommended.
> **Prices:** Appetizers $3.50–$7; main courses $9.50–$24; lunch $6–$11.50; pretheater dinner $17. AE, DC, MC, V.
> **Open:** Lunch Mon–Fri 11:30am–2:30pm; dinner Sun–Tues 5–9pm, Wed–Sat 5–11pm; late suppers daily.

In the heart of the University of Pennsylvania campus (Wharton specifically) is Palladium, the latest enterprise of co-owners Roger Harman and Duane Ball. Strictly speaking, Palladium is an elegantly appointed full-service restaurant and bar; it's reminiscent of an old-time faculty club—chesterfields and wing chairs with footstools face an old stone fireplace, while leaded-glass windows, oak wainscoting, and an ornate ceiling add the final touches. In the spacious dining room the atmosphere is similar, if slightly less cozy. The prices here are a little high to make the Palladium a student hangout, but they're quite reasonable given this restaurant's quality. You can choose à la carte dishes, a fixed-price menu, or a pretheater special.

Menus change completely four times a year, but crab cakes, boneless chicken breast, and eggplant are staples. All main dishes are accompanied by potatoes au gratin (good enough to be a meal in themselves) and a mélange of fresh vegetables.

The desserts do not quite live up to the standard set by the main courses, although the cold lime mousse is quite pleasantly tart. Pastries, homemade ice cream, and ices also are offered. Watch the (largely student) service, which is at best uneven, and sometimes downright slow.

Downstairs is The Gold Standard, a cafeteria that heats up with comedy, dinner theater, and the like.

★ **White Dog Café,** 3420 Sansom St. ☎ 386-9224.
> **Cuisine:** AMERICAN. **Reservations:** Recommended.
> **Prices:** Appetizers $5–$6; main courses $14–$19; desserts $6; lunch $8–$15. AE, DC, MC, V.

Open: Lunch Mon–Fri 11:30am–2:30pm; dinner Mon–Thurs 5:30–10pm, Fri–Sat 5:30–11pm, Sun 5–10pm; brunch Sat–Sun 11am–2:30pm. Frequent theme dinners and parties.

Judy Wicks is one of Philadelphia's great citizens: She led the fight against the University of Pennsylvania to save this block of Sansom Street and has evolved into a smart, tough, and fun-loving entrepreneur. All this comes through in the White Dog Café. The name is indebted to the mystic and theosophist Madame Blavatsky, who resided here a century ago. Blavatsky was about to have an infected leg amputated, when a white dog in the house slept across the leg and cured all. It's still got cure-all food under chef/partner Kevin von Klause.

You'll enter two row houses with the dividing wall knocked out and with the most sophisticated kitchen equipment and electronics concealed behind an eclectic mélange of checkered tablecloths, antique furniture and lights, and white dogs, dogs, and dogs. The friendly pups are everywhere—on the menu, holding matchbooks, pouring milk, and in family photographs.

From Sansom Street, the three-counter bar specializes in such all-American beers as McSorley's Ale, New Amsterdam, and Anchor Steam, as well as inexpensive American wines by the glass or bottle. Dining areas lie to the rear and right—there are several, and the White Dog has completed an ambitious glassed-in porch across the rear.

The staff offers frequently changing menus as well as "theme" dinners based on the season or a particular American region. Two delicious constants are the fresh rolls and muffins, vestiges of Judy's original bakery concept for the White Dog. The appetizers include Yucatán chicken soup with coriander and lime and brook trout with apple horseradish. The grilled vegetables served with hummus dip are light and delicious.

The White Dog attracts everyone, from Penn students to the mayor. Just next door at 3424 Sansom St., **The Black Cat** (☎ **386-6664**) offers more of Judy's antiques and crafts; living-room articles are sold in the living room and so on. It's open Tuesday through Thursday from 11am to 11pm, Friday and Saturday from 11am to midnight, and 11am to 9pm Sunday and Monday.

Inexpensive

New Deck Tavern, 3408 Sansom St. ☎ **386-4600.**

Cuisine: AMERICAN. **Reservations:** Recommended.
Prices: Main courses $6–$11.
Open: Lunch, dinner, and late supper, daily 11am–2am.

Virtually next door to the White Dog (see above), the New Deck Tavern is less of a restaurant than a relaxed watering hole, with truly Irish beers and barmaids and a 37-foot solid cherry-wood bar. The Tavern specializes in crab cakes and homemade soups. Try to catch Dottie Ford, a secretary to Penn's physics department, on the piano nightly between 7 and 9pm; she has an amazing range of thousands of show and other tunes, built up over the past 50 years.

The Restaurant, 4207 Walnut St. ☎ **222-4200.**

> **Cuisine:** ECLECTIC. **Reservations:** Required on weekends, accepted after 3pm.
> **Prices:** $13.50 prix fixe for appetizer and main course; extra $3 for desserts. AE, CB, DC, MC, V.
> **Open:** Dinner only, Tues–Sat 5:30–10pm.

The Restaurant is simply the final project for students at the Restaurant School, a cooking school central to Philadelphia dining and restaurateurs that emphasizes business and management. After eight months of instruction, teams plan a menu and kitchen protocol, then take over the ground floor for eight weeks at a time.

So why eat in this restored Victorian? There are several reasons, so Philadelphians say. The food is never downright bad and is often quite good. A month of Texan turkey recipes once left most people cold, but the following month a New Orleans menu was worth three times the price. In fact, it's popular to check out the month's crop, and it's not unusual for a good team to attract sufficient financial backing to set up elsewhere in town. Since the students are paying for the right to cook your meal, the prices are extremely low. The restaurant has acquired a liquor license and offers a fine selection of apéritifs, wines, and cocktails. You can count on at least one soup, one salad, and five main courses.

★ **Zocalo,** 36th St. and Lancaster Ave. (1 block north of Market St.). ☎ **895-0139.**

> **Cuisine:** MEXICAN. **Reservations:** Recommended.
> **Prices:** Appetizers $4–$6.50; main courses $9–$15; three-course prix-fixe dinner $13.95 Mon–Thurs. AE, DC, MC, V.
> **Open:** Lunch Mon–Fri noon–2:30pm; dinner Mon–Thurs 5:30–10pm Fri–Sat 5:30–11pm, Sun 5–9:30pm.

This sparely decorated restaurant presents contemporary Mexican cuisine, from all the provinces, using fresh ingredients. It's undoubtedly the best Mexican place around, and its food is priced accordingly—from such traditional dishes as carne asada to such modern classics as fresh shrimp in adobo. There's lively Latin music on most nights, with a pleasant deck in back for use in summer.

Budget

Le Bus, 3402 Sansom St. ☎ **387-3800.**

> **Cuisine:** AMERICAN. **Reservations:** Recommended.
> **Prices:** Main courses $5–$9. No credit cards.
> **Open:** Mon–Fri 7:30am–10pm, Sat 7:30am–11pm, Sun 10am–2pm.

Le Bus actually used to be one; stationary, it dispensed simple fare from four wheels in the funkier days of Sansom Street. It has since moved indoors to a simple row house, with the expected contemporary art on the walls, an uncluttered decor and bar, and even a neon sign. You'll still learn about the homemade breads, baked goods, vegetarian lasagne, chili, soups, and salads from a blackboard over the counter, though, and you must bus them yourself to your table.

Expect the main courses to be under $9, with unusual spices. The apple pie with sour cream is a wonderful dessert. A second Le Bus has opened at 4266 Main St. in Marrayunk with the same menu.

New Delhi, 4004 Chestnut St. ☎ **386-1941.**

> **Cuisine:** INDIAN. **Reservations:** Not required.
> **Prices:** Main courses $4.50–$9; all-you-can-eat lunch buffet $5.95 daily; dinner buffet $8.95 Mon–Thurs only. AE, MC, V.
> **Open:** Mon–Thurs noon–10pm, Fri–Sat noon–11pm.

New Delhi is a fairly good Indian restaurant near the University of Pennsylvania campus with an all-you-can-eat, 26-item buffet. It boasts quality ingredients, a tandoor clay oven, and friendly service. Look for discount coupons in student tabloids.

5 Chinatown

Moderate

Golden Pond, 1006 Race St. ☎ **923-0303.**

> **Cuisine:** CHINESE. **Reservations:** Recommended.
> **Prices:** Appetizers $3.50–$7.50; main courses $7.50–$16. Lunch special $5.95. MC, V.
> **Open:** Mon–Fri 11:30am–10pm, Sat–Sun noon–11pm.

This very stylish Hong Kong–style place costs a bit more than others in the neighborhood, but the impeccable service and the obviously fresh preparation are worth it. Wing Ming Tang, the chef, is a survivor of the Tiananmen Square riot in 1989 and has years of Hong Kong training. This Chinese cuisine features some potato dishes, chicken, duck, and seafood, but no pork or beef. It's one of the few places that serves brown rice.

Inexpensive

 Harmony Vegetarian Restaurant, 135 N. 9th St. ☎ 627-4520.

> **Cuisine:** CHINESE. **Reservations:** Recommended.
> **Prices:** Appetizers $3.95–$5.95; main courses $6.95–$12.95. MC, V.
> **Open:** Lunch, daily 11:30am–3pm; dinner Sun–Thurs 3–10pm, Fri–Sat 3–11pm.

This winner of the 1991 *Travel/Holiday* Good Value dining award is intimate and candlelit and prohibits smoking. Despite the menu listings for meat and fish, absolutely everything is made with vegetables (that also means no eggs or dairy). George Tang makes his own gluten by washing the starch out of flour; this miracle fiber is then deep-fried and marinated as appropriate to simulate "beef" or "chicken" or even "fish." Raves go to the hot-and-sour soup and the various mushroom dishes. BYOB.

Imperial Inn, 142 N. 10th St. ☎ **627-5588.**

> **Cuisine:** CHINESE. **Reservations:** Recommended.
> **Prices:** Appetizers $2.95–$6.95; main courses $7.95–$12.95. AE, CB, DC, MC, V.

Open: Lunch, daily 11:30am–3pm; dinner Mon–Thurs 3pm–1am. Fri–Sun 3pm–2am.

The Imperial Inn, with another location at 942 Race St. (☎ **627-2299**), has shown its true staying power in Chinatown under proprietor Luis Sust. The North 10th Street location, opened in 1980, serves an enormous variety of Szechuan, Mandarin, and Cantonese dishes.

Lunch here features dim sum, appetizer-size dishes that are trundled around on carts for diners to take as the fancy strikes them, with $1.50 the average cost per dish. It's a great form of instant gratification for samples. For dinner, the lemon chicken features a sautéed boneless breast in egg batter, laced with a mild lemon sauce. You can order a full-course dinner, which includes a choice of soup, rice, a main course, and a dessert for about $3 more than the main course itself.

Budget

★ **Capital,** 1008 Race St. ☎ **925-2477.**
   Cuisine: VIETNAMESE. **Reservations:** Recommended.
   Prices: Main courses $2.75–$6.75. MC, V.
   Open: Daily 11am–10pm.

The positive restaurant reviews placed at every table are not merely a major part of the decor, which was upgraded in 1993. Capital is one of the best spots in town for Vietnamese cuisine, which needs some explanation. Look for ground pork, sweet or pungent herbs and greens, and slight French touches. *Bun thit nuong* is a small, savory serving of pork with garlic flavor over rice noodles. You must bring your own bottle of liquor or wine.

Joe's Peking Duck House, 925 Race St. ☎ **922-3277.**
   Cuisine: CHINESE. **Reservations:** Recommended.
   Prices: Appetizers $2.50–$4.95; main courses $5.95–$10.95. No credit cards.
   Open: Daily 10:30am–11:30pm.

Chef Joe Poon, a graduate of the Culinary Institute of America, churns out Chinatown's best Peking duck, Szechuan duck, and barbecued pork with consistent quality. More recent menus have grown in low-fat items like steamed sea bass with light black-bean sauce. The decor is unassuming.

Ray's Coffee Shop, 141 N. 9th St. ☎ **922-5122.**
   Cuisine: CHINESE. **Reservations:** Not required.
   Prices: Main courses $6–$13; coffee $2.80–$5. AE, DC, MC, V.
   Open: Mon–Thurs 9am–10pm, Fri 9am–midnight, Sat 9:30am–midnight, Sun 11am–9pm.

I predict that the popularity of this place skyrockets after the Convention Center opens, since it features an unusual combination of subtle Taiwanese cuisine (dumplings are especially touted) and a selection of dozens of exotic coffees, each brewed to order in smart little glass siphons. The iced coffee here is great.

Shiao Lan Kung, 930 Race St. ☎ **928-0282.**

Cuisine: CHINESE. **Reservations:** Not necessary.
Prices: Appetizers $3.25–$8.95; main courses $5–$10.75. AE, CB, DC, MC, V.
Open: Sun–Thurs 4pm–3am, Fri–Sat 4pm–4am.

This modest place is very close to the Convention Center, and the Lee family unassumingly turns out fresh and adventuresome dishes like jellyfish as well as most standards. It won the "Best of Philly" award for Chinese cuisine in 1992. The Pa-chen tofu in hot pot has ham, barbecued pork, fish balls, and several vegetables thrown together with unusual subtlety.

6 Specialty Dining

Local Favorites

⭐ **Reading Terminal Market,** 12th and Arch Sts. ☎ **922-2317.**
💲 **Cuisine:** INTERNATIONAL/AMERICAN. **Reservations:** None.
Prices: Depends on vendor. Cash only at about half the vendors.
Open: Mon–Sat 8am–6pm. Public rest rooms. Many vendors close at 5pm.

The Reading Terminal Market has been a greengrocer, snack shop, butcher, fish market, and sundries store for smart Philadelphians since the turn of the century. The idea was to use the space beneath the terminal's tracks for the food business so that commuters and businesses could stock up easily and cheaply.

The basic format is rows of dozens of stalls, now half English covered market with cool brick floors and smells of fresh provender and baked bread and half gourmet grocer/charcuterie. It's again a wonderful place to snack and browse.

What's at Reading Terminal exactly? Scrapple, mangoes, clam chowder, pretzels—you name it, if it's fresh and unpackaged. The northwest corner (12th and Arch streets) is where most of the "retail," as opposed to restaurant or institutional, Amish farm products come to market. You can still see the Amish in the big city on their market days of Wednesday and Saturday, and you can buy sticky buns at **Beiler's Pies,** soft pretzels made before your eyes at **Fisher's,** and individual egg custards (75¢) and chicken potpie at **The Dutch Eating Place.** If you're in the market for meat, **Harry Ochs** and **Halteman Family** have the most extensive selections, with great country hams and local honey as well. **Reading Terminal Cheese Shop and Salumeria** offers gourmet cheeses and tinned goods, while **Margerum's,** now in its fourth generation, sells flours, spices, and coffee beans from barrels and kegs. The best coffee sold is **Old City Coffee's.**

If your stomach rumbles uncontrollably by now, **Terminal Bakery** will still it with terrific bagels (40¢) or **Braverman's** will fill it with egg challah ($3.50), as well as danish and other pastry. For more protein, **Pearl's Oyster Bar** practically gives away six cherrystone clams for $3, and a shrimp platter with french fries, bread, and cole-slaw goes for $4. Or try **Coastal Cave Trading Co.,** which has great clam chowder ($2.95), oyster crackers, and smoked fish. Just inside 12th Street, **Bassett's** purveys Philadelphia's entry in the best American ice-cream contest at $1.50 a cone. The shakes ($3.15) are no less enticing, and the turkey sandwiches ($4.95) are simply the best anywhere. And a new contender, **Old Post Road Farm,** has a cherry pie that tastes just like cherry.

The renovation of the market has left it with many more stools and counters. **Jill's Vorspeise** has a great selection of hearty soups, for starters. A lunch like linguine with clam sauce will cost $3 at **By George Pasta & Pizza; Spataro's,** an old-time favorite, vends fresh buttermilk, cottage cheese, and huge slabs of fresh pies. The **12th Street Cantina** sells not only tasty enchiladas and burritos but authentic ingredients, like blue cornmeal. Some consider **Olivieri Prince of Steaks**—a third generation of Pat's down in South Philly—the best in town. And a new **Beer Garden** can draw pints of Yuengling Porter and Dock Street Beer, among other more mass-market brews.

Hoagies & Steak Sandwiches

I've already mentioned Jim's Steaks at 400 South St. (☎ **928-1911**).

BUDGET

Lee's Hoagies, 44 S. 17th St. ☎ **564-1264.**

> **Cuisine:** AMERICAN. **Reservations:** Not accepted.
> **Prices:** $4–$10. No credit cards.
> **Open:** Mon–Fri 10:30am–8pm; Sat 10:30am–6pm.

For more than 30 years Lee's hoagies have captured the hearts and mouths of many native Philadelphians, at a low-slung complex between Market and Chestnut streets and also on Chestnut itself between 13th and 14th streets. The regular hoagie (basically an elongated spicy cold-cuts sandwich) measures about eight inches long, the giant about twice as long. They will create various combinations, such as the Italian (four meats and provolone) and the turkey (with provolone and mayonnaise)—order these a day in advance. Lee's minors in steak sandwiches, served with fried onions and sauce.

★ **Pat's King of the Steaks,** 1237 E. Passyunk Ave. (between 9th and Wharton Sts). ☎ **468-1546.**

> **Cuisine:** AMERICAN. **Reservations:** Not accepted.
> **Prices:** $3.95–$10. No credit cards.
> **Open:** 24 hrs.

Pat's, so its adherents claim, serves the best steak sandwiches this side of the equator. The location and hours make for an interesting mix at the take-out counter.

★ **Tacconelli's,** Somerset St. at Aramingo Ave. ☎ **425-4983.**

> **Cuisine:** ITALIAN. **Reservations:** Required; place pizza orders in advance.

Prices: Pizzas $5.50–$12. MC, V.
Open: Dinner only, Wed–Sun 4–9pm.

A real insider recommendation for pizza is Tacconelli's—not, as you'd think, in South Philly, but north of the new discos along Christopher Columbus Boulevard (formerly Delaware Avenue). Tacconelli's is open until whenever the crusts run out (about 9pm). It's imperative to call ahead to reserve the type of pizza you want, which is prepared in a brick oven. The white pizza with garlic oil and the spinach and tomato pies are particularly recommended. To get here, take the Frankfort subway line from Market Street to Somerset Street, then walk eight blocks east. If you drive from Society Hill, take Front Street north, make a right onto Kensington Avenue, then make another right onto Somerset.

Hotel Dining

HISTORIC AREA

Moderate

 Azalea, Omni Hotel, 4th and Chestnut Sts. ☎ **931-4260.**
Cuisine: AMERICAN. **Reservations:** Recommended.
Prices: Appetizers $4.75–$12.75; main courses $13.50–$26.75; breakfast $6.25–$13.75; lunch $8.50–$13.75. AE, CB, DC, MC, V.
Open: Breakfast Mon–Fri 6:30–10:30am, Sat–Sun 7–1am; lunch, daily 11am–2pm; dinner Sun–Thurs 5:30–10pm, Fri–Sat 5:30–11pm.

For imaginative interpretations of American produce, including local dishes, this is one of the two best spots in town, with a treetop view of Independence National Historical Park. Azalea features arched windows, chandeliers, and comfortable armchairs.

The menu selections include such traditional Pennsylvania Dutch specialties as chicken-corn soup with saffron and apple fritters, shad in sorrel sauce (what saved the troops at Valley Forge), and pheasant potpie. The menus change seasonally, and Kennett Square mushrooms, Lancaster County persimmons and quince, and elderberry preserve make an appearance. The local brook trout is sealed in cornmeal, then topped with smoky bacon. The desserts offer a choice of five freshly made sorbets or an old-fashioned apple-and-sour-cherry pie.

Inexpensive

Society Hill Hotel, 301 Chestnut St. ☎ **925-1919.**
Cuisine: AMERICAN. **Reservations:** Not required.
Prices: Appetizers $2.50–$4.95; main courses $4.95–$12.95. AE, CB, DC, MC, V.
Open: Daily 11am–1am; Sun brunch 11am–2:30pm.

This is a very pleasant, lively spot opposite Independence National Historical Park, with outdoor bar service during the summer. The light menu includes burgers and club sandwiches, along with omelets and salads. Ted Gerike makes this one of the city's top piano bars.

CENTER CITY

Very Expensive

The Dining Room, The Ritz-Carlton Philadelphia, Liberty Place (between Chestnut and Market Sts. at 17th St.). ☎ **563-1600.**

Cuisine: CONTEMPORARY/INTERNATIONAL. **Reservations:** Required. **Prices:** Dinner $32 (two courses), $38 (three courses), or $44 (four courses); lunch $35.
Open: Breakfast Mon–Sat 6:30–11am; lunch and Sun brunch 11:30am–2:30pm; dinner Tues–Sat 6–10pm. **Closed:** Sun and Mon dinner, Mon lunch.

Chef Troy Thompson and sommelier David Fischer preside over an operation that is elegant in every way. The room itself is stunning, with large crystal chandeliers, royal carpets, dark cabinets, and hand-blown cobalt-blue goblets. If you have reason to leave your seat, you'll find that your napkin is refolded when you return.

The menu has been lightened and reduced to six to seven choices per course. It's too dependent on seasonal market choices to quote from, so look for garnishes or reductions of fruit and root vegetables from Amish County or New Zealand.

★ **The Fountain,** The Four Seasons Hotel, One Logan Square (between 18th St. and the Franklin Parkway). ☎ **963-1500.**

Cuisine: INTERNATIONAL. **Reservations:** Required. **Prices:** Appetizers $6–$13; main courses $18–28; lunch $8–$17; prix-fixe four-course menu $45. AE, CB, DC, MC, V.
Open: Breakfast Mon–Fri 6:30–11:30am, Sat–Sun 7–11am; lunch, daily 11:30am–2:30pm; dinner, daily 6–11pm; brunch Sun 10am–2:30pm. Fri and Sat dessert and dancing in Swann Lounge.

The Zagat Restaurant Survey's 1992 edition ranked this Philadelphia's second most popular restaurant (behind Le Bec-Fin) and *Food & Wine* magazine chose it as one of America's top 25. The views partially explain why: unparalleled plumes from the Swann Fountain in Logan Circle on one side, and the hotel's own court-yard cascade on the other. The chief reason is the wonderful cuisine, expertly prepared and quietly served in expansive surroundings.

The menu is complicated and understated, and my recommendation is to accept the $45 prix-fixe menu rather than go à la carte for 35% more. After a complimentary canape or two, you might have filet of skate with capers, a mesclun salad with pear and purple potato, sautéed lamb tenderloin and veal kidneys with mustard-seed sauce, a cheese tray, and fresh fruit pastry. A favorite à la carte starter is the pierogi of foie gras in Savoy cabbage with truffles. The main courses include salmon filet and pheasant with bacon and more Savoy cabbage.

Grill Room, The Ritz-Carlton Philadelphia, Liberty Place (between Market and Chestnut Sts. at 17th St.). ☎ **563-1600.**

Cuisine: AMERICAN/ENGLISH. **Reservations:** Required. **Prices:** $41 average for dinner; $30 for lunch.
Open: Breakfast 6:30–11am; lunch Mon–Sat 11:30am–2:30pm; dinner, daily 5:30–10pm.

The Ritz-Carlton's Grill Room has become one of the city's chief spots for business lunches, and is easily equal to its formal Dining Room. The entrance bar features a marble bar and an antique wood-burning fireplace and opens into a clublike atmosphere for 85 with mahogany paneling and period furnishings and paintings. Under executive chef Thomas von Muenster (a veteran of the Ritz-Carlton in Boston), the Grill serves steaks, chops, and fish for lunch and dinner. A special Cuisine Vitale selection identifies the calories and nutritional values of six dishes.

Expensive

 210, Rittenhouse Hotel, 210 W. Rittenhouse Sq. ☎ **546-9000,** ext. 2534.

Cuisine: CONTEMPORARY FRENCH. **Reservations:** Required.
Prices: Appetizers $8–$12; main courses $21–$32.50; breakfast $5.75–$9.50; à la carte desserts $5–$7. Four-course tasting menu $55, Fri–Sat only.
Open: Breakfast Mon–Sat 6:30–11am; lunch Mon–Fri 11:30am–2:30pm; dinner Mon–Sat 6–10:30pm.

210 is the flagship of this luxury hotel's dining rooms. The sweeping windows look out over Rittenhouse Square, with contemporary art and cherry floors around. Tiny spotlights dramatize the floral table centerpieces.

The menu changes constantly; typical appetizers include beggars' purses of exotic mushrooms with escargots and a mosaic of seafood carpaccios, while main courses include a seared "scallopine" cut salmon with cucumber and vidalia-onion relish. Tiny pots of exotically flavored crèmes brûlée come in a basket of spun sugar. Even the breakfasts veer into fantasyland, with savory blintzes and sour-cream waffles.

Moderate

Michel's, Latham Hotel, 17th and Walnut Sts. ☎ **563-9444.**

Cuisine: FRENCH/AMERICAN. **Reservations:** Recommended.
Prices: Appetizers $4–$10; main courses $13–$19; breakfast $2–$9; lunch $7–$13.
Open: Breakfast 6:30–10:30am Mon–Fri, 7:30am–11:30am Sat–Sun; lunch 12:30am–2:30pm daily; dinner 5:30–10:30pm daily.

Michel Richard, a flamboyant French chef who found his true home in California, has been opening up a set of Eastern outposts, following his book *Home Cooking with a French Accent.* Michel's has a whimsical art-gallery feel. The cuisine aims to amuse and amaze you: who else would stack a smoked salmon terrine with salmon mousse so it resembles a pastry? If you *do* want puff pastry, you can have it around almost anything, including crab cakes. Desserts are magnificent, and a dozen wines are available by the glass.

Dining with a View

I've already mentioned **210,** with a view of Rittenhouse Square; **The Fountain** at The Four Seasons, overlooking Logan Circle's fountains;

Meiji-en, on the Delaware waterfront; and the **Chart House,** also on the Delaware River.

Moderate

Founders Atop the Bellevue, Broad and Walnut Sts.
☎ 893-1776.

Cuisine: CONTINENTAL. **Reservations:** Recommended.
Prices: Appetizers $4.95–$11.95; main courses $14.95–$26.95. AE, CB, DC, MC, V.
Open: Breakfast Sat–Sun 7–10am; lunch Sat–Sun 11:30am–2:30pm; dinner Mon–Sat 5:30–11pm, Sun 5:30–9pm.

Founders is actually the keystone of the Bellevue Hotel's restaurants, and its 19th floor location makes it attractive for fans of views and elegant dining rooms, given its arched windows, flourishes and swags of draperies, and plush armchairs. It's another winner in the 1994 *Conde Nast Traveler's* readers poll for America's top 50 restaurants. The "founders" are the statues of Philadelphia luminaries that surround you. There's also live entertainment.

Top of Centre Square, 1500 Market St. ☎ 563-9494.

Cuisine: INTERNATIONAL. **Reservations:** Recommended.
Prices: Appetizers $3.95–$6.95; main courses $12.95–$21.95; lunch $5.95–$11.95 AE, CB, DC, MC, V.
Open: Lunch Mon–Fri 11:30am–3pm; dinner Mon–Thurs 5:30–10pm, Fri–Sat 5:30pm–midnight, Sun 4:30–9pm.

Situated on the 41st floor of an office building directly west of City Hall, this modern restaurant with bilevel seating wraps around the city, from the two rivers to surrounding states. The lunch menu focuses on sandwiches, pastas, and quiches; the dinner menu features salmon, fish, ribs, and steaks. It's not the best food for the price, but the views are wonderful.

Dining Complexes ———————————————

I've already described the outstanding **Reading Terminal Market.**
The top new choice in town is the ★ S **Food Court at Liberty Place** on the second level (accessible by escalator or elevator) of Liberty Place between Chestnut and Market streets and 16th and 17th streets, in the heart of Center City. Reading Terminal alumni like **Bain's Deli, Bassett's Original Turkey,** and **Original Philly Steaks** are joined by **Mandarin Express, Mentesini Pizza, Sbarro,** and **Chick-fil-A.** Best of all, the food court is spotless, large, and reasonable, with full lunches from $3.50. You'll find it easy to keep your eyes on the kids as they wander. The Food Court is open Monday to Saturday from 9:30am to 7pm, Sunday from noon to 6pm.

Downstairs at the Bellevue is a sparkling 1993 effort to attract a clientele willing to pay less than upscale prices while using South Broad Street at Walnut Street. It's very appealing with bright tiles, great lighting and public restrooms, and quiet center tables surrounding food-court vendors such as **Tien-bo Chinese Express** (check out the $4.25 tempura), **Mentesini Pizza, Rocco's Italian Hoagies**

($4.85 and up), **Bookbinder's Seafood Bar,** and the **Gourmet Deli** and **Syrinka's Polish Restaurant.**

Another good collection of snacks is at **The Food Court** at the Gallery, on Market at 9th Street. The Gallery parades ropes of people up and down four floors of shops under a massive glass roof, and the lowest level near Gimbels houses an enclave of oyster bars; ice-cream stands; and stalls with baked potatoes, Greek snacks, and egg rolls.

The first floor of the **Bourse,** 21 N. 5th Street (just east of the Liberty Bell), has 10 snack/restaurant operations, all moderately priced and designed for take-out to be eaten at the tables that fill this cool and stunning restoration of the 1895 merchant exchange. Names of representative stalls include **Sbarro's** for pizza and pasta, **Bain's Delicatessen** for turkey sandwiches, and for sandwiches **Grande Olde Cheesesteak.**

Light, Casual & Fast Food

Girasole, 1305 Locust St. ☎ 985-4659.

   Cuisine: ITALIAN. **Reservations:** Recommended.
   Prices: Appetizers $3.95–$6.95; main courses $8.95–$15.95. AE, CB, DC, MC, V.
   Open: Lunch Mon–Fri noon–2:30pm; dinner Mon–Thurs 5–10:30pm, Fri–Sat 5–11pm.

Although it's a handsome restaurant, Girasole is prime grazing ground for its antipasto salad of tiny shrimp and white beans and for its terrific pizzas with irregular crusts and fresh ingredients, cooked in a wood-burning oven.

Mango Bay, 264 S. 16th St.☎ 735-3316.

   Cuisine: CARIBBEAN/AMERICAN. **Reservations:** Optional.
   Prices: Appetizers $3.50–$6.95; main courses $6.95–$14.95. AE, CB, DC, MC, V.
   Open: Mon noon–11pm, Tues–Sat noon–midnight, Sun 11:30am–midnight.

Restaurateur Steve Poses—legendary in town for departed spots such as Frog and The Commissary—has largely abandoned the field for catering, but retains this location as a delightful 1994 trip to the tropics. Look for lots of curries with saffron-flavored rice and stewed vegetables, and daily grilled fish specials. Chutneys range from mango and pineapple to tomato.

Marabella's, 1420 Locust St. ☎ 545-1845. Also Benjamin Franklin Pkwy. at 17th St. ☎ 981-5555.

   Cuisine: INTERNATIONAL. **Reservations:** Not accepted for dinner.
   Prices: Appetizers $2.95; main courses $7.95–$14.95; lunch $3–$6. AE, DC, MC, V.
   Open: Mon–Thurs 11:30am–11pm, Fri–Sat 11:30am–midnight, Sun 3–11pm.

A colorful and upbeat setting that's great for families, Marabella's offers a menu and a noise level to match. Pizzas, simple Italian grazing breads and salads, and mesquite-grilled fish are available without the pretense of a meal in several courses. (See also page 111).

Sfuzzi, 1650 Market St. (One Liberty Place). ☎ **851-8888.**

Cuisine: ITALIAN. **Reservations:** Recommended.
Prices: Appetizers $4–$6; main courses $9–$15. AE, CB, DC, MC, V.
Open: Lunch Mon–Sat 11:30am–3pm; dinner Mon–Wed 5:30–10pm, Fri–Sat 5:30–11pm, Sun 5–9pm; Sunday brunch 10:30am–2:30pm.

Clean, bright, and modern, Sfuzzi has a silent *S*. The service at the bar or at the tables concentrates on pastas, pizzas, desserts, and such Italian specialties as crispy pizza, fried calamari with aioli, and crispy chicken breast with romano cheese dustings.

Zanzibar Blue, 305 S. 11th St. ☎ **829-0300.**

Cuisine: CONTINENTAL. **Reservations:** Not required.
Prices: Appetizers $3.95–$8.95; main courses $7.95–$15.95; Sunday brunch $15.
Open: Dinner Sun–Thurs 5:30–10pm, Fri–Sat 5:30–11pm; late supper, daily to 1am; Sun jazz brunch 11am–2:30pm.

This café and restaurant between Pine and Spruce streets is in a renovated building, with nightly jazz and roomy, sophisticated seating. The menu features bouillabaisse, crab cannelloni, Caesar salad, and bruschetta.

Sunday Brunch

Nearly every restaurant in Philadelphia offers Sunday brunch, ranging from standard bagels with spreads to full English breakfasts. The entries above provide full descriptions of **Carolina's, Chart House, Downey's, Famous Deli, Swann Lounge** and **The Fountain** at The Four Seasons (generally voted the best in town), and **White Dog Café** (the funkier favorite).

Afternoon Tea

The advent of true luxury hotels in Philadelphia has brought exquisite afternoon teas to the first-floor lounge at the **Omni Hotel,** the **Cassatt Lounge at the Rittenhouse Hotel** (the most cheery, with a beautiful outdoor garden), the **Swann Lounge at The Four Seasons Hotel,** and **The Ritz-Carlton.** The **Dickens Inn** in Head House Square does a more solid, English burgher version. See the above listings for fuller descriptions.

Ice Cream & Desserts

Bassett's Ice Cream (☎ **925-4315**) at Reading Terminal has long claimed supremacy for its rich and smooth flavors. The king of the hill may have been dethroned by **Hillary's** (☎ **922-4931**), a relative newcomer at South and 5th streets, at Front and Chestnut streets, and at Chestnut and 20th streets. All three open at noon and stay open late. **More Than Just Ice Cream,** 1141 Pine St., features Bassett's and Häagen-Dazs as bases for splendid creations.

Late-Night/24-Hour

Philadelphia is not the most vivacious of cities late at night, and you're most likely to find late-night or all-night food either at bars known to close at 2am, or on South Street. I have already mentioned Cutters, Downey's, Dock Street Brewing Company, Los Amigos, Pat's King of the Steaks, and the Sam Adams Brew House as well as most Chinatown locales.

Copabanana, 4th and South Sts. ☎ **923-6180.**

Cuisine: AMERICAN. **Reservations:** Not required.
Prices: Burgers $4.95–$7.50; Tex-Mex main courses $6.95–$10.95. AE, MC, V.
Open: Daily noon–1am.

People watching is a favorite pastime at this tropical neon fantasy bar and grill overlooking South Street. It features Tex-Mex food and gourmet burgers, with upbeat tapes providing atmosphere.

Melrose Diner, 1501 Snyder St. (intersection of 15th St., Passyunk Ave. and Snyder St., 1 block west of S. Broad. St.). ☎ **467-6644.**

Cuisine: DINER. **Reservations:** Not accepted.
Prices: Breakfast $2–$5; lunch and dinner $4–$10. No credit cards.
Open: 24 hrs.

Somewhere between kitsch and postmodern, the Melrose's logo of a coffee cup with a clock face and knife-and-fork hands is eternal. Scrapple and eggs, creamed chipped beef, and the like are dished out 10 blocks north of the sporting stadiums in South Philly. They do all their own baking.

Pizzeria Uno, 509 S. 2nd St. ☎ **592-0400;** and 18th and Locust sts. ☎ **790-9669.**

Cuisine: ITALIAN. **Reservations:** Not required.
Prices: Pizzas $8.45 and up. AE, CB, DC, MC, V.
Open: Sun–Thurs 11:30am–midnight, Fri–Sat 11:30am–1:30am.

Established in 1943, this string of dark-green bar/cafés, festooned with signs and brass rails, serves a reliable deep-dish Chicago pizza that's more like a meal-on-bread than a traditional pizza. The 1721 Locust St. location, just off Rittenhouse Square, is very convenient.

Picnic Fare

Charcuterie Francaise, 30th Street Station. ☎ **222-3299.**

Yes, Philadelphia's Amtrak station has finally spruced up in terms of all sorts of foods to go. This stop has six different chicken salads, beef bourguignon, and unusual pasta salads. The French breads are excellent. If you're not satisfied or are looking for a little less priciness, try the nearby Bain's Deli for sandwiches or Ro & Sons for salads.

Famous Deli, 4th and Bainbridge Sts. ☎ **922-3274.**

Before South Street turned funky, it was a mostly Jewish neighborhood, and under three generations of Auspitzes the 70-year-old Famous has weathered the demographics in fine style. The deli roasts its own turkey and does a lot of carry-out of lox, whitefish, pastrami, and corned beef. It seats about 125 with the 1994 addition of an enclosed porch. It stocks all the Sunday papers too.

Foodtek, 26 S. 2nd St. ☎ **238-1115;** and 308 South St.
☎ **592-7377.**

These unassuming storefronts on two of the historic area's busiest blocks open up in back to a wonderful deli/breakfast seating area, with provisions ranging from sliced meats to stuffed quail. There is a bakery and a small greenmarket too.

Coffee Bars

My top choices are: **The Coffee Shop,** 130 S. 17th St. (near Liberty Place), open daily from 1993, with lighter and more full-bodied blends on hand. It also has a full espresso bar and excellent muffins, scones ($1.50), and biscotti. **Old City Coffee,** at 221 Church St. (behind Christ Church), at Reading Terminal Market and 2 Penn Center Plaza, near City Hall. Coffee selection is rich, varied, and strong. **Dean and DeLuca Café,** at 1601 Market St.—an absolutely stunning corner space—and in the Art Alliance Building on Rittenhouse Square. Baked goods, sandwiches, and salads as well as take-out desserts.

Frommer's Cool for Kids: Restaurants

Ben's Restaurant (☎ **448-1200**) in the Franklin Institute at Logan Circle (p. 140). Ben's is well set up for kids with cafeteria food, hamburgers, and hot dogs. You can enter with or without museum admission.

Chinatown Between 9th and 11th streets and Race and Vine streets are lots of family-oriented places.

Cutter's Grand Café and Bar (p. 104) Lunch and dinner menus for children feature a $3.25 peanut butter and jelly sandwich, $5 fettuccine Alfredo, grilled cheese sandwiches, and fish-and-chips. Try for a window banquette.

Food Court at Liberty Place Kids have their choice of cuisines from among 25 stalls, and they can wander without going out of sight.

Marabella's (p. 106, 123) A natural in Center City; its pizzas, burgers, and grilled chicken come quickly and as you order them, and the noise and the color are cheerful. You'll have plenty of family company.

7

What to See & Do in Philadelphia

CONSIDER THE SIGHTSEEING POSSIBILITIES—THE MOST HISTORIC SQUARE MILE in America; more than 90 museums; innumerable colonial churches, row houses, and mansions; an Ivy League campus; more impressionist art than you'd find in any place outside of Paris; and leafy, distinguished parks, including the largest one within city limits in the United States. Philadelphia has come a long way from what it was in 1876, when a guidebook recommended seeing the new Public Buildings at Broad and Market streets, the Naval Yards, the old YMCA, and the fortresslike prison.

Most of what you'll want to see within the city falls inside the original grid plan, between the Delaware and Schuylkill rivers and South and Spring Garden streets. In fact, it's possible to organize your days into walking tours relatively easily—see Chapter 8, "Strolling Around Philadelphia," for suggestions. Even if you ramble on your own, nothing is that far away. A stroll from City Hall to the Philadelphia Museum of Art takes about 25 minutes, although you'll undoubtedly be sidetracked by the flags and flowers along the Parkway. A walk down Market or one of the "tree" streets (Chestnut, Spruce, Pine, Locust) to Independence National Historical Park and Society Hill should take a little less time—but it probably won't, since there's so much to entice you on the way.

Suggested Itineraries

If You Have 1 Day

Start at the Liberty Bell in Independence National Historical Park, then move south through Independence Hall and on to residential Society Hill, which is interwoven with U.S. history. In the evening, see what's on at the Academy of Music, the Annenberg Center at the University of Pennsylvania, or the Spectrum for sports.

If You Have 2 Days

Day 1   Follow the itinerary given above.

Day 2   Starting at City Hall, walk up the Benjamin Franklin Parkway to Logan Circle and spend the afternoon at Franklin Institute or the Philadelphia Museum of Art. Try to circle back to Rittenhouse Square and the Liberty Place complex before closing.

If You Have 3 Days

Days 1–2   Follow the itinerary given above.

Day 3   Spend the morning in Old City viewing its Christ Church and Elfreth's Alley, then explore the Delaware River waterfront at Penn's Landing. Finally, either visit the New Jersey State Aquarium by ferry to Camden or continue shoreward to eclectic South Street. At night, hop by water taxi among the riverfront clubs and restaurants.

Did You Know?

- The "hex" signs that adorn barns and houses in Pennsylvania Dutch Country were a sign to travelers that German was spoken within.

- It is still against the law in Philadelphia to sleep in a barber shop and to take a cow to Logan Circle.

- The first public protest in America against slavery was held at the Germantown Friends (Quaker) Meeting House in 1688.

- The Benjamin Franklin Parkway is one of the widest streets (250 feet) in the world.

- Early fire-insurance companies offered rewards for stopping fires. This led to street battles between rival volunteer brigades racing to arrive at a blaze first, often while buildings burned down!

- It was in Philadelphia that Charles Goodyear superheated sulfur to harden India rubber, at the same time preserving its pliancy.

If You Have 5 Days or More

Days 1–3   Follow the itinerary given above.

Day 4   Explore the Rittenhouse Square/South Broad Street area, with a visit to the Academy of Fine Arts, winding up with a stroll through Reading Terminal Market (it closes at 5pm) and Chinatown.

Day 5   Fairmount Park's Zoo and many restored colonial mansions beckon. If you hunger for more Georgian, make a trip to Germantown for the afternoon.

1   The Top Attractions

Of course, the attractions below only scratch the surface. Depending on your interests, the Philadelphia Zoo, Fairmount Park, South Philadelphia's Italian Market, the Rosenbach Museum, the Afro-American Historical and Cultural Museum, the University of Pennsylvania campus, or the Museum of American Jewish History might be tops. They'll be covered either later in this chapter or mentioned in Chapter 8, "Strolling Around Philadelphia."

Independence National Historical Park, "America's most historic square mile." Visitor Center at 3rd and Walnut Sts. ☎ **215/597-8974;** TDD **215/597-1785** or **215/627-1776** for 24-hour recording.

Is there anyone who doesn't know about the Liberty Bell in Independence Hall? It may not be there anymore, but you get the point: The United States was conceived on this ground in 1776, and the future of the young nation was assured by the Constitutional Convention held here in 1787. The choice of Philadelphia as a site was natural because of its centrality, wealth, and gentility. The delegates argued at Independence Hall (then known as the State House) and boarded and dined at City Tavern. Philadelphia was the nation's capital during Washington's second term, so the U.S. Congress and Supreme Court met here for 10 years while awaiting the construction of the new capital at Washington, D.C. From the first penny to the First Amendment, Philadelphia led the nation.

The National Historical Park comprises 40 buildings on 45 acres of Center City real estate (see Walking Tour 1 in Chapter 8 for more information). Independence Hall and the Liberty Bell in its glass pavilion lie between 6th and 5th streets. The Visitor Center, at the corner of 3rd and Walnut streets, is well equipped to illustrate the early history of this country, in a neighborhood that ranks as a superb example of successful revitalization. Fifty years ago, this area had become overgrown with warehouses, office buildings, and rooming houses. The National Park Service stepped in, soon followed by the Washington Square East urban-renewal project now known as Society Hill. Buildings were bought and then torn down to create Independence Mall, a wide swath of greenery opposite Independence Hall. To the east, gardens replaced edifices as far as the Dock Street food market, which was replaced by Society Hill Towers in 1959. Graff House, City Tavern, Pemberton House, and Library Hall all were reconstructed on the original sites; Liberty Bell Pavilion, Franklin Court, and the Visitor Center are contemporary structures that were erected for the Bicentennial of the Declaration of Independence celebrations.

A park ranger must lead you through Independence Hall, and you must reserve a place for the free and frequent guided tours of the Bishop White House and the Todd House. This can be done in person at the **Visitor Center,** 3rd and Chestnut streets (☎ **597-8974,** voice or TDD), which should be your first encounter with the park. Here you can pick up a map of the area and information in any of 10 languages. The modern bell tower houses a 5-ton bell given by Queen Elizabeth II of England to this country in 1976, and it rings at 11am and 3pm. The gift shop sells mementos and park publications, and every 30 minutes the center shows a John Huston feature, *Independence,* without charge.

Admission: Free tour of Independence Hall by guide on a first-come, first-served basis. Some of the park's building interiors require reservations. Other adjacent historic buildings have separate admissions.

Open: Daily 9am–5pm, often later in summer. **Subway:** SEPTA Market-Frankford Line to 5th and Market streets or 2nd and Market streets. **Bus:** No. 76 or any Chestnut Street Transitway bus from Center City. **Car:** From I-76, take I-676 east to 6th Street (last exit before the Ben Franklin Bridge), then turn south (right) along Independence Mall. From the Ben Franklin Bridge, make a left onto 6th Street and follow the same directions as above. From I-95 southbound, take the Center City exit to 2nd Street. From I-95

northbound, use the exit marked "Historic Area." Turn left on Columbus Boulevard (formerly Delaware Avenue) and follow it to the
exit for Market Street (on right). **Parking:** Meters are along most
streets; parking facilities (all $10 per day) are at 2nd and Sansom
streets, at Independence Mall between Arch and Market streets, and
at the corner of Dock and 2nd streets.

⭐ **Independence Hall,** Chestnut St. between 5th and 6th Sts.
Even if you knew nothing about Independence Hall, flanked by Old
City Hall to the left and Congress Hall to the right, you could tell
that noble and important works took place here. From an
architectural standpoint, the ensemble is graceful and functional;
from the standpoint of history and American myth, it's unforgettable.
Independence Square sets you thinking about the boldness of forming
an entirely sovereign state from a set of disparate colonies and about
the strength and intelligence of the representatives who gathered here
to do it. Although these buildings are best known for their national
role, remember that city, county, and state governments used them
at various times too.

The French and Indian War (1754–63) required troops who, in
turn, required money, and King George III saw no reason why the
colonists shouldn't pay for their own defense through taxes. The
colonists disagreed, and the idea that the king harbored tyrannical
thoughts swept through the colonies but was felt most strongly in
Virginia and Massachusetts. Philadelphia, as the wealthiest and most
culturally anglophile of the seacoast cities, was leery of radical
proposals of independence, as Franklin was in his role as American
agent in London. But the news that British troops had fired on citizens
defending their own property in Concord pushed most moderates
to reconsider what they owed to England and what they deserved as
free people endowed with natural rights.

The Second Continental Congress convened in May 1776 in the
Pennsylvania Assembly Room, to the left of the Independence Hall
entrance. Each colony had its own green baize–covered table, but not
much of the original room's furnishings escaped use as firewood when
British troops occupied the city in December 1777. The Congress
acted quickly, appointing a tall Virginia delegate named George
Washington as commander of the Continental Army. After the failure
of a last "olive branch" petition, the Congress, through John Adams,
instructed each colony's government to reorganize itself as a state.
Thomas Jefferson worked on a summary of why the colonists felt
that independence was necessary. The resulting Declaration of
Independence, wrote noted historian Richard Morris, "lifted the
struggle from self-interested arguments over taxation to the exalted
plane of human rights." Most of the signatories used Philip Syng's
silver inkstand, which is still in the room. The country first heard
the news on July 8 in Independence Square.

Before and after the British occupied the city, Independence Hall
was the scene of the U.S. national government. Here the Congress
approved ambassadors, pored over budgets, and adopted the Articles

Philadelphia Attractions

of Confederation, a loose and problematic structure for a country composed of states. Congress moved to New York after the war's end, and it grudgingly allowed delegates to recommend changes.

The delegates who met in the Assembly Room in Philadelphia in 1787 did more than that—they created a new Constitution that has guided the country for more than 200 years. Jefferson's cane rests

Spring Garden St.

8th St.
7th St.
6th St.
5th St.
4th St.
3rd St.
2nd St.
Front St.

Callowhill St.

Franklin St.

95

Vine St.

Franklin Sq.

Delaware Ave.

Benjamin Franklin Bridge

676

30

Race St.

Federal Reserve Bank

11

12
Cherry St.

13
Elfreth's Alley

U.S. Mint

14

Arch St.

15

Delaware River

(Christopher Columbus Blvd.)

Filbert St.

U.S. Federal Bldg.
16

Independence National Park

95

Market St.

17

5TH & MARKET

18 5TH ST.

19

2ND ST.

The Bourse

20

Bank St.

2ND ST.

Chestnut St.

Jeweler's Row

22 **23**

24

25 **27**

21

26

(i) **Visitor's Center**

Walnut St.

28

Penn's Landing

Willings Alley

W. Wash. Sq.

Locust St.

Dock St.

Washington Sq.

S. Wash. Sq.

8th St.
7th St.
6th St.
5th St.
4th St.
3rd St.

Maitis St.

Spruce St.

29

30

SOCIETY HILL

Pine St.

Head House Sq.

Lombard St.

South St.

Information ⊕

Marine Corps Memorial Museum **25**	Rodin Museum **2**
Mother Bethel A.M.E. Church **31**	Second Bank of the U.S. **24**
Norman Rockwell Museum **21**	Shops at Liberty Place **8**
Old City Hall **23**	Society Hill **29**
Penn's Landing **28**	Todd House **26**
Philadelphia Maritime Museum **20**	U.S. Mint **12**
Philadelphia Museum of Art **1**	
Please Touch Museum **4**	

here, as does a book of Franklin's. Washington, as president of the convention, kept order from the famous "Rising Sun Chair." Delegates were mature, urbane (24 of the 42 had lived or worked abroad), and trained to reason, and many had experience drafting state constitutions and laws. They decided on approaches to governance that are familiar today: a bicameral Congress, a single ex-

Did You Know?

- Ben Franklin's kite-flying experiment in 1752 took place at what is now the corner of 10th and Ludlow streets.

- Thirty-two bridges span the Schuylkill River within the city limits.

- George Washington lived in a mansion at the corner of 5th and Chestnut streets for his entire two terms as president.

- Philadelphian Robert Green's chance decision to combine ice cream and soda water has refreshed millions since 1861.

- W. C. Fields's epitaph does *not* read, "On the whole, I'd rather be in Philadelphia."

- The U.S. Congress held a rare session outside the capital for the special July 16, 1987, bicentennial celebration of the U.S. Constitution at Independence Mall.

- The first law school (1790) and medical school (1765) in America were established at the University of Pennsylvania.

- The oldest U.S. fire-insurance company, the Philadelphia Contributorship (1752), still offers a standing toast to George Washington at its monthly board meetings.

ecutive, an independent judiciary, and a philosophical belief in government by the people and for the people. No wonder John Adams called the convention "the greatest single effort of national deliberation that the world has ever seen."

Across the entrance hall from the Assembly Room, the courtroom served as Pennsylvania's Supreme Court chamber. Like the court at Williamsburg, Virginia, this room exemplifies pre–Bill of Rights justice—for example, your ranger guide will probably point out the tipstaff, a wooden pole with a brass tip that was used to keep onlookers subdued. Other period details include little coal boxes to keep feet warm on chilly days. This is one of the first courtrooms in America to hear the argument that disagreement with a political leader isn't sedition, one of the great concepts in modern Anglo-American law.

The stairwell of Independence Hall held the Liberty Bell until 1976. The ranger will conduct you upstairs to the Long Gallery, the largest Pennsylvania room of its time. Now it's set up as a banquet hall with a harpsichord (some of the guides even play) and a rare set of maps of the individual 13 colonies. Its view of Independence Mall is superb.

Two smaller rooms adjoin the Long Gallery. To the southwest, the royal governors of Pennsylvania met in council in a setting of opulent blue curtains, silver candlesticks, and a grandfather clock. Beneath a portrait of William Penn, governors met with foreign and Native American delegations, in addition to conducting normal business. On the southeast side, the Committee Room fit the whole

Pennsylvania Assembly while the Second Continental Congress was meeting downstairs. More often, it stored the assembly's reference library or arms for the city militia.

As you descend the stairs, look at calm **Independence Square,** with its elm trees and statue of Commo. John Barry. The clerk of the Second Congress, John Nixon, first read the Declaration of Independence here, to a mostly radical and lower-strata crowd (Philadelphia merchants didn't much like the news at first, since it meant a disruption of trade, to say the least).

Tours: A park ranger must lead you through Independence Hall; free tours leave every 15 minutes. Avoid waits by arriving early.

Open: Summer, daily 9am–9pm; winter, daily 9am–5pm. **Bus:** 76.

Liberty Bell, Chestnut St. between 5th and 6th Sts.

You can't leave Philadelphia without seeing the Liberty Bell. During the first minute of 1976 it was taken out of Independence Hall and put in its own glass Liberty Bell Pavilion across the street, once the site of the Executive Mansion.

The Liberty Bell, America's symbol of independence, was commissioned in 1751 to mark the 50th anniversary of another noble event: William Penn, who governed Pennsylvania by himself under Crown charter terms, agreed that free colonials had a right to govern themselves, so he established the Philadelphia Assembly under a new Charter of Privileges. The bell, cast in England, cracked as it was tested, and the Philadelphia firm of Pass and Stow recast it by 1753. It hung in Independence Hall to "proclaim liberty throughout the land" as the Declaration of Independence was announced and survived a bumpy trip to an Allentown church in 1777 so that the British wouldn't melt it down for ammunition. The last time it tolled was in 1846 to celebrate Washington's birthday. The term Liberty Bell was coined by the abolitionist movement, which recognized the potency of its inscription in the fight against slavery.

You can no longer touch the bell, but you can photograph it. You can even see it through the glass walls at night. The brick arcades with terrazzo floors and marble benches one block north of the bell were built for the 1976 bicentennial, but they have been considered white elephants outside of special festivals and concerts.

Admission: Free.

Open: Summer, daily 9am–8pm; rest of year, daily 9am–5pm. **Bus:** 76.

⭐ **Franklin Court**, Chestnut St. between 3rd and 4th Sts., with another entrance at 314 Market St.

Franklin Court may just be the most imaginative, informative, and downright fun museum run in America by the National Park Service. Designed by noted architect Robert Venturi, it was very much a sleeper when it opened in April 1976, because the Market and Chestnut streets' arched passages give little hint of the court within and the exhibit below.

Franklin Court once held the home of Benjamin Franklin, who'd resided with his family in smaller row houses in the neighborhood.

Like Jefferson at Monticello, he planned many of the time-savers and interior decorations of the house; but unlike Jefferson, Franklin spent the building period as colonial emissary first to England, then to France. His wife, Deborah, oversaw the construction, as the engraved flagstones show, while Ben sent back continental goods and a constant stream of advice. Unfortunately, they were reunited only in the family plot at Christ Church Burial Ground, since Deborah died weeks before the end of Ben's 10-year absence. Under the stewardship of his daughter Sarah and her husband, Richard Bache Franklin Court provided a gentle home for Ben until his 1790 death.

Since archeologists have no exact plans of the house, a simple frame in girders indicates the dimensions of the house and the smaller print shop. Excavations have uncovered wall foundations, bits of walls, and outdoor privy wells, and these have been left as protected cutaway pits. This is all very interesting—but enter the exhibition entrance for the fun. After a portrait and furniture gallery, a mirrored room reflects Franklin's almost limitless interests as a scientist, an inventor, a statesman, a printer, and so on. At the Franklin Exchange, dial various American and European luminaries to hear what they thought of Franklin.

Frommer's Favorite Philadelphia Experiences

Afternoon Tea at the Swann Lounge   The quintessential luxury tea is held at The Four Seasons, overlooking one of the city's finest squares with its fountains on both sides.

A Nighttime Stroll Through Independence Square   The combination of history, elegance, and proportion among the three basic buildings that contained America's first government always induce a sense of wonder at this country's good fortune in its founding citizens.

Barnes Foundation   Admission to this private Merion art collection is restricted—actually, closed until 1996 when the collection returns from touring—and the collection itself is overwhelming in its impressionist coverage and thematic groupings.

Regattas Along the Schuylkill   On all spring weekends along Boathouse Row just north of the Philadelphia Museum of Art, crews race each other every five minutes or so, with cheering friends along the riverbanks.

Reading Terminal Market   From Amish custards and Bassett's ice cream to Bain's turkey sandwiches and the food of the 12th Street Cantina, this is the motherlode of unpackaged, fresh, honest-to-goodness provisions. It celebrated its centennial in 1993.

Open-House Tours   If you're in the city at the right times, don't miss tours of restored mansions in Society Hill, Rittenhouse Square, or Fairmount Park for some true connoisseurship in interior design and Americana.

The middle part of the same hall has a 15-minute series of three climactic scenes in Franklin's career as a diplomat. On a sunken stage, costumed doll figures brief you, and each other, on the English Parliament in 1765 and its Stamp Act; the Court at Versailles when its members were wondering whether to aid America in its bid for independence; and the debates of the Constitution's framers in 1787, right around the corner at Independence Hall. Needless to say, Ben's pithy sagacity wins every time.

On your way in or out on the Market Street side, stop in the 1786 houses that Ben rented out. One is the Printing Office and Bindery, where you can see colonial methods of printing and bookmaking in action. Next door, get a letter postmarked at the Benjamin Franklin Post Office (remember that Ben was postmaster general too!). Employees still hand stamp the marks. Upstairs, a postal museum is open in summer.

Admission: Free.

Open: Daily 9am–5pm, including the post office and postal museum. **Bus:** 76.

The Top Museums

⭐ **Philadelphia Museum of Art,** 26th St. and Ben Franklin Pkwy. ☎ **763-8100** or **684-7500** for 24-hour information.

Even on a hazy day you can see America's third-largest art museum from City Hall—resplendent, huge, a beautifully proportioned Greco-Roman temple on a hill. Because the museum, established in the 1870s, has relied on donors of great wealth and idiosyncratic taste, the collection does not aim to present a comprehensive picture of Western or Eastern art. But its strengths are dazzling—it's undoubtedly one of the finest groupings of art objects in America, and no visit to Philadelphia would be complete without at least a walk-through.

The museum is designed simply, with L-shaped wings off the central court on two stories. A major rearrangement of the collections has just been completed, and they now mix paintings, sculptures, and decorative arts within set periods. The front entrance (facing City Hall) admits you to the first floor. Special exhibition galleries and American art are to the left; the collection emphasizes that Americans came from diverse cultures, which combined to create a new, distinctly national esthetic. French- and English-inspired domestic objects like silver predominate in the Colonial and Federal galleries—but don't neglect the fine rooms of Amish and sturdy Shaker crafts, more German in origin. The 19th-century gallery has many works of Philadelphia's Thomas Eakins, which evoke the spirit of the city in watercolors and oil portraits.

Controversial 19th- and 20th-century European art galleries highlight Cézanne's monumental *Bathers* and Marcel Duchamp's *Nude Descending a Staircase,* which doesn't seem nearly as revolutionary as it did in 1913. The recent gift of the McIlhenny $300-million collection of paintings is one of the last great donations of this type possible and adds French impressionist strength.

Upstairs is a chronological sweep in 83 galleries of European arts from medieval times through about 1850. The John G. Johnson Collection, a Renaissance treasure trove, has been integrated with the museum's other holdings. Roger van der Weyden's diptych *Virgin and Saint John* and *Christ on the Cross* is renowned for its exquisite sorrow and beauty. Van Eyck's *Saint Francis Receiving the Stigmata* is unbelievably precise (borrow the guard's magnifying glass). Other masterpieces include Poussin's frothy *Birth of Venus* (the USSR sold this and numerous other canvases in the early 1930s, and many were snapped up by American collectors) and Rubens's sprawling *Prometheus Bound.* The remainder of the floor takes you far abroad— to medieval Europe, 17th-century battlefields, Enlightenment salons, and Eastern temples.

The museum has excellent dining facilities as well. A cafeteria, open from 10am to 2:30pm Tuesday through Friday and 10am to 3pm Saturday and Sunday, dispenses simple hot lunches and salad plates for about $4. The Bauhaus Café across the way, open 11:45am to 2:15pm Tuesday through Saturday, Sunday 11am to 2pm, and Wednesday 5 to 7pm, has a $4 minimum and take-your-own service.

The PMA has moved into the 20th century with recent shows of Jonathan Borofsky and Anselm Kiefer and a blockbuster on Picasso's still lifes. A massive exhibit on Cézanne's paintings, watercolors, and drawings—exclusive to the PMA in this country—will be *the* hot cultural item in town from May through August of 1996, with 340,000 visitors expected.

Admission: $6 adults, $3 students; children under 5 free. Free Sun 10am–1pm. Parking is free and plentiful.

Open: Tues–Sun 10am–5pm; Wed evening hours to 8:45pm with music, talks, and socializing. **Bus:** 76.

Museum of American Art of the Pennsylvania Academy of Fine Arts, 118 N. Broad St. at Cherry St. ☎ 972-7600.

Located three blocks north of City Hall, the Museum of American Art of PAFA, the first art school in the country (1805) and at one time the unquestioned leader of American beaux arts, in 1976 got a healthy dose of Cinderella treatment as its headquarters celebrated its centennial at the same as the U.S. bicentennial. At the end of all the scrubbing, repainting, and stuccoing, Philadelphians were amazed again at the imagination of the Frank Furness masterpiece built in 1876. Go for the American paintings and sculpture or for the building itself—but go.

The ground floor houses an excellent bookstore and card shop, new exhibitions (often of Philadelphia artists), a café, and the academy's classrooms. A splendid staircase, designed from archways to light fixtures by Furness, shines with red, gold, and blue walls. The bottom-left corner of the mezzanine wall was left unrestored—you can see how dingy the entire building was. Each May, half the museum is devoted to the annual academy school exhibition.

As is evident from the PAFA galleries, such early American painters as Gilbert Stuart, the Peale family, and Washington Allston congregated in Philadelphia, because it was America's capital and wealthiest city. The main galleries feature works from the museum's collection of over 6,000 canvases. The rotunda has been the scene of occasional Sunday concerts ever since Walt Whitman came here to listen spellbound. The adjoining rooms display works from the illustrious years of the mid-19th century, when PAFA probably enjoyed its most innovative period.

Tours: Leave from the Grand Stairhall Mon–Fri at 11am and 2pm (only at 2pm during summer weekends).

Admission: $5 adults, $3 seniors and students. Half-price Sat 10am–1pm.

Open: Tues–Sat 10am–5pm; Sun 11am–5pm. **Bus:** C, 48.

Franklin Institute Science Museum, 20th St. and Benjamin Franklin Pkwy. ☎ **448-1200** or **564-3375** for a taped message.

The Franklin Institute Science Museum isn't just kid stuff—everyone loves it because it's a thoroughly imaginative trip through the worlds of science that shows us their influence on our lives. The complex covers four floors of a handsome neoclassical building, with large recent additions. The museum actually has three parts. The first is the home of the Franklin National Memorial, with a 30-ton statue of its namesake and a collection of authentic Franklin artifacts and possessions.

The second part is a collection of 1940s through 1970s science- and technology-oriented exhibition areas that were pioneers in hands-on displays, from a gigantic walk-through heart with heartbeat recordings and explanations, to ship models and the Hall of Aviation, with its small planes and a chance to sit in a cockpit of a Wright brothers' biplane. For a hair-raising experience, plug into a Van de Graaff generator at the lightning gallery. On the third floor, an energy hall bursts with Rube Goldberg contraptions, noisemakers, and light shows. The nearby Discovery Theater gives afternoon shows featuring liquid air and other oddities. The fourth floor specializes in astronomy and mathematical puzzles. The basement Fels Planetarium (☎ **563-1363**) rounds out the picture.

The third part of the Franklin Institute is the result of an ambitious 1991 campaign to construct a Futures Center addition—with $22 million from city and state and $36 million from private sources. Just past the Franklin National Memorial on the second floor, you'll enter an energy-charged atrium with cafés, ticket counters, and ramps and stairs leading to the new exhibits. Just beyond is a separate-admission Omnimax arena, showing films ranging from undersea explorations to the Rolling Stones in spectacular 70mm format. Besides the two-level atrium are eight permanent, interactive exhibits taking you into the 21st century with Disney World–style pizzazz, including ones on space, earth, computers, chemistry, and health. My personal favorites are the video driving exercise in "Future Vision," "The Jamming Room" of musical synthesizers, and the "See Yourself Age" computer program in "Future and You." The texts throughout are witty and disarming.

Of course, you'll eventually get hungry—with a family, the institute's a full afternoon. Your choices are excellent: a vending-machine space in the **Wawa Lunchroom** on the first floor, open only to museum goers; the new all-American with a nutritional twist **Ben's Restaurant** on the second floor, accessible without museum admission and open Monday to Friday from 8:30am to 2:30pm, Saturday and Sunday from 9am to 3:30pm; and the **Omni Café** in the Futures Center lobby, open daily from 11am to shortly before museum closing and serving beer and wine. For dessert, vendors outside sell Philadelphia soft pretzels with plenty of mustard.

Admission: This is confusing and depends on what you want. Basic to exhibitions and Futures Center: $8.50 adults, $7.50 children. Planetarium, Omniverse, and laser shows: $6 adults, $5 children. Combinations of the two: $13.50 adults; $11.50 children.

Open: Science Center, daily 9:30am–5pm; Futures Center, Mon–Wed 9:30am–5pm, Thurs–Sat 9:30am–9pm, Sun 9:30am–6pm. **Bus:** 33, 76.

2   More Attractions

Architectural Highlights

Benjamin Franklin Bridge, entrance at 5th and Vine Sts.

An old fixture on the Olde City landscape has jumped into the 21st century—the Benjamin Franklin Bridge, designed by Paul Cret, one of the architects of the Parkway across town. The largest single-span suspension bridge in the world (1.8 miles) when it was finished in 1926, it carries cars and commuter trains and also has a foot/bicycle path along its south side. For the bicentennial of the U.S. Constitution, a Philadelphia team, including Steven Izenour (of Venturi, Rauch, and Scott Brown), a leading American architect and planner, created a computer-driven system for illuminating each and every cable. At night Philadelphians are treated to the largest lighting effects short of Ben Franklin's lightning itself.

Admission: Free.

Open: Daily 6am–dusk. **Bus:** 50.

City Hall, Broad and Market Sts. ☎ **686-9074.**

When construction of City Hall began in 1871, it was planned to be the tallest structure in the world. But that elaborate 1901 wedding cake by John McArthur, Jr., with an inner courtyard straight out of a French château, was dated in more ways than one, and it still arouses wildly differing reactions. Also gracing City Hall is Calder's 37-foot-tall statue of William Penn.

You may wish to wander inside its vast floors, which range from breathtaking to bureaucratically forlorn; both inside and out, City Hall boasts the richest sculptural decoration of any American building. The Mayor's Reception Room (Room 202) and the City Council Chamber (Room 400) are especially rich.

The highlight of City Hall is the **tower view.** The Juniper Street entrance is most convenient, but you can take any corner elevator to the seventh floor and follow the red tape (always indicative of city government). In this case, it leads to two escalators and a waiting area for the tower elevator. The elevator up to the Penn statue's recently renovated shoestrings, at 480 feet, can hold only eight people, and the outdoor cupola cannot hold many more. On the way, notice how thick the walls are—City Hall is the tallest building ever constructed without a skeleton of steel girders, so that white stone stretches 6 feet thick at the top and 22 feet at ground level. (The need for repair increases as the building approaches its centenary. There's a 1990 bolster of hand-riveted wrought iron now, which you can see around the clock mechanism.) The simply stupefying view from the top encompasses not only the city but also the upper and lower Delaware Valley and port, western New Jersey, and suburban Philadelphia. It's windy up there, though. If you look straight down, you can see more of the hundreds of sculptures designed by Calder, the works of whose descendants—Alexander Sterling Calder (1870–1945) and Alexander Calder (1898–1976)—beautify Logan Circle and the Philadelphia Museum of Art.

Admission: Free.

Open: Daily 10am–3pm. During school year, Mon–Fri 10am–noon reserved for school groups. Last tour at 2:45pm. **Bus/Subway:** Most lines converge beside or underneath the building.

Fisher Fine Arts (Furness) Library, 220 S. 34th St. at Locust Walk on the University of Pennsylvania campus. ☎ **898-8325.**

Like the Pennsylvania Academy of Fine Arts building (see above), this citadel of learning has the characteristic chiseled thistle of Frank Furness, although it was built a decade later from 1888 to 1890. The use of 1890s leaded glass here is even richer. The library now houses, appropriately, the fine arts library of the University of Pennsylvania.

Admission: Free.

Open: During academic year only, Mon–Fri 9am–10pm; summer hours, Mon–Fri 9am–5pm. **Bus:** 44.

Pennsylvania Convention Center, between 11th and 13th Sts. and Market and Race Sts. ☎ **418-4728.**

$522,000,000—that's quite an investment! With the July 1993 opening of the Convention Center, Philadelphia made clear that the future of the area depends on its ability to welcome tens of thousands of visitors weekly. The statistics are staggering: with 440,000 square feet of exhibit space, it's larger than 30th Street Station. But what's really great about the Convention Center is how solid, elegant, and in keeping with its surroundings it is. Architects Thompson, Ventulett, Stainback & Associates shoehorned blocks of brick and limestone between I-76 in the back and just five blocks from Independence National Historic Park in the front.

Unless you're one of the millions the PCC hopes to lure in for a meeting, you'll need to take the public tour for a peek inside. The highlight is a stupendous Grand Hall on the second level, evoking the Train Shed and Headhouse of the Reading Terminal it once was; gray and black Mexican marble alternates with waterfalls, steel, and terrazzo, with huge granite pylons for heating and cooling the mammoth space. Esplanades and corridors contain a veritable museum of 52 living artists (35 from Philadelphia) in one of the most successful public art projects of our time. By 1995, the Market Street entrance should be restored and have escalators up to the Train Shed, and the Marriott being constructed next door will have a skywalk into the Great Hall. And don't forget—the incomparable Reading Terminal Market is downstairs!

Admission: Public tours free; most shows charge admission.

Open: Public tours Tuesdays and Thursdays at 11:30am, 12:30am, 1:30pm, and 2:15pm. Enter at the northwest corner of 12th and Arch Streets. **Bus/Subway:** Rail lines (including Airport Express) stop at Market East Station; SEPTA at 11th and Market and 13th and Market; buses 12, 17, 33, 44.

Philadelphia Merchants Exchange, Walnut and 3rd Sts.
☎ 597-8974.

This sloped site, alongside one of the city's original creeks emptying into a Delaware cove, was used by hometown architect William Strickland from 1832 to 1834 as a forerunner of a stock-and-trading market. It's a pity that this building, once obviously central to city life, isn't open to the public, because the exterior is fascinating—a Greek semicircular front end on the river side and a strong coffer of a building with a portico facing the city. The tower was built to provide instant information on arriving ships.

Admission: Not open to the public. **Bus:** 21, 42.

Cemeteries

Christ Church Burial Ground, 5th and Arch Sts. (enter on 5th St.).

This 1719 expansion of the original graveyard of Christ Church (see below) contains the graves of Benjamin Franklin and his wife, Deborah, along with those of four other signers of the Declaration of Independence and many Revolutionary War heroes. It's a remarkably simple and peaceful place. There are always pennies on Ben's grave; tossing them there is a local tradition of wishes for good luck.

Admission: Free.

Open: Due to vandalism, open by appointment only now, when church staff is available. **Bus:** 48, 50.

Laurel Hill Cemetery, 3822 Ridge Ave., East Fairmount Park.
☎ 228-8200.

How come you find Benjamin Franklin buried in a small, flat plot next to a church (see above) while Civil War Gen. George Meade is buried in a bucolic meadow? Basically, the views of death and the contemplation of nature got more romantic in the 19th century, and Laurel Hill was a result of that romanticism. Laurel Hill (1836), the first American cemetery designed by an architect, was the second (after Mount Auburn in Cambridge) to develop funerary monuments—even small Victorian palaces. Set amid the rolling, landscaped hills overlooking the Schuylkill, its 100 acres also house plenty of tomb sculpture, Pre-Raphaelite stained glass, and art nouveau sarcophagi. People picnicked here a century ago, but there's nothing but walking allowed now.

Admission: Free, although restrictions may apply, since it's still in use as a private institution. The Friends of Laurel Hill arrange tours (☎ 228-8817).

Open: Tues–Sat 9:30am–1:30. **Directions:** Go north on East River Drive; make a right on Ferry Road, go one block to Ridge Avenue, and turn right. The entrance is a half mile along on the right. **Bus:** 61.

Mikveh Israel Cemetery, Spruce St. between 8th and 9th Sts.

☎ **922-5446.** (synagogue number).

Philadelphia was an early center of American Jewish life, with the second-oldest synagogue (1740) organized by English and Sephardic Jews. While this congregation shifted location and is now adjacent to the Liberty Bell, the original cemetery—well outside the city at the time—was bought from the Penn family by Nathan Levy and later filled with the likes of Haym Solomon, a Polish immigrant who helped finance the revolutionary government, and Rebecca Gratz, the daughter of a fine local family, who provided the model for Sir Walter Scott's Rebecca in his *Ivanhoe.*

Admission: Free.

Open: Summer Mon–Fri 10am–4pm; off-season, contact synagogue or park service. **Bus:** 47, 90.

Churches & Synagogues

Arch Street Meeting House, 4th and Arch Sts. ☎ **627-2667.**

This plain but imposing brick building dates from 1804, but William Penn gave the land to his Society of Friends in 1693. In this capital city of Quakers, each year during the last week in March, 104 Monthly Meetings (local congregations) send 13,000 representatives for worship and "threshing sessions." They use a spartan chamber, with hand-hewn benches facing one another. Other areas of the meetinghouse display Bibles, clothing, and implements of Quaker life past and present, along with a simple history of the growth of the religion and the life of William Penn.

Admission: Free. Guided tours year-round.

Open: Mon–Sat 10am–4pm. Services Thurs 10am and Sun 10:30am. **Bus:** 17, 33, 48, 50.

Christ Church, 2nd St., a half block north of Market St.

☎ **922-1695.**

The most beautiful colonial building north of Market Street has to be Christ Church (1727–54). Its spire gleams white from anywhere in the neighborhood, now that the buildings to the south have been replaced by a grassy park and a subway stop. The churchyard also has benches, tucked under trees or beside brick walls.

Christ Church, dating from the apex of English Palladianism, follows the proud and graceful tradition of Christopher Wren's churches in London. As in many of them, the interior spans one large arch, with galleries above the sides as demanded by the Anglican church. Behind the altar, the massive Palladian window—a central columned arch flanked by proportional rectangles of pane—was the wonder of worshipers and probably the model for the one in Independence Hall. The main chandelier was brought over from England in 1744. As in King's Chapel in Boston, seating is by pew—Washington's is marked with a plaque.

With all the stones, memorials, and plaques, it's impossible to avoid history. William Penn was baptized at the font, which All Hallows' Church in London sent over. Penn left the Anglican church at age 23 (he spent most of his 20s in English jails because of it), but his charter included a clause that an Anglican church could be founded if 20 residents requested it, which they did. The socially conscious Philadelphians of the next generations chose Anglicanism as the "proper" religion, switching to Episcopalianism after the Revolution.

There's also a small gift shop.

Admission: Free, although donations are welcome.

Open: Mon–Sat 9am–5pm, Sun 1–5pm. Sun services at 9 and 11am. **Closed:** Mon–Tues Jan 1–Mar 10 and major holidays. **Bus:** 5, 17, 33, 48.

Gloria Dei, 916 Swanson St., near Christian and Delaware Aves. ☎ **389-1513.**

Take Swanson Street under I-95 at Christian Street in Queen Village and then a turn onto Water Street to reach Gloria Dei, or Old Swedes' Church. The National Park Service administers this oldest church in Pennsylvania (1700). At its dedication, the self-styled "Hermits of the Wissahickon" performed a public concert on viola, trumpets, and kettledrums. Inside the enclosing walls, you'll think yourself back in the 1700s, with a miniature parish hall, a rectory, and a graveyard amid the greenery. The one-room museum directly across from the church has a map of the good old days, and the graves of tubby Gov. Johan Printz and president of the Confederated States John Hanson lie nearby.

The thin, simple church interior has plenty of wonderful details. Everybody loves the ship models suspended from the ceiling: The *Key of Kalmar* and *Flying Griffin* carried the first Swedish settlers to these shores in 1638. And catch the silver crown in the vestry—any woman married here wears it during the ceremony.

Admission: Free.

Open: Apr–Oct, daily 9am–5pm. By appointment in the off-season. **Bus:** 5, 64, 79.

Mother Bethel African Methodist Episcopal Church, 419 S. 6th St. ☎ 925-0616.

This National Historic Landmark site is the oldest piece of land continuously owned by blacks in the United States. Richard Allen, born in 1760, was a slave in Germantown and bought his freedom in 1782, eventually walking out of St. George's down the street to found the African Methodist Episcopal order, today numbering some 5,000,000. This handsome, varnished-wood-and-stained-glass 1890 building is their mother church.

Admission: Free (donations welcome).

Open: Tues–Wed, Fri–Sat, 10am–3pm; Sun 2–4pm. Sun service, 10:45am.

Old St. Joseph's Church, Willings Alley near 4th and Walnut Sts. ☎ 923-1733.

At its 1733 founding, St. Joseph's was the only place in the English-speaking world where Roman Catholics could celebrate mass publicly. The story goes that Benjamin Franklin advised Father Greaton to protect the church physically, since religious bigotry wasn't unknown even in the Quaker city. That's why the building is so unassuming from the street, a fact that didn't save it from damage during the anti-Catholic riots of the 1830s. Such French allies as Lafayette worshiped here. The present building (1838) is Greek Revival merging into Victorian, with wooden pews and such unusual colors as mustard and pale yellow, but the interior has preserved a colonial style unusual in a Catholic church.

Admission: Free.

Open: Mon–Fri 10:30am–2pm, Sat 10:30am–6:30pm, Sun 7am–4pm. One daily mass Mon–Sat, four on Sun. **Bus:** 21, 42, 50.

St. Peter's Episcopal, 3rd and Pine Sts. ☎ 925-5968.

St. Peter's (1761) was originally established through the bishop of London and has remained continuously open since. So like all pre-Revolutionary Episcopal churches, St. Peter's started out as an Anglican shrine. But why was this so, with Christ Church at 2nd and Market? In one word—mud. In the words of a local historian, "the long tramp from Society Hill…was more and more distasteful to fine gentlemen and beautiful belles.…"

Robert Smith, the builder of Carpenters' Hall, continued his penchant for red brick, pediments on the ends, and keystoned arches for gallery windows. Not much has ever changed inside, with its white box pews. Unlike in most churches, the wineglass pulpit is set into the west end, but the chancel is at the east, so the minister had to do some walking during the service. George Washington and Mayor Samuel Powel sat in pew 41. The 1764 organ blocks the east Palladian window. The steeple outside, constructed in 1842, was designed by William Strickland to house a chime of bells, which are still played.

The graveyard contains seven Native American chiefs, victims of the 1793 smallpox epidemic. Painter C. W. Peale, Stephen Decatur of naval fame, Nicholas Biddle of the Second Bank of the United States, and other notables also are interred here.

Admission: Free.

Open: Tues–Sat 9am–4pm, Sun 1–4pm. Guided tours Sat 10am–noon, Sun 1–3pm. **Bus:** 50, 90.

University

University Of Pennsylvania, 34th and Walnut Sts. ☎ 898-5000.

This private, now coeducational, Ivy League institution was founded by Benjamin Franklin and others in 1740; it boasts America's first medical (1765), law (1790), and business (1881) schools. Penn's liberal arts curriculum, dating to 1756, was the first to combine classical and practical subjects.

The university now has 4 undergraduate and 12 graduate schools, spanning over 100 academic departments. Its progress and excellence have been revitalized in the last two decades, thanks to extremely successful alumni and fund-raising drives. The total college enrolls 22,000 students, and the 260-acre campus includes the **University Museum of Archaeology and Anthropology,** the **Annenberg Center for the Performing Arts,** and the **Institute for Contemporary Art.**

Historic Buildings & Monuments

Betsy Ross House, 239 Arch St. ☎ 627-5343.

One colonial home everybody knows about is this one, restored in 1937 and distinguished by the Stars and Stripes outside. Elizabeth (Betsy) Ross was a Quaker needlewoman, married in Gloria Dei Church and newly widowed in 1776. So she worked as a seamstress and upholsterer out of her home on Arch Street (nobody is quite sure if No. 239 was hers, though). Nobody knows if she did the original American flag of 13 stars set in a field of 13 red and white stripes, but she was commissioned to sew for the American fleet ship's flags that replaced the earlier Continental banners.

The house takes only a minute or two to walk through, and the wooden stairwell was designed for shorter colonial frames—certainly not Washington's! Since the house is set back from the street, the city maintains the Atwater Kent Park in front, where Ross and her last husband are buried. The upholstery shop, now a gift shop, opens into the period parlor. Other rooms include the cellar kitchen (standard placement for this room), tiny bedrooms, and model working areas for upholstering, making musket balls, and the like. Note such little touches as reusable note tablets made of ivory; pine cones, used to help start hearth fires; and the prominent kitchen hourglass.

Admission: Free, but suggested contribution of $1 adult, 25¢ child.

Open: Summer, daily 9am–6pm; rest of year, daily 9am–5pm. **Bus:** 5, 17, 33, 48.

Carpenters' Hall, 320 Chestnut St. ☎ 925-0167.

Carpenters' Hall (1773) was the guildhall for—guess who?—carpenters; at the time the city could use plenty, for 18th-century Philadelphia was the fastest-growing urban area in all the colonies and perhaps in the British Empire outside of London. Robert Smith, a Scottish member of the Carpenters' Company, designed the building (like most carpenters, he did architecture and contracting as well).

He also designed the steeple of Christ Church, with the same calm Georgian lines. It's made of Flemish Bond brick in a checkerboard pattern, with stone window sills, superb woodwork, and a cupola that resembles a saltshaker.

You'll be surprised at how small Carpenters' Hall is because such great events transpired here. In 1774 the normal governmental channels to convey colonial complaints to the Crown were felt inadequate, and a popular Committee of Correspondence debated in Carpenters' Hall. The more radical delegates, led by Patrick Henry, had already expressed treasonous wishes for independence, but most wanted to exhaust possibilities of bettering their relationship with the Crown.

What's in there now isn't much—an exhibit of colonial building methods; some portraits, including a Gilbert Stuart; and Windsor chairs, which seated the First Continental Congress. If some details look as if they're from a later period, you're right: The fanlights above the north and south doors date from the 1790s, and the gilding dates from 1857.

Admission: Free.

Open: Tues–Sun 10am–4pm (hours are curtailed because the Carpenters' Company still maintains it). **Bus:** 21, 42, 76.

Declaration House [Graff House], 7th and Market Sts.
☎ 597-2505.

Bricklayer Jacob Graff constructed a modest three-story home in the 1760s, figuring on renting out the second floor for added income. The Second Continental Congress soon brought to the house a thin, red-haired tenant—Thomas Jefferson—who was in search of a quiet room away from city noise. If the Declaration of Independence is any indication, he found it, because he drafted it here between June 10 and June 18, 1776.

The reconstruction uses the same Flemish Bond checkerboard pattern (only on visible walls; it was too expensive for party walls) for brick, windows with paneled shutters, and implements that the house exhibited in 1775. If you compare it with Society Hill homes, it's tiny and asymmetrical, with an off-center front door. You'll enter through a small garden and see a short film about Jefferson and a copy of Jefferson's draft (which would have forbidden slavery in the United States, had the clause survived debate). The upstairs rooms are furnished as Jefferson would have seen them.

Admission: Free (part of Independence National Historical Park).

Open: Daily 9am–5pm. **Bus:** 17, 33, 48, 76.

★ Elfreth's Alley, 2nd St. between Arch and Race Sts.
☎ 574-0560.

The modern Benjamin Franklin Bridge shadows Elfreth's Alley, the oldest continuously inhabited street in America. Most of colonial Philadelphia looked much like this: cobblestone lanes between the major thoroughfares; small two-story homes; and pent eaves over doors and windows, a local trademark. Note the busybody mirrors that let residents see who is at their door (or someone else's) from the second-story bedroom. In 1700 the resident artisans and tradesmen worked with shipping, but 50 years later haberdashers, bakers, printers, and house carpenters set up shop. Families moved in and out rapidly, for noisy, dusty 2nd Street was the major north-south route in Philadelphia. Jews, blacks, Welsh, and Germans made it a miniature melting pot. Because of luck and the vigilant Elfreth's Alley Association, the destruction of the street was averted in 1937. The minuscule, sober facades hide some ultramodern interiors, and there are some restful shady benches under a Kentucky Coffee Bean tree on Bladen Court, off the north side of the street.

Number 126, the 1755 **Mantua Maker's House** (cape maker), built by blacksmith Jeremiah Elfreth, now serves as a museum and is the only house open to the public. An 18th-century garden in back has been restored, and the interiors include a dressmaker's shop and upstairs bedroom. You can also buy colonial candy and gifts and peek in some of the open windows on the street. On the first weekend in June all the houses are thrown open for inspection—don't miss this.

Admission: $1 adults, 50¢ children, $2.50 families.

Open: Daily 10am–4pm. **Bus:** 5, 48, 76.

Masonic Temple, 1 N. Broad St. ☎ **988-1917.**

Quite apart from its Masonic lore, the Temple—among the world's largest—is one of America's best on-site illustrations of the use of post–Civil War architecture and design, because the halls are more or less frozen in time and because no expense was spared. There are seven lodge halls, designed to capture the seven "ideal" architectures—Renaissance, Ionic, Oriental, Corinthian, Gothic, Egyptian, and Norman (notice that Renaissance was the most contemporary style architect James Windrim could come up with!). Many of the Founding Fathers, including Washington, were Masons (this is actually the preeminent Masonic Temple of American Freemasonry), and the museum has preserved their letters and emblems. Lafayette and Andrew Jackson also were Masons.

Admission: Free.

Open: Tours Mon–Fri at 10 and 11am and 1, 2, and 3pm, Sat at 10 and 11am only. **Bus:** 17, 33, 44, 48, 76.

Pennsylvania Hospital, 8th and Spruce Sts. ☎ **829-3971.**

Pennsylvania Hospital, like so much in civic Philadelphia, owes its presence to Benjamin Franklin, who devised a rudimentary matching-grant scheme so that the Assembly wouldn't feel it was subsidizing something that private citizens didn't want. This was the first hospital in the colonies, and it seemed like a strange venture into social welfare at the time. Samuel Rhoads, a fine architect in the Carpenters' Company, designed the Georgian headquarters; the east wing, nearest 8th Street, was completed in 1755, and a west wing matched it in 1797. The grand Center Building by David Evans completed the ensemble in 1804. The marble pilasters and arched doorway of the middle structure add curving grace to the anchorlike wings. Instead of a dome, the hospital decided on a surgical amphitheater's skylight.

In spring, the garden's azaleas brighten the neighborhood, and the beautifully designed herb garden is equally popular.

The hospital was the workplace of Philadelphia's many brilliant doctors, among them Philip Syng Physick, Benjamin Rush, and Caspar Wistar. The entrance on 8th Street, between Spruce and Pine, highlights the Benjamin West painting, *Christ Healing the Sick in the Temple.*

Admission: Free.

Open: Mon–Fri 9am–5pm. Guided tours are no longer obligatory; copies of a walking tour itinerary are available from the Marketing Department on the second floor of the Pine Street building. **Bus:** 47, 90.

★ **Powel House,** 244 S. 3rd St. ☎ **627-0364** or **925-2251.**

If Elfreth's Alley (see above) leaves you wondering about how someone really well-to-do lived in colonial Philadelphia, head for the Powel House. Samuel Powel was mayor, and he and his wife, Elizabeth, hosted every Founding Father and foreign dignitary around. (John Adams called these feasts "sinful dinners," which shows how far Samuel had come from a Quaker background.) He spent most of his 20s gallivanting in Europe, thanks to the family's wealth, collecting wares for this 1765 mansion.

Unbelievably, this most Georgian house was slated for demolition in 1930 because it had become a decrepit slum dwelling. Period rooms were removed to the Philadelphia Museum of Art and the Metropolitan Museum of Art in New York. But the Society for the Preservation of Landmarks saved it and has gradually refurnished the entire mansion as it was. The yellow satin Reception Room, off the entrance hall, has some gorgeous details, such as a wide-grain mahogany secretary. Upstairs, the magnificent ballroom features red damask drapes whose design is copied from a bolt of cloth found untouched in a colonial attic. There is also a 1790 Irish crystal chandelier and a letter from Benjamin Franklin's daughter referring to the lively dances held here. An 18th-century garden lies below.

Admission: $3 adults, $2 students; children under 6 free.

Open: Guided tours only, Tues–Sat 10am–4pm, Sun 1–4pm. Tours are given whenever a group of six or more congregates; be sure to arrive at least 30 minutes before closing. **Bus:** 50, 76, 90.

Libraries & Literary Attractions

Athenaeum of Philadelphia, 219 S. 6th St. (Washington Square East). ☎ **925-2688.**

The age when a group of private subscribers could fund the dissemination of useful knowledge—or even keep tabs on it in diverse fields—has long since passed, but a 15-minute peek into the Athenaeum will show you one of America's finest collections of Victorian-period architectural design and also give you the flavor of private 19th-century life for the proper Philadelphian. The building, beautifully restored in 1975, houses almost 1 million library items for the serious researcher in American architecture. Changing exhibitions of rare books, drawings, and photographs fill a recently constructed first-floor gallery.

Admission: Free.

Open: Mon–Fri 9am–5pm. Permission to enter and guided tours are given on request. **Bus:** 21, 42, 90.

Free Library of Philadelphia, Central Library, 19th and Vine Sts. ☎ **686-5322.**

Across Logan Circle from the Academy of Natural Sciences (see below), the Free Library of Philadelphia rivals the public libraries of Boston and New York for magnificence and diversity. The library and its twin, the Municipal Court, are plagiarisms of buildings in the Place de la Concorde in Paris (the library's the one on the left). If you're hungry, the rooftop cafeteria is one of the nicest locations for a snack and one of the only Parkway dining areas.

The main lobby and the gallery always have some of the institution's riches on display—from medieval manuscripts to modern bookbinding. Greeting cards and stationery are sold for reasonable prices too. The second floor houses the best local history, travel, and resource collection in the city. The local map collection is fascinating. The third-floor rare-book room hosts visitors on Monday to Friday from 9am to 5pm. If you're interested in manuscripts from the 19th century, children's literature, incunabula, and early American hornbooks, this is the place.

There's also an active concert and film series.

Admission: Free.

Open: Mon–Wed 9am–9pm, Thurs–Fri 9am–6pm, Sat 9am–5pm, Sun 1–5pm. **Bus:** 76.

Edgar Allan Poe National Historical Site, 532 N. 7th St. ☎ **597-8780.**

The acclaimed American author lived here from 1843 to 1844. "The Black Cat," "The Gold Bug," and "The Tell-Tale Heart" were published while he was a resident. It's a simple place—after all, Poe was badly off most of his life—and the National Park Service keeps it unfurnished. An adjoining building contains basic information on Poe's life and work, along with a reading room and slide presentation. The Park Service also runs intermittent discussions and candlelight tours on Saturday afternoons.

Admission: Free.

Open: Tues–Sat 9am–5pm. **Bus:** 47.

Rosenbach Museum and Library, 2010 Delancey Place (between Spruce and Pine Sts). ☎ **732-1600.**

The Rosenbach specializes in books: illuminated manuscripts, parchment, rough drafts, and first editions. If you love the variations and beauty of the printed word, they'll love your presence.

You're not allowed absolute freedom in the opulent town-house galleries, nor free rein among the 30,000 rare books and 270,000 documents. But the admission fee allows you a 75-minute tour with one of the genteel volunteer guides. Some rooms preserve the Rosenbachs' elegant living quarters, with Hepplewhite furniture and Sully paintings. Others are devoted to authors and illustrators: Marianne Moore's Greenwich Village study is reproduced in its entirety, and the Maurice Sendak drawings represent only the tip of the iceberg—or the forest. The second-floor foyer holds the original manuscript of Joyce's *Ulysses* and first editions of Melville, in Melville's own bookcase. And the third-floor special exhibitions explore anything from the colors used in illuminated manuscripts to children's books. Don't miss the shop, tucked behind the entrance, for bargains in greeting cards and a superb collection of Sendak.

Admission: $5 adults, $3.50 children under 18 and seniors.

Open: Tues–Sun 11am–4pm. **Closed:** Aug. If you have a special scholarly interest, contact the library before you visit. **Bus:** 17, 90.

Markets

Italian Market, 9th St. between Christian and Federal Sts.

While touring South Philadelphia, be sure to visit the Italian Market, where you can buy the freshest produce, pasta, seafood, and other culinary delights—this is what shopping used to be like before supermarkets and malls. It's hardly pristine—in cold weather, vendors light fires in the trash cans for warmth—but it's vibrant. It's increasingly safe and interesting to head for the market from South Street, which has been gentrified from Front to Ninth streets. Only a couple of blocks filled with notable Italian restaurants—Ralph's, Felicia's, and Palumbo's—separate South Street from the market proper. Fast-talking vendors, opera-singing butchers, and try-it-before-you-buy-it cheese merchants hawk their wares here. **Fante's Cookware** is famous nationally.

Open: Daily, dawn to dusk. **Bus:** 47, 64.

⭐ **Reading Terminal Market,** 12th and Arch Sts. ☎ 922-2317.

The Reading Terminal Market has been a greengrocer, snack shop, butcher, fish market, and sundries store for smart Philadelphians since the turn of the century. The idea was to use the space beneath the terminal's tracks for the food business so that commuters and businesses could stock up easily and cheaply. It's survived everything, even the new Convention Center upstairs.

What's at Reading Terminal exactly? You'll find scrapple, mangoes, clam chowder, and pretzels—you name it, if it's fresh and unpackaged, it'll be there. This is where most of the "retail," as opposed to restaurant or institutional, Amish farm products come to market. Chapter 6, "Philadelphia Dining," provides a fuller description of the individual vendors and local specialties, but there is a pleasant central beer garden with seating as well as many bar-stool and café-table setups by individual vendors.

Open: Mon–Sat 8am–6pm. Many vendors close at 5pm. **Bus:** 17, 33, 44, 48.

More Museums & Exhibitions ———————

Academy of Natural Sciences, 19th St. and Benjamin Franklin Pkwy. ☎ **299-1000.**

If you're looking for dinosaurs, the Academy is the best place to find them. Kids love the big diorama halls, with cases of several species mounted and posed in authentic settings. A $2.5-million permanent display, "Discovering Dinosaurs," features more than a dozen specimens, including a huge Tyrannosaurus rex with jaws agape. This was joined in late 1991 by "What on Earth!" on geology; many of the displays are hands-on or interactive. The North American Hall, on the first floor, has enormous moose, buffalo, and bears. A small marine exhibit shows how some fish look different in ultraviolet light and how the bed of the Delaware has changed since Penn landed in 1682.

The second floor features groupings of Asian and African flora and fauna. Many of the cases have nearby headphones that tell you more about what you're seeing. Five or six live demonstrations are given here every day; the handlers are expert in conducting these sessions with rocks, birds, plants, and animals. Several daily Eco Shows are given in the auditorium downstairs too. The Egyptian mummy, a priest of a late dynasty, seems a bit out of place.

Upstairs, "Outside In" is a touchable museum designed for children under 12, with a model campsite, fossils, minerals, shells, and other unbreakables. It stimulates almost every sense: Children can see, feel, hear, and smell live turtles, mice, bees in a beehive, and snakes (all caged) and wander around mock forests and deserts. "Outside In" is open Monday to Friday from 1 to 4pm, Saturday and Sunday and holidays from 10am to 5pm. Admission here is part of the general admission. A large bird hall and a hall of endangered species round out the picture, along with frequent films. There's a brown-bag lunchroom and vending area with drinks and snacks.

Admission: $6 adults, $5.50 seniors, $5 children 3–12; under 3 free.

Open: Mon–Fri 10am–4:30pm, Sat–Sun and holidays 10am–5pm. **Bus:** 32, 33, 76.

Afro-American Historical and Cultural Museum, 7th and Arch Sts. ☎ **574-0380.**

Three blocks northwest of the Liberty Bell is the only building in America specifically constructed to display the history of African Americans. It's built in five split levels of ridged concrete, meant to evoke African mud housing, off a central atrium and ramp. As you ascend, you follow the path from African roots through to the role blacks have played in U.S. development. The specific exhibitions do change.

The ground floor contains the admissions office, the gift shop, and the African Heritage Gallery (here's your chance to see photographs of original cornrow hairstyles and customs). The second level, concentrating on slavery and captivity, is undoubtedly the most dramatic and informed section. It emphasizes that the slave trade was hardly exclusive to, or even predominant in, North America, and that it persisted in South America until 1870.

The upper three levels, dealing with black history and culture after emancipation, lose some focus since blacks slowly gained acceptance and/or visibility in so many areas of American life. Black cowboys, inventors, athletes, spokespeople, businesspeople—all are presented, along with such organizations as the NAACP and CORE and the civil rights movements of the 1960s.

Admission: $3.50 adults, $1.75 children and seniors.

Open: Tues–Sat 10am–5pm. **Bus:** 47, 48.

American-Swedish Historical Museum, 1900 Pattison Ave. ☎ **389-1776.**

Modeled after a 17th-century Swedish manor house, this small museum chronicles 350 years of the life and accomplishments of Swedish Americans. Specific rooms highlight John Ericsson, inventor of the Civil War ironclads, and 19th-century opera singer Jenny Lind. Seasonal festivals are part of the mix here: In April, the museum hosts *Valborgsmassoafton* (Spring Festival), with folk dancing, singing, and refreshments; and St. Lucia's Day in December is a softly lit Christmas precursor.

Admission: $2 adults, $1 students and seniors; children under 12 free.

Open: Tues–Fri 10am–4pm, Sat noon–4pm. **Bus:** C.

Atwater Kent Museum, The History Museum Of Philadelphia, 15 S. 7th St. ☎ **922-3031.**

Across the street from the Balch Institute (see below), the small Atwater Kent Museum occupies the former home of the Franklin Institute. Using more artifacts than the Visitor Center, the Atwater Kent shows you what Philadelphia was like from 1680 to 1880. The founder, you may remember, built most of America's early radios, and much of this fortune benefited Philadelphia gardens and societies. Nothing was too trivial to include—the collection jumps from dolls to dioramas, from cigar-store Indians to period toy shops. Sunbonnets, train tickets, rocking horses, ship models, and military uniforms are all part of the display.

Admission: $2 adults, $1 children.

Open: Tues–Sat 10am–4pm. **Bus:** 17, 33, 42, 76.

Balch Institute for Ethnic Studies, 18 S. 7th St. ☎ **925-8090.**

Everyone comes from someplace—and the United States is virtually the only country where everyone (except the Native Americans) comes from someplace else and knows it and is proud of it. The institute has a terrific library that covers everything you've always wanted to know about your roots, if you're one of more than 100 ethnicities. The exhibition "Freedom's Doors" made the point that one-third of all immigrants disembarked not at New York but at Boston, Miami, New Orleans, Los Angeles, and so forth. To the left, the exhibits change every couple of months; they range from ethnic images in World War I posters to African crafts.

Admission: Free, although donation requested.

Open: Mon–Sat 10am–4pm. **Bus:** 17, 33, 42, 76.

⭐ **Barnes Foundation,** 300 N. Latches Lane, Merion Station, PA 19066. ☎ 215/667-0290.

Take a train, a taxi, a bus, or a car, or even walk if you have to—if you're interested in art, the Barnes Foundation will stun you with its magnificence. Albert Barnes crammed his French provincial mansion with over 1,000 masterpieces—180 Renoirs, 80 Cézannes, innumerable impressionists and postimpressionists, and a generous sampling of European art from the Italian primitives onward. **Note:** because much of the collection is touring, and the galleries are being renovated, the Barnes will not be open until late 1995.

Barnes believed that art has a quality that can be studied scientifically—for example, one curve will be beautiful and hence art, and another that's slightly different will not be art. That's why the galleries display antique door latches, keyholes, keys, and household tools with strong geometric lines right next to the paintings. And the connections beg to be drawn between neighboring objects—an unusual van Gogh nude, an Amish chest, and New Mexico rural icons. Virtually every first-rank European artist is included: Degas, Seurat, Bosch, Tintoretto, Lorrain, Chardin, Daumier, Delacroix, Corot, and so forth. This is not a bad use of a fortune derived from selling patent medicine!

At press time, the Barnes is changing from the archaic rigidity that used to govern its policies, since the first generation of trustees has passed on. Until now, the foundation admitted only 200 visitors on Friday, 200 on Saturday, and 100 on Sunday.

Admission: Undetermined at press time.

Open: Undetermined at press time. **SEPTA:** Take Paoli local train to Merion; walk up Merion Avenue and turn left onto Latches Lane. **Bus:** 44 to Old Lancaster Road and Latches Lane. **Car:** I-76 (Schuylkill Expressway) north to City Line Avenue, then south on City Line 1 1/2 miles to Old Lancaster Road. Turn right onto Old Lancaster, continue 4 blocks and turn left onto Latches Lane.

Hill-Physick-Keith House, 321 S. 4th St. ☎ 925-7866 or 925-2251.

As with the Powel (p. 149) and Bishop White (p. 182) homes, the Hill-Physick-Keith House combines attractiveness through design and interest through history on Society Hill. This home is, if anything, the area's most impressive—it's freestanding but not boxy, gracious but solid. Built during the 1780s boom, it soon wound up housing the father of American surgery, Philip Syng Physick, a very professional name for a physician. The usual pattern of descendants, neglect, and renovation has applied here, on an even grander scale.

All the cloths and wallpapers were fashioned expressly for use here, and the mansion as restored is a landmark of the Federal style from about 1815. The drawing room opens onto a lovely 19th-century walled garden and shows the excitement caused by the discovery of the buried city of Pompeii by including a Roman stool and

18th-century Italian art. Many of the furnishings in the upstairs parlor were lent by the Society of Cincinnatus, among them an inkstand tarnished by Ben Franklin's fingerprints. Dr. Physick treated Chief Justice Marshall, and Marshall's portrait and gift of a wine stand testify to the doctor's powers.

Admission: $4 adults, $2 students and seniors; children under 6 free.

Open: Tues–Sat 10am–4pm, Sun 1–4pm. Guided tours are for six or more only; last tours are given 30 minutes before closing. As with other houses on Society Hill, it's occasionally rented for parties and receptions, so call beforehand. **Bus:** 50, 90.

Historical Society of Pennsylvania, 1300 Locust St.
☎ 732-6200.

This museum houses the finest collection of colonial furniture and art in Center City. Only members and scholars are admitted to the archives, but the museum exhibits sprawl over the first floor of this solid turn-of-the-century building. It helps if you have a basic background of local history, since almost every notable of the city (and some famous out-of-towners such as Napoléon's brother Joseph and George Washington, both of whom lived here) has a portrait or chair represented.

Admission: $2.50 gallery for adults; $1.50 children 6–18 and seniors; $5 library.

Open: Tues and Thurs–Sat 10am–5pm, Wed 10am–9pm. **Closed:** All major holidays. **Bus:** 21, 23, 42, 76, C.

National Museum of American Jewish History, 55 N. 5th St.
☎ 923-8811.

This is the only museum that's specifically dedicated to preserving and presenting Jewish participation in the development of the United States. Don't expect to walk into another colonial structure. The complex was built in the aftermath of the 1950s clearance that allowed for Independence Mall, although the congregation connected to it, Mikveh Israel, was established in Philadelphia in 1740 (see the "Cemeteries" listing, above). The walkway between 4th and 3rd streets displays an 1876 statue by Sir Moses Ezekiel, an English lord born in America, symbolizing religious freedom. It was fittingly given by the Jewish congregation in Philadelphia, and you can see how much lower the street level was a century ago. You'll enter close to 4th Street (passing Christ Church Cemetery, with Ben Franklin's grave the major attraction here) into a dark-brick lobby that serves both the museum and the adjoining Mikveh Israel Synagogue. The museum starts with a permanent exhibition, "The American Jewish Experience: From 1654 to the Present," combining dry-mounted reproductions of portraits and documents, actual books and letters, and utensils and religious articles to attest to the diversity and vitality of American Jews. It's a fascinating show, and the museum should be proud of sponsoring its recent tour. Smaller rotating exhibitions supplement this presentation. Official annual attendance clocks in at more than 40,000, but it's usually cool and restful and makes a good break from a hot Independence Park tour. A small gift shop is attached.

Admission: $2.50 adults, $1.75 students, seniors, and children; children under 5 free.

Open: Mon–Thurs 10am–5pm, Fri 10am–3pm, Sun noon–5pm.
Bus: 17, 33, 48, 50.

Norman Rockwell Museum, 6th and Sansom Sts. (lower level). ☎ 922-4345.

The Norman Rockwell Museum in the corner of the old headquarters of the Curtis Publishing Company on Washington Square exhibits about 320 of his famous covers for the *Saturday Evening Post.* Only a couple of these are the original paintings and sketches, although a re-creation of Rockwell's studio has an unfinished one on the easel. You can see the classic Four Freedoms posters, which stimulated war-bond sales in World War II. The gift shop has more Rockwelliana than you could imagine.

Admission: $2 adults, $1.50 seniors; children under 12 free.

Open: Mon–Sat 10am–4pm, Sun 11am–4pm. **Bus:** 21, 42, 90.

Please Touch Museum, 210 N. 21st St. ☎ 963-0667.

The museum is the first in the country designed specifically for children seven years and younger. Dedicated to a unique fun-filled educational, cultural, hands-on experience, the converted factories provide a window to the creative, exuberant, and receptive in us all. The location is great—just off the Parkway, two blocks south of Franklin Institute—and it's one of the best indoor activities for a younger family, Philadelphian, or tourist.

The museum shows its thoughtful design at the lobby: A separate gift shop, with plenty of cute and challenging items, can be entered without paying admission. Once you're in, you can park strollers, check coats, and buy tickets at counters that cater to kids. Exciting hand-on exhibits like "Growing Up" encourage parent/child participation and focus on specific social, cognitive, and emotional areas of child development. "Studio PTM," installed in 1993, allows children to experience being behind the camera and on stage in a television studio, including sound effects and camera angles. "Move It!," an exhibit on Philadelphia transportation, has brought together a SEPTA bus driver's seat, a toy-sized Delaware River barge port, and the old monorail from Wanamaker's. My own kids love "Nature's Nursery," with toy animals revealed through various pushes and pulls; "Play in Motion," which mixes gymnastics and science; and "Foodtastic Journey," with an extensive play farm to supermarket to kitchen route.

The Please Touch Museum is not a day-care center; you cannot simply drop the kids off, and you won't want to. Educational activities like storytelling or crafts are available daily from 11am to 3:30pm. It's also a great place to celebrate a child's birthday, if you care to plan ahead.

Admission: $6.50 adults and children, $5 seniors; maximum of three kids per adult. Voluntary donation Sun 9–11am and Wed 3–4:30pm. No strollers inside, but Snuglis available.

Open: Daily 9am–4:30pm. **Bus:** 7, 48, 76.

Rodin Museum, Benjamin Franklin Pkwy. between 21st and 22nd Sts. ☎ **763-8100.**

The Rodin Museum exhibits the largest collection of the master's work—129 sculptures, 72 drawings, and several sketchbooks—outside the Musée Rodin in Paris. It has inherited a little of its sibling museum's outer facelessness, making a very French use of space within and boasting much greenery without. Entering from the Parkway, virtually across the street from the Franklin Institute (see above), you'll contemplate *The Thinker* contemplating other things, then pass through an imposing arch to a front garden of hardy shrubs and trees surrounding a fish pond. Before going into the museum, study the *Gates of Hell.* These gigantic doors reveal an awesome power to mold metal by the force of passionate imagination.

The galleries were restored to their original sparkle in 1989. The main hall holds authorized casts of *John the Baptist, The Cathedral,* and *The Burghers of Calais.* Several of the side chambers and the library hold powerful erotic plaster models, along with Steichen photographic portraits of Rodin.

Admission: Donation requested. Free with same-day admission ticket from the Philadelphia Museum of Art (see above).

Open: Tues–Sun 10am–5pm. **Bus:** 76.

U.S. Mint, 5th and Arch Sts. ☎ **597-7350.**

The U.S. Mint building was the first authorized by the government during Washington's first term. Fortunately for us, the present edifice, diagonally across from Liberty Bell Pavilion (see above), turns out enough cash to keep us all solvent, about 1,500,000 coins every hour. This is one factory tour that's quite stingy with free samples, but a self-guided walk through the process has its own rewards.

The coinage process involves melting raw metal, rolling it to coin thinness, punching out blanks from these sheets, and pressing designs on them. The metal slabs and coils look cherry red from the heating they undergo, and after the coins are done a counting machine automatically sews lots of 5,000 into bags, headed for Federal Reserve Banks. Points along the route have prerecorded explanations, if you wish to listen (ever wonder how the layers in composite coins stick together?).

Admission: Free.

Open: Basic hours 9am–4:30pm. Sept–April, Mon–Fri only; Sat-added May–June; open-daily July–Aug. **Closed:** New Year's Day, Christmas. **Bus:** 5, 48, 76.

The University of Pennsylvania Museum of Archaeology and Anthropology, 33rd and Spruce Sts. ☎ **898-4890.**

Higher buildings may have left its Romanesque brickwork more secluded, but considering its contents, this museum has still seen quite a bit of the world. The University of Pennsylvania, which celebrated its centennial in 1986–87, got into archeology and anthropology on the ground floor, and hundreds of excavations have endowed it with Benin bronzes, biblical inscriptions, Mesopotamian masterpieces, Pre-Columbian gold, and artifacts of every continent.

The museum is intelligently explained. The basement Egyptian galleries, including colossal architectural remains from Memphis and "The Egyptian Mummy: Secrets and Science," are family favorites. Probably the most famous excavation display, located on the third floor, is a spectacular Sumerian trove of jewelry and household objects from the royal tombs of the ancient city of Ur. Adjoining this, huge cloisonné lions from Peking's (now Beijing's) Imperial Palace guard Chinese court treasures and tomb figures. The Ancient Greek Gallery in the classical-world collection, renovated in 1994, has 400 superb objects such as red-figure pottery—a flower of Greek civilization— and an unusual lead sarcophagus from Tyre that looks like a miniature house. Other galleries display Native American and Polynesian culture and a small but excellent African collection of bronze plaques and statues.

The glass-enclosed Museum Café, overlooking the museum's inner gardens, serves cafeteria-style snacks and light meals from 8:30am to 3:30pm weekdays, 10am to 4pm Saturday, and 1 to 5pm Sunday. The Museum Shop has cards and objects brought back by world-hopping graduate archeologists, and The Pyramid Shop has children's items. There's also a very active range of events throughout the year.

Admission: $5 donation adults, $2.50 students and seniors; free for children under 6.

Open: Tues–Sat 10am–4:30pm, Sun 1–5pm. **Closed:** Mon, holidays, and summer Sun Memorial Day–Labor Day. **Bus:** 21, 30 (from 30th Street Station), 40, 42, and 90.

Neighborhoods

Philadelphia is a collection of neighborhoods more than it is a uni-fied metropolis. Many neighborhoods have special interest for the visitor because of their history, ethnicity, architecture, or attractions. Below are short descriptions designed to alert you to the possibilities of several neighborhoods. Many individual attractions are discussed elsewhere in this chapter.

CHINATOWN

By 1885 several hundred Chinese lived in the area centered around Race Street between 8th and 11th streets, which today is known as Chinatown.

Nowadays it's largely a commercial neighborhood, with Chinese restaurants, groceries, and gift shops abounding. (Also of interest to tourists is the fact that it's only five minutes from the new Convention Center and many of the city's largest and cheapest parking facilities are located here.) Strolling through Chinatown, you'll pass under the **Chinese Friendship Gate** at 10th and Arch streets, the largest authentic Chinese gate outside China.

See Chapter 6 for specific restaurant recommendations.
Bus: 17, 23, 33, 44, 48.

GERMANTOWN

On the original route west to Reading, Germantown is one of the most ancient settlements in Philadelphia, and it was founded by German émigrés attracted by Penn's religious tolerance. See Chapter 11 for more details.

Transportation: SEPTA commuter rail or bus 23 from Center City.

MANAYUNK

★ This neighborhood, four miles up the Schuylkill River from Center City, has rocketed to gentility in the last five years, with many of the city's hottest boutiques, galleries, and café/restaurants on Main Street, overlooking a 19th-century canal adjoining the river. Emerging from 19th-century textile mills and abandoned storefronts, Manayunk now celebrates a June-long renaissance, replete with pro-cycling races, open houses, and street fairs. There's not much here in the way of highbrow history, but it's still a picturesque and vital place for an afternoon stroll.

Favored restaurants include **Jake's,** 4365 Main St. (☎ **483-0444**), now a second-generation hit with strong multicultural flavors; **Kansas City Prime,** 4417 Main St. (☎ **482-3700**), a reasonable and splashy steak-and-lobster catch; **Le Bus,** 4266 Main St. (☎ **487-2663**), for comforting down-home hearth meals and breads; and **Sonoma's,** 4411 Main St. (☎ **483-9400**), frigid in decor but "Italifornian" in cuisine. For a break from strolling, the 1993 **Manayunk Farmers Market** at 4120 Main St. has a food court and canal-side deck, along with free parking (a rarity here) and 25 great stalls; open Thursday through Saturday from 8am to 7pm, Sunday 9am to 5pm. I also love **Le Petite Gourmet,** across from Le Bus at 4311 Main St.

Bus: 27, 32, and 61 from Center City; Main Street is the continuation of East River Drive (Kelly Drive) above the Philadelphia Museum of Art.

OLDE CITY

★ Olde City, a rough rectangle overshadowed by the Benjamin Franklin Bridge just north of Independence National Historical Park, is an eclectic blend of row houses dating from William Penn's time, 19th-century commercial warehouses, and 20th-century rehabs à la SoHo in New York City. Highlights from this era include **Christ Church, Elfreth's Alley** (the oldest continuously inhabited street in the country), and **Loxley Court,** between 321 and 323 Arch Street. Many of these 17th- and 18th-century row houses crumbled as loft warehouses accommodated Victorian port activity. The neighborhood gentrified very rapidly from the 1960s until the late 1980s, with lots of crafts and art galleries and their artists. If you're interested in either the very old or the very new, this is the place to spend a few hours, and the odd alleyways between the city grid streets provide nooks for quaint and quiet cafés and shops. The first Friday night of every month is like a giant block party, with all the galleries and stores open until 8pm. See Walking Tour 2 in Chapter 8.

Transportation: SEPTA bus or subway line to 2nd Street. Bus 5 goes north on 3rd Street, south on 2nd Street.

QUEEN VILLAGE & SOUTH STREET

QUEEN VILLAGE   On a pleasant day you'll want to walk south from Society Hill along the Delaware or 2nd Street (known as "Two Street" among old Philadelphians). The Swedish originally settled this area, along with river islands below the confluence with the Schuylkill. The National Park Service administers **Gloria Dei** (1700), the Swedes' oldest church in the state, and the **American-Swedish Historical Museum** is nearby. Lots of small, reasonable cafés and bistros here.

Bus: 64.

SOUTH STREET   Located below Society Hill and above Queen Village, South Street was the city limit in the plan Thomas Holmes drew up for William Penn. Artists, free spirits, and late-night activity do make it the most bohemian area of Center City. At any hour of the day or night, you'll find something happening on South Street.

Don't look for history here. Most of the colonial structures on South and Bainbridge streets succumbed years ago to drab storefronts. With many bookstores, hoagie shops, handcrafted contemporary furniture stores, natural-food stores, European cafés, and art galleries, the South Street renaissance spreads from 2nd to 9th streets, with offshoots into Bainbridge.

Bus: 40.

SOCIETY HILL

This neighborhood, loosely bounded by Walnut and Lombard streets and Front and 7th streets, takes its name from a group of businessmen, the Free Society of Traders, who William Penn persuaded to settle here. Today it's a fashionable section of the old city, just south of Independence National Historical Park, where you can stroll among restored Federal, colonial, and Georgian homes. Two of Philadelphia's finest houses, the **Hill-Physick-Keith House,** 321 S. 4th St. and the **Powel House,** 244 S. 3rd St., are open for guided tours (see the full descriptions, above). For further coverage, see Walking Tour 1 in Chapter 8.

Bus: 5, 21, 40, 42, 76.

SOUTH PHILADELPHIA

The rest of the nation first heard of South Philadelphia when Sylvester Stallone brought his Rocky character to silver-screen fame (ironically, the character is definitely from another "hood," Kensington), but this community was one of the earliest settlements along the Delaware. Dutch and Swedish settlers arrived here in the early 17th century and since then have been joined by people of many nations. Successive waves of Jewish and Italian immigrants arrived at Pier 53 in the 19th and 20th centuries. In the 1940s southern blacks joined a longstanding black community, and since the 1950s many Lebanese, Koreans, and Southeast Asians have made South Philly their home. Today it is Philadelphia's most colorful and ethnically diverse neighborhood, although the stereotypes and most of the restaurants and bars are Italian.

Transportation: The Broad Street subway line runs through South Philadelphia with stops at Ellsworth-Federal, Tasker-Morris, Snyder, Oregon, and Pattison streets. Buses through the neighborhood are 5, 23, 47, 50.

UNIVERSITY CITY

West Philadelphia was farmland that didn't begin to be settled until the first permanent bridge across the Schuylkill in the 1810s. Things didn't really pick up until the **University of Pennsylvania** moved here from 9th and Chestnut streets in the 1870s, though. You ought to wander through the main campus, both for the architecture and for the suitably preppie students. Locust Street has been converted into a walk, and if you stroll west you'll come to an intersection with mobile fruit and refreshment vendors; they're out daily, with student-size prices. On the way back, enter the original college quadrangle, built in 1895 but based on Oxford and Cambridge models, with just a touch of Dutch gables. When classes are in session, the *Daily Pennsylvanian* lists cultural events, such as **Annenberg Theater** productions. This area is also home to **Drexel University: Children's Hospital** and **University Hospital:** and the **Civic Center,** host of many quality shows from boats to horticulture and antiques. **Bus:** 21, 42.

Outdoor Art & Plazas

Since the late 1950s, Philadelphia has required that all new developments dedicate 1% of the total cost of the project toward public art. As a result, a burst of modern art has joined the inevitable war memorials, Alexander M. Calder's massive program for city Hall, and the early sculpture placed in Fairmount Park. Of the dozens of pieces, the most notable seem to be Claes Oldenburg's 1976 *Clothespin,* an enigmatic symbol of union opposite City Hall at 15th and Market streets; Robert Indiana's 1978 *LOVE,* a slickly ironic statement opposite the Visitors Center at 16th Street and John F. Kennedy Boulevard; Isamu Noguchi's 1984 *Bolt of Lightning—Franklin Memorial,* at the entrance to the Franklin Bridge at 5th and Vine streets; and, of course, the replica of Rocky Balboa in victory, at the entrance to the Sports Complex in South Philadelphia.

Parks & Gardens

Bartram's Gardens, 54th St. and Lindbergh Blvd. ☎ **729-5281.**

On the banks of the Schuylkill 20 blocks below the University of Pennsylvania in West Philadelphia, historic Bartram's Gardens is the birthplace of American horticulture and a reawakening Sleeping Beauty of an institution. Started in 1731, the National Historic Landmark includes the original and just-restored Bartram 1731 homestead and 44 acres of natural gardens. John and William Bartram were America's first botanists and naturalists. The city purchased the estate in 1891, but only in the last decade have the gardens been researched and "unmothballed."

Admission: Grounds free; house $4.50 adults, $2 children 6–18; under 6 free. Tours $4.50–$9.

Open: May–Oct, Wed–Sun, 10am–4pm; Nov–Apr, Wed–Fri, 10am–4pm. Parking is available. **Bus:** 52.

★ Benjamin Franklin Parkway

The Parkway, a broad diagonal swath linking City Hall to Fairmount Park, wasn't included in Penn's original plan. In the 1920s, however, Philadelphians thought that a grand boulevard in the style of the Champs Elysées was appropriate. In summer, a walk from the Visitors Center to the "Museum on the Hill" becomes a flower-bedecked and leafy stroll; but all year round, institutions, public art, and museums enrich the avenue with their handsome facades. Most of the city's parades and festivals pass this way too. Bus route 76 goes both ways every 20 minutes.

Logan Circle, outside the Academy of Natural Sciences (see above), used to be Logan Square before the Parkway was built, and it was a burying ground before becoming a park. The designers of the avenue cleverly made it into a low-landscaped fountain, with graceful figures cast by Alexander Sterling Calder. From this point, you can see how the rows of trees make sense of the diagonal thoroughfare, although all the buildings along the Parkway are aligned with the grid plan. Under the terms of the city permit, The Four Seasons Hotel now landscapes and tends Logan Circle, to magnificent effect.

★ Fairmount Park

The northern end of the Benjamin Franklin Parkway leads into Fairmount Park, the world's largest landscaped city park, with 8,700 acres of winding creeks, rustic trails, and green meadows, plus 100 miles of jogging, bike, and bridle paths. In addition, this park features more than a dozen historical and cultural attractions, including some of America's finest colonial mansions, as well as gardens, boathouses, America's first zoo, and a Japanese teahouse. See the map on the facing page and the description (p. 165) of Philadelphia Zoological Gardens.

Bus: 76 to the Museum of Art entrance; 38 or 76 to the upper end.

Penn's Landing

Philadelphia started out as a major freshwater port, and its tourism and services are slowly nudging it back to the water after 50 years of neglect. You can always see freighters moving along the Delaware, but in the 20th century Philadelphia turned its back on the urban waterfront, building I-95 between the city and its port. In 1945, 155 "finger" piers jutted out into the river; today, only 14 remain. Since 1976 the city has added on parts of a complete waterfront park at Penn's Landing, on Columbus Boulevard (formerly Delaware Avenue) between Market and Lombard streets, with an assembly of historic ships, performance and park areas, cruise facilities, and a marina Penn's Landing has a piecemeal but pleasantly spacious feeling.

Fairmount Park

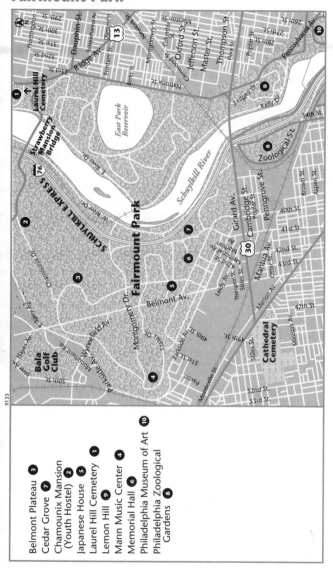

Belmont Plateau **3**
Cedar Grove **7**
Chamounix Mansion (Youth Hostel) **2**
Japanese House **5**
Laurel Hill Cemetery **1**
Lemon Hill **9**
Mann Music Center **4**
Memorial Hall **6**
Philadelphia Museum of Art **10**
Philadelphia Zoological Gardens **8**

Attractions in and Near the Water: Several ships and museums are berthed around a long jetty at Spruce Street. Queen Elizabeth "parked" her yacht *Britannia* here in 1976. From the north down, these attractions are the Philadelphia Maritime Museum's **Workshop on the Water** (☎ 925-7589), a wood boatbuilding shop and classroom housed in a 1939 lighter barge (open from May through

October only, Wednesday to Sunday from 9:30am to 4:30pm); the **USS** *Becuna* (☎ **922-1898**), a guppy-class submarine, commissioned in 1944 to serve in Admiral Halsey's South Pacific fleet; the **USS** *Olympia* (☎ **922-1848**), Admiral Dewey's own flagship in the Spanish-American War (☎ **922-1898**), with a self-guided three-deck tour (admission to both the *Olympia* and the *Becuna* is \$3.50 for adults, \$1.75 for children under 12; both are open daily from 10am to 5pm); a **water taxi** (☎ **351-4170**) at \$3 one ride or \$5 all day that serves the restaurants and clubs on the piers north of the Benjamin Franklin Bridge as well as the New Jersey State Aquarium in Camden; and the *Liberty Belle II* (☎ **629-1131**), a harbor cruise boat. Anchoring the southern end is the **Chart House** restaurant (see Chapter 6 for details).

Another group of boats occupies the landfill directly on the Delaware between Market and Walnut streets. In front of the Port of History and Maritime museums at Walnut Street, the *Riverbus* (☎ toll free, **800/634-4027**) plies a round-trip route to the New Jersey State Aquarium in Camden every half hour (\$2 adults, \$1.50 children). The *Gazela Primiero,* a working three-masted, square-rigged wooden ship launched from Portugal in 1883, has visiting hours on Saturday and Sunday from 12:30 to 5:30pm when it's in port. Adjoining are the *Barnegat Lightship* and *Jupiter* a tugboat; all the above are operated by the Philadelphia Ship Preservation Guild (☎ **923-9030**); admission \$3 adults, \$2 students.

Museums: Opposite Walnut Street, between the two dock areas, the contemporary poured-concrete structure north of the Olympia jetty is the **Port of History Museum.** The museum was opened by the city in December 1981 as a center for international exhibitions of the fine arts, crafts, and design. The **Philadelphia Maritime Museum** now at 321 Chestnut St., will be moving the Maritime to this much-underused site, if \$2.7 million needed for renovations comes through. It's open Wednesday to Sunday from 10am to 4:30pm; admission is \$2 for adults, \$1 for children. Even if you don't go in, take in the great views from the upper terraces.

Plaza and Park Areas: On a walk north along the river, charts help you identify the Camden shoreline opposite and the funnels of passing freighters. The hill that connects the shoreline with the current Front Street level has been enhanced with the festive **Great Plaza,** a multitiered, tree-lined amphitheater that hosts many Visitors and Convention Bureau festivals, such as Jambalaya Jam. The terrace itself is a wonderfully landscaped and informative view of quirky facts about the site and city, with plenty of benches. At Delaware Avenue and Spruce Street, the sober 1987 **Philadelphia Vietnam Veteran Memorial** lists 641 local casualties.

Bus: 21 on Chestnut Street to Front Street. No. 42 east on Chestnut Street to 2nd Street, down 2nd Street to Dock Street, and then down to Walnut Street. **On Foot:** Pedestrian walkways across Front Street on Market, Chestnut, or Walnut street; Front Street connects directly at Spruce Street. **Car:** Take I-95 northbound or southbound. Take Exit 16 and make a left onto Columbus Boulevard. From I-76, take I-676 to I-95 south. Ample parking is available on site.

★ **Philadelphia Zoological Gardens**, 34th St. and Girard Ave. ☎ **243-1100.**

The Philadelphia Zoo was the nation's first, opened in 1874, but by the late 1970s the 42 acres tucked into West Fairmount Park were run-down and had few financial resources. It has since become a national leader with more than 1,500 animals—many of them endangered species—in interesting and comfortable habitat settings.

The latest attractions are the white lions: two females arrived in June 1993, and one had a cub in April 1994, among a pride of six cats. The 1992 $1^1/_2$ acre, $6-million Carnivore Kingdom houses snow leopards and jaguars; feeding time is around 11am for smaller carnivores, 3pm for tigers and lions. The "World of Primates" exhibit gives you the illusion of forest life among gorillas, orangutans, and ring-tailed lemurs. The monkeys themselves now have a new home on four naturally planted islands, where a variety of primate species live together naturally (summer only; segregated in Primate Pavilion in winter).

The old Bird House has been changed to the new Jungle Bird Walk, where you can walk among free flying birds. Glass enclosures have been replaced with wire mesh so that the birds' songs can now be heard from both sides.

As part of the zoo's concern to educate zoo visitors about animal life, a spectacular children's exhibit, the Treehouse ($1), was opened in 1985. It contains six larger-than-life habitats for kids of all ages to explore—oversize eggs to hatch from, an oversize honeycomb to crawl through, and a four-story ficus tree to climb through and see life from a bird's-eye view. The very popular Camel Rides ($1.50) start next to the Treehouse. A Children's Zoo (50¢) portion of the gardens lets your kids pet and feed some baby zoo and farm animals; this closes 30 minutes before the zoo proper. Pony rides ($1) are also given here.

Other exhibits cover polar bears, the Reptile House, which bathes its snakes and tortoises with simulated tropical thunderstorms, and cavorting antelopes, zebras, and giraffes that coexist on the "African Plains" exhibit. For a quick survey, consider the Monorail Safari ($2 for adults, $1.50 for children, 50¢ more on weekends; operated April to November). It circumnavigates the zoo in 20 minutes and has a prerecorded narrative.

The zoo has several snack areas and the Picnic Grove has been recently refurbished with new landscaping and Victorian benches and tables. A cafeteria-style restaurant, that lets you sit in its airy, sky-lit dining room or at outdoor tables, stands next to the Rare Mammal House.

Admission: $8 adults, $5.50 seniors and children 2–11; under 2 free. A family membership for $40 might be worth it. Parking spaces for 1,800 cars; $4 per vehicle. Fidelity Bank MAC ATM machine near North Gate.

Open: Daily, Mon–Fri 9:30am–5pm, Sat–Sun 9:30am–6pm. Closed on Thanksgiving Day, Christmas, and New Year's Day. **Bus:** 76. **Trolley:** 15.

⭐ **Thomas H. Kean New Jersey State Aquarium,** 1 Riverside Dr., Camden, N.J. 08103. ☎ **609/365-3300.**

The aquarium opened in 1992 as a first step in reclaiming the once-vital (and now denuded) Camden waterfront with a hotel and marina, trade center, and office and commercial development. As an aquarium, it fills a true niche in the Delaware Valley.

Up to 3,000 fish live here. The main attraction is a 760,000-gallon tank, the second largest (next to Epcot Center's) in the country, with stepped seat/benches arranged in a Greek amphitheater on the first floor. Three times a day, a diver answers questions through a "scuba phone." This window wall is by far the best; parents of younger children will find few other flat edges for them to stand on for views. This tank also contains sharks, rockfish, a shipwreck, and a mock-up of the underwater Hudson canyon off the Jersey coast. Also on the first floor is an open-air New Jersey beach setting complete with shorebirds, a pine barrens stream, and salt marsh. The second floor has "Dangers of the Deep," a 1994 shark exhibit with 30 sharks, along with more didactic explorations of ocean life, fish senses, and water babies. Touch tanks are on both floors.

Between the ticket pavilion and the building is a reproduction of a Delaware Water Gap brook stocked with trout and a 170,000-gallon outdoor tank with nine Atlantic seals. The Riverview Café serves basic fast-food; outdoor seating is frequently windy.

Admission: $9 adults, $7.50 students and seniors, $6 children 2–11; children under 2 free. Reserved admission through Ticketmaster, toll free **800/922-6572,** recommended (handling charge). *Delawhale Riverbus* ferry from Port of History Museum at Penn's Landing is $3 adults, $1.50 children, each way.

Open: Daily, 9:30am–5:30pm. **Closed:** Thanksgiving Day, Christmas, and New Year's Day. **Directions by Car:** From I-676 eastbound (Vine Street Expressway/Ben Franklin Bridge or westbound from I-295/New Jersey Turnpike, take Mickle Boulevard exit and follow signs.

3 Cool for Kids

Philadelphia is one of the country's great family destinations: It has a great many attractions for different types of kids, and because it's so walkable and neighborhoodlike, a respite or an amenity is never far away. Since so many of the family attractions are explained in more detail elsewhere in this or other chapters, I'll restrict myself to a list of the basics. See "Fast Facts: Philadelphia" in Chapter 4 for babysitting options.

A monthly publication on what to do with kids in Philadelphia, *Metrokids,* is available at the Visitors Center, 16th Street and John F. Kennedy Boulevard.

MUSEUMS & SIGHTS   In Center City, there are the **Please Touch Museum,** 210 N. 21st St.; **Franklin Institute,** Benjamin Franklin Parkway and 20th Street; and the **Academy of Natural Sciences,** the Parkway and 19th Street. The **Free Library of Philadelphia Children's Department** across Logan Circle at Vine and 19th streets is a joy, with a separate entrance, 100,000 books and microcomputers in a playgroundlike space, and weekend hours. Around Independence Hall are the **Liberty Bell** at Market and 5th streets; **Franklin Court,** between Market and Chestnut streets at 4th Street; the waterfront at **Penn's Landing,** off Front Street; and, of course, the guided tour of **Independence Hall.** You can also take the ferry from Penn's Landing to the new **aquarium** in Camden. In Fairmount Park you'll find the **zoo** in West Fairmount Park.

SHOPPING AREAS   These include **Liberty Place** on Chestnut Street between 16th and 17th streets, with a wonderful food court and distinguished rotunda and escalators; **The Gallery** at Market East, at Market and 8th streets; the **Bourse** at Chestnut and 5th streets; and the outdoor **Head House Square** at Spruce and 2nd streets. Also, see the children's fashions and toys sections of Chapter 9.

PLAYGROUNDS   **Rittenhouse Square** at 18th and Walnut streets has a small playground and space to eat and relax. Other imaginative urban playgrounds on this side of Center City are **Schuylkill River Park** at Pine and 26th streets and at 26th Street and the Benjamin Franklin Parkway, opposite the art museum. From Society Hill, try **Delancey Park** at Delancey between 3rd and 4th streets (with lots of fountains and animal sculptures to climb on) or **Starr Garden** at 6th and Lombard streets. The best in Fairmount Park is the **Smith Memorial** (head north on 33rd Street, then take a left into the park at Oxford Avenue).

EXCURSIONS   There are **Sesame Place,** based on public TV's *Sesame Street,* in Langhorne, the 1993 Carousels at *Peddler's Village* in Lahaska, and the working and participatory **Quarry Valley Farm** in Lahaska—all in Bucks County; plus there's **Ridley Creek State Park** and its 17th-century working farm in Montgomery County. And for fascinating real life, try a couple of days on a working Amish farm.

ENTERTAINMENT   The **Philadelphia Marionette Theater** has heavily reserved programs in Belmont Mansion in West Fairmount Park; call **879-1213** for details.

The **Philadelphia Museum of Art** has dedicated itself to producing Sunday-morning and early-afternoon programs for children, without fail and at minimal or no charge. Your kids could wind up drawing pictures of armor or watching a puppet theater about dragons, visiting a Chinese court, or playing with Picasso-style cubism. Call **763-8100** or **684-7500** for 24-hour information.

4 Organized Tours

BUS TOURS   Those double-decker buses decked out like trolleys, clanging along the city streets, are from **American Trolley Tours** (☎ 333-0320). Tours of historic areas, conducted by guides in the climate-controlled vehicles, leave mornings and afternoons from the Visitors Center at 16th Street and John F. Kennedy Boulevard and from the Independence National Park Visitor Center at 3rd and Walnut streets. Cost is $10 Adults, $5 children.

WALKING TOURS   To explore the 4-block historic district at your own pace with the benefit of a prerecorded commentary, you can rent an Audio Walk and Tour cassette player and tape. The narration describes each attraction as you walk from site to site. An illustrated souvenir map comes with the tape. Players and cassettes are available daily from **AudioWalk and Tour,** Norman Rockwell Museum, 6th and Sansom streets (☎ 925-1234), on Washington Square. It's open from 10am to 6pm on Monday to Saturday, 11am to 5pm on Sunday. The charge is $8 for one person, $16 for two to six people. If you prefer to purchase the cassette and use your own recorder, the cost is $10.95.

   If you wish to stroll through this area or one of the other neighborhoods without the benefit of prerecorded commentary, consult the walking tours described in Chapter 8.

   Many specific-interest tours—African-American Philadelphia, architectural walks, Jewish sites in Society Hill, the Italian Market—exist: check the Visitors Center (☎ 215-636-3300) for information.

CANDLELIGHT STROLLS   From May through October, evening tours of the historic area, led by costumed guides, leave from Welcome Park at 2nd and Walnut streets at 6:30pm. Tours of Olde City (Friday) and Society Hill (Saturday) take 90 minutes; the cost is $5 for adults, $4 for seniors and children. Call **735-3123** for reservations with **Centipede Tours, Inc.,** 1315 Walnut St.

HORSE & CARRIAGE TOURS   To get the feel of Philadelphia as it was (well, almost—asphalt's a lot smoother than cobblestones!), try a narrated horse-drawn carriage ride. Operated daily by the **76 Carriage Co.** (☎ 923-8516), tours begin at 5th and Chestnut streets in front of Independence Hall from 10am to 5pm, with later hours in summer. Fares range from $10 for 15 minutes to $20 for 30 minutes, with a maximum of four per carriage. Reservations are not necessary.

BOATING TOURS   Two choices are available at Penn's Landing. The *Spirit of Philadelphia* (☎ 923-1419) at the Great Plaza combines lunch, brunch, or dinner with a cruise on a 600-person passenger ship, fully climate-controlled, with two enclosed decks and two open-air decks. Trips, which require reservations, are $20 and up, for 2- or 3-hour trips.

The *Liberty Belle II* (☎ 629-1131) boards, from Lombard Street Circle, near the Chart House restaurant at the southern end of Penn's Landing, and can, accommodate up to 475 passengers on three decks. Meals and prices are comparable.

With the opening of the new Thomas H. Kean New Jersey State Aquarium, the new *Riverbus* (☎ toll free **800/634-4027**) provides a 10-minute crossing from a landing just outside the Port of History (and soon-to-be Maritime) Museum at Penn's Landing. There's a large interior to the ferry, and the views of the Philadelphia skyline are great, although the aquarium is the only possible destination in New Jersey. Departures from Penn's Landing are on the quarter hour and every half hour thereafter; from Camden, on the hour and half hour. Summer hours are Monday to Friday from 7am to 6:45pm, Saturday from 9am to 11:45pm, and Sunday from 9am to 7:45pm; from mid-September through mid-May, the weekend hours are curtailed at 6:45pm. One-way fares are $3 for adults, $1.50 for children and seniors.

Philadelphia Water Taxi visits all the attractions on the Delaware River waterfront, with stops at restaurants, clubs, Penn's Landing, and the aquarium. It swings by every 30 minutes, day and night; if you have a specific request, call **800/225-0256** and give code 44221 for automatic paging. One-trip fare is $3, and a $5 pass is good all day and night.

---

5 · Sports & Recreation

Spectator Sports ─────────────

Philadelphia fields teams in every major sport and boasts a splendid complex at the end of South Broad Street to house them all. **Veterans Stadium** (☎ 686-1776) is a graceful bowl with undulating ramps that can seat 58,000 for the Phillies in baseball and 68,000 for the Eagles in football. **The Spectrum II,** being built at press time, will house the pro hockey and basketball teams; until it does, these teams will continue to rely on **The Spectrum** (☎ 336-3600), which also functions as one of the best rock-concert forums around. It also hosts the U.S. Pro Indoor Tennis Championships.

All these are next to one another and can be reached via a 10-minute subway ride straight down South Broad Street to Pattison Avenue ($1.50). The same fare will put you on the SEPTA bus C, which goes down Broad Street slower but with a bit more safety late at night.

Professional sports aren't the only game in town, though. Philadelphia has a lot of colleges, and **Franklin Field** and the **Palestra** dominate West Philadelphia on 33rd below Walnut Street. The Penn Relays, the first intercollegiate and amateur track event in the nation, books Franklin Field on the last weekend in April. Regattas pull along the Schuylkill all spring, summer, and fall, within sight of Fairmount Park's mansions.

A call to Teletron (☎ toll free **800/233-4050**) or TicketMaster (☎ **212/507-7171** in New York, **215/336-2000** in Philadelphia) can get you tickets in many cases before you hit town.

BASEBALL   The 1993 National League pennant-winning **Philadelphia Phillies,** Box 7575, Philadelphia, PA 19101 (☎ **463-1000** for ticket information, **463-5300** for daily game information), play at Veterans Stadium, Broad Street and Pattison Avenue. Day games usually begin at 1:35pm, regular night games at 8:05pm on Friday, at 7:35pm on other days. When there's a twilight doubleheader, it begins at 5:35pm. The huge computerized scoreboard and the antics that follow a Phillies home run will leave you laughing and amazed.

Tickets for the Phillies have been increasing rapidly in cost; box seats overlooking the field are around $15, and the cheapest bleacher seats are $6, if you're over 14.

Don't forget to book now for the July 9, 1996, all-star game.

BASKETBALL   The **Philadelphia 76ers,** Box 25050, Philadelphia, PA 19147, play about 40 games at the Spectrum between early November and late April. Call **339-7676** for ticket information; tickets range from $9 to $39. There's always a good halftime show, and the promotion department works overtime with special nights, especially involving 76ers T-shirts.

There are five major college basketball teams in the Philadelphia area, and the newspapers print schedules of their games. Most games are at the Palestra, with tickets going for $4 to $6. Call **898-4747** to find out about ticket availability.

BICYCLING   The CoreStates Pro Cycling Championship, held each June, is actually a top world event in the cycling world. The 156-mile races starts and finishes along the Benjamin Franklin Parkway, and watching the cyclists climb "The Wall" in Manayunk is terrifying.

BOATING   From April to September, you can watch regattas on the Schuylkill River, which have been held since the earliest days of "the Schuylkill Navy" a century ago. The **National Association of Amateur Oarsmen** (☎ **769-2068**) and the **Boathouse Association** (☎ **686-0052**) have a complete schedule of races. The Dad Vail Regatta is one of the best known.

FOOTBALL   Football, without a doubt, is Philadelphia's favorite sport. It will take all your ingenuity to come up with tickets for a game, since all **Philadelphia Eagles** games (at Veterans Stadium, Philadelphia, PA 19148) are popular, especially now that their young, talented team is getting on track. Call **463-5500** for ticket advice. The games start at 1 or 4pm, and tickets cost up to $45.

HORSE RACING   The racing closest to Philadelphia is at **Garden State Park,** N.J. 70 and Haddonfield Road in Cherry Hill, New Jersey (☎ **609/488-8400**), which runs thoroughbred races in the spring and harness (standard bred) races in the fall. Call for exact schedules, but the first post time is usually 7:30pm Wednesday through Saturday.

For more thoroughbred horse racing, **Philadelphia Park** (the old Keystone Track) has races every day except Monday from January 1 to February 13 (post time is 12:30pm) and from June 15 to December 31 (post time is 1pm). The $2.50 admission includes parking and a program; the park is on Street Road in Bensalem, half a mile from Exit 28 on the Pennsylvania Turnpike. Call **639-9000** for information.

Off-Track Wagering Parlor and Dining, 7 Penn Center, 1635 Market St., on the concourse and lower mezzanine levels (☎ **245-1556**), features 270 color video monitors and an ersatz art deco design; it brings the wagering to you in the comfort of Center City.

ICE HOCKEY The Spectrum rocks to the **Philadelphia Flyers,** led by star Eric Lindros, from fall to spring, and their tickets are even harder to get than the Eagles'. Call **755-9700** for ticket information; if you can find some, they'll cost between $12 and $23.

TENNIS Philadelphia has several world-class tournaments annually. February brings the **Comcast U.S. Professional Indoor Championships** at the Spectrum, with $600,000 in prize money; call **947-2530** for information. The women's invitational held at Haverford College (☎ **896-1000**) in late September has attracted top players, including Martina Navratilova, and Advanta sometimes brings the **Virginia Slims tour** to the Civic Center in November. The late-summer **USTA Senior Men's Grass Court Championships** at Germantown Cricket Club (☎ **438-9900**) can bring you face-to-face with former greats.

TRACK & FIELD The city hosts the **Penn Relays,** the oldest and still the largest amateur track meet in the country, in late April at Franklin Field. There's a November annual **Marathon** and a September **Philadelphia Distance Run,** a half-marathon; the latter is becoming a world-class event. Call **686-0053** for more details.

Recreation

I can't begin to make a complete list of the number of leisure sports and recreations in which you can indulge while in Philadelphia, so contact the Department of Recreation (☎ **686-3600**). The following is merely a sample:

BICYCLING Plaisted Hall, the Fairmount Park rental spot for bikes and boats, burned in 1993; there are plans to reconstruct it, but no public rentals at press time. If you do get or have a bicycle, the biking is flat near the Schuylkill on either side but loops up sharply near Laurel Hill Cemetery or Manayunk.

Call the **Bicycle Club of Philadelphia** at **440-9483** for specific neighborhood rental recommendations.

BOATING As above, city rowers and sailors must await Plaisted Hall's reconstruction. Outside of the city, try **Northbrook Canoe Co.,** north of Route 842 in Northbrook on Brandywine Creek

(☎ 793-2279) or **Point Pleasant,** on Route 32, seven miles north of the New Hope exit on I-95, with canoeing, inner tubing, and rafting on the Delaware River (☎ 297-8823).

FISHING   It's true that **Pennypack Creek** and **Wissahickon Creek** are stocked from mid-April through December with trout and muskie and provide good, even rustic, conditions. A required license of $12.25 for Pennsylvania residents or $20.25 for out-of-staters is available at such sporting-goods stores as I. Goldberg or at the Municipal Services Building near the Visitors Center. Out of the city, **Ridley Creek** and its **state park** (☎ 566-4800) and **Brandywine Creek** at Hibernia Park (☎ 384-0290) are stocked with several kinds of trout.

GOLF   The city of Philadelphia operates 5 municipal courses out of the more than 100 in the region. All have 18 holes, and the current fees range from $14 to $21 on Monday to Friday and $16 to $24 on Saturday and Sunday. Call **877-8813** or the numbers below for more information on **Cobbs Creek and Karakung** (two adjacent courses in West Philadelphia, which are considered the best), 7800 Lansdowne Ave. (☎ 877-8707); **Franklin D. Roosevelt,** 20th Street and Pattison Avenue (☎ 462-8997); **J.F. Byrne,** Frankford Avenue and Eden Street (☎ 632-8666); **Juniata,** M and Cayuga streets (☎ 743-4060); and **Walnut Lane,** Walnut Lane and Henry Avenue (☎ 482-3370).

Among the better county-operated courses outside the city are **Montgomeryville Golf Club,** Route 202 (☎ 855-6112); **Paxon Hollow Golf Club,** Paxon Hollow Road in Marple Township (☎ 353-0220); and **Valley Forge Golf Club,** 401 N. Gulph Rd., King of Prussia (☎ 337-1776).

HEALTH CLUBS   The Four Seasons, the Rittenhouse, Sheraton Society Hill, or The Hotel Atop the Bellevue have in-house facilities at an additional charge. Most other moderately priced hotels have at least a few exercycles and an aerobics space; the KormanSuites, four blocks from Logan Circle, has a full gym room, pool, and tennis court. Near Society Hill, the top health club that admits per-day guests is **Gold's Gym** with Ron Jaworski, 834 Chestnut St. (☎ 592-9644). Opened in fall 1988, it provides an understanding staff, large Universal weight machines, free weights, and several aerobics classes daily. The cost is $10 per guest, and it's open Monday to Friday from 6am to 10pm, Saturday and Sunday from 8am to 5pm. Another alternative closer to midtown is the **12th Street Gym,** 204 S. 12th St. (☎ 985-4092), a revamped version of a 1930s men's club with a pool, courts for squash and racquetball, and weights and aerobics rooms. It's open Monday to Friday from 5:30am to 11pm, Saturday from 7am to 7pm and Sunday from 9am to 7pm. The basic rate is $10 per guest.

HIKING   **Fairmount Park** (☎ 686-3616) has dozens of miles of paths, and the extensions into Wissahickon Creek are quite unspoiled, with dirt roads and no auto traffic. Farther afield,

Horseshoe Trail (☎ **664-0719**) starts at Routes 23 and 252 in Valley Forge State Park and winds 120 miles west marked by yellow horseshoes until it meets the Appalachian Trail.

HORSEBACK RIDING There are many riding trails in Fairmount Park, the Wissahickon, and Pennypack Park within city limits, and Chester and Brandywine counties are famous for horsemanship, from fox hunting to the Winterthur Point-to-Point races. Unfortunately, insurance costs have made it unprofitable for most riding stables to allow visitors to rent horses. The only riding stable within city limits that does is **Harry's Riding Stables** (☎ **335-9975**), 2240 Holmesburg Ave., Philadelphia, PA 18136, near Pennypack Park. It's open seven days a week from 9am to 8pm, and seven or eight horses are always available, with rates of $20 per hour for guided trail rides with western saddles. The easiest directions from Center City are via I-95 north. Take the Academy Road exit, following the exit ramp to the left onto Academy until the first light; then turn left onto Frankford Avenue and continue for two miles. After a hill, there's an intersection with a railroad trestle that passes above Frankford. Before going under it, take the dirt road on the left and follow 300 yards to the white barn building on the right.

ICE SKATING It rarely gets cold enough in Philadelphia for ponds and creeks to freeze over. Although the city operates several artificial rinks, your best bet for finding a rink near Center City is the **University of Pennsylvania Class of '23 Rink**, 3130 Walnut St. (☎ **387-9223**). It's open daily to the public for about two hours in the afternoon.

RUNNING & JOGGING Here again, **Fairmount Park** has more trails than you could cover in a week. An 8.2-mile loop starts at the front of the Museum of Art, up the east bank of the Schuylkill, across the river at Falls Bridge, and back down to the museum. At the north end, Forbidden Drive along the Wissahickron has loops of dirt/gravel of five miles and more, with no traffic. The Benjamin Franklin Bridge path from 5th and Vine Street is 1.8 miles each way.

SWIMMING Philadelphia has 86 municipal swimming pools, and many hotels have small lap versions. Municipal pools are open daily from 11am to 7pm and are free. Two of the best are **Cobbs Creek,** 63rd and Spruce streets, and **FDR Pool,** Broad and Pattison in South Philadelphia. Call **686-1776** for details.

TENNIS Some 115 courts are scattered throughout **Fairmount Park,** and you can get a tourist permit for their use by calling **686-0152.** You might also try the University of Pennsylvania's indoor courts at the **Robert P. Levy Tennis Pavilion,** 3130 Walnut St. (☎ **898-4741**). Rates are $27 for two visitors until 4pm, $31 for two after 4pm.

8

Strolling Around Philadelphia

PHILADELPHIA IS PROBABLY THE MOST COMPACT, WALKABLE MAJOR CITY IN the United States, just as it was in 1776. It's fascinating to see the progress of the centuries and unexpected juxtapositions on a random walk, always noting that the nearer you are to the Delaware, the older (and smaller) the buildings are likely to be. The walking tours mapped out below are specifically designed to enhance your ability to cover the most worthwhile attractions and to recoup your strength along the way.

Walking Tour 1
Historic Highlights & Society Hill

Start   Visitor Center, 3rd and Walnut streets.
Finish   City Tavern, 2nd and Walnut streets; optional extension to Penn's Landing.
Time   6–7 hours.
Best Time   Start between 9 and 11am to avoid hour-long waits for Independence Hall tours.

Start your tour at the:

1. **Visitor Center** in Independence National Historical Park, 3rd and Walnut streets. This handsome brick building was built for the 1976 bicentennial celebration and maintains spotless restrooms and cool benches as well as providing pamphlets and maps of the park, free tickets (limited in number) for the Bishop White and Todd Houses (see below), and information about special tours or special daily events. The John Huston–directed film *Independence* is shown without charge every half hour. There is a small exhibition area and a substantial quality gift shop and bookstore.

Just opposite the Visitor Center is the:

2. **First Bank of the United States** (1795), not open to the public but a superb example of Federal architecture, is as old and as graceful as a Roman rotunda. The idea for this building derived from Alexander Hamilton. The reliance on the currencies of the 13 new states hampered commerce and travel, and he proposed a single bank for loans and deposits. The bank started in Carpenters' Hall but moved here on the completion of the building. The mahogany American eagle on the pediment over the Corinthian entrance columns is a famous—and rare—example of 18th-century sculpture.

Behind the First Bank, the Park Service cleared much of the block (as throughout the Historic Park area), leaving historic structures and establishing 18th-century gardens and lawns. To the right, a walkway leads to the midblock:

3. **Carpenters' Hall,** which was a newly built guildhall when the First Continental Congress met here in 1774

(see Chapter 7 for a fuller description). Just north of this, you'll find:

4. **New Hall,** a modern copy of a hall built in 1791 for rent by the Carpenters' Company. With the federal government based in Philadelphia until Washington, D.C., was habitable, the U.S. government took the space as the first headquarters of the War (now Defense) Department. This building now houses the Marine Corps Museum, since the marines were founded at Tun Tavern nearby; you can see uniforms and swords that fought on "the shores of Tripoli" as well as the medals that decorated those uniforms.

   A few steps north on Chestnut Street proper is:

5. **Pemberton House,** another reconstruction. Joseph Pemberton, a Quaker merchant of sugar and Madeira, had just built this fine Georgian home when the Second Continental Congress cut back on British imports, in the aftermath of the gunfire at Concord and Lexington. After Pemberton went bankrupt, the house was razed in 1862, only to be reconstructed a century later. The development of the infant U.S. army and navy are the subjects here. The exhibit features continuous showings of a military history of the Revolutionary War, which followed a slow pattern of British advances, defeats, and regroupings to the south. The main theater of battle moved from Boston in 1775 to New York, New Jersey, and Pennsylvania in 1777 and 1778, with a final bottleneck for the British at Chesapeake Bay in 1781. The second floor's highlight is the model gun deck of a frigate, with instructions on maneuvering for a naval battle.

   The other side of Chestnut Street is a handsome collection of 19th-century banks and commercial facades, including the 1867 **First National Bank** at no. 315 and the **Philadelphia National Bank** at no. 323. The Chestnut Street entrance to:

6. **Franklin Court** is nestled here (see Chapter 7 for a full description of this wonderful tribute to Benjamin Franklin's final home and spirit).

   Virtually across Chestnut Street at no. 321 is the:

7. **Philadelphia Maritime Museum** (☎ **925-5439**). It's been a marvelous museum here for about 25 years, but it may be merging with the Port of History Museum at Penn's Landing (see Chapter 7). If it hasn't yet, it's a fine exploration of how the Delaware Valley influenced the history and trade of the region. The building itself is an unusual Victorian specimen, in yellow brick and granite facings. Admission is $2.50 for adults, $1 for students and seniors. The museum is open Tuesday to Saturday from 10am to 5pm, Sunday from 1 to 5pm.

   Walk west along Chestnut Street or back in the gardens, crossing 4th Street until you get to the midblock:

Walking Tour
Historic Highlights & Society Hill

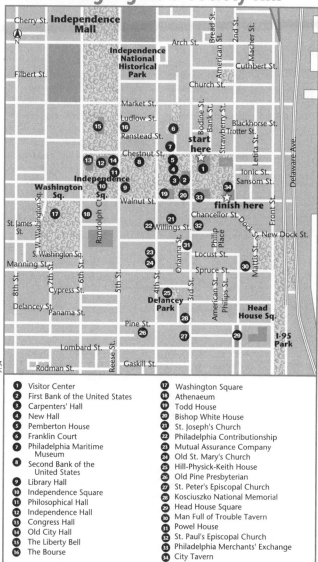

1. Visitor Center
2. First Bank of the United States
3. Carpenters' Hall
4. New Hall
5. Pemberton House
6. Franklin Court
7. Philadelphia Maritime Museum
8. Second Bank of the United States
9. Library Hall
10. Independence Square
11. Philosophical Hall
12. Independence Hall
13. Congress Hall
14. Old City Hall
15. The Liberty Bell
16. The Bourse
17. Washington Square
18. Athenaeum
19. Todd House
20. Bishop White House
21. St. Joseph's Church
22. Philadelphia Contributionship
23. Mutual Assurance Company
24. Old St. Mary's Church
25. Hill-Physick-Keith House
26. Old Pine Presbyterian
27. St. Peter's Episcopal Church
28. Kosciuszko National Memorial
29. Head House Square
30. Man Full of Trouble Tavern
31. Powel House
32. St. Paul's Episcopal Church
33. Philadelphia Merchants' Exchange
34. City Tavern

8. **Second Bank of the United States.** Its strong
   Greek columns have corroded somewhat, but the bank still
   holds interest. The Second Bank was chartered by Congress
   in 1816 for a term of 20 years, again at a time when the
   country felt that it needed reliable circulating money. The
   building (1819–24), designed like the Merchants Exchange

by William Strickland, is adapted from the Parthenon, and the Greeks would have been proud of its capable director, Nicholas Biddle. An elitist to the core, he was the man Andrew Jackson and his supporters had in mind when they complained about private individuals controlling public government. Urged by Henry Clay for reasons of political capital, Biddle asked prematurely for the renewal of the charter, making this the issue of the 1832 presidential election. "Old Hickory" vetoed the charter and won the election; this increased the money supply but ruined Biddle and the bank.

The federal government bought the building in 1844 for about half its original cost of $500,000 and used it as the Customs House until 1934. The National Park Service uses it as a portrait gallery of early Americans. The collection contains many of the oldest "gallery portraits" in the country, painted by Charles Willson Peale and once displayed in the Long Room of Independence Hall. Sully, Neagle, Stuart, and Allston also are represented.

Refueling Stop

A **tea garden** in the adjoining holly garden, staffed by the Friends of Independence National Historical Park, provides ice cream and cool drinks from noon to 5pm from mid-May to mid-September.

Just west of the Second Bank lies:

9. Library Hall, the 1954 reconstruction of Benjamin Franklin's old Library Company, which was the first lending library of its type in the colonies. The Library Company is now at 1314 Locust St. (see Walking Tour 3, below); this graceful Federal building houses the library of the American Philosophical Society based across the street. The collection is entrancing, including Franklin's will, a copy of William Penn's 1701 Charter of Privileges, and Jefferson's own handwritten copy of the Declaration of Independence. The exhibits center on the history of science in America. The library's hours follow the park schedule.

The pull of great government will lead you across 5th Street to:

10. Independence Square, where on July 8, 1776, John Nixon read the Declaration of Independence to the assembled city. You'll be at the back of the official trio of **Independence Hall, Congress Hall,** and **Old City Hall** on Chestnut Street between 5th and 6th streets.

On your right is:

11. Philosophical Hall, the home of the American Philosophical Society. The society is a prestigious honor roll of America's outstanding intellects and achievers founded by Ben Franklin. The building's interior is not open to the public, but look for traces of old Georgian springing into new Federal architecture, such as fan-shaped windows, larger windows, and more elaborate doorsteps. In Franklin's day, philosophers were more often than not industrious young men with scientific and learned interests, so the society included mostly intellectually advanced citizens.

To your left is:

12. **Independence Hall,** grand, graceful, and one of democracy's true shrines (see Chapter 7 for a full description). Ranger-led 35-minute tours depart every 15 minutes or so. The two flanking buildings, **Old City Hall** (Supreme Court Building) and **Congress Hall,** were intended to balance each other, and their fanlighted doors, keystoned windows, and simple lines reward you from any angle. They were used by a combination of federal, state, county, and city governments during a relatively short period (this can get confusing).

13. **Congress Hall** (1787) held the U.S. Congress for 10 years; Washington departed public life from here. The House of Representatives met downstairs, and the place looks somewhat modern with wall-to-wall carpeting and venetian blinds. It's hard to get mahogany desks and leather armchairs of such workmanship now, though. Washington was inaugurated here in 1793 and John Adams in 1797. Look for the little corners where representatives could smoke, take snuff, and drink sherry during recess. Watching the House and Senate from the balconies became a popular social activity, and if debate was boring one could always admire the ceiling moldings.

14. **Old City Hall** (1790), at the corner of 5th and Chestnut streets, contained the only unaccounted-for branch of the federal government, the U.S. Supreme Court under Chief Justice John Jay. (Until the present City Hall anchored Center Square, this was the City Hall from 1800 to 1870.) The park uses the restored courthouse to describe the judiciary's first years.

Across Chestnut Street from this central trio is:

15. **The Liberty Bell,** once located in Independence Hall, was moved for the bicentennial celebration to the special glass pavilion across Chestnut Street (see Chapter 7 for a full description).

Just to the east of the Liberty Bell is:

16. **The Bourse,** a superb example of late Victorian architecture. It has been renovated as a mall in the form of two arcades surrounding an expansive skylit atrium. The Bourse, built from 1893 to 1895 as a merchants exchange, handsomely combines a brick-and-sandstone exterior with a cool and colorful interior.

Refueling Stop

The Bourse's spacious, cool ground-floor **Food Court** is open Monday, Tuesday, and Thursday from 10am to 6pm; Wednesday, Friday, and Saturday until 8pm; and Sunday from 11am to 6pm.

Now cut through Independence Square to the greenery at the southwest corner. This is Washington Square:

17. Washington Square, seems a little unbalanced since Independence National Historical Park opened up the block to the northeast—but it's just as expansive and even more leafy than when it was the town's pasture. In the 1840s, this was the center of fashionable Philadelphia; but many handsome structures have been razed to make room for chunky offices and apartment houses. Only the 1823 southwest corner Federals, the **Meredith-Penrose House** and its neighbors, give you a sense of what was lost. It now holds the Tomb of the Unknown Soldier from the Revolutionary War, complete with eternal flame. The square has also housed Philadelphia publishing for 150 years, with **Lea and Febiger** and **J. B. Lippincott** at no. 227. The massive white building on the north face has been redeveloped, but the Curtis Publishing Co. once sent out the *Saturday Evening Post* and other magazines from here. The **Norman Rockwell Museum** in the corner section pays tribute to the *Post*'s frequent illustrator (see Chapter 7 for a fuller description). As you enter, admire that luminous mosaic mural *The Dream Garden:* Tiffany Studios executed a drawing by Maxfield Parrish, and the 1916 hand-fired masterpiece must be worth a fortune.

That solid, Italianate Revival brownstone (1845–47) on Washington Square East is the:

18. Athenaeum, a corner of virtually unchanged 19th-century society (see Chapter 7 for a fuller description).

Society Hill wasn't named that because only the upper crust of Philadelphia lived there in colonial times, although they did. The name refers to the Free Society of Traders, a group of businessmen and investors persuaded by William Penn to settle here with their families in 1683. The name applies to the area east of Washington Square between Walnut and Lombard streets. Most of Philadelphia's white-collar workers, clerics, teachers, importers, and politicos have lived and worked here.

In 1945 nobody would have considered walking through the decrepit and undesirable neighborhood, despite the hundreds of colonial facades. That's all changed now because of a massive urban-renewal project. Many new housing developments fit in discreet courts; they, too, use simple brick facades that blend with the Georgian exteriors superbly.

It's a good idea for you to know something about colonial and Federal architecture as you stroll about the vital blocks because many homes aren't open to individual tours. Brick is everywhere, since English settlers found clay by the Delaware's banks—but the types and the construction methods have varied over 150 years. Generally, houses built before the 1750s, such as the **Trump House** at 214 Delancey St., have two-and-a-half stories, with two rooms per floor and a dormer window jutting out of a steep gambrel roof. An eave usually separates the simple door and its transom windows from the second level. Careful bricklayers liked to alternate the long and short sides of bricks, called "stretchers" and "headers"; this was named Flemish Bond, and the headers often were glazed to create a checkerboard pattern. Wrought-iron boot scrapers flank the doorsteps.

Houses built in Philadelphia's colonial heyday soared to three or four stories—taller after the Revolution—and adopted heavy Georgian cornices (the underside of a roof overhang) and elaborate doorways. The homes of the truly wealthy, such as the **Powel House** at 244 S. 3rd St. and the **Morris House** at 235 S. 8th St., have fanlights above their arched brick doorways; the **Davis-Lenox House** at 217 Spruce St. has a simple raised pediment. Since the Georgian style demanded symmetry, the parlors often were given imaginary doors and windows to even things out. The less wealthy lived in "trinity" homes—one room on each of three floors, named for faith, hope, and charity. Few town houses stood on individual plots; the **Hill-Physick-Keith House** at 321 S. 4th St. is the exception that proves the rule.

Federal architecture, which blew in from England and New England in the 1790s, is less heavy (no more Flemish Bond for bricks) and more graceful (more glass, with delicate molding instead of wainscoting). Any house such as the **Meredith House** at 700 S. Washington Sq., with a half story of marble stairs leading to a raised mahogany door, was surely constructed after 1800. Greek Revival elements such as rounded dormer windows and oval staircases became the fashion from the 1810s on. Three of the few Victorian brownstones at 260 S. 3rd St. once belonged to Michel Bouvier, Jacqueline Kennedy Onassis's great-great-grandfather.

If you're here in May, don't pass up **Philadelphia Open House** to view the bandbox interiors of dozens of homes (volunteered by proud owners). Call **215/928-1188** for information.

Of course, houses aren't all there is to Society Hill. Georgian and Federal public buildings and churches, from **Head House Square** and **Pennsylvania Hospital** to **St.**

Peter's and **St. Paul's,** may make you feel as if you'd stumbled onto a movie set. But all of the buildings are used—and the area works as a living community today. Fine restaurants and charming stores cluster south of Lombard, too, especially around Head House Square (1803) at 2nd and Lombard streets.

Continuing on your tour, leave the Athenaeum and walk west one block on St. James Street, then go north on 5th Street and take a right turn onto Walnut Street for two blocks. As you walk down Walnut to 3rd Street, the restored row houses will catch your eye, with their paneled doors and shutters, bands of brick or stone between floors, and small lozenges of painted metal. These last are fire-insurance markers—all early American cities had terrible fire hazards, and Philadelphia, led by Benjamin Franklin, was the first to do anything about them. Groups of citizens formed such companies as the Philadelphia Contributionship, which suggested prevention strategy with leather fire buckets and lightning rods. The plaques of leafy green trees (on the Mutual Assurance Company) or four clasped hands (on the Contributionship) functioned as advertisements but also helped the firemen identify which houses they were responsible for saving. Now the houses belong to park offices and the Pennsylvania Horticultural Association, which maintains an 18th-century formal garden. At the corner of Fourth and Walnut streets is the:

19. Todd House (1775). Tours (for 10 at a time) are required, and tickets by advance reservation are available gratis at the Visitor Center. John Todd, Jr., was a young Quaker lawyer of moderate means. His house cannot compare to that of Bishop White, but it is far grander than Betsy Ross's. Todd died in the 1793 epidemic of yellow fever, and his vivacious widow married a Virginia lawyer named James Madison, the future president. The Todds lived and entertained on the second floor, since Todd used the ground-floor parlor as his law office.

Farther down Walnut toward 3rd Street is the other park-run dwelling, the:

20. Bishop White House, at no. 309. Tours (for 10 at a time) are required; again, free tickets can be obtained at the Vision Center. This house is on one of the loveliest row-house blocks in the city, giving the park a life-size example of how a pillar of the community lived in Federal America. Bishop White (1748–1836) studied for the Anglican priesthood in England, then returned home to tend Christ Church; he later founded Episcopalianism after the break from the mother country. He traveled abroad with Benjamin West and was Franklin's warm friend, which his upstairs library shows. White stayed out of politics as an expression of his belief in the separation of church and state. Notice the painted cloth floor in the entrance hall—after 20 varnishings, it survived muddy boots remarkably well. And, in case you take the indoor "necessity" for granted, remember that outhouses provided the only relief on most colonial property. The library shows "modern" tastes, with Sir Walter Scott's Waverley novels, the *Encyclopaedia Britannica,* and even the Koran alongside traditional religious texts. The collection has survived intact.

Across the street, the park has purchased property and made a garden that exposes the side of:

21. **St. Joseph's Church,** the first Roman Catholic church in Philadelphia (see Chapter 7 for a description). It's much more intriguing if you enter through Willing's Alley and walk back to 4th Street and south half a block because an iron gate and archway conceal it well.

Not many tourists know about them, but the headquarters of 18th-century fire-insurance companies are open to the public, in the heart of Society Hill. In a neighborhood that was as moneyed and as crowded as this one, fire was a constant danger. Groups of subscribers pledged to help one another in case of fire—there were no fire departments in those days! Ironically, many companies required a complete inventory of the possessions before they would set premiums, and these inventories have guided modern restorers of run-down town houses. You can see the insurance plaques on the upper facades of many homes. In fact, the:

22. **Philadelphia Contributionship** (1836), 212 S. 4th St. (below Walnut Street), has used the "Hand-in-Hand" mark since 1752. This facade is all Greek Revival—with a gorgeous limestone entrance, columns, and balustrades leading to the front door. Architect Thomas Walter also designed the dome and the House and Senate wings on the U.S. Capitol. Entrance to the building is free, and it's open Monday to Friday from 10am to 3pm. The normal exhibition displays old leather fire-fighting equipment, desks with inkwells, and the original policy statement and list of members. If you call **627-1752** ahead of time, you'll get to view some of the gorgeous boardrooms, with their veined marble fireplaces and maple dining-room chairs.

Just below Locust Street on the same block is the:

23. **Mutual Assurance Company,** at no. 240. The company combines two splendid row houses built in 1750 and 1826. Mutual's firemark is a green tree, because when Philadelphia Contributionship decided to stop insuring houses close to sidewalk trees in 1784, Mutual went for the arbor-loving market. It's well worth a tour—call **925-0609** to arrange one and enter through the garden on Locust Street. The furniture (mostly Empire, with some

Hepplewhite) and art are as outstanding as the pedigree. The back parlor of the Cadwallader House has famous portraits of Washington and Franklin.

Just opposite the Mutual is **Bingham Court,** a 1967 adaptation within the Society Hill idiom of brick row houses. A few doors down 4th Street is:

24. **Old St. Mary's Church,** the most important Roman Catholic church during the Revolution (this was the "Sunday" church, as opposed to St. Joseph's weekday chapel). The interior is fairly prosaic, but the paved graveyard is a picturesque spot for a breather, with some interesting headstones and memorials.

The corner of Spruce and 5th streets is a good place to take a breath, with the town houses of **Girard Row** in front of you. Half a block to the west at 426 Spruce St., Thomas U. Walter, the architect of the Capitol's dome in Washington and a master of Greek Revival, designed a Baptist church in 1830 that has been modified as the **Society Hill Synagogue** (run by Romanian immigrants at the turn of the century and by Conservative Jews more recently).

A half-block down 4th Street is the:

25. **Hill-Physick-Keith House,** at no. 321, possibly the nicest residential structure in Society Hill (see Chapter 7 for a fuller description). Take a few steps east on adjoining Cypress Street to reach **Delancey Park,** a delightful playground with sturdy activities and a group of stone bears that are perfect for photo props.

More Georgian and Federal church facades appear at the corners of 4th and Pine streets. One is Old Pine:

26. **Old Pine Presbyterian,** with its enormous raised facade and forbidding iron fence, didn't always look like a Greek temple, but that's what makes it worth seeing (it's free and open daily from 9am to 5pm). The Penns granted the Presbyterians this land in perpetuity, and the first sanctuary took shape in 1768. The double Corinthian columns, inside and out, were added in 1830, after the occupying British soldiers burned most of the interior. Everything is linear at Old Pine: The portico leads into a rectangle of pews, and slim pillars support a gallery with an elaborately carved rail of flowers and dentils. The altar will surprise you—it's just a dais backed by elaborate columns and entablature. You'll find it hard to believe that this filigree is of wood and not clay or plaster.

Old Pine Community Center on the block south to Lombard Street leads to South Street's funky shopping and nightlife district just beyond. Walk east on Pine Street to:

27. **St. Peter's Episcopal Church** (1761), an example of classic Georgian simplicity (see Chapter 7 for a fuller description).

Farther east, at 301 Pine St., is the:

28. **Kosciuszko National Memorial,** a double 1775 Georgian that housed this Polish engineer and soldier who turned the tide for American forces at Saratoga. He returned to the United States, exiled from Poland, in search of a pension from Congress and lived here in 1797 while pursuing this.

Now follow Pine Street to 2nd Street, the major north-south route through Philadelphia in colonial days. Open markets were a big part of urban life. In fact, no colonial native would recognize Market Street today without its wooden sheds that covered stalls from Front to 6th streets and its narrow cart paths on both sides. One place he or she would recognize, though, is:

29. **Head House Square,** built in 1803 in the middle of 2nd Street as a place where fire companies and shoppers could congregate. Head House itself, that brick shed with a cupola that once held a fire bell, trails a simple brick arcade between Pine and South streets. In those days, market took place on Tuesday and Friday at dawn. Butter and eggs were sold on the west side, meat under the eaves, and herbs and vegetables on the river side. Fish sellers were relegated to the far sidewalks (it isn't hard to imagine why). Now, in summer, craftspeople spread out their goods, especially on weekends.

Refueling Stop

Dickens Inn, 421 S. 2nd St., and several other Head House Square restaurants make excellent lunch or snack stopovers; Dickens Inn (open from 11:30am daily) has an English afternoon tea, as well as a tempting ground-floor bakery. For great on-street chocolate chip cookies or brownies, go to **Koffmeyer's Bakery** on 2nd near Lombard.

Now head up 2nd Street, perhaps cutting in to Delancey Street between 2nd and 3rd streets, north on Philip Street's quaint court, and back to 2nd on Spruce Street. Across the street from the 1765 **Abercrombie House** (one of the tallest colonial dwellings in America) is the:

30. **Man Full of Trouble Tavern,** at 127 Spruce St. This place re-creates a big part of Capt. James Abercrombie's life. The Knauer Foundation has restored the tavern to its original appearance with Delft tiles, a cagelike bar, and tables with Windsor chairs and pewter candlesticks. The 1760 tavern bordered Little Dock Creek then, and sailors and dock workers ate, drank, and roughhoused here nightly. The attic held a mariner's flophouse—you'll wonder how because of the narrow gables called pent eaves. Admission is now by group appointment only.

Just up the hill are **Society Hill Towers** (1964), the I. M. Pei twins that signaled the 20th century and stick out like 30-story sore thumbs today. It's best to walk west back to 3rd Street, then north to a stunning block of row-house mansions including **Bishop Stevens** at no. 232, with its cast-iron balcony; **Atkinson House** at no. 236, which today conceals an indoor pool; and **Penn-Chew House** at no. 242, owned by the grandson of William and the last colonial governor of Pennsylvania. The one of these mansions that you can enter is:

31. Powel House, at 244 S. 3rd St. This home of Philadelphia's last colonial and first U.S. mayor beats the Bishop White House by far (see Chapter 7).

Across the street is:

32. St. Paul's Episcopal Church (1761), at 225 S. 3rd St., founded because of another example of Philadelphia's religious tolerance. Christ Church on Market Street had a young clergyman, William McClenachan, who preached such radical notions as the separation of church and state. Since the High Anglican church refused to license his speech, St. Paul's was set up as his "bully pulpit," and the money for the Georgian hall was raised through donations and lotteries. Now it houses the headquarters of the denomination's community services, inside beautiful pre-Revolutionary wrought-iron gates and marble-topped enclosing walls. If you head for the second floor (open Monday to Friday from 9am to 5pm), you can still see most of the original chancel.

Standing at the corner of 3rd and Walnut streets, you can't miss the:

33. Philadelphia Merchants' Exchange (1832), a masterwork by William Strickland (described in Chapter 7). It's not open to the public. Heading toward 2nd Street and the river, you'll cross one of my favorite spaces, a broad area of cobblestones covering Dock Street (Dock Creek in Penn's day) and the Delaware River beyond. The **Ritz 5** movie house on your left offers fine independent fare; the **Pasta Blitz** just beyond is the umpteenth restaurant trying to make it in this unwelcoming site. Soon you'll approach the reconstructed:

34. City Tavern restaurant and gardens from the rear. This was the most opulent and genteel tavern and social hall in the colonies and the scene of many discussions among the Founding Fathers. Unlike most of the city's pubs, it was built in 1773 with businessmen's subscriptions, to assure its quality. In fact, George Washington met with most delegates to the Constitutional Convention for a farewell dinner here in 1787. The park now operates the City Tavern as a concession, which serves lunch and dinner (see Chapter 6).

If you choose to continue toward the Delaware via the pleasant pedestrian extension of Walnut Street and the staircase at its end, you'll pass between the new **Sheraton Society Hill** hotel and the famed **Old Original Bookbinder's** restaurant, winding up more or less in front of the **Port of History Museum** on the waterfront. Consult the "Penn's Landing" description in the "Neighborhoods" section of Chapter 7 for more details.

Walking Tour 2
Olde City

Start   Visitor Center, 3rd and Walnut streets.
Finish   Market Place East, 7th and Market streets.
Time   3–5 hours.
Best Time   No later than 3pm, to avoid museum closings. If contemporary art and socializing is your interest, the first Friday of every month brings special late hours for all galleries, all cafés, and many historic attractions.

Olde City is an intriguing blend of 18th- and even 17th-century artisan row houses, robust 19th-century commercial structures, and 20th-century rehabs of all of the above featuring artist lofts and galleries. See it now; many property owners would rather demolish than rehab, and classics on 110–112 S. Front St. for example, were destroyed despite public outcry in March 1994. Walk out the south entrance of the **Visitor Center** and along the narrow lane adjoining **City Tavern** to:

1. **Welcome Park,** the site of the Slate Roof House where William Penn granted the "Charter of Privileges" (now at the Library Hall off Independence Square) in 1701. The pavement bears a massive and whimsical map of Penn's City, with a time line of his life and times on the walls.

   Next door is the **Thomas Bond House,** a restored 1769 Georgian row house that's now a bed-and-breakfast (see Chapter 5 for more information). Walk along the block-long **AMC Olde City 2** cinemas to:

2. **Front Street,** which actually lapped at the river's edge throughout colonial times. A walk north brings you to **Hillary's Ice Cream** at the corner of Chestnut Street and the possibility of exploring Penn's Landing (see "Neighborhoods" in Chapter 7 for a description) via a beautifully terraced park. However, head back to the florid **Corn Exchange Bank** at 2nd and Chestnut streets, then turn right onto one of the liveliest blocks in the historic area.

Refueling Stop

The block of "Two Street" between Chestnut and Market contains good restaurants such as **Serrano's, Los Amigos,** and **Rib-It** (see Chapter 5 for details). My favorite is the quiet, cool seating for 40 at the rear of **Foodtek Market and Café,** with great hot and cold charcuterie. It's open on Monday to Thursday from 7:30am to 1am, on Saturday and Sunday until 2am.

Once you hit Market Street (High Street in colonial times), you'll find a different world of sharp discount clothing and wholesale toy stores. The many alleyways between Front and 5th streets, with names like **Trotter Street, Black Horse Alley, Bank Street,** and **Strawberry Lane,** testify to the activities and preoccupations of colonial residents. A particular favorite facade of mine is that of the:

3. **Norwegian Seaman's Church,** at 22 S. 3rd St. This William Strickland 1837 gem with Corinthian columns and granite steps is now a nightclub called Revival. If you haven't taken Walking Tour 1, go now to:

4. **Franklin Court,** the final home and reconstructed post office of Benjamin Franklin between 3rd and 4th streets. Standing on Market Street, you'll find the graceful spire of:

5. **Christ Church,** which is unmissable. Urban renewal removed the unsightly buildings that hid its walls from Market until the 1950s (see Chapter 7 for a fuller description of revolutionary Philadelphia's leading place of worship and its restful benches and adjoining cemetery).

It may be a bit early for another refueling stop, but the block of Church Street directly to the west of the church contains **Old City Coffee** at no. 221, a favorite place for marvelous coffee and light lunches. If by the time you get here the end of the day is approaching, duck underneath the Market Street ramp to I-95 at Front Street to reach **Panorama's** wine bar and bistro.

Walk north along Front Street for four short blocks to get the flavor of 1830s warehouses, such as the **Girard** at 18–30 N. Front St. and **Smythe** at 101 Arch St. If you continued north and east, you would come to the attractive new clubs and restaurants on the water, such as **Meiji-en, Rock Lobster,** and **The Beach Club.** Instead, take a left onto:

6. **Elfreth's Alley** (from 1702), the oldest continuously occupied group of homes in America (see "More Attractions" in Chapter 7 for a full description). The homes are tiny, and you can enter no. 126. Several courts are perfect for wandering.

Back on 2nd Street with its china and restaurant supply stores, you might detour north for a minute to look at **2nd Street Art Building,** housing the Clay Studio and NEXUS galleries, or to visit the:

7. **Fireman's Hall Museum,** at Quarry Street, housed in an 1876 firehouse.

Walking Tour—Olde City

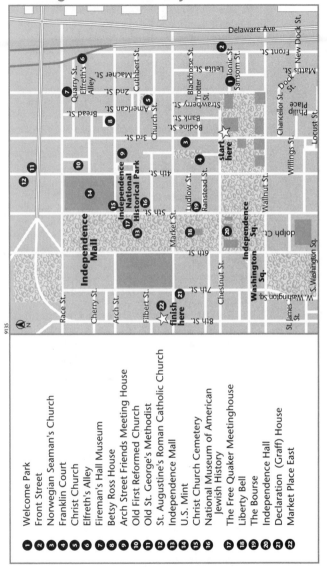

Welcome Park
Front Street
Norwegian Seaman's Church
Franklin Court
Christ Church
Elfreth's Alley
Fireman's Hall Museum
Betsy Ross House
Arch Street Friends Meeting House
Old First Reformed Church
Old St. George's Methodist
St. Augustine's Roman Catholic Church
Independence Mall
U.S. Mint
Christ Church Cemetery
National Museum of American Jewish History
The Free Quaker Meetinghouse
Liberty Bell
The Bourse
Independence Hall
Declaration (Graff) House
Market Place East

Then head south to Arch Street, turning right onto it to the:

8. **Betsy Ross House,** at no. 239 (see Chapter 7 for full details). It's a short walk through the house, but there's a large garden. Directly opposite are the **Mulberry Market,** an upscale deli with seating in the rear, and **Humphry Flags** if you're feeling patriotic.

Cross 3rd Street to the **Hoop Skirt Factory** at 309–313 Arch St., a light 1875 factory renovated in 1980, and the charming **Loxley Court** just beyond, designed by carpenter Benjamin Loxley in 1741. It stayed within the family until 1901. On the south side of the street is the:

9. **Arch Street Friends Meeting House,** the largest Quaker meetinghouse in America, a simple 1805 structure with a substantial history (see Chapter 7 for details). You could keep walking straight west one block to Independence Mall, but I recommend that you take a slightly gritty walk north on 4th Street to:

10. **Old First Reformed Church,** at 151 N. 4th St. Built in 1837 for a sect of German Protestants, the building survived a late 19th-century stint as a paint warehouse. Note that this church functions as a small and always full youth hostel during July and August nights (see Chapter 5 for details). Crossing under the gloomy piers of the **Benjamin Franklin Bridge,** you'll see:

11. **Old St. George's Methodist,** at 235 N. 4th St., the cradle of American Methodism and the scene of fanatic religious revival meetings in the early 1770s. The bridge was in fact built farther south to preserve it. On the other side of the street, below Vine, is one more church:

12. **St. Augustine's Roman Catholic Church.** It's another 18th-century building, this one built for German and Irish Catholics who couldn't make it south of Market Street. Villanova University, and the Augustinian presence in the United States, started here. This building is actually an 1844 structure, built to replace the original, which burned down during anti-Catholic riots. Now, keep walking west along the bridge to 5th Street, then head south along:

13. **Independence Mall,** a swath of urban renewal that bit off more than the Historical Park could chew. At the upper end of the Mall (Florist Street) is the bicycle and pedestrian entrance to the Benjamin Franklin Bridge; biking and walking across the bridge make thrilling but time-consuming expeditions. It's best to head down 5th Street, stopping at the:

14. **U.S. Mint,** one of the three places in the country that churns out U.S. coinage (see Chapter 7 for its hours and description). Just south of the U.S. Mint is:

15. **Christ Church Cemetery,** the resting place of Benjamin and Deborah Franklin and other notables (toss a coin through the opening in the brick wall for luck), and also the:

16. **National Museum of American Jewish History,** at 55 N. 5th St. The city of Philadelphia has a history of distinguished Jewish involvement in town affairs

almost as long as the life of the town itself. The museum, connected to the city's oldest congregation, commemorates this story (see Chapter 7 for a fuller description). You'll notice how much lower street level used to be by looking at the statuary outside.

In Independence Mall, a small building across from the Franklin graves is the:

17. **Free Quaker Meetinghouse,** run by the Park Service. These "Fighting Quakers," such as Betsy Ross, were willing to support the Revolutionary War; since this violated the tenets of pure Quakerism, they were read out of Arch Street Friends.

Now, recross Market Street to see the:

18. **Liberty Bell,** if you haven't seen it yet (see Chapter 7 for details). Near the Liberty Bell is:

19. **The Bourse,** a 19th-century exchange that now contains a food court and pleasant urban mall (a refueling stop described in Walking Tour 1). Reenter Independence Mall and you'll be in front of:

20. **Independence Hall,** with its two flanking buildings, **Congress Hall** and **Old City Hall.**

Continue west along Chestnut Street to 7th Street, and turn right onto a historic block containing the **Atwater Kent Museum** of city memorabilia, the **Balch Institute of Ethnic Studies,** and:

21. **Declaration (Graff) House,** a reconstruction of the lodgings where Thomas Jefferson drafted the Declaration of Independence. It is run by the National Park Service, with free daily admission. (All of the above are described more fully in Chapter 7.)

From the old to the new: Right behind Graff House on Market Street is a huge McDonald's designed for children; directly opposite it on Market Street is:

22. **Market Place East,** the converted and rehabilitated former home of Lit Brothers Department Store, a wrought-iron palace that's a block long (see the full description in Chapter 9). The below-ground food area contains an **Au Bon Pain** and **Pagano's** charcuterie.

Walking Tour 3
Midtown & the Parkway

Start   Visitors Center, 16th Street and John F. Kennedy Boulevard.
Finish   Logan Circle, intersection of 19th Street, Race Street, and the Benjamin Franklin Parkway.
Time   6 hours.
Best Time   No later than noon, to avoid museum closings.

Worst Time   Sunday, when many stores are closed, and Monday, when most museums are shuttered.

This tour encompasses the confident heart of 19th-century Philadelphia. If you've already sampled the charm and excitement of historic Philadelphia, the downtown area and southwest of Center City may seem anticlimactic. But there's plenty to see here, too, starting with the massive French Renaissance City Hall. Center Square and its environs were farmland or parkland during the 18th century. But as commercial buildings and loft warehouses began to dominate Olde City, old Philadelphia families began to consider Rittenhouse Square to be the fashionable part of town. Individual dwellings, such as Hockley House (1875) at 235 S. 21st St. and the present Art Alliance Building on Rittenhouse Square, coexist with attractive row houses such as those at 18th Street and Delancey Place. Churches, the Academy of Fine Arts (at Broad and Cherry), the Academy of Music (at Broad and Locust), and such private clubs as the Union League (at Broad and Sansom) enhanced the Victorian life-style.

The 20th century has added international-style skyscrapers to Penn Center, notably the PSFS Building and such postmodern structures as I. M. Pei's Commerce Square (41 stories, at Market and 21st streets) and Helmut Jahn's One and Two Liberty Place (61 and 54 stories, respectively, three blocks east). This is also a wonderful shopping, cultural, and restaurant area, catering to up-to-the-minute tastes.

Start your walking tour at the:

1. **Visitors Center,** run by the Philadelphia Convention and Visitors Bureau at 16th Street and John F. Kennedy Boulevard. The Visitors Center has it all in a shiny wedding cake of a building that's open daily from 9am to 6pm. Half-priced tickets to many evening events are sold here as well.

   Passing by Robert Indiana's *LOVE* statue, you'll reach:

2. **City Hall.** You can't help knowing where City Hall is, at the intersection of Broad and Market streets. This fanciful, exuberant hodgepodge graced with a huge statue of William Penn has free tours and elevators to the viewing area at Penn's feet. Until Liberty Place was built, Penn's hat was by custom the tallest point within city limits. (See Chapter 7 for full details.)

   Everyone wonders what that chiseled-looking building just north of City Hall with the single tower is—a church? No, it's the:

3. **Masonic Temple,** one of the world's largest (see Chapter 7 for a full description).

   Continue two blocks up North Broad Street to:

4. **Pennsylvania Academy of Fine Arts,** founded in 1804. This 1876 building is now overshadowed by the Philadelphia Museum of Art as "the" museum in town, but it hosts an excellent blend of the best in old and new

Walking Tour–Midtown & The Parkway

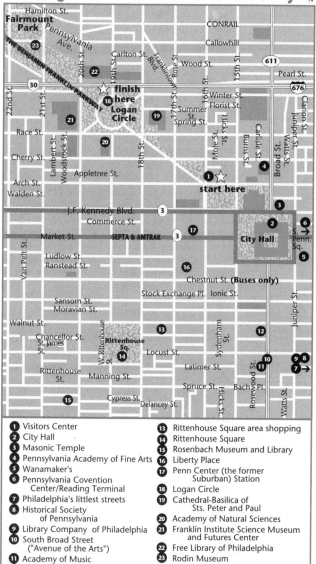

- 1 Visitors Center
- 2 City Hall
- 3 Masonic Temple
- 4 Pennsylvania Academy of Fine Arts
- 5 Wanamaker's
- 6 Pennsylvania Covention Center/Reading Terminal
- 7 Philadelphia's littlest streets
- 8 Historical Society of Pennsylvania
- 9 Library Company of Philadelphia
- 10 South Broad Street ("Avenue of the Arts")
- 11 Academy of Music
- 12 Hotel Atop the Bellevue
- 13 Rittenhouse Square area shopping
- 14 Rittenhouse Square
- 15 Rosenbach Museum and Library
- 16 Liberty Place
- 17 Penn Center (the former Suburban) Station
- 18 Logan Circle
- 19 Cathedral-Basilica of Sts. Peter and Paul
- 20 Academy of Natural Sciences
- 21 Franklin Institute Science Museum and Futures Center
- 22 Free Library of Philadelphia
- 23 Rodin Museum

American art, in a wonderful renovated High Victorian building (see Chapter 7 for details).

Now backtrack to City Hall and head east through:

5. **Wanamaker's,** now a shadow of its former self but still an impressive department store. It features an enormous pipe organ; an atrium; and "the Iggle," a central statue of our national bird that has been a rendezvous for generations of shoppers (see Chapter 9 for details).

Back on Market Street, you'll pass the classic international style **Philadelphia Savings Fund Society (PSFS) Building** skyscraper at 12th Street. Directly opposite that is:

6. **Reading Terminal,** once a commuter terminal but now the facade of the brand-new **Pennsylvania Convention Center** (see Chapter 7 for tour details). The **Reading Terminal Market,** midblock just north of Market Street, is one of the country's great surviving urban food markets (see Chapter 6 for the delicious details).

Three blocks south, Locust and 12th streets are the center for:

7. **Philadelphia's littlest streets,** a group of wonderfully charming row houses tucked into alleys and courtyards. My favorites are the art clubs of **South Camac Street** between 12th and 13th streets and between Locust and Spruce streets, followed by **Manning, Sartain, Quince,** and **Jessup** streets, between 11th and 12th streets at the same latitude. If you care to continue two blocks south, you'll find **Antique Row** lining Pine Street with galleries between 9th and 12th streets.

The 1300 block of Locust Street has two wonderful collections. The finest collection of colonial furniture and art in Center City won't be found at any museum but at the:

8. **Historical Society of Pennsylvania,** 1300 Locust St. (see Chapter 7 for a full description). The modern, connected:

9. **Library Company of Philadelphia,** at no. 1314, is the current home of Ben Franklin's original lending library. It contains 300,000 volumes, including Lewis and Clark's records of their 1804 expedition. Grand old houses lie across the street at no. 1319 and no. 1321 Locust.

From here, walk past the Doubletree Hotel Philadelphia to:

10. **South Broad Street,** once the undisputed cultural capital of the city, now picking up steam as a revitalized "Avenue of the Arts." For reasons of safety and convenience, the city is pushing to link this stretch in an unbroken series of theaters and performance halls. So far, the Philadelphia College of Art at Broad and Pine has become the University of the Arts; the ArtsBank renovation is complete; and construction of new homes for the Philadelphia Orchestra (funding is virtually assured) and for The Wilma Theater is pending. The:

11. **Academy of Music** is modeled on La Scala in Milan. It is open for daytime tours or evening performances of the Philadelphia Orchestra, one of the best ensembles in the country (see Chapter 10 for details). Walk one block north (passing Philadelphia's most opulent health club) to the:

12. **Hotel Atop the Bellevue,** the current incarnation of a grand 1901 hotel. Thomas Edison designed the lighting fixtures; it's worth a peek at the former lobby, now the site for the **Shops at the Bellevue** and the below-ground **Food Court** (public restrooms and refueling available). (see Chapters 5 and 6 for full information).

   Keep walking north to the **Union League** at Broad and Sansom streets, the most evident of Philadelphia's many private clubs; this one was formed and constructed in the flush of Civil War sentiment for the Republican party. Then backtrack to Walnut Street and next turn left to:

13. **Rittenhouse Square area shopping.** The blocks between Broad and 18th are dotted with the city's finest independent stores (see Chapter 9 for a full listing). You'll pass the city's and (probably the country's) highest concentration of great restaurants per foot!

Refueling Stop

   For a physical and intellectual pick-me-up, the second floor of **Borders,** the city's best bookstore at 1727 Walnut St., has a comfortable espresso bar with racks of newspapers and magazines. It's open Monday to Friday from 7am to 10pm, Saturday from 9am to 9pm, and Sunday from 11am to 7pm. **The Coffee Shop,** 130 S. 17th St., has several blends going and excellent muffins and scones.

14. **Rittenhouse Square** functioned as the city's center of social prestige roughly from 1870 through 1930, or until proper Philadelphians discovered that they could live in the Main Line suburbs permanently. Despite the construction of apartment houses to replace such mansions as **McIlhenny House** at the southwest corner, it still adds a touch of elegance to the city, bolstered by the **Curtis School of Music** at Locust Street and the **Rittenhouse Hotel** (though not by the jagged architecture it inherited). The park itself has splendid curving walks around whimsical fountains and decorative pools, with sunlight or winter chill dappling through the trees.

   South and west of Rittenhouse Square are unusual turn-of-the-century town houses ranging from severe Georgian to fanciful neomedieval. A favorite "summary" street of styles is **Delancey Street,** between Spruce and Lombard streets. If you detour as far west as 20th Street, you'll be rewarded with the interiors and garden of:

15. **Rosenbach Museum and Library,** at no. 2010, a shrine of book collectors and lovers of literature (see Chapter 7 for a full description).

   From Rittenhouse Square, head north on 18th Street to Chestnut Street, taking a right and following a block to:

16. **Liberty Place,** a tremendously inviting 1991 urban mall and superb family refueling stop at the second-floor food court. (See Chapter 6 for the cuisine and Chapter 9 for the shops.)

   Walking east one block, then north one block, you'll see the Visitors Center. Look northwest, and begin your stroll along Benjamin Franklin Parkway. The Parkway connects City Hall with the welcoming arms of the Philadelphia Museum of Art, just over a mile away, swirling through Logan Circle and its fountain en route. The last decade's explosive growth of the new corporate headquarters in town has solidified the many grand cultural institutions built on its edges. If you visit the cultural attractions, you can pick up a "Parkway Passport" offering discounts on most local restaurants—and vice versa.

   Walking up from the **Visitors Center** at 16th Street and John F. Kennedy Boulevard, you'll pass:

17. **Penn Center (the former Suburban) Station,** a compact art deco terminal whose street level has been transformed into the inviting **Marathon Grill.** Be aware that an underground concourse linking the station to City Hall also contains dozens of shops, services, and food vendors. A left turn brings you onto the Parkway itself.

   Two blocks up, the Parkway intersects with Cherry and 17th streets. On the Parkway's north side, **Friends Select School,** a leading Quaker-founded preparatory school, occupies new headquarters in the Pennwalt Building, while on the south side, **Marabella's** dishes up Tuscan pastas and antipasti for hungry grazers. One block west on Cherry Street, **Dock Street Brewing Co.** dispenses American bistro fare and beer, freshly brewed on the premises, in a relaxed setting. A block farther, past **TGI Friday's** and the rounded marble tower of the **Embassy Suites Hotel** lies:

18. **Logan Circle.** Originally a square, it was converted with the Parkway construction. This most corporate and institutional setting of all of William Penn's original city parks has the lowest buildings surrounding it. The highlight is the 1920 **Swann Fountain,** designed by Alexander S. Calder with evocations of the three waters (Delaware, Schuylkill, Wissahickon) that nourish Philadelphia.

   At the eastern end of Logan Circle is the:

19. **Cathedral-Basilica of Sts. Peter and Paul.** Built in 1846, this sober Roman church with a copper dome made the statement that Catholics would recover and populate a newer part of Center City after the anti-Catholic riots of the early 1840s.

   Continue walking clockwise around Logan Circle. The four-story **Four Seasons Hotel** was sensitively designed not to intrude architecturally; furthermore, the hotel renovated the Swann Fountain in the mid-1980s and maintains its

hothouse gardens. Afternoon tea at the **Fountain Café**
within is a quintessential Philadelphia experience.

Just past 19th Street on Logan Circle is the:

20. **Academy of Natural Sciences,** displaying flora and
fauna from the world over, from dinosaurs to contemporary
volcanoes (see Chapter 7 for details).

Next to the academy is **Moore College of Art,** with its
street-level exhibition space open to the public. Taking up
the whole west side of Logan Circle is the neoclassical
facade of the:

21. **Franklin Institute Science Museum and
Futures Center,** a top attraction (see the details in
Chapter 7). Don't forget that even without admission you
can eat at the entranceway **Ben's Café.** With a detour two
blocks south on 21st Street, you'll come to the **Please
Touch Museum** (also see Chapter 7).

To the north side lie both the:

22. **Free Library of Philadelphia,** with a wonderful
Children's Library as well as research and circulating
collections and an inexpensive rooftop cafeteria (again,
Chapter 7 has the details) and the twin **Municipal Court
Building.**

If you continue up toward the **Philadelphia Museum
of Art** on the north side of the Parkway from the Free
Library, two blocks up you'll come to the ancillary
collection of the:

23. **Rodin Museum,** bequeathed to the city in the 1920s
and renovated in 1989. It has a very pleasant outdoor
sculpture garden in a leafy atmosphere (see the full
description in Chapter 7).

9

Philadelphia Shopping A to Z

IN COLONIAL DAYS, PHILADELPHIA WAS ONE OF THE MOST INTERESTING shopping marts in the world. Franklin's *Autobiography* tells of his surprise on coming to breakfast one morning to find a china bowl and silver spoon: "Luxury will enter families and make a progress in spite of principle."

Philadelphia has plenty of goods to help luxury enter your life. It's close enough to New York City to get high-fashion and international wares, especially in the specialty shops around Rittenhouse Square. Also, remember that there is no sales tax on clothing; other items are taxed at 7%.

Most stores stay open during regular business hours on Monday to Friday, on Saturday, and later on Wednesday evening. Some are also open on Sunday.

Antiques

Philadelphia is one big attic that's full of the undervalued heirlooms and cast-offs of previous generations. Pine Street from 9th to 12th streets boasts about 25 stores, many of which do their own refinishing. Germantown Avenue in Chestnut Hill also has a concentration of shops. As in any antique market, you'll have to bring a lot of expertise to any store and you'll have to trust your dealer. There are usually dozens of antique markets every week in the Delaware Valley. Consult the "Weekend" section of the *Philadelphia Inquirer* for details.

Calderwood Gallery, 221 S. 17th St. ☎ **732-9444.**

This is an international resource for French art nouveau and art deco furnishings, which are beautifully displayed. The prices are reasonable compared to those in New York City.

Freeman Fine Arts, 1808 Chestnut St. ☎ **563-9275.**

The dean of auction houses in town since 1805 stages a full auction every Wednesday (viewing on Monday and Tuesday). They specialize in most Americana. Special fully cataloged auctions for jewelry and fine furniture are held here several times annually; regular auctions include standard home furnishings and some fine pieces.

★ **Gargoyle's,** 512 S. 3rd St. ☎ **629-1700.**

In Society Hill, my personal favorite is Gargoyles, which has everything from toothpick holders to mantels and bars. Although much of the stock is American, there's also a delightful selection of English pub signs, dart boards, and the like. Several large items have been salvaged from 19th-century buildings and businesses.

Jansen Antiques, 1036 Pine St. ☎ **592-1670.**

The displays of Victorian and art deco furnishings and jewelry here are unusually uncluttered compared to others in the neighborhood.

M. Finkel and Daughter, 936 Pine St. ☎ **627-7797.**

Look here, one of the true anchors of the Pine Street neighborhood, for folk art, furniture, and painting in general and bright Amish quilts and needlework in particular.

Reese's Antiques, 928-930 Pine St. ☎ **922-0796.**

This place is not quite as wonderful as the cigar-store Indian out front, and the help can be nearly as somnolent, but Reese's is one of the oldest Pine Street shops, featuring a large selection of china and silver.

⭐ **W. Graham Arader III Gallery,** 1308 Walnut St. ☎ **735-5977.**

Arader has become one of the country's leading rare book, map, and print dealers in the past 15 years because of its aggressive purchasing and higher pricing. You'll find a variety of interesting items here.

Art Galleries

The line between museums that exhibit studio artists, such as the Pennsylvania Academy of Fine Arts (PAFA), and galleries that promote sales is smaller here than in many other cities. The line between art and crafts is fine also (see "Crafts" below for more listings). Many of the less traditional galleries are in the colonial district or on South Street.

AIA Bookstore and Design Center, 117 S. 17th St. ☎ **569-3188.**

This recently renovated gallery specializes in architectural renderings, watercolors, and drawings. Connected to it is an excellent bookstore (see below).

The Eyes Gallery, 402 South St. ☎ **925-0193.**

The Eyes Gallery presents a cheerful assortment of Latin American folk art, including Santos and retablos. Also included are one-of-a-kind articles of clothing and jewelry spread over three floors. Open every day of the week.

Gilbert Luber Gallery, 1220 Walnut St. ☎ **732-2996.**

Here you can find superb Japanese and Chinese antique and contemporary graphics and art books. The gallery is branching into antique and contemporary Thai objects.

Gross-McCleaf Gallery, 127 S. 16th St. ☎ **665-8138.**

Now in its 25th year, this gallery features exhibits of regional painters. The focus is on painterly realism, including landscape, still life, and figurative work.

Helen Drutt, 1721 Walnut St. ☎ **735-1625.**

Among the private galleries, Helen Drutt has influential shows of crafted objects of fiber, clay, and metal—both beautiful and utilitarian. Winter hours are Wednesday to Saturday 10am to 5pm; summer hours are Wednesday and Thursday from 11am to 5pm and Friday from 11am to 4pm.

Janet Fleisher, 211 S. 17th St. ☎ **545-7562.**

This is the city's undisputed doyenne of Native American and Pre-Columbian artifacts and crafts, with some modern folk art as well.

Locks, 600 Washington Sq. S. ☎ **629-1000.**

This is another powerhouse gallery for paintings, sculptures, and mixed-media works. Gallery 1 is frequently devoted to group theme shows, and the smaller Gallery 2 usually focuses on a single artist.

Makler, 225 S. 18th St. ☎ **735-2540.**

Makler presents the weightiest contemporary artists, such as Louise Nevelson and Jim Dine. By appointment only.

⭐ **Newman Galleries,** 1625 Walnut St. ☎ **563-1779.**

The oldest gallery in Philadelphia (it was founded in 1865), Newman Galleries provides a very strong representation of Bucks County artists and of American sculptors and painters in general. Custom framing and art conservation are also available.

⭐ **Philadelphia Art Alliance,** Rittenhouse Square, 251 S. 18th St. ☎ **545-4302.**

The three floors of local talent here are chosen by the alliance's committee of laymen and artists. Most of the material—pottery, sculpture, and hangings—already has a stamp of approval. The new Dean & De Luca café helps too.

Rosenwald-Wolf Gallery, University of the Arts, 333 S. Broad St. at Pine St. ☎ **875-1116.**

This gallery features works not only by faculty but also by distinguished visitors. Student shows are held in May through July.

Schmidt/Dean, 1636 Walnut St. ☎ **546-7212.**

Opened in 1988, Schmidt/Dean specializes in contemporary painting prints, photographs, and sculpture.

The School Gallery of the Pennsylvania Academy of Fine Arts, 1301 Cherry St. ☎ **569-2797.**

The building is a wonderful school with student and faculty exhibits that change frequently during the year. Hours are Monday, 10am to 5pm; Tuesday through Friday 10am to 7pm; Saturday 10am to 4pm.

Schwartz Gallery, 1806 Chestnut St. ☎ **563-4887.**

They are specialists in 19th- and 20th-century paintings, particularly those with Philadelphia connections.

⭐ **Snyderman Gallery,** 103 Cherry St. ☎ **238-9576.**

Snyderman Gallery is one of my favorites. It recently moved from South Street to a 6000-square-foot space in Olde City. The gallery now focuses primarily on painting, sculpture, and studio artists working in wood, clay, and glass.

Art Supplies

Taws, 1527 Walnut St. ☎ **563-8742.**

A fine selection of artists' materials and studio furnishings can be found here, convenient to Center City. There are also some interesting decorative pieces and gifts.

Bookstores

AIA Bookstore and Design Center, 117 S. 17th St. at Sansom St. ☎ **569-3188.**

Boasting some of the finest shelves you'll see anywhere, this bookstore also offers an excellent downstairs gallery of architectural renderings, watercolors, and drawings. A double "Best of Philly" award winner.

Book Trader, 501 South St. ☎ **925-0219.**

If you're on South Street and feel like browsing or just resting, Book Trader has a fine paperback collection and benches, along with a resident cat. It's open until midnight on most nights. You can also find a good selection of out-of-print books, American fiction, and used LPs, tapes, and CDs.

The Bookstore of the University of Pennsylvania, 3729 Locust Walk at 37th St. ☎ **898-7595.**

Obviously, you'll find complete course readings for thousands of courses, but you'll also find excellent selections of quality fiction and nonfiction and children's books. The Bookstore carries stationery, gifts, and has a film-developing service as well.

★ **Borders,** 1727 Walnut St. ☎ **568-7400.**

Started by the Borders brothers in Minneapolis, this bookstore is a dream come true and has quickly become a cultural center of Rittenhouse Square. It features a great staff and a greater selection, computerized searches, hundreds of serious magazines and periodicals, attention to local writers, an active reading series in the evening, and even a second-floor espresso bar with newspapers! There's a great children's book section with toys and storytelling hours on most Saturdays.

Brentano's, The Shops at Liberty Place, 1625 Chestnut St. ☎ **557-8443.**

Here you'll find a fine collection of bestsellers, a local-interest collection, classics, and glossy coverage of contemporary affairs.

Encore, 609 Chestnut St. ☎ **627-4557.**

Bestsellers are sold here at 35% off, the best discount in town. Nothing goes for full price, and you can often pick up exactly what you've been looking for. Additional Encore bookstores are located at Commerce Square at Market and 21st streets (☎ **567-8630**) and at 205 S. 38th St. (☎ **382-5700**).

The Joseph Fox Bookstore, 1724 Sansom St. ☎ **563-4184.**

This bookstore has choice selections in art, graphic design, architecture, photography, current and classic fiction, and books for children.

Rizzoli, Shops at the Bellevue. ☎ unavailable at press time.

A branch of an upscale New York bookstore is checking into the old Gucci location here. In addition to the renowned collection of art and coffee-table books, they'll include an espresso bar, children's books, music books, CDs, and international magazines.

Tower Books, 425 South St. ☎ **925-9909.**

Tower Books has extended the concept of massively stocked merchandise from recordings into books and magazines. It's open every night until midnight.

China, Silver & Glass

Keystone Silver, 602 Washington Sq. S. ☎ **922-1724.**

About 50% of the business here is repair—replating, polishing, or replacing parts—but Keystone also sells plate and sterling and antique and modern reproductions. Hours are 10am to 4pm weekdays, and 10am to 1pm Saturday (except July and August).

Niederkorn Silver, 2005 Locust St. ☎ **567-2606.**

Antique baby items, dressing-table adornments, napkin rings, picture frames, and Judaica are featured here. Also on display is Philadelphia's largest selection of period silver, including works of such fine crafters as Jensen, Tiffany, and Spratling. Open Tuesday through Saturday.

Colonial Reproductions

Fried Brothers, 467 N. 7th St. ☎ **627-3205,** or toll free **800/356-5050.**

Near the Edgar Allan Poe National Historical Site, Fried Brothers specializes in hardware suitable for colonial buildings and furnishings. If you admire the doorknobs in Society Hill, you'll see the like here.

Crafts

Philadelphia artisanry has always commanded respect. The tradition lingers on, in both small individual workshops and cooperative stores. The Olde City section, north of Society Hill, has seen a mushrooming of contemporary crafts and design stores. The Craft Show held every November is one of the top five in the country.

For outdoor crafts vendors, check **Independence Mall** during summer weekends, although flea-market items seem to predominate there. **Head House Square** becomes a bustling bunch of booths all day Saturday and on Sunday afternoons from April through September.

Agape, 1116 Pine St. ☎ **922-2804.**

From a cramped storefront with a loft, Agape offers import and export items that are striking and sophisticated, with very low-priced specials on fine furniture and jewelry.

★ **The Black Cat,** 3424 Sansom St. ☎ **386-6664.**

Next door to the White Dog Café, Judy Wicks has set up a charming arts-and-crafts store that's open until 9pm Monday through Wednesday, 11pm Thursday through Sunday. Livingroom knick-knacks are displayed in a living room and so forth. Also, there's a small number of antiques and near antiques.

The Fabric Workshop Museum, 1315 Cherry St., 5th floor.
☎ **922-7303.**

This place is a bit out of the way, unless you're coming from the new Convention Center, but don't miss the bags, scarves, ties, and umbrellas of Venturi and Red Grooms designs.

Moderne, 111 N. 3rd St. ☎ **923-8536.**

This Olde City stalwart gives a slant to European art deco furniture. It offers a very good selection of American and French ironworks—furniture and decorative items. They've also branched out into the sale of books and fabrics appropriate to 20th-century design.

OLC, 152–154 N. 3rd St. ☎ **923-6085.**

OLC, in the Olde City, has 6,000 feet of sophisticated lighting and furnishings displayed in a museum-quality setting that's been cited by the American Institute of Architects.

★ **Thos. Moser Cabinetmakers**, 210 W. Washington Sq.
☎ **922-6440.**

Tucked away off West Washington Square, between Walnut and Locust Streets, is one of the country's great craftsmen of wooden furniture—or his store at least, since Tom Moser lives and works out of Maine. The beds, cabinets, desks, and chairs here are inspired by Shaker and other rural American designs, and the execution and finishes are wondrous. Custom furniture inquiries are welcome.

The Works Gallery, 319 South St. ☎ **922-7775.**

The specialties here are ceramics, glass creations, and furniture transcending the boundary between craft and art. Photography is also tucked in between rooms.

Department Stores

Strawbridge & Clothier, 8th and Market Sts. ☎ **629-6000.**

Strawbridges have run this department store for over a century, and it has quietly anchored the Market East neighborhood in the midst of bad times, and it will hopefully do so during the expected Convention Center boom. Now connected to the Gallery mall, it carries a full line over three stories; its prices and boutiques are moderately scaled, with frequent sales of 20% to 30% off. It contains an underrated but excellent food hall too.

★ **Wanamaker's**, between Market and Chestnut and 13th and Juniper Sts. ☎ **422-2000.**

Wanamaker's deserves special mention. This was one of the first of the great department stores in the country, and Philadelphians found the prospect of buying fine merchandise from soap to fireplaces tremendously exciting. The present building (1902–10) fills a city block and is modeled ingeniously on Renaissance motifs, which give its 12 stories proportion and grace.

Ralph Lauren now has a first-floor boutique in Wanamaker's. The store also contains various snack bars. On the first floor, there's an Adrien Arpel salon, a chiropodist on call at the shoe salon, and an estate-jewelry counter. On the mezzanine, you'll find a service center with a post office, a film developer, a travel bureau, a dry cleaner, and an optometrist. The retail area has shrunk from eight to five floors, with three stories of commercial offices on top. A five-story court presents Christmas shows with a massive 30,000-pipe organ; this court also hosts daily organ concerts at 11:15am and 5:15pm.

Discount Shopping

Daffy's, 17th and Chestnut Sts. ☎ **963-9996.**

Bonwit Teller occupied this handsome four-story site for decades, and from December 1992 Daffy's has presented excellent value for name and house brands for men, women, and children. Prices are 40% to 75% off regular retail, and men's and women's Italian suits, fine leather items, and lingerie are particular bargains. Open daily (Sundays noon to 6pm). And Kirk Windra does terrific windows.

Eddie Bauer Outlet Store, 1400 Walnut St. ☎ **569-9691.**

Better known through its catalog, Eddie Bauer is tucked into an excellent location for superior preppie/outdoor men's and women's clothes. Items are (mostly) overstocks rather than defective, and discounting starts at 30% and goes beyond 50%, although selection is not complete. Open daily (Sundays noon to 5pm).

Ron Friedman Co., 14 S. 3rd St. ☎ **922-4877.**

Save 40 to 60% on American and imported leather handbags, wallets, and briefcases.

House of Bargains, 1939–1943 Juniper St. ☎ **465-8841.**

A South Philly institution for children's clothes, with a remarkable assembly of brand names anywhere from 40 to 80% off retail prices. Actually located at the intersection of South Broad Street and Passyunk Avenue.

Night Dressing, 2100 Walnut St. ☎ **563-2828.** Also at 724 S. 4th St. ☎ **627-5244.**

Locations in Rittenhouse Square and Society Hill carry Lily of France, Olga, Warners, and so forth, almost all at half-price. New arrivals almost daily. Big selection of sleepwear and robes. Some bathing suit cover-ups.

Sherman Brothers, 1520 Sansom St. ☎ **561-4550.**

Here over 35 years, and recently expanding into the suburbs, Sherman Brothers has the city's best collection of fine men's shoes like Cole Haan, Allen Edmonds, and Bally, as well as difficult sizes. Discounted 10 to 25% every day.

Fashion

Look for the more conservative styles in the many stores around Rittenhouse Square and in the department stores and the more sharply styled or contemporary fashions on South Street and in the malls. Buying clothes from the outlets of national stores, ranging from The Gap to Burberrys, could save you money because clothing comes without any state sales tax in Pennsylvania.

CHILDREN'S FASHION

Born Yesterday, 1901 Walnut St. ☎ **568-6556.**

Right on Rittenhouse Square, this store fits babies, boys to size 8, and girls to size 14. The fashions are always current, with a good selection of classics. This is a great store for new parents and grand-parents and doting aunts and uncles, with an attentive staff.

The Children's Boutique, 1717 Walnut St. ☎ **563-3881.**

This place features many all-cotton, color-coordinated outfits by local designers and a good selection of top-of-the-line traditional children's clothes. The store also has a large infant department and stocks some toys.

Gap Kids, 432 South St. ☎ **629-1232.**

Here you'll find high-quality, casual clothes that mix and match well—and can be exchanged or returned cheerfully at hundreds of locations nationwide. There's another location at 1718 Walnut St. (☎ **546-7010**).

Kamikaze Kids, 527 S. 4th St. ☎ **574-9800.**

Aggressively styled fashion wear is sold here. The stock ranges from tights to hair ornaments—everything the urban chic child needs. It also stocks incredible Halloween costumes. The items are not cheap.

K.I.D.S. Children's Shoe Boutique, 56 N. 3rd St. ☎ **592-9033.**

Somewhere between a postmodern carnival and a shoe store, this place is very convenient to Franklin Court and other Independence Hall sites.

Wanamaker's, between Market and Chestnut and 13th and Juniper sts. ☎ **422-2000.**

This store has an excellent children's department, with clothes rang-ing from onesies to dress for special occasions. There are frequent sales.

MEN'S FASHION

Black Tie, 1120 Walnut St. ☎ **925-4404.**

If formal wear is a sudden necessity, sales and rentals can be found at Black Tie. It carries Lord West, After Six, Bill Blass, and other suave styles, as well as custom tailoring and accessories and shirts.

Bottino Shoes, 121 S. 18th St. ☎ **854-0907.**

Look here for sharper, more avant-garde European (and particularly Italian) men's and women's fashions.

★ **Boyd's,** 1818 Chestnut St. ☎ **564-9000.**

Under the Gushner family, Boyd's has moved "uptown" to a beau-tifully restored blue-and-white commercial palace. It's the largest in the city, with 65 tailors on site, and has European and American lines of all types, as well as alterations for a variety of fine designers such as Ermenegildo Zegna. Boyd's still has its valet and has added a café.

Brooks Brothers, 1500 Chestnut St. ☎ **564-4100.**

Brooks Brothers won't steer you wrong on perfectly acceptable items for business and casual wear; slimmer men should head for the Brooksgate section because the regular styles are cut generously.

Wayne Edwards, 1521 Walnut St. ☎ **563-6801.**

This stretch of Walnut Street is really the block for fashion. Wayne Edwards sports a slightly larger selection of contemporary styles than nearby Allure.

WOMEN'S FASHION

A number of the following women's clothing stores could set up successfully in any fashion capital of the world.

Ambitions, 212 S. 17th St. ☎ **546-1133.**

Specializing in larger sizes, Ambitions carries a full selection of fashionable clothing and accessories.

Ann Taylor, 1713 Walnut St. ☎ **977-9336.**

This conservative retailer stumbled by dropping the Joan & David shoe line and delving into cheaper garments, but it is working on a revitalization and a reemphasis on quality. Look for markdowns to rebuild trade.

★ **Boyd's,** 1818 Chestnut St. ☎ **564-9000.**

Boyd's, a superb men's fashion mansion, leapt into the women's wear game in fall 1993 with a third floor boutique. Look for classic suits, dresses, and casual wear by European designers such as Istante by Gianni Versace, Vestimenta, and Encore by YSL.

Compagnie Internationale Express Limited, 1730 Chestnut St. ☎ **563-1301.**

This local shop of Leslie Wexner's Express empire has middle-priced contemporary styles and friendly help. The enticements are up front, with the cashiers far in the rear.

Dan's Shoes, 1204 Chestnut St. ☎ **922-6622.**

Fully guaranteed and tremendously discounted designer shoes are found here. It's more like a bazaar than a full-service store, but there are some real finds along with the regular stuff. There's another store at 1733 Chestnut St. (☎ **568-5257**).

Daffy's, 17th and Chestnut Sts. ☎ **963-9996.**

The third and fourth floors of the former Bonwit Teller building are devoted to women's wear. Prices are 40 to 75% off regular retail, and women's Italian suits and leather handbags are noteworthy. The first floor carries more sporty items. Open daily (Sundays noon to 6pm).

★ **J. Crew,** Liberty Place, 1625 Chestnut St. ☎ **977-7335.**

This store offers a nice merging of casual with formal clothes, all brightly colored and softly styled, plus beautiful cable-knit sweaters. It's a meeting place for high-school and college-aged students.

Knit Wit, 1721 Walnut St. ☎ **564-4760.**

Now in a chic new location, Knit Wit specializes in the latest in contemporary fashions and accessories for women.

Naana's Tailors, 41 N. 2nd St. ☎ **627-9251.**

Whether it's letting out that dress or an emergency repair, Naana's can take care of it in a hurry. Hours are 10am to 7pm, Monday through Saturday; noon to 5pm Sundays.

⭐ **Nan Duskin,** in the Rittenhouse Hotel, 210 W. Rittenhouse Sq. ☎ **735-6400.**

A Rittenhouse Square fixture for more than 40 years, Nan Duskin carries the creations of the finest European and American designers. It's the premier venue in town for national couturiers.

One Night Stand, 132 S. 17th St. ☎ **568-9200.**

Elegant designer dresses suitable for formal wear are for rent or sale here. Even the mayor's wife stops by. It's open Monday to Friday until 6pm, Saturday until 5pm.

Mendelsohn, 229 S. 18th St. ☎ **546-6333.**

Offered here are stylish clothes for the mature woman with fashion sense. This place feels like a throwback to an earlier, pleasant era in Rittenhouse Square.

Plage Tahiti, 128 S. 17th St. ☎ **569-9139.**

A selective store, Plage Tahiti has original but adaptable clothes. As the name suggests, French bathing suits are a constant.

Rodier of Paris, 135 S. 18th St. ☎ **496-0447.**

This expensive, fashion-forward retailer is now back in Rittenhouse Square, after an untimely fling at The Bourse. The sophisticated clothing offered is designed and manufactured in France.

Toby Lerner, 117 S. 17th St. ☎ **568-5760.**

With an intimate setting for clothes, accessories, and jewelry, this spot is in one of the most affluent neighborhoods in town—and the prices reflect this. It's celebrating a 20th anniversary with selections from Armani, Anne Klein, Barbara BVI, Montana, and others.

Victoria's Secret, 1721 Chestnut St. ☎ **567-1034.**

This very popular specialist in lingerie and accessories now carries a full line of women's clothing at excellent prices. It's always crowded.

WOMEN'S, MEN'S & CHILDREN'S FASHIONS

Banana Republic, 1716 Walnut St. ☎ **735-2247.**

This mail-order success story, combining safari retail and travel accessories and books, has moved into retail. There's another store in Chestnut Hill at 8506 Germantown Ave. (☎ **242-2882**).

Burberrys Limited, 1705 Walnut St. ☎ **557-7400.**

Burberrys has all the suits, raincoats, and accessories suitable for a gentleman or a lady.

Filene's Basement, 1608–1612 Chestnut St. ☎ **864-9080.**

The legendary off-price retailer could not have opened in fall 1993 in a more central spot, with three floors of everything from lingerie to shoes and suits. Prices are generally 30 to 60% off full retail price.

The Gap, 1524 Chestnut St. ☎ **564-3862.**

The Gap features casual styles in predictable colors for men and women. As in Baby Gap, you know exactly what you're getting, and you can make an easy exchange or get a refund at any Gap around the country. Other locations are at 5th and South streets

(☎ **627-7334**), 1710 Walnut St. (☎ **732-3391**), The Gallery at Market East (☎ **625-4962**), and virtually all area malls.

Polo/Ralph Lauren, The Shops at the Bellevue, Broad and Walnut Sts. ☎ **985-2800.**

The new Polo/Ralph Lauren has its own private elevator and fabulous settings for the plushest suitings in town.

Urban Outfitters, 1801 Walnut St. ☎ **569-3131.**

Housed in a turn-of-the-century mansion on the corner of Rittenhouse Square, this store has been branching off from the conservative preppy look. The basement has an unusual children's, home-furnishings, and book selection. There's another store at 4040 Locust St. (☎ **387-0373**).

Florists

Local flower stores abound. You can also call 24-hour service for FTD through **Flower World** (☎ **567-7100** or toll free **800/257-7880**).

Bloomies, 1200 Spruce St. ☎ **732-3262.**

This florist is open late every day and provides prompt delivery for phone orders.

Flower Market, Concourse of 2 Penn Center. ☎ **563-5478.**

The Flower Market has cornered the Rittenhouse Square market. A dozen prize roses, gift boxed, go for $25, and most of the world's standard blooms as well as plants, dish gardens, and arrangements, are available at good prices. The Flower Market delivers to Philadelphia and to the surrounding suburbs. Hours are 7am to 6:30pm Monday through Friday.

Food

⭐ **The Reading Terminal Market** at 12th and Market streets, with its dozens of individual booths and cafés, has been recommended in Chapter 6. Also, see the "Picnic Fare" section at the end of Chapter 6.

⭐ **Chef's Market,** 231 South St. ☎ **925-8360.**

The premier gourmet store in Society Hill is Chef's Market, with a staggering array of charcuterie, cookbooks, and condiments. Would you believe this place stocks breads and cakes supplied by 20 bakeries?

Italian Market, 9th St. between Christian and Wharton Sts.

The Italian Market comes straight out of another era, with about 150 pushcarts and open stalls selling fresh goods and produce, cheese, and some clothes from Tuesday through Saturday (the end of the week is better). Many shops are open until noon on Sunday. Particular favorites are **DiBruno's** at 930 S. 9th St. for cheese, **Sarcone and Sons** at 758 S. 9th St. for bread, and the pound cake at the **Pasticceria** at 9th and Federal streets. You can always snack on fried dough or pastries along the route, as well as save money or pick up an espresso machine at **Fante's.** To reach the market, head five blocks south of South Street; SEPTA bus 47 goes south on 8th Street from Market.

Michelfelder's Lunchmeats, Inc., 1234 Market St. ☎ **568-7948.**
Michelfelder's has links of German and domestic wurst, plus lunch sandwiches. There is another store at the Gallery at Market East (☎ **627-2288**).

Pagano's Gourmet, Market Place East, 701 Market St.
☎ **922-7771.**
Pagano's stocks a large selection of cheeses, deluxe meats, exotic condiments, and breads and crackers. Gift packages and box lunches are prepared from $7.95. The original **Pagano's Cheesery** is at 1507 Walnut St. (☎ **568-0891**). There's another Pagano's Gourmet in Penn Center Station Concourse, beneath 17th Street and John F. Kennedy Boulevard (☎ **557-0423**), and a Pagano's Gourmet Café at 601 Walnut St. (☎ **627-5656**).

La Petite Boulangerie, 16th St. and John F. Kennedy Blvd.
☎ **977-9495.**
A new entrant, La Petite Boulangerie has two Center City locations for croissants, baguettes, and the like. The location listed above has some café seating. The other location (no seating) is at 19 N. Juniper St. (☎ **751-1035**).

R&W Delicatessen, 19th and Walnut Sts. ☎ **563-7247.**
The deli nearest to Rittenhouse Square, R&W has plenty of fixings for do-it-yourself lunches, including hearty noodle pudding.

Rago, 258 S. 20th St. ☎ **732-0444.**
A small gem of a store just north of Spruce Street, Rago is run by the same family that operates Fratelli Rago, a fine Italian trattoria three blocks away.

Gifts

Amy & Friends, 2124 Walnut St. ☎ **496-1778** or **232-3714.**
You have to put up with a fair amount of free-flowing disorder to enjoy this place, but there's a truly eclectic assortment of antiques and bric-a-brac, including Classic Writing, a boutique specializing in top-quality fountain pens.

Bernie Robbins Co., 1625 Sansom St. ☎ **563-2380.**
Arranged for quick selection, Bernie Robbins Co. is a high-class catalog showroom, and the values on jewelry, technological wonders, luggage, and appliances are excellent. You can also order by mail.

Country Elegance, 269 S. 20th St. ☎ **545-2992.**
Unique gifts and home accessories, along with a great selection of fine and antique linens, are sold here. It's open Monday to Friday until 7pm and Saturday until 6pm.

Crabtree & Evelyn, The Shops at Liberty Place, 1625 Chestnut St.
☎ **665-9184.**
Crabtree & Evelyn, the very English emporium, purveys fine toiletries and comestibles for the discriminating. Their marmalade's famous, but those badger-bristle shaving brushes and those soaps

make terrific gifts as well. There's another store at The Bourse
(☎ 625-9256).

Dandelion, 1718 Sansom St. ☎ **972-0999.**

Proprietor Beth Fluke has traveled to see, and buy, it all, and has a
discriminating sense of handcrafted jewelry and gifts from the American Southwest, the Near East, and East Coast artisans. A great place
for wedding or birthday gifts—that is, sophisticated pieces at many
different price levels. Nice selection of blank cards too.

Details, 131 S. 18th St. ☎ **977-9559.**

Sumptuous gifts, such as picture frames and stationery, are sold at
the former Papier Cache, a turn-of-the-century town house.

Mineralistic, 608 S. 4th St. ☎ **922-7199.**

Crystals and semiprecious stones and pendants, along with New Age
tapes and the like, are sold at this store, at the intersection of South
Street and Society Hill. There's also a store on Main Street in
Manayunk.

Touches, 225 S. 15th St. ☎ **546-1221.**

This is an upscale boutique with clothing and accessories, leather
goods, boxes, perfume bottles, handmade jewelry, frames, and baby
gifts.

Urban Outfitters, 1801 Walnut St. ☎ **569-3131.**

Urban Outfitters specializes in campus-trendy furniture, clothing,
health foods, kitchen equipment, and fabrics such as Marimekko.

Jewelry

Philadelphia is known for all types of jewelry—traditional, one-of-
a-kind, heirloom, and contemporary. Most of the city's jewelers
occupy two city blocks at **Jeweler's Row,** centering on Sansom
and 8th streets.

Bailey, Banks & Riddle, 16th and Chestnut Sts. ☎ **564-6200.**

Established in 1832, Bailey, Banks, and Biddle has extraordinary
silverware and stationery as well as jewelry. It's an enormous store
(or museum, if you're not looking to spend).

L. Switt, 130 S. 8th St. ☎ **922-3830.**

Don't let the crotchety help at I. Switt scare you away; the store does
beautiful traditional settings at reasonable prices.

Jack Kellmer, 717 Chestnut St. ☎ **627-8350.**

With a magnificent marble showroom, Kellmer imports diamonds
by the dozen and sells unusual gold and diamond jewelry.

★ **J.E. Caldwell & Co.,** Chestnut and Juniper Sts. ☎ **864-7800.**

This is another big and traditional store, founded in 1839. It stocks
watches and silver as well as jewelry. It also does repairs, and the
building has just been magnificently renovated.

Jeweler's Row, between Sansom and Walnut Sts. and 7th and 8th Sts.

This area contains more than 350 retailers, wholesalers, and
craftspeople. Particularly noted is **Sydney Rosen** at 714 Sansom St.

(☎ **922-3500**). **Robinson Jewelers,** 107 S. 8th St. (☎ **627-3066**), specializes in Masonic jewelry and watch repair.

Tiffany & Co., The Shops at the Bellevue, 1414 Walnut St.
☎ **735-1919.**

This fabled silver and jewelry store features exquisite service. Though many items are very expensive here, there are plenty of attractive items under $100.

Luggage

Robinson Luggage Company, Broad and Walnut Sts.
☎ **735-9859.**

Here you'll find a great selection of leather, along with discounted travel accessories and briefcases.

Travel-Wise, 132 S. 18th St. ☎ **563-7001.**

This Rittenhouse Square store carries gadgets and gifts as well as luggage. It's open Monday through Saturday 10am to 6pm.

Malls & Shopping Centers

Franklin Mills, 1455 Franklin Mills Circle. ☎ **632-1500.**

About 15 miles northeast of Center City on the edge of Bucks County (follow the signs from I-95 [take Exit 22 north] or from Pa. 276 [take Exit 28 south]), the former Liberty Bell racetrack opened in mid-1989 as Franklin Mills, the city's largest mall, with 1.8 million square feet devoted to 250 discount and outlet stores. There's parking for more than 9,000 cars in four color-coded zones. For entertainment the **49th Street Galleria** has bowling, roller skating, miniature golf, batting cages, and rides and games. (Open Monday to Thursday from 10am to 11pm, Friday and Saturday until midnight, and Sunday until 9pm). If you can't stop there, two ancillary malls are a 61-checkout-lane (that's right, 61 lanes) **Carrefour** supermarket/department store and a 30-store **Home and Design Centre.**

Franklin Mills is open Monday to Saturday from 10am to 9:30pm and Sunday from 11am to 6pm. SEPTA trains go right to the complex.

The Gallery/Gallery II, 8th to 11th and Market Sts. ☎ **625-4962**

The Gallery and Gallery II are built on four levels accommodating more than 200 stores and restaurants around sunken arcades and a glass atrium. The J. C. Penney department store, at the 10th Street corner of Market Street, has fit in Gimbel's shoes. The **food court** has over 25 snack bars and take-out spots. The **Hard Shell Café** at the street corner of 9th and Market, offers "all-you-can-eat" specials. Stores offer running shoes, books, pets, cameras, jewelry, fresh produce, toys, and all the clothing that you could ever need. **Strawbridge & Clothier,** one of America's last independent department stores still in family hands, connects over 9th Street with merchandise of slightly higher quality and prices.

The Gallery/Galleria II is open Monday, Tuesday, Thursday, and Saturday from 10am to 7pm, Wednesday and Friday from 10am to 8pm, and Sunday from noon to 5pm.

Market Place East, Market Street between 7th and 8th Sts.
☎ **592-8905.**

The century-old Lit Brothers Department Store was a sprawling assembly of wrought-iron facades that introduced hundreds of thousands to their first adult clothes. It has been recently and beautifully resuscitated. The ground floor has attracted classy tenants—including **Ross Dress for Less, Dress Barn,** and **The Main Event.** An upbeat complex of restaurants and night-time entertainment features **Mike Schmidt's,** and **Rich's La Bella Vita Ristorante.** There is garage space nearby.

Market Place East is open from 10am to 6pm Monday to Saturday. Same stores are open from 11:30am to 5:30pm Sunday. The food court and bars downstairs are open from about 7am to midnight most days.

Shops at the Bellevue, Broad and Walnut Sts.

The lower floors of the Bellevue Hotel have been turned into a very upscale collection of top names in retailing. Browsing here is quite low-key; you'll feel that the wares are displayed in a private club. **Polo/ Ralph Lauren** is the third largest in the world, with three floors of mahogany-and-brass splendor and a private elevator. Other tenants include **Tiffany & Company,** with its extraordinary jewelry, silver, and accessories; **Suhey Rosan** for women's fashion; **Vigant** luggage; **Alfred Dunhill** of London; and **Neuchatel Chocolates.** Dining is at **Ciboulette** on the mezzanine (see p. 99), the **Palm Restaurant,** or the new lower-level food court.

Shops at the Bellevue is open from 10am to 6pm Monday to Saturday (to 8pm Wednesday).

★ **The Shops at Liberty Place,** Chestnut St. between 16th and 17th sts. ☎ **851-9055.**

The Liberty Place development is the real thing: It's the handsome 60-story tower that supplanted City Hall as the city's tallest spire, and it contains 70 stores and stalls that together achieve an ambience and a comfort level that are the finest in the city. It's beautifully designed and signed, with many street exits and entrances that curve and converge on a soaring, glass-domed rotunda with teal-blue and brass accents. Representative of the retailers are **Rand McNally** for maps and children's games; **Brentano's** for books; **The Coach Store** for luggage; **Compagnie Internationale Express** for casual clothes; **Handblock** for high-quality Indian clothes and fabrics; and **Jos. A. Bank** and **J. Crew** for traditional clothes. The second floor is a wonderfully convenient, reasonable court where you can eat on the run, with hundreds of well-kept tables and chairs around quality food stalls. Provident Bank operates an automatic teller machine inside near 17th Street, and the garage directly underneath holds 750 cars. The Shops at Liberty Place are open Monday to Saturday from 9:30am to 7pm and Sunday from noon to 6pm.

South Street, just south of Society Hill.

This once-funky area has turned into big business. Because restaurants and nightlife now line South Street from Front to 8th streets, many of the 180 stores here are open well into the evening and offer goods ranging from the gentrified to the somewhat grotesque. Along with national reps of **The Gap** and **Tower Records,** the stores I recommend are these: **Queen Village Flowers,** 700 S. 2nd St. (☎ **925-0484**); the **Works Crafts Gallery,** 319 South St. (☎ **922-7775**); antique and contemporary fashions at **Xog,** 340 South St. (☎ **925-0907**); and terrific books and records at **The Book Trader,** 5th and South streets (☎ **925-0219**).

Recordings & Music

Jacobs Music Co., 1718 Chestnut St. ☎ **568-7800.**

Known primarily as a piano store (since 1900), Jacobs is Center City's best source of sheet music for serious and pop musicians alike (in the same building as Theodore Presser).

Nathan Muchnick, 1725 Chestnut St. ☎ **564-0209.**

Classical rarities are sold here.

Third Street Jazz and Rock, 20 N. 3rd St. ☎ **627-3366** or **800/486-8745.**

With 20 years experience and 25,000 CDs in stock, Jerry Gordon has one of the finest collections of jazz in the country. Also featured are new wave, Caribbean, and African music.

★ **Tower Records,** 610 South St. ☎ **574-9888.**

The champion of South Street's recent stores has to be the Los Angeles–based Tower Records, which moved into the former Ripley Music Hall. Its philosophy is to stock virtually all current recordings at lower prices, and the Tower Records Classical Annex across the street at no. 537 (☎ **925-0422**) has even lower prices. It's open 15 hours every day.

Sporting Goods

Finish Line Sports, 1915 Walnut St. ☎ **569-9957.**

This store has a great location right off Rittenhouse Square, but it's quite small and primarily for athletic shoes and fashion-conscious accessories. However, Finish Line is expanding into sportswear of all types.

★ **The Original I. Goldberg,** 902 Chestnut St. ☎ **925-9393.**

An army-navy paradise and then some, I. Goldberg provides at excellent prices the basic goods that you'll need for anything in the outdoors, with styles from the determinedly antifashion to the up-to-the-minute. The selection is very large, but the help is harried.

Tobacco

Holt's, 114 S. 16th St. ☎ **563-0763.**

Holt's is renowned throughout the country for its selection of pipes and tobaccos. There are enough fresh cigars here to fill every humidor in Congress, plus an excellent pen selection.

Toys

 **Einstein Presents of Mind,** 1624 Chestnut St. ☎ **665-3622.**

From Russian dolls to origami, from fossils to Babar the Elephant—it's all here for the 1990s family. The space, just across from Library Place, is wonderful, and the staff creates a sense of festival with the constantly changing displays.

Past Present Future, 24 S. 18th St. ☎ **854-0444.**

Past Present Future sells soft sculpture, custom and wooden handmade toys, and puzzles. I've seen plenty of adults whiling away some time in here. There's also a good selection of toys and gifts for adults, including craft jewelry.

Wine & Liquor

After the repeal of Prohibition, Pennsylvania decided not to license private liquor retailing but to establish a government monopoly on alcohol sales. You, or any tavernkeeper or restaurateur, can find liquor only in state stores (or at a vineyard within the state). They are usually open Monday to Wednesday from 9am to 5pm and Thursday to Saturday until 9pm. The selection has improved greatly in recent years. You cannot, however, buy chilled beer or champagne—just what's on the shelf. (Try a delicatessen or licensed supermarket for the bubbles.)

Near Independence Hall, **Old City Liquor,** 32 S. 2nd St. ☎ **625-0906,** looks—and acts—almost like a nonstate store. It's open Monday and Tuesday from 11am to 7pm and Wednesday to Saturday from 9am to 9pm.

Also in the Independence Hall Area, try the **Bourse Building,** 5th and Chestnut streets (☎ **560-5504**); 32 S. 2nd Street (☎ **625-0906**) or **Society Hill Shopping Center** (☎ **922-4224**). In the City Hall Area, there are state stores at 1318 Walnut St. (☎ **735-8464**) and 265 S. 10th St. (☎ **922-6497**). Around Rittenhouse Square, you might try **The Wine Reserve,** at 205 S. 18th St. (☎ **560-4529**), an upscale version of a state store, opened in early 1990. Consumers can browse freely among such opulent surroundings as a slate floor and a mahogany counter and shelves. Bottles of some 800 wines are stacked horizontally—a first in Philadelphia! In University City there's a state store at 4049 Walnut St. (☎ **222-3547**).

10

Philadelphia Entertainment & Nightlife

I F YOU ASK PHILADELPHIANS TO NAME THE BIGGEST CHANGE IN THEIR CITY over the last 20 years, the explosion of entertainment and nightlife possibilities will rank right up there with Independence National Historical Park and the restaurant renaissance. From sound-and-light shows at Independence Hall to sound-and-light shows at the Columbus Boulevard dance clubs, there's enough pizzazz and activity in this city to fill months of idle evenings.

The city itself seems a little surprised with its newfound vitality, since Philadelphia's always been known for its sedate domestic pleasures. But with the gentrification of Center City neighborhoods and the preservation of a safe urban environment, such spots as the piers along the Delaware River, Olde City north of Society Hill, and the northwest quadrant of Center City have joined South Broad Street and Rittenhouse Square as lively areas for café- or barhopping and live entertainment.

This doesn't mean that Philadelphia has let its preeminence in cultural affairs slide. A project to make South Broad St. into "Avenue of the Arts" is picking up steam, with the new **ArtsBank** performance space, the revitalized **Merriam Theater,** and an impending new home for the Philadelphia Orchestra. The Academy of Music presents a full season of the marvelous Philadelphia Orchestra and the financially struggling but artistically vital Pennsylvania Ballet. Two or three theaters offer road productions and preliminary versions of Broadway shows, and the Walnut Street Theatre has been going strong since 1809. The city is rich in resources for all: movies, cabaret, jazz, and dance.

The best sources for what's current are the "Weekend" supplement of the *Philadelphia Inquirer* (it comes out on Friday) and a publication called *Welcomat,* 25,000 copies of which are distributed throughout Center City. Most hotel lobbies carry it, as does the Visitors Center, which is also an excellent information source. For monthly happenings, consult the front section of *Philadelphia* magazine.

In May 1996, the city plans an ambitious International Festival of the Arts to present premieres all over town in dance, music, opera, and theater; visual art exhibitions and installations; and works by major visiting artists.

Discounts

For further inducement, check out **Upstages** at the Visitors Center, 16th Street and John F. Kennedy Boulevard (☎ **567-0670**). It has half-price tickets for up to 50 events each week (open Tuesday to Saturday from 10am to 5pm). There's a small service charge. You can even call before you stop by, to see what's on.

Senior citizens can receive discounts of about 10% or $5 per ticket or more at many theaters, including the Annenberg Center, American Music Theater Festival, and Wilma Theater. Concert halls generally make rush or last-minute seats available to students at prices under $10; these programs sometimes extend to adults as well. Groups can generally get discounts of 20% to 50% by calling well in advance.

1 The Performing Arts

Music, theater, and dance are presented regularly all over the city. I have restricted the venues below to Center City and West Philadelphia, where you'll be most of the time and where the quality of entertainment tends to be highest. There's really no off-season for the performing arts in Philadelphia; when the regular seasons of the Philadelphia Orchestra or Pennsylvania Ballet end, the outdoor activities that make Philadelphia so pleasant take over.

Major Performing Arts Companies

OPERA COMPANIES

Opera Company Of Philadelphia, 30 S. 15th St. 20th floor. ☎ **928-2100.**

This company presents full stagings of four operas per year at the Academy of Music. The performances take place on Monday, Tuesday, Thursday, or Friday evenings and there are Sunday matinees; seating preference given to season subscribers. Such international opera stars as Benita Valente (who lives down the street), Elena Filipova, and Vinson Cole appear in about half of the productions. They have snagged Luciano Pavarotti to judge and host an annual International Voice Competition, with the winner receiving a role in a production the following season.

   Prices: Tickets $17–$130.

CLASSICAL MUSIC

All-Star Forum, 1530 Locust St. ☎ **735-7506.**

Moe Septee, Philadelphia's top concert impresario, brings recital soloists, chamber groups, dance troupes, and occasionally theater groups to the Academy of Music on weekday nights at 8pm or on Sunday at 3pm. The talent is world-class.

   The All-Star Forum also presents the **Philadelphia Pops** in four series per year. Bridging the symphonic and the popular under acclaimed pianist Peter Nero, the Pops sells out for most performances.

   Prices: Tickets $12.50–$42.50.

Concerto Soloists Of Philadelphia, 825 Walnut St. ☎ **574-3550.**

Marc Mostovoy has assembled a group of excellent New York visitors and homegrown Curtis graduates for full seasons of chamber music. The concerts take place at the **Walnut Street Theater** and the **Church of the Holy Trinity** (☎ **567-1267**) near Rittenhouse Square at 19th and Walnut streets.

⭐ **Curtis Institute Of Music,** 1726 Locust St. ☎ **893-5252.**

Philadelphia has a surfeit of really excellent musicians and programs, many of them springing from the world-famous Curtis Institute, which was led for many years by Rudolf Serkin; it is now led by Gary Groffman. Curtis itself has a small hall that's good for chamber works, just off Rittenhouse Square; call **893-5260** for a schedule of the mostly free concerts, operas, and recitals. Student recitals are on Mondays, Wednesdays, and Fridays. The Curtis Opera Theater presents full-scale productions.

Philadelphia Chamber Music Society, 135 S. 18th St. ☎ 569-8587.

Celebrating its 10th season in 1995, the PCMS is committed to bringing renowned international soloists and chamber musicians to the city such as Gil Shaham, Mitsouko Uchida, and the Tokyo String Quartet, along with the Music From Marlboro group long nurtured by the former head of Curtis, Rudolf Serkin. Except for a few "run-outs" at Haverford, all 30 concerts are at the Pennsylvania Convention Center's 600-seat auditorium. Ticket prices for this quality of artist are exceptionally low.

Prices: Tickets $10–15.

★ The Philadelphia Orchestra, regular season Sept–May at the Academy of Music, Broad and Locust Sts. ☎ 893-1900 or 893-1999 to charge tickets.

For many people, a visit to Philadelphia isn't complete without hearing a concert given by the smooth, powerful ensemble under Wolfgang Sawallisch. The orchestra achieved renown under Leopold Stokowski, then was led for 44 years by the legendary Eugene Ormandy and for 12 years by Riccardo Muti. The Philadelphia has built a reputation for virtuosity and balance that only a handful of the world's orchestras can match.

The backbone of its year is the subscription schedule at the Academy of Music. The average season includes 102 concerts: 30 on Saturday evenings, 18 each on Tuesday and Thursday evenings and Friday afternoons, 12 on Friday evenings, and 6 on Sunday afternoons. The orchestra also offers nonsubscription and youth programs. In summer it moves to Mann Music Center for six weeks of free concerts (see below). More tickets to individual performances are available than in the past, with certain dress rehearsals open and fewer subscriptions sold.

Prices: Tickets $10–$78. Try to buy well in advance of the date for best seats. Student rush seats for $7 are sold at 7:30pm for all Tuesday and Thursday concerts. Unreserved amphitheater seats for $4 are sold at 1:30pm on Friday and 7pm on Friday and Saturday.

★ The Philadelphia Orchestra, summer season at Mann Music Center, George's Hill near 52nd St. and Parkside Ave. ☎ 567-0707.

During the 6-week summer season at Fairmount Park, the orchestra's concerts at the Mann Music Center under Charles Dutoit fill up quickly. Special SEPTA buses travel here from Center City, and there's plenty of free parking on Parkside Avenue. Concerts are on Monday, Wednesday, and Thursday at 8pm. You must have a ticket to be admitted as a seat holder, although unreserved tickets are free. To get them, write Robin Hood Dell Concerts, Department of Recreation, P.O. Box 1000, Philadelphia, PA 19105. Two's the limit, and requests made too far in advance will be returned.

If you haven't got tickets for seats, join approximately 15,000 others who sit on the grassy slopes above the orchestra. Don't forget the blankets and insect repellent.

Prices: Reserved seats $12–$45.

Relache Ensemble. Various venues. Office at 11 S. Strawberry St. ☎ **574-8246.**

This contemporary music group of about a dozen instrumentalists has expanded into copresenting world music or cutting-edge performances at, primarily, the new ArtsBank on South Broad Street, but also at the Mandell Theatre at the Annenberg Center. Relâche strikes a refreshing balance between interesting and overintellectualized choices, and has a particular affinity for young composers.

Prices: Tickets $10–$25.

THEATER COMPANIES

American Music Theater Festival, 123 S. Broad St., Suite 2515. ☎ **893-1570** or **567-0670** for ticket charges.

Founded in 1984, this group presents music theater in all major forms—opera, musical comedy, cabaret, and experimental. Lee Breuer's *The Gospel at Colonus* and Anthony Davis's *X* are two of nearly 40 productions of national interest, mostly at Play's & Players on 1714 Delancey St. American Music Theater also copresents a great cabaret series at Hotel Atop the Bellevue.

Prices: Tickets $10–$40.

Arden Theatre Company, St. Stephen's Alley, 10th and Ludlow Sts. ☎ **829-8900** or UPSTAGES at **567-0670.**

Arden is a professional troupe dedicated to presenting the greatest stories told by the greatest storytellers. To date, Arden has mounted 27 productions, including 11 world premieres. Arden performs in a new 200-seat theater, located on the site where Ben Franklin flew his kite in 1752.

Prices: Tickets $14–$22.

Philadelphia Drama Guild [PDG], 100 N. 17th St. ☎ **563-7530.** Box office **898-6791.**

PDG, quickly rising to national prominence under artistic director Mary B. Robinson, puts on five productions annually at the Annenberg Center. Tickets are available from the subscription director at the above address or at the theater door. A recent season included top-quality productions of Brian Friel, Sean O'Casey, August Wilson, and William Shakespeare. The season runs from late October through early April.

Prices: Tickets $12–$33.50. Discounts for students and seniors.

Philadelphia Festival Theatre For New Plays, 1515 Locust St., 7th floor. ☎ **735-1500.**

The PFTNP was founded in 1981 to help develop and produce new plays at the highest level; since 1990, they've gotten into new translations, adaptations, commissions, and coproductions. They have 2,100 subscribers for a season of four plays, using the new Philadelphia ArtsBank on Broad and South streets.

Prices: Tickets $10–$25.

Walnut Street Theatre, 9th and Walnut Sts. ☎ **574-3550.**

Founded in 1809, the Walnut Street Theatre continues its distinctive role in the history of the American stage. The regional Walnut Street Company as well as numerous local and touring attractions play here. It was renovated in 1971, and the orchestra pit can seat 50 musicians.

In the 1,052-seat theater, the resident company presents five plays from September through June; both subscriptions and single tickets are available. In 1986 the company began a Studio Theater Season, presenting new and more experimental works in the 75-seat and 90-seat studio spaces at 825 Walnut St., adjoining the theater. Barrymore's Café is a welcome downstairs addition.

Prices: Tickets $22–$39, with $5 student rush. Wed is singles night, with half-price tickets and reception.

The Wilma Theater, 2030 Sansom St. ☎ **963-0249;** box office **963-0345.**

The premier modern theater company in town has to be The Wilma Theater, which has grown to receive national acclaim and grants from the National Endowment for the Arts. Recent seasons featured new plays by Athol Fugard, Tom Stoppard, Charles Ludlam, and Lanford Wilson. They're hoping to build new headquarters on South Broad Street.

DANCE COMPANIES

Local troupes vie successfully with such distinguished visitors as Alwin Nikolais, Pilobolus, and the Dance Theater of Harlem. Contact the **Philadelphia Dance Alliance,** an organization that appears at WHYY's Forum Theater and includes most of the performing dance companies in the city, at 135 S. 23rd St., Philadelphia, PA 19103 (☎ **564-5270**).

Movement Theatre International [MTI], 3700 Chestnut St. ☎ **382-0606.**

MTI—which has assumed operations at a tabernacle temple near the University of Pennsylvania campus—goes well beyond modern dance to present vaudeville, clown theater, mime, circus acts, and classical dance-drama. It produces an annual festival.

Prices: Tickets usually $15.

★ **Pennsylvania Ballet,** 1101 S. Broad St. at Washington Ave. ☎ **551-7014.** Box office at Academy of Music **893-1930,** at Merriam **875-4829.**

Founded in 1963, this nationally renowned company almost went under in 1991 but was rejuvenated under young director Christopher d'Amboise, son of choreographer Jacques d'Amboise, and later by Roy Kaiser. The company performs at the Academy of Music and the Merriam (formerly Shubert) Theater during the yearly season. Its Christmas-season performances of Tchaikovsky's *Nutcracker,* with the complete Balanchine choreography, is a new city tradition. Each of the company's dozens of performances from September through June offers something old, something new, maybe something blue, and always something interesting.

Prices: Tickets $15–$65, *Nutcracker* performances $20–$80.

Major Concert Halls & All-Purpose Auditoriums

In addition to performances at the following major institutions, look for the many concerts presented in churches, especially around Rittenhouse Square; the city suffers from a dearth of medium-size concert halls.

Academy of Music, Broad and Locust Sts. ☎ **893-1935** for general information, **893-1930** for ticket availability.

In the early 19th century constructing an Academy of Music was a proposal much discussed by the cultured movers and shakers in Philadelphia. At the time, opera was the hallmark of culture, and Philadelphia lagged behind New York and Boston in the construction of a music hall equipped for it. The cornerstone was laid in 1852. Modeled on La Scala in Milan, it's grand, ornate, acoustically problematic, and is used some 300 evenings annually. The academy was refurbished in 1986, but it remains a symphony of Victorian crimson and gold, with original gaslights still flaming at the Broad Street entrance. The marble planned for the facade has never been added, and the brick and glass seem to suit Philadelphia far better.

The Philadelphia Orchestra has been a resident since its inception, playing same 100 dates annually, however, they'll be moving within a decade to a brand-new hall one block south. When that happens, look for many more touring orchestras to touch base here. Other days are given over to opera and ballet performances, travel films, and other events.

Box Office: Open Monday to Saturday from 10am to 5:30pm (8:30pm on event dates) and Sunday from 1pm on event dates. Tickets for any one event go on sale four weeks before at the box office. You can write for tickets from one month ahead of curtain time. The address is Academy of Music Box Office, Broad and Locust streets, Philadelphia, PA 19102; include a self-addressed stamped envelope.

Tours: $3; reservations required ☎ **893-1935**.

Prices: Tickets $12–$45, depending on event.

Painted Bride Art Center, 230 Vine St. ☎ **925-9914.**

It's hard to know what to call the Painted Bride Art Center, near the entrance to the Benjamin Franklin Bridge. It's an art gallery with contemporary tastes, but it also stays open for business and energy, in various forms—folk, electronic and new music, jazz, dance, and theater. Although its director claims that the room can hold 300, the official seat count for the main hall is 60.

Prices: Tickets $8–$20.

Theaters

At any time, there will be at least one Broadway show in Philadelphia, on the way into or out of New York. There'll also be student repertory, professional performances by casts connected with the

University of Pennsylvania, small-theater offerings in neighborhoods of Center City, and cabaret or dinner theater in the suburbs.

Annenberg Center, 3680 Walnut St. ☎ **898-6791.**

Located on the beautiful University of Pennsylvania campus and endowed by publisher and ambassador Walter Annenberg, the Annenberg Center offers both international and national companies from September through June in performances of theater, dance, music, and plays for children. Of the two stages, the **Harold Prince Theater** generally has more intimate productions, and usually the more avant-garde choices. The **Zellerbach Theater** can handle the most demanding lighting and staging needs.

Regional organizations presenting annual seasons include the Philadelphia Drama Guild and Philadelphia Festival Theatre for New Plays. In May, the center presents an International Theatre Festival for Children, a 5-day event that attracts a regional audience. It's easily reached by bus or subway/surface line.

Box Office: Open noon–6pm weekdays, with extended hours during performances. TDD phone is **898-4939**.

Prices: Vary with performance. Discounts for students and seniors.

Artsbank, 601 S. Broad St. at South St. ☎ **545-0590** or box office **567-0670.**

One of the cornerstones of the new Avenue of the Arts project, the 1994 ArtsBank is a gift of the William Penn Foundation, which realized that there wasn't enough quality, affordable performance space in Center City. The 238-seat theater has a sprung (that's bouncy) wood floor and state-of-the-art computerized lighting and sound. Relâche, Arden Theatre, Philadelphia Festival Theatre for New Plays, and University of the Arts students will be just a few of the performing artists.

Prices: Depends on event.

The Forrest, 11th and Walnut Sts. ☎ **923-1515.**

Of the Philadelphia theaters listed here, the Forrest is the best equipped to handle big musicals like *Crazy for You,* and it hosts several during the year, along with other short-running plays and concerts. Performances are usually on Monday to Saturday at 8pm and on Wednesday and Saturday at 2pm.

Prices: Tickets $15–$40, but the 1992 *Phantom of the Opera* production topped out at $100.

The Merriam Theater, Broad and Locust Sts. ☎ **732-5446.**

The Merriam, belonging to the newly rejuvenated University of the Arts, hosts many of Broadway's top touring shows in addition to popular artists like Patti LaBelle, Barry Manilow, comedians, magicians, and the Pennsylvania Ballet. It's an ornate turn-of-the-century hall, renovated to some degree for uses never foreseen during the vaudeville era.

Prices: Tickets $15–$60.

2   The Club & Music Scene

The minimum legal drinking age in Pennsylvania is 21. Bars may stay open until 2am; establishments that operate as private clubs can serve until 3am.

★ Delaware Waterfront

With huge spaces of fantasyland and night lights shimmering off the water—the unused piers and warehouses of Delaware Avenue (renamed Christopher Columbus Boulevard in 1992, but nobody likes this) both north and south of the Ben Franklin Bridge exploded as a social scene in the early 1990s. Although many waterfront spots serve passable food (I recommend **Meiji-en, Eli's Pier 34,** and **The Chart House**), they shine most for nightlife. If you're driving, park at Pier 24 at Callowhill Street, between **Rock Lobster** and **Kat Man Du,** three blocks north of the bridge ($5) or at Eli's Pier 34 ($3). Once there, the 26-foot water taxis with surrey tops are great; a one-way ride is $3, or you can pay $5 for an open ticket good for 24 hours. They run every 30 minutes to most locations, from 11am to 11pm Monday through Thursday and until 2am Friday and Saturday. Most clubs charge admission of $10 to $15 during peak hours and take major credit cards.

Start about three blocks north of the intersection of Columbus Boulevard and Spring Garden Street and work south to:

Maui, Pier 53, 1143 N. Columbus Blvd. ☎ **423-8116.**

Lush tropical foliage out of "Gilligan's Island," outdoor beach grill, the city's biggest dance floor, and King Sunny Ade live music at deafening levels. Crowd is in their 20s and 30s.

Beach Club at Pier 42, 945 N. Columbus Blvd. ☎ **829-1900.**

This outdoor-only beach setting is Atlantic City in a block: the city's biggest sandbox; volleyball games; wonderfully wacky cocktails: beach-stand food, Friday pig roasts, very casual attire.

Aztec Club/Kokomo Bay, 939 N. Columbus Blvd.
☎ **574-5730/574-1920.**

The Aztec Club is a cavernous room set with bamboo, mock Easter Island head carvings, and Aztec pillars. Friday evening brings a huge buffet, with the loudest live music and DJs on the river. Kokomo Bay is even more fantastic, with a lagoon, a 30-foot waterfall, and a volcano that erupts at midnight. Stick with hand-held food at the café.

Eighth Floor, 800 N. Columbus Blvd. ☎ **922-1000.**

Open in June 1994, this very upscale spot attracts a style-conscious 30s and 40s crowd. The wraparound waterfront view is terrific.

Egypt, 520 N. Columbus Blvd. at Spring Garden St. ☎ **922-6500.**

On the land side of Columbus Boulevard, this bi-level dance floor features concert light and sound systems in a campy "oasis" setting.

Kat Man Du/Elizabeth at Kat Man Du, Pier 25, 417 N. Columbus Blvd. ☎ **629-1101** or **627-5151.**

Kat Man Du was the first (1988) and remains the most pleasant outdoor island getaway complete with palm trees, white-sand beaches, world dance music, daiquiries and an island "mall" with travel agency. Reasonably priced outdoor pit barbecue, plenty of secluded nooks, and $5 admission. Elizabeth is a docked riverboat, and quite upscale. Dancing is to classic rock.

Dave & Buster's, Pier 19, 325 N. Columbus Blvd. ☎ **413-1951.**

Traffic is huge for this urban country club with video arcades, electronic golf, billiards, and blackjack.

Rock Lobster, 221 N. Columbus Blvd. ☎ **627-7625.**

At the corner of Race Street, just north of Ben Franklin Bridge and on the Marina, is this long-awaited blend of top nightclub/disco and good restaurant. It serves hundreds of moderately priced lunches and dinners daily, in a 4,000-square-foot tent or al fresco area designed to look like a Maine yacht club. Crowd is in their 30s, 40s, and 50s.

Admission: No cover until 9pm, then normally $5 Mon–Thurs, $7 Fri–Sat. Higher when national acts appear.

Eli's Pier 34, 735 S. Columbus Blvd. ☎ **923-2500.**

This club is set apart from the rest of the waterfront night spots, at Fitzwater Street, just south of the historic ships at **Penn's Landing** and **The Chart House.** It's also the most restful, with the longest pier extending in to the Delaware River, and it touts its year-round seafood at reasonable prices. Live music nightly and an oldies dance party on Fridays.

Cabaret & Nightclubs

Ethel Barrymore Room, in the Hotel Atop The Bellevue, Broad and Locust Sts. ☎ **893-1776.**

In collaboration with the American Musical Theater Festival, major cabaret stars such as Julie Wilson are presented in this classic setting every winter and spring. Old-timers will recognize this room as the Bellevue-Stratford's original home.

Admission: $25 cover.

The Lounge at the Omni, 4th and Chestnut Sts. ☎ **925-0000.**

This lounge is a very posh spot, with dark woods and Oriental carpets, a crackling fireplace, a piano trio, and large picture windows surveying Independence National Historical Park across the street. It stays open past midnight on weekends.

Middle East, 126 Chestnut St. ☎ **922-1003.**

Dinner followed by belly dancing and eastern Mediterranean music makes a fine evening for scores of Philadelphians nightly. Councilman Jim Tayoun presides, and many of his family members help in various capacities. If you've never seen it, don't worry about taking the kids to see belly dancing: It's quite an art and as pure as the driven snow.

Admission: $10 minimum with show.

Comedy Clubs

Comedy Cabaret, 126 Chestnut St. ☎ **625-5653**.

This addition to the Middle East complex operates from Wednesday (open stage) to Saturday nights. Shows are on Friday at 8:30 and 11pm and on Saturday at 8 and 11pm. There is a separate $10 admission.

Funny Bone, 221 South St. ☎ **440-9670**.

Because of its neighborhood, the Funny Bone is a bit free-form. Shows are on Tuesday to Thursday at 8:30pm, on Friday and Saturday at 8:30 and 11pm, and on Sunday at 8:30pm. Admission is $8 on weeknights and $10 on weekends.

Folk & Country Music

Boot N Saddle, 1131 S. Broad St. ☎ **336-1742**.

In the heart of South Philly, this cash-only place features live country music every Friday and Saturday night in the back, with seating at tiny tables. There's a large island bar in the front. It's open Monday to Saturday until 2am.

D'Medici Restaurant, 824 S. 8th St. ☎ **922-3986**.

On Friday and Saturday, Dave Morris and his band bring this otherwise sedate Italian restaurant in South Philadelphia to life with renditions of Sinatra, Mel Tormé, Tony Bennett, and other neighborhood favorites. There's no cover charge.

Tin Angel Acoustic Cafe, 20 S. 2nd St. ☎ **574-2900**.

This new club, very conveniently located in Serrano, is riding the "unplugged" wave with artists like John Wesley Harding, Dan Hicks, and Susan Werner. Open Wednesdays through Saturdays.

Admission: Wed, no cover for open-mike evenings; other nights $8–$15.

Triangle Tavern, 10th and Reed Sts. ☎ 467-8683.

If you're in search of where Rocky Balboa would go to sing along with the band, go no further than this place, which couldn't be cheaper. The help really participates. See Chapter 6 for a restaurant review.

Rock Music

Chestnut Cabaret, 38th and Chestnut Sts. ☎ **382-1201**.

The Chestnut Cabaret, in the heart of University City, is committed to bringing the best in local, regional, and even national acts in rock, pop, jazz, reggae, blues, and rhythm and blues on Tuesday to Saturday nights. It does not serve food.

Admission: Cover varies, but no minimum.

J. C. Dobbs, 304 South St. ☎ **925-4053**.

Dobbs features rock bands, both crude and smooth, every night until 2am. The upstairs serves food until 1am, and the air is always leaden. It's a hard-drinking place, with lots of energy when the band is good.

Admission: $5 at most.

Khyber Pass Pub, 56 S. 2nd St. ☎ **440-9683.**

This is one of the most popular spots to hear jazz, funk, and rock nightly. There's live entertainment from 9:30pm until 1 or 2am, depending on the crowd and the day. Khyber Pass is named after the route the British took to get through Pakistan, and it's somebody's version of what a British overseas officers' club would look like. It does have a certain atticlike charm, nevertheless, and English ales and Irish stout are served.

Admission: $5 cover most nights.

North Star Bar, 27th and Poplar Sts. ☎ **235-7827.**

North Star, located near the Philadelphia Museum of Art, has photo exhibits and poetry readings. Rock groups perform five nights a week in a recently glassed-in courtyard. You'll see an older bar as you enter. It's a very comfortable place to drink, and the spicy chicken wings are fine.

Admission: $5–$8.

Revival, 22 S. 3rd St. ☎ **627-4825.**

This beautiful 1837 church now features techno, house, and alternative music Monday through Saturday nights. Revival has two floors, including the city's largest nonpier club dance floor, and six bars.

Admission: $1–$10, for ages 21 and over. Takes credit cards.

Spectrum, Electric Factory Concerts, Broad and Pattison Sts. ☎ **569-9416** or **568-3222;** box office at Spectrum **336-3600.**

Most of the events that the Electric Factory sponsors, from Willie Nelson to Phil Collins, take place at the **Spectrum,** the city's main indoor arena, in South Philly. As with most rock concerts, tickets at the door are next to impossible to obtain. They're usually distributed through TicketMaster or Ticketron.

Jazz & Blues

Philadelphia is one of the great American venues for jazz. The Peco Energy Jazz Festival takes place over President's Day weekend in February and June brings the Mellon PSFS Jazz Festival produced by George Wien. Increasingly, major cultural venues like the Philadelphia Museum of Art are getting into the act. For specific information, write or call Mill Creek Jazz and Cultural Society, 4624 Lancaster Ave., Philadelphia, PA 19131 (☎ **215/473-2880**).

Blue Moon Jazz Club, 21 S. 5th St. at The Bourse. ☎ **413-2272.**

This pub has nightly sets at 9:30pm. Shirley Scott, Mickey Roker, or assorted quartets perform Wednesday to Saturday, with open sessions Sunday to Thursday. There's no cover charge.

Carolina's, 261 S. 20th St. ☎ **545-1000.**

This popular restaurant features a jazz trio on Saturday night. It's a favorite singles spot, with not bad bistro dining, though cramped.

Liberties, 705 N. 2nd St. above Fairmount Ave. ☎ **238-0660.**

A carved walnut bar and high-backed booths highlight this pub with a changing schedule of jazz trios. It's a favorite haunt of local artists and musicians. Live music is featured nightly from 8:30pm to 12:30am.

Morgan's, 17 E. Price St., Germantown, PA. ☎ **848-2640** or **844-6067** for schedule. **Directions:** North on Germantown Ave. for 2¼ miles after intersection with North Broad St. East Price St. is 1 block beyond Chelten Ave.

Another place for serious jazz is Morgan's, an unassuming building in Germantown that happens to house top talent in a terrific environment.

> **Admission:** $8–$15.

The Saloon, 7th and Catharine Sts. ☎ **627-1811.**

Deep in the heart of South Philly, The Saloon features Victorian antiques which accent a fine Italian restaurant. If you want to hear mellow music, head upstairs by the glossy mahogany bar. The Saloon bar is open Wednesday to Saturday until 12:30am. The drinks average $2.50.

> **Admission:** Free.

Zanzibar Blue, 305 S. 11th St. ☎ **829-0300.**

This place features the best of the city's jazz bands. The ambience is elegant—Denzel Washington loved it while filming *Philadelphia*—so you may wish to dress up for a visit. Zanzibar is open until 2am nightly; there's also a jazz brunch ($15) on Sunday.

> **Admission:** $8–$10.

Dance Clubs

BALLROOM DANCING

Social Club, 2009 Sansom St., 2nd floor. ☎ **564-2277.**

There's no live entertainment, but Social Club's sound system is programmed with mambos, foxtrots, and swing. Most attendees are members, but nonmembers are welcome.

> **Admission:** $10.

DISCOS

The two hottest areas in town right now are the Delaware waterfront (see above) and the booming northeast between City Hall and the Museum of Art.

The Bank, 600 Spring Garden St. ☎ **351-9404.**

The Bank, a taxi ride away from Center City, was created by the same people who started Chestnut Cabaret. It offers one of the city's largest dance floors, situated in a shabby yet chic renovated 1872 Frank Furness–designed bank. A young but sophisticated crowd, both collegiate and grunge.

> **Admission:** Thursdays $10, Fridays $7, Saturdays $5.

The Black Banana, 3rd and Race Sts. ☎ **925-4433.**

Even though this is technically a private club, nonmembers are admitted. You can dance to cool postmodernism until 3am. Videos are shown on the first floor, and the dance floor is on the second. American Express is accepted.

> **Admission:** $15.

Circa, 1518 Walnut St. ☎ **545-6800.**

This new club is absolutely the greatest: it tastes like the Mediterranean, looks like beaux arts, and feels like Manhattan. Thursdays through Saturdays, following the excellent dinner (see Chapter 6), the main room is cleared to accommodate stylish throngs on a wooden dance floor until 2am. Music is DJ-spun house and pop.

Admission: $10 cover Fri–Sat after 9pm, $8 after 10pm.

Monte Carlo Living Room, 2nd and South Sts. ☎ **925-2220.**

There's a brass plaque on the door stating that proper attire is required (coats and ties for men, dresses for women). The way to do the Monte Carlo is to dine romantically and well, then dance the night away at the piano bar and old-style disco upstairs, with a tinkling fountain illuminated in alternating reds and blues and sentimental artwork. The surfaces (including the ceiling) are very mirrored, with wood railings and flowered carpets leading to different levels. It's open Monday to Saturday from 6pm to 2am. There's dancing to continental crooners after 9:30pm, with a DJ playing Top 40 releases between sets.

Admission: $10, unless you've dined downstairs or are a member.

Quincy's, at the Adam's Mark, City Line Ave. at Monument Rd. ☎ **581-5000.**

The top choice in this flashy suburban-mall area is Quincy's. Clean sounds emanate from good bands, there's lots of wood paneling and old brass, and there are backgammon tables galore. Quincy's also provides one of the best happy hours anywhere, with incredible buffet tables. There's a singles dance on Sunday from 5 to 10pm, with no cover charge.

Admission: Free–$10.

Xero, 613 S. 4th St., half block south of South St. ☎ **629-0565.**

This has been one of the most solid and successful bar/restaurant/club scenes in town since the early 1990s. Thursdays bring a complete food, drink, and dance package for $5, and alternative DJs set the mood on weekends. Happy hours 7 to 9pm on Fridays and Saturdays.

GAY DANCE CLUBS

Hepburn's, 254 S. 12th St. ☎ **545-8088.**

This is Philadelphia's only bar primarily for women, open nightly until 2am. Downstairs is a quiet bar, with etched glass and a community bulletin board; dinners are served Wednesday–Saturday. Upstairs are two bars and a crowded disco. No credit cards are accepted.

Admission: Free.

Woody's, 202 S. 13th St. ☎ **545-1893.**

Woody's party atmosphere also attracts many straights. The original bar is downstairs, and a sandwich counter has been added alongside. The disco adjoining the upstairs lounge features trompe l'oeil Atlases holding up a roof of stars. Free two-step lessons on Tuesdays, 5 to 6pm.

Admission: $5–$10 Fri–Sat.

3 The Bar Scene

Bridget Foy's South St. Grill, 200 South St. ☎ **922-1813.**

Newly renovated and with a fine open-style grill at reasonable prices, Bridget Foy's offers a nice, mellow atmosphere with no pressure to socialize if you don't feel like it and the company to keep you entertained if you do. It's open every evening until 1am. Situated at the lower corner of Head House Square, the establishment features a lively sidewalk café in summer.

Cutters Grand Cafe And Bar, 2005 Market St. ☎ **851-6262.**

This is the quintessential 1990s bar: long, high, massively stocked, with businesslike high-tech systems and a friendly and elegant atmosphere. The destination, in the new IBM building at Commerce Square, makes it a fine postbusiness meeting place.

TGI Friday's, 18th St. and the Parkway. ☎ **665-8443.**

It's hard to believe that a place this obviously corporate in intent and atmosphere could make it—but it has become a favorite of the younger crowd that populates Logan Circle's new office towers. There's standing room only at the outdoor terrace on summer evenings for the happy-hour buffet and socializing.

Pubs & Wine Bars

Bridgid's, 726 N. 24th St. ☎ **232-3232.**

This tiny, very friendly horseshoe-shaped bar near the Philadelphia Museum of Art stocks a superb collection of Belgian beers, including an array from fruit- to hops-originated brews. A tapas menu is also available at the bar.

Dock Street Brewing Co. Brewery And Restaurant, 18th and Cherry Sts., 2 Logan Square. ☎ **496-0413.**

This is the epitome of the 1990s—a comfortable, moderate place that brews and sells only its own beers, nestled into a top corporate corner. Offered at two separate bars are up to six varieties of beer at $2.50 per glass (or a sampler of all six for $3.50), painstakingly brewed within the last month. You can even inspect the spotless fermenting vats to the right of the bar.

Houlihan's Old Place, 18th St. and Rittenhouse Square. ☎ **546-5940.**

Houlihan's Old Place isn't exactly old, and the decor is more that of Albert Hall with peppy graffiti than that of an Irish pub. But it's one of Center City's most active pubs, especially among young professionals and older students. The decor and noise level are determinedly eclectic and on the loud side. Mixed drinks start at $2.50. A substantial dining area serves lunch, dinner, and Sunday brunch.

The Irish Pub, 1123 Walnut St. ☎ **925-3311.** Also at 2007 Walnut St. ☎ **568-5603.**

With one located across from the Forrest Theatre and the other off Rittenhouse Square, both Irish Pubs pack in hundreds of good-natured professionals, of both genders and all ages. There is Irish and American folk music in the front, but you can get far away and a floor down if you wish. Both are open until 2am nightly.

Jeannine's Bistro, 10 S. Front St. ☎ **925-1126.**

This is a more moderate effort by Jeanne Mermet, situated above her La Truffe. Guitar and violin music are offered on the weekend, though the bistro is open only until 10:30pm. The ambience of plush pillows, padded bench seats, and candlelight is charming. About 20 wines are available by the glass at $4.50 to $7 each.

Odeon, 114 S. 12th St. ☎ **922-5875.**

Odeon is the closest you'll get to Paris in Center City. It offers a fine assortment of both wines by the glass—the cruvinet holds 16—and fine beers, both U.S. and international. There are also more than 20 single-malt scotches. I recommend the bar as a dining spot, with its recent change to moderate bistro fare.

Panorama, 14 N. Front St. at Front and Market Sts. ☎ **922-7800.**

Panorama is at the rear of Penn's View Inn but separate from the moderately priced Italian restaurant. Its curving wine bar features 120 different selections by the glass. Most cost about $5. There's piano entertainment. Panorama is open Monday to Saturday until 1am, Sunday until 10:30pm.

Samuel Adams Brew House, 1516 Sansom St. ☎ **563-2326.**

The Brew House was opened in the late 1980s as an offshoot of the Sansom Street Oyster House downstairs. Three beers are regularly brewed right here: a light ale, an amber ale, and a dark porter. The bar of aged wood and etched glass was imported from Great Britain.

Serrano, 20 S. 2nd St. ☎ **928-0770.**

Serrano—which now also holds Tin Angel Acoustic Cafe—offers a wonderful collection of brews in an intimate setting. It is also on one of the Historic District's nicest blocks. The old wooden bar has antique stained glass behind it, and the wood fire is spiced. Try one of the local brewer's products, Stoudt's unpasteurized ($5.95 per bottle).

Piano Bars

Downey's, Front and South Sts. ☎ **625-9500.**

Downey's is a terrific Irish pub with a contemporary flair. Many of the local professional athletes head here after a game to relax upstairs, downstairs, or at the café tables outside. The new upstairs bar has

classy skylights set into the original tin-plate ceiling and the obligatory Irish coin nailed to the portal. The music's upstairs on piano
and accompaniment nightly from 8pm to 1am on Friday and
Saturday. At Sunday brunch (11:30am to 3pm) a strolling string
quartet punctuates the atmosphere. A beautiful new wraparound
second-floor deck offers waterfront views for dining or cocktails.

1701 Cafe, in the Warwick Hotel, 17th and Locust Sts.
☎ **545-4655.**

Open 24 hours, 1701 Café offers plenty of smooth, sophisticated
peace and quiet. There's something about comfortable chairs and
marble-topped bars that draws in everyone from hotel guests to
students. Of course, the cool music helps, played Wednesday to
Saturday from 9pm to 1am and Sunday from 8pm to midnight. Light
meals are available on the café side, and if you're at the bar you know
where you stand, which isn't nearby. Jazz predominates.

The Society Hill Hotel, 3rd and Chestnut Sts. ☎ **925-1919.**

The Society Hill Hotel, a renovated 1832 shell, has a dozen rooms
upstairs—but the bar has all of Society Hill excited. It's one of the
few modern bars in town that's sophisticated but not glitzy, and the
outdoor café makes it even more charming on a summer eve. (Why
don't more places follow their lead and screw hooks into the
undersides of tables and counters so that women can hang their purses
and pocketbooks safely but conveniently?)

Gay Bars

See also "Gay Dance Clubs," above.

247 Bar, 247 S. 17th St. ☎ **545-9779.**

Animal heads and pine paneling mark this macho stalwart in the
Rittenhouse Square area. There are pool tables and plenty of TVs
for sports watching.

The Venture Inn, 255 S. Camac St. ☎ **545-8731.**

The quaint block has this charming bar and restaurant as a
centerpiece. The dining room features candlelight and a fireplace,
with intimate seating. Dinners are a real value. No credit cards are
accepted.

4 More Entertainment

Readings

Borders Book Shop and Espresso Bar, 1727 Walnut St.
(☎ 568-7400), runs one of the country's top series of author readings in an elegant setting that's steps from Rittenhouse Square. In a
recent month, authors included Anna Quindlen, Marilyn French,
Nancy Lemann, Spalding Grey, Michael Pollan, and Meg Pei. Readings usually are at 7:30pm on weekdays and at 2pm on weekends.

Salons

Judy Wicks at the White Dog Café, 3420 Sansom St. (☎ **386-9224**), has instituted salon meals, tapping into local academics, artists, and her own contacts. Issues addressed include domestic and foreign policy, the arts, and social movements. Dinner talks include a three-course dinner for $25 per person, and reservations are recommended. A great singles activity for the intellectually curious.

Spectacles

The **Benjamin Franklin Bridge** has been outfitted with special lighting effects by the noted architectural firm Venturi, Rauch and Scott Brown. The lights are triggered into mesmerizing patterns by the auto and train traffic along the span. Some summers **Independence Hall** is the scene of a 9pm sound-and-light show with 1776 as its theme.

Movie Theaters

HISTORIC AREA

Ritz 5 Movies, 214 Walnut St. ☎ **925-7900/1.**

This is the single best Historic District Area choice for independent releases. It has five comfortable screening rooms and shows sophisticated—often foreign—fare. The first daily matinee performances cost $4. There are more screens in this part of town; Ritz has also constructed a fiveplex behind The Bourse and the new Omni Hotel at 4th and Chestnut streets (☎ **440-1180**).

CENTER CITY

Standard studio releases are offered at **United Artists at Rittenhouse Square** 1907–1911 Walnut St. (☎ **567-0320**), and **United Artists Sam's Place I and II,** 1826 Chestnut St. (☎ **972-0538**). Action films are screened at **Sameric 4,** 1908 Chestnut St. (☎ **567-0604**), and **AMC Midtown 2,** Chestnut Street at Broad Street (☎ **567-7021**).

Roxy Screening Room, 2023 Sansom St. ☎ **561-0114.**

The Theatre of the Living Arts runs this room, which offers Center City's only cinémathèque of first-run and foreign films. Tickets cost $5.50; $4.50 for students; $3.75 seniors.

UNIVERSITY CITY

International House, 3701 Chestnut St. ☎ **387-5125.**

International House presents a fine series of foreign films, political documentaries, and the work of independent filmmakers. Admission is $3.50.

AMC Walnut Mall 3, 3925 Walnut St. ☎ **222-2344.**

This theater screens intelligent releases for the College Crowd from the United States and abroad. The popcorn is outstanding.

11

Easy Excursions from Philadelphia

The SAME BOATS THAT BROUGHT PENN'S QUAKERS ALSO BROUGHT THE settlers of Germantown, an agricultural retreat that many wealthy colonials called home in summertime. Other pioneers fanned out into the Delaware Valley to the south, Bucks County to the north, and what is now Pennsylvania Dutch Country to the west. Much of this area remains lush and unspoiled, although development-versus-environment struggles are becoming pointed. The major attractions of the countryside are historical: colonial mansions and inns, early American factories or businesses, and battlegrounds of the Revolution and the Civil War.

1 Germantown & Chestnut Hill

Germantown

Germantown, a district within Philadelphia's city limits, is far enough away from Center City stamping grounds to make it an excursion destination. The area was settled in the 1680s, by non-Quaker immigrants seeking a better life. Even though time has faded the handwriting, few other American streets have as much to tell about past American life at every level, from the nation's first summer White House to breweries. Many of these still bear scars from the Battle of Germantown, an attempt by the Revolutionary forces to recapture occupied Philadelphia.

ORIENTATION   Addresses of interest stretch approximately from no. 4500 to no. 6610 Germantown Ave., a hilly 3-mile walk (once a Native American trail) in itself. If you start touring from upper Germantown (as I recommend), it's all downhill.

INFORMATION   The fastest route by public transport is the R8 commuter train to Chestnut Hill West; from Reading Terminal or Suburban Station, get off at Queen Lane (Middle) or Tulpehocken Avenue (Upper), four blocks west. By car from Center City, head north on the Schuylkill Expressway, and the Roosevelt Boulevard/U.S. 1 exit will bring you to the Wayne-Wissahickon turnoff in lower Germantown.

WHAT TO SEE

⭐ **Cliveden,** 6401 Germantown Ave. ☎ **848-1777.**
Georgian through and through, Cliveden was built in the 1760s for the chief justice of Pennsylvania, in the Palladian county-seat tradition used by Woodford and Mount Pleasant in Fairmount Park. Note the pockmarks of bullets from the Battle of Germantown. Cliveden was donated in 1972 to the National Trust for Historic Preservation.
   Admission: $6 adults and seniors, $4 children.
   Open: Tues–Sat 10am–4pm, Sun 1–4pm. The guided tour is obligatory. **Closed:** Jan–Mar.

⭐ **Ebenezer Maxwell Mansion,** 200 W. Tulpehocken St. at Greene St. ☎ **438-1861.**

This house is a bit off the avenue, but it's an ornate and classic Victorian mansion (rare in Philadelphia) that's worth a visit, especially when bedecked at Christmas. There's also a public garden.

Admission: $3 adults, $2 children over 6 and seniors.

Open: Wed–Sun 1–4pm.

Wyck, 6026 Germantown Ave. ☎ **848-1690.**

Wyck combines the treasures of nine generations of the same Quaker family, but it's not too richly ornamented, since they were Quakers. William Strichland did notable alterations in 1824 to the colonial house. The garden has over 35 varieties of roses.

Admission: $3 adults, $2 children and seniors.

Open: Tues, Thurs, and Sat 1–4pm. **Closed:** Winter.

Deshler-Morris House, 5442 Germantown Ave. ☎ **596-1748.**

A 1975 renovation of a 1752 home, with a 1772 addition, the Deshler-Morris boasts an impressive history: General Howe stayed here during the British occupation of the city, and George Washington waited out the yellow fever epidemic of 1793 to 1794 here. The "necessary" in the garden seats 12!

Admission: $1.

Open: Tues–Sat 1–4pm; other times by appointment. **Closed:** Jan–Mar.

DINING

If you set aside Tuesday or Friday afternoon for the jaunt, the **Farmer's Market** at West Haines Street (near Wyck, or three blocks north of Chelten Avenue) will revive you with egg custard, cheeses, scrapple, and other Pennsylvania Dutch foods. It's open on Tuesday from 9am to 4pm and on Friday from 9am to 6pm.

Chestnut Hill

Farther up Germantown Avenue lies Chestnut Hill, an enclave of suburban gentility—even exclusivity—with a historic "Main Street" flavor. It was once filled with chestnut trees, and it is still the highest point within city limits. Just to the south and west is Wissahickon Creek Park, an extension of Fairmount Park that was purchased and cleared of all commercial development by the city in the 1860s; the stunning rambles and walks have been compared to Alpine gorges. You can stop by the **Chestnut Hill Welcome Center,** 8426 Germantown Ave., Chestnut Hill PA 19118 (☎ **247-6696**), or simply ramble among the galleries, restaurants, shops, and boutiques.

⭐ **Morris Arboretum,** entrance at 101 Hillcrest Ave. between Germantown and Stenton Aves. ☎ **247-5882.**

A 1932 gift to the University of Pennsylvania, this arboretum is an elaborately landscaped country estate as well as a collection of 3,500 trees and shrubs assembled for scientific study. The stone mansion is long gone, but maps indicating the Japanese Garden, English Park, and Wissahickon Creek meadow are available at the gate house. This place is great for families.

Admission: $3 adults, $1 students and seniors.

Open: Mon–Fri 10am–4pm, Sat–Sun 10am–5pm. **Directions:** Take Germantown Avenue north for .9 mile on Bethlehem Pike, then make a left onto Stenton Avenue; make a left on Hillcrest and follow it for .2 miles.

WHERE TO STAY

Moderate

 Chestnut Hill Hotel, 8229 Germantown Ave., Philadelphia, PA 19118. ☎ **215/242-5905** or toll free **800/628-9744.** 28 units. AC TV TEL

Rates (including continental breakfast): $85 single, $95 double; $100 deluxe single, $110 deluxe double. Children under 12 free in parents' room. **Parking:** Free.

This stucco and cement hotel, built in 1899, was renovated and expanded to include shops and restaurants in 1983. It's comfortable, with first- and second-floor lounges, but the 28 rooms differ in size. Sharing space are two pleasant restaurants: **J. B. Winberie** (☎ **247-6710**) and **Pollo Rosso** (☎ **248-9338**), as well as a farmer's market.

WHERE TO DINE

Inexpensive

Campbell's Place, 8337 Germantown Ave. ☎ **242-2066.**

Cuisine: CONTINENTAL/AMERICAN. **Reservations:** Not required.
Prices: Main courses $7–$12 lunch, $6.95–$14.95 dinner. No credit cards.
Open: Lunch Sat noon–5pm; dinner Tues–Sat 5–10pm. Bar is open until 1am.

This is basically a good neighborhood tavern for informed tastes, with a varied menu of pasta dishes, steaks, and Chinese wok cooking.

Under The Blue Moon, 8225 Germantown Ave. ☎ **247-1100.**

Cuisine: CONTINENTAL. **Reservations:** Recommended.
Prices: Appetizers $3.50–$5.25; main courses $13.75–$18 MC, V.
Open: Dinner Tues–Thurs 6–9pm, Fri–Sat until 10pm.

The top choice in the neighborhood for almost two decades, this restaurant offers unusual international dishes such as sesame-pecan chicken and a fabled duck. There's a sensibly priced but interesting wine list.

---

2 Bucks County & Nearby New Jersey

Bucks County, at most an hour by car from Philadelphia, is bordered by the Delaware River to the east and Montgomery County to the west. Historic estates and sites, along with the antique stores and country inns they've spawned, abound. Many artists and authors, including Oscar Hammerstein II, Pearl Buck, and James Michener, have gained inspiration from the natural beauty, which has survived major development so far. A newer interest is "ecotourism"—the area is great for gentle outdoor activities. Nearby New Jersey offers scenic routes for bicycling and walking as well as fine restaurants.

GETTING THERE   The best automobile route into Bucks County from Center City is I-95 (north). Pa. 32 (which intersects I-95 in Yardley) runs along the Delaware, past Washington Crossing State Park to New Hope, which connects to Doylestown by U.S. 202. By train, the R5 SEPTA commuter rail ends at Doylestown, with connections to New Hope and Lahaska.

INFORMATION   To find out more about the hundreds of historic sites, camping facilities, and accommodations here, contact the **Bucks County Tourist Commission,** 152 Swamp Rd., Doylestown, PA 18901 (☎ **215/345-4552** or toll free **800/836-2825**). You can also write to or stop by the **New Hope Information Center,** South Main and Mechanic streets, Box 141, New Hope, PA 18938 (☎ **215/862-5880**); it's open Monday to Friday from 9am to 5pm, Saturday and Sunday from 10am to 6pm.

What to See & Do

Sesame Place, 100 Sesame Rd., Langhorne, PA 19047 (junction of U.S. Rte. 1 and I-95). ☎ **215/752-7070.**

At this hands-on family play park 30 minutes from Center City, kids climb through three stories of sloping, swaying fun on the Nets and Climbs or crawl through tubes and tunnels amid splashing fountains and showers of spray at Mumford's Water Maze. As of 1994, a festive Amazing Alphabet parade involves everyone with pushing, pulling, and confetti. Physical fitness is also a major new theme. The kids will want their swimsuits for the Rubber Duckie and Runaway Rapids (locker rooms are provided). All of the best-loved "Sesame Street" characters perform in stage revues at the Circle Theatre and stroll for photo ops. Indoors, the air-conditioned Computer Gallery has puzzles, Mix 'n' Match Muppets, logic games, and more than 70 computer activities for kids 3 to 13. Everyone will love the Rainbow Room, where every movement reveals a splash of stunning colors. There's even an Adult Oasis. Sesame Place is an Anheuser-Busch Theme Park planned in conjunction with Children's Television Workshop.

Admission: $20.95 adults and children 3–15, $17.80 seniors over 55. Twilight admission $14.95. Second-day tickets $12.95 with validated first-day ticket. **Parking:** $4 per day. **Note:** Many hotels in the area offer discount tickets in their package rates.

Open: May to mid-June Mon–Fri 10am–5pm, Sat–Sun 10am–8pm. Late June to Aug, daily 9am–8pm, Sept–Oct Sat–Sun only 9am–8pm.

Pennsbury Manor, Rte. Pa. 9 (Tyburn Rd.) from U.S. 1 (intersects I-95) or U.S. 13, Morrisville, PA 19067. ☎ **215/946-0400.**

William Penn planned his very English plantation and manor at Pennsbury Manor, along the Delaware 24 miles north of

Philadelphia on Route 32 (River Road). On it, he designed a self-sustaining (and obviously pre-Georgian) estate, replete with a smokehouse, an icehouse, a barn, an herb garden, a plantation office, and a boathouse. The various dependencies and the manor itself were demolished but were rebuilt to the smallest detail in 1939.

Pennsbury Manor boasts the largest collection of 17th-century antiques in the state, spread over four floors of the manor. On a sunny day, it's a treat to inspect the carefully labeled herb garden, step inside the icehouse for a cool respite, and watch the guinea fowl (more popular than chickens in 1600s) wandering along the golden brick paths.

Admission: $5 adults, $2.50 seniors and students 5–17; children under 5 free.

Open: Tues–Sat 9am–5pm, Sun noon–5pm. Last tour at 3:30pm.

Fallsington, south off U.S. 1 at Tyburn Rd., Fallsington, PA 19054. ☎ **215/295-6567.**

When Penn was in residence and wished to worship, he'd go to Fallsington, 6 miles north of Pennsbury Manor. This colonial village grouped around the Quaker meetinghouse has been preserved virtually intact. Take Pa. 13 north to Tyburn Road (Pa. 9), then turn right and follow the road.

Admission: $3.50 adults, $2.50 seniors, $1 students 6–18.

Open: Mon–Sat 10am–4pm, Sun 1pm–4pm. Special Fallsington open-house days are the second Sat in May and Oct.

Washington Crossing State Park, Intersection of Pa. 532 and Pa. 32 (River Rd.), 3 miles north of I-95 from Exit 31, P.O. Box 103, Washington Crossing, PA 18977. ☎ **215/493-4076.**

A trip along the Delaware via Route 32, through Morrisville and Yardley, will bring you to Washington Crossing State Park, 500 acres that are open year-round. Most people know that Washington crossed a big river in a small boat on Christmas Eve of 1776. This was the place, although the Durham boats on display in the boat barn used to hold 30. The state park is divided into an upper and a lower section separated by three miles; Washington left from the lower park. You can sip a glass of punch at **Old Ferry Inn** (1752), where he ate before the assault, and tour the bird sanctuary and the Memorial Building at the point of embarkation.

The **Wild Flower Preserve** in the upper park is really a 100-acre arboretum, flower garden, and shrub preserve rolled into one; it contains 15 different paths, each emphasizing different botanical wonders. The **Thompson-Neely House** ($1 admission, good for the Old Ferry Inn also) was intact when General Washington, Brigadier General Stirling, and Lt. James Monroe decided on the year-end push into New Jersey. Next to the Wild Flower Preserve is the stone **Bowman's Hill Tower;** it will reward you (or the children) with a view of this part of the Delaware Valley, which would probably belong to the British Commonwealth if Washington's troops hadn't routed the Hessians in 1776.

An annual reenactment of the historic crossing takes place here on Christmas.

Admission: Free to the Visitor Center and its 30-minute film. Tours following screenings of historic buildings are $2.50 adults, $1 children over 6.

Open: Buildings Mon–Sat 9am–5pm, Sun noon–5pm. Grounds, daily 9am–8pm or sunset.

New Hope & Lambertville

Four miles from Washington Crossing, along River Road (Pa. 32), punctuated by lovely farmland (as opposed to U.S. 202's factory outlets), you'll come upon New Hope, a former colonial town turned artists' colony. It's somewhat commercial by now. The weekend crowds can get fierce, and parking is cramped, but once on foot you'll enjoy the specialty stores, restaurants, and galleries. Lambertville, across the Delaware in New Jersey, has rather pedestrian architecture but more scenic routes along the river and, many say, better restaurants.

Among the attractions of the New Hope area are the following.

Bucks County Playhouse, 70 S. Main St. (P.O. Box 313), New Hope, PA 18938. ☎ **215/862-2041.**

This is the center of New Hope entertainment with summer theater that features Broadway hits and musical revivals. It's a former gristmill with a seating capacity of almost 500.

Admission: Tickets $15–$20.

Open: Apr–Dec Wed–Sun evenings and Wed and Thurs matinees.

New Hope Mule Barge, New and South Main Sts., New Hope, PA 18938. ☎ **215/862-2842.**

For a while in the early 1800s canals were thought to be the transport revolution in England and the eastern United States. Coal was floated down this one in the 1830s from mines in the Lehigh Valley, and the barges are still pulled by mules. The barges run April through October and leave from New Street.

Admission: $6.95 adults, $5.50 for students, $4.25 children under 12.

Open: May 1–Oct 15, six launchings daily. Apr and Oct 16–Nov 15, reduced launchings on Wed, Sat, and Sun.

Parry Mansion Museum, Main and Ferry Sts., New Hope, PA 18938. ☎ **215/862-5652.**

One of the loveliest old homes in town, this mansion was erected in 1984 by the elite of New Hope. The Parry family lived in this 11-room Georgian until 1966, and the rooms are decorated in different period styles of 1775 (whitewash and candles) to 1900 (wallpaper and oil lamps).

Admission: $4 adults, $3 seniors.
Open: May–Dec Fri–Sat 1–5pm.

Bucks County

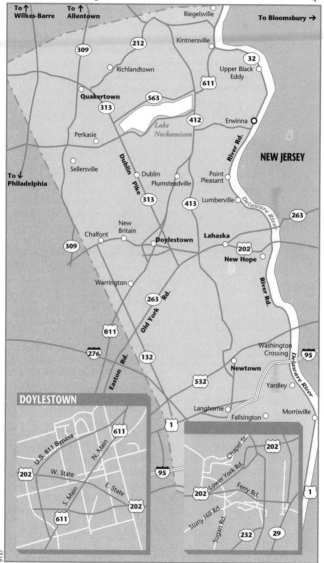

Peddler's Village, U.S. 202 and Rte. 263, Lahaska, PA 18931.
☎ 215/794-4000.

Five miles west of New Hope, on Route 202, Peddler's Village looks antique, but the appeal to customers is timeless and most of the merchandise is contemporary. It's not a country market; the prices are marked up considerably, but the ambience and convenience are attractive. The 1993 **Carousel World** can spin the family on a 1926 restored carousel, along with other fine examples of this art ($3.75 adults, $2.50 children). **Jenny's** on Route 202 at Street Road (☎ **794-5605**) is for elegant continental dining in an atmosphere of brass and stained glass. The specialties of the **Cock 'n' Bull** (☎ **794-7055**) are a massive buffet on Tuesday and Thursday and the beef burgundy served in a loaf of bread that's baked in the hearth. The 60 rooms in the **Golden Plough Inn,** are scattered throughout the village.

Admission: Free.

Open: Most stores Mon–Sat 10am–5pm, Fri until 8pm. Special Strawberry Festival in May.

COUNTRY WALKING & BICYCLING

Walking or riding along the Delaware River or along the canals built for coal hauling on either side can be the highlight of a summer. The two most convenient routes are the following.

In Stockton, N.J., take Route 263 just over the Delaware to Pennsylvania. Then park your car, cross the old bridge on foot or bicycle, and follow the towpath on the Pennsylvania side north toward Lumberville and its cute general store, three miles away. The **Lumberville Store Bicycle Rental Co.** (Route 32, Lumberville, PA 18933; ☎ **215/297-5388**) has all kinds of bicycles for rent at moderate day rates. It's open April to mid-October daily from 8am to 6pm.

The second route, just south of Lumberville, follows River Road south and west to Cuttalossa Road, which winds past an alpine chalet, creeks, ponds, and sheep grazing and clanking their antique Swiss bells. **Cuttalossa Inn,** Cuttalossa Road, Lumberville, PA 18933 (☎ **215/297-5082**), offers high-class cuisine in a spectacular setting.

OTHER ATTRACTIONS

Other transport-based attractions of the New Hope area are a **covered-bridges tour** (call **215/345-4552** for information about this self-guided free tour); **river tubing** at Point Pleasant Canoe, up the Delaware from New Hope at upper Black Eddy and Riegelsville (☎ **215/297-8181**), for two to four hours of relaxing family fun; and a **steam railway** out of New Hope (☎ **215/862-2707**).

COOL FOR KIDS

Quarry Valley Farm, 2302 Street Rd., Lahaska, PA 18931.
  ☎ **215/794-5882.**

On Street Road near Peddler's Village, Quarry Valley Farm is a working ménage of a hayloft for exploring, barnyard animals for petting, ponies for riding, and even cows for milking.

Admission: $6 adults, $5.50 children under 12

Open: Daily 10am–5pm.

Rice's Country Market, Solebury, PA 18963. ☎ **215/297-5993.**
Rice's Market is the real thing—a quality market of country goods and crafts. Amish wares are sold in the main building, along with antiques and collectibles; many outdoor stalls get taken also.

Admission: $5, including parking.

Open: Tues 6am–noon. Get there early. **Directions:** Route 263 south toward Peddler's Village (Route 202), right onto Aquetong Road for two miles, then a right onto Green Hill Road.

WHERE TO STAY

New Hope and its New Jersey neighbor across the Delaware River, Lambertville, have well-deserved reputations for their country inns and restaurants. All used to require 2-day stays and frown on children, but Sesame Place's success is changing this. The listings here only scratch the surface; other choices might include **Inn at Phillips Mill** in New Hope (☎ **215/862-2984**) or **The Buchsville House** in Kintnersville (☎ **215/847-8948**).

Country Inns

⭐ **Centre Bridge Inn,** P.O. Box 74, Rte. 32, New Hope, PA 18938. ☎ **215/862-2048.** 9 rms. AC
Rates: $60–$105 weekday single or double; $90–$135 weekend single or double. AE, MC, V. **Parking:** Free.

Situated beside the Delaware River 3¹/₂ miles north of New Hope, the current building is the third since the early 18th century. Many of the elegant guest rooms have canopy, four-poster, or brass beds; wall-high armoires; modern private baths; outside decks; and views of the river or countryside. Five rooms have TVs.

Evermay-On-The-Delaware, River Rd., Erwinna, PA 18920. ☎ **610/294-9100.** Fax 610/294-8249. 16 rms, 1 carriage house suite. AC TEL
Rates (including continental breakfast and 4pm tea): $55–$80 single; $85–$160 double; $200 suite. MC, V. **Parking:** Free.
Thirteen miles north of New Hope on River Road in Erwinna lies this gracious historic inn. Combining privacy with a romantic setting overlooking the Delaware, Evermay once hosted the Barrymores for croquet weekends. The inn now offers rooms with luxurious antique furnishings. At a 7:30pm seating on Friday, Saturday, Sunday, and holidays, the formal dining room offers an excellent prix-fixe six-course $48 dinner that's open to the public as well; reserve well in advance.

⭐ **Whitehall Inn,** 1370 Pineville Rd., New Hope, PA 18938. ☎ **215/598-7945.** 6 rms (4 with bath). AC TEL
Rates: $130–$180 per night, single or double. Includes four course breakfast and 4pm high tea. Two-night minimum. AE, DC, MC, V. **Parking:** Free.

Four miles outside New Hope is this 18th-century manor house on a former horse farm, complete with a pool. Mike and Suella Wass serve magnificent four-course breakfasts, and their "innsmanship" is nationally known, with such touches as fresh fruit bowls, a bottle of mineral water in every room, and afternoon tea concerts.

Hotels and Motels

Comfort Inn, 3660 Street Rd., Bensalem, PA 19020. ☎ **215/245-0100** or toll free **800/458-6886.** 141 rms. AC TV TEL
Rates: $43–$58 single; $53–$68 double. Includes good continental breakfast. AE, DC, MC, V.
Parking: Free.

For moderate lodgings in Bucks County, this is one of the best choices, off I-95 about 20 miles from Washington Crossing and 5 miles from Sesame Place. The inn is a modern, bright three-story property with either two double beds or a king-size bed in each room. There's also an exercise room. There's only one elevator, so get used to the stairs.

New Hope Motel In The Woods, 400 W. Bridge St., New Hope, PA 18938. ☎ **215/862-2800.** 28 rms. AC TV
Rates: $54 single; $64 double. AE, DC, MC, V. **Parking:** Free.

Just a mile west of town is this motel tucked in a peaceful woodland setting off Route 179. For over 30 years, it has offered modern ground-level rooms with private baths and standard motel amenities. Open all year, it has a swimming pool that's open during the summer.

Sheraton Bucus County Hotel, 400 Oxford Valley Rd., Langhorne, PA 19047. ☎ **215/547-4100** or toll free **800/325-3535.** 167 rms. A/C TV TEL
Rates: $125–$135 single or double. AE, DC, MC, V. **Parking:** Free.

This festive, modern 14-story hotel opened right across the street from Sesame Place in 1987. The soundproof guest rooms have oversized beds and quilted fabrics, many with extra sofa beds. Other facilities include a health club, a swimming pool and sauna, and a full-service restaurant.

WHERE TO DINE

Karla's, 5 W. Mechanic St., New Hope, PA 18938. ☎ **215/862-2612.**
Cuisine: INTERNATIONAL. **Reservations:** Recommended for dinner.
Prices: Appetizers $3.50–$8; main courses $13–$19; lunch $3.95–$7.95. AE, DC, MC, V.
Open: Sun–Thurs 11am–10pm, Fri–Sat 11am–4am.

In the heart of New Hope, next door to the Information Center, this lively and informal restaurant offers three settings—a sunlit conservatory with ceiling fans, stained glass, and plants; a gallery room with local artists' works; and a bistro with marble tabletops. The eclectic menu offers grilled rib-eye steak, veal francese, and chicken breast with Thai ginger sauce. The lunch items are tamer.

Odette's Fine Country Dining, S. River Rd. and Rte. 32, New Hope, PA 18938. ☎ **215/862-3000.**
Cuisine: INTERNATIONAL. **Reservations:** Recommended.

Prices: Appetizers $6.95–$8.95; main courses $14.95–$24.95; lunch $6.95–$9.95. AE, DC, MC, V.
Open: Lunch Mon–Sat 11:30am–3pm; dinner Mon–Fri 5–10pm, Sat 5–11pm, Sun 3–10pm; brunch, Sun 10:30am–2:30pm.

Surrounded by the river and the canal on the southern edge of town, this elegant restaurant has been an inn since 1794. The previous owner, Odette Myrtil, was a Ziegfeld Follies girl whose memorabilia adorns the place. The menus are seasonal and change thrice annually, providing nice twists on standard bases of steak, seafood, duck, and veal. There is also a weekend cabaret.

Doylestown Area

The triangle where U.S. 202 (west of New Hope), Pa. 313 (south of Scranton), and U.S. 611 (that's North Broad Street in Philadelphia) intersect defines Doylestown, the county seat. It's a pleasant town just to walk around, but three interesting collections in town invite you indoors. They were all endowed by the same man, Dr. Henry Chapman Mercer (1856–1930). Mercer was a collector, local archeologist, and master of pottery techniques.

WHAT TO SEE

★ **Fonthill Museum,** E. Court St., off Swamp Rd. (Rte. 313), Doylestown, PA 18901. ☎ **215/348-9461.**

Not many people can call their home a castle, but Dr. Mercer could, and the castle even was built with reinforced concrete of his own design. The core of the building is a 19th-century farmhouse, but towers, turrets, and tiles have been amassed beyond belief. All the rooms are of different shapes, and each has tiles of Mercer's collection set into the chamber.

Admission: $5 adults, $4.50 seniors, $1.50 children.

Open: Mon–Sat 10am–5pm, Sun noon–5pm. **Closed:** New Year's Day, Thanksgiving Day, and Christmas. Guided tours only; reservations are recommended.

Moravian Pottery And Tile Works, Swamp Rd., Doylestown, PA 18901. ☎ **215/345-6722.**

Down the road on Pa. 313, the Moravian Pottery and Tile Works was Dr. Mercer's next big project. It's also made of reinforced concrete. If you go to the State Capitol in Harrisburg, you can see over 400 mosaics from here that illustrate the history of Pennsylvania. The working ceramists at the pottery today turn out tiles, mosaics, and pottery available through the museum shop.

Admission: $2.50 adults, $1 youths, $2 seniors.

Open: Daily 10am–4:45pm. Tours are given every 30 minutes. **Closed:** Major holidays.

★ **Mercer Museum,** Pine St. at Ashland St., Doylestown, PA 18901. ☎ **215/345-0210.**

Mercer Museum displays thousands of early American tools, vehicles, cooking pieces, looms, and even weather vanes. Mercer had the collecting bug in a big way, and you can't help being impressed with the breadth of the collection and the castle that houses it. It rivals the Shelburne, Vt., complex—and that's 35 buildings on 100 acres! The open atrium rises five stories, and suspends a Conestoga wagon, chairs, and sleighs as if they were Christmas-tree ornaments. During the summer, a log cabin, a schoolhouse, and other large bits of American life are open for inspection.

Admission: Museum and library, $5 adults, $4.50 seniors, $1.50 youths.

Open: Mon–Sat 10am–5pm, Sun noon–5pm, Tues 5–9pm. Spruance Library (Bucks County history), Tues 1–9pm, Wed–Sat 10am–5pm. **Closed:** Thanksgiving Day and Christmas.

WHERE TO DINE

★ **Sign of the Sorrel Horse,** Old Bethlehem Rd., Quakertown. ☎ **215/536-4651.**

Cuisine: FRENCH. **Reservations:** Required. Jackets recommended for men. **Directions:** Go 10 miles north of Doylestown on Route 313. Take Route 563 north for 2 miles, then turn left onto Old Bethlehem. The restaurant is a quarter mile on the left.

Prices: Appetizers $4.50–$11.95; main courses $16.95–$24.95. MC, V.

Open: Dinner only, Wed–Sun 5:30–9pm.

This is the best restaurant in the Doylestown area, with a husband-and-wife team who have trained at the Cordon Bleu school. It contains three dining rooms in a 1749 building, overlooking the kitchen herb gardens. The menu is rich, with smoked sea scallops, lobster, and filet mignon—all served with fresh reductions and mousses. The ice cream is homemade with honey, not sugar. **Note:** Jon Atlim is contemplating moving to the former Pear & Partridge on Old Easton Road, just outside Doylestown.

3 Montgomery County

Montgomery County is a region of rivers, hills, fall foliage, and Main Line suburban development. It's best known for Valley Forge, Washington's winter headquarters at the nadir of the Revolutionary War, but it has everything from a Frank Lloyd Wright synagogue (Beth Sholom in Elkins Park) to Pennsylvania Dutch festivals (the Goschenhoppen Folk Festival held in mid-August in East Greenville).

INFORMATION I can't describe more than a few of the major attractions here, so call or write to the **Valley Forge Convention and Visitors Bureau,** 600 W. Germantown Pike, Plymouth Meeting, PA 19462 (☎ **610/834-1550** or toll free **800/345-8112**), for particulars on recreation, annual events, campgrounds, and historic sites.

Valley Forge

WHAT TO SEE

Valley Forge National Historical Park, Rte. 23 and N. Gulph Rd., Valley Forge, PA 19481. ☎ **610/783-1077.**

Only 30 minutes from central Philadelphia and a half-day excursion in itself now, Valley Forge was hours of frozen trails away in the winter of 1777 to 1778. The Revolutionary forces had just lost the battles of Brandywine and Germantown. While the British occupied Philadelphia, Washington's forces repaired to winter quarters near an iron forge where the Schuylkill met Valley Creek, 18 miles northeast. A sawmill and gristmill were supposed to help provide basic requirements, but they had been destroyed by the British. Some 12,000 men and boys straggled into the encampment, setting up quarters and lines of defense.

Unfortunately, the winter turned bitter, with six inches of snow and iced-up rivers. Critical shortages of food and clothing, along with damp shelters, left nearly 4,000 men diseased and unfit for duty. Almost 2,000 perished, and many others deserted. Congress, which had left Philadelphia hurriedly, couldn't persuade the colonies to give money to alleviate the conditions. Nevertheless, the forces slowly gained strength and confidence, due in part to the Prussian army veteran Baron von Steuben, appointed by Washington to retrain the Continental Army under his revised and distinctly American "Manual of Arms." By springtime the Continentals were an army on which their new allies, the French, could rely. Replicas of their huts, some of the officers' lodgings, and later memorials dot the park today.

Start your visit at the **Visitor Center** (☎ **215/783-7700**), located at the junction of Pa. 23 and North Gulph Road. A 15-minute film depicting the encampment is shown here every half hour. Also at the Visitor Center is a museum containing Washington's tent, an extensive collection of Revolutionary War artifacts, and a bookstore.

Highlights within the park include the **National Memorial Arch;** an 1865 covered bridge; the **Isaac Potts House** (1770), which Washington commandeered as his headquarters; and the 1993 Monument to Patriots of African Descent.

If you're here in late April or early May, you'll see the magnificent dogwood blossoms.

That Gothic chapel (1903) houses the **Washington Memorial Chapel** (it's free, with Sunday carillon recitals in the bell tower at 2pm), next to the Valley Forge Historical Society Museum (see below). Like the memorial arch, the chapel seems to honor an American hero in a peculiarly European way, with flags and stained-glass medievalism.

Admission: Free; $2 adult admission to historic buildings.

Guided Tours: Autotape tour is $8 for two hours; tour bus service from the Visitor Center, $5.50 adults, $4.50 ages 5 to 16, toddlers, free.

Open: Daily 8:30am–5pm, later in summer. **Directions:** Access is from Exit 24 of the Pennsylvania Turnpike or Exit 25 of the Schuylkill Expressway (I-76) to Route 363. Follow the signs. By bus, take SEPTA no. 45 from the Visitors Center at 16th Street and John F. Kennedy Boulevard to King of Prussia Plaza, then take the hourly no. 99 bus to the park.

Valley Forge Historical Society Museum, Rte. 23, Valley Forge. ☎ **610/783-0535.**

The museum, next to Washington Memorial Chapel, has a large collection of Washingtoniana and the deposits of history.

Admission: $2 adults, $1.50 seniors, $1 children 2–12.

Open: Mon–Sat 9:30am–4:30pm, Sun 1–4:30pm. **Closed:** Easter Day and Christmas.

Mill Grove, Audubon and Pawlings Rds., Box 25, Audubon PA 19407. ☎ **610/666-5593.**

Two miles north of Valley Forge (take Audubon Road, which parallels Route 422, and make a left off Pa. 363 just over the Schuylkill River), **Mill Grove** preserves 170 acres of wildlife sanctuary around the home of the young John James Audubon. Now the fieldstone mansion with Georgian touches and a kitchen wing is decorated with murals of birdlife and Audubon's observance of it. Outside, miles of walks among nature's calls and chirps make it easy to linger here for an afternoon. You're welcome to walk but not to picnic or pick.

Admission: Free.

Open: Museum, Tues–Sun 10am–4pm. Grounds, dawn to dusk. **Closed:** Major holidays.

SHOPPING

King of Prussia Court and Plaza, near junction of U.S. 202 and Pa. 363, half mile south of I-276; 3 miles south of Valley Forge National Historical Park via Rte. 422. ☎ **215/265-5727.**

People have always been drawn to King of Prussia because of its name. The King of Prussia mall, called the Court and Plaza, is now one of the finest in the country, with 300 establishments in three separate sections. The major stores of the 130 include Bloomingdale's, Strawbridge & Clothier, and Sears. And by 1996, a 135-store expansion will add a Lord & Taylor, a Nordstrom's, and much more. Choose from 15 restaurants, 12 shoe stores, 6 jewelers (including Bailey, Banks, and Biddle of Center City in Philadelphia), and 24 clothing stores.

Open: Mon–Sat 10am–9:30pm, Sun 11am–5pm.

WHERE TO STAY

Comfort Inn At Valley Forge, 550 W. DeKalb Pike, King of Prussia, PA 19406. ☎ **610/962-0700** or toll free **800/222-0222.** Fax 610/962-0218. 121 rms. AC TV TEL

Rates: 75 single; $85 double. Weekend packages from $75. AAA and CAA discounts are available. AE, DC, MC, V. **Parking:** Free.

This inn is only a mile from the Valley Forge National Park, which makes it good for families. It has five floors. VCRs are built into the TVs.

Facilities: Coin-operated laundry; fitness center.
Services: Complimentary newspaper; free HBO.

Sheraton Valley Forge Hotel, N. Gulph Rd. and 1st Ave., Valley Forge, PA 19406. ☎ **610/337-2000** or toll free **800/325-3535.** Fax 610/768-3222. 327 rms, 72 fantasy suites. AC MINIBAR TV TEL
Rates: $110–$120 single; $120–$130 double; from $160 suites. AE, DC, MC, V. **Parking:** Free.

This is a busy high-rise complex with rooms, suites, five restaurants, and two lounges, all of primary interest to getaway weekenders. The fantasy suites, ranging from Caveman, Wild West, and Pre-Raphaelite to Futurist, are remarkably popular.

Dining: Five restaurants, including Lily Langtry's and Chumley's Steak and Sea Food.

Facilities: Health club ($15 additional) open until 12:30am, with Nautilus machines, racquetball courts, a whirlpool, a tanning bed, and a steam room; outdoor pool; dedicated no-smoking floors.

Services: Valet parking, complimentary newspapers.

West of Valley Forge

WHAT TO SEE

Ridley Creek State Park, Pa. 3 (West Chester Pike) 3 miles past Newtown Square, Sycamore Mills Rd., Media, PA 19063.
☎ **610/566-4800;** and **Colonial Pennsylvania Plantation,** within park, P.O. Box 150, Edgemont, PA 19028.
☎ **610/566-1725.**

Ridley Creek State Park is about 15 miles west of Center City, 17 miles from the Valley Forge interchange, and 7 miles north of Media and I-95 via Pa. 352. It has two unusual attractions: the bonafide Colonial Pennsylvania Plantation, handed down straight from William Penn's charter; and a superb park with miles of picnic areas, playgrounds, and hiking and cycling trails. The plantation is the best example in the area of how a "yeoman," or common, family lived in virtual self-sufficiency on a colonial farm. It's staffed mostly by talented schoolteachers who come summer after summer to build wood fences, garden and grow corn, tend pigs and shear sheep, and weave cloth for clothes. Children love it.

Admission: Park, Free. Plantation $2.50 adults, $1.50 seniors and children 4–12.

Open: Park, daily 8am–dusk. Plantation, Apr–June and Oct Fri–Sun 10am–5pm; July–Aug Thurs–Sun 10am–5pm.

Skippack Village, on Pa. 73.

Skippack Creek, which feeds into the Schuylkill near Mill Grove, runs along Pa. 73 near the junction of Pa. 113. To get to Skippack Village, follow Pa. 363 north to Pa. 73. The main entrepreneurs have refurbished about 40 colonial and Federal manses as restaurants and shops. As you'd expect, antiques and collectibles rate high on the popularity list, but you can also pursue casual clothes and international dolls. The restaurants here include the moderately priced **Trolley Stop** (☎ **610/584-4849**).

WHERE TO DINE

Skippack Roadhouse, 4022 Skippack Pike (Rte. 73), Skippack. ☎ **610/584-4231.**

Cuisine: AMERICAN. **Reservations:** Recommended.
Prices: Main courses $8–$12 at lunch, $13–$24 at dinner. AE, DC, MC, V.
Open: Lunch Mon–Sat 11:30am–2:30pm; dinner Mon–Thurs 5–9pm, Fri–Sat 5–10pm, Sun 4:30–8:30pm. Jazz on Fri and Sat.

This is an elegant, charming country roadhouse—with a white tile bar, mirrors, and fresh flowers—composed of six intimate dining rooms. The extensive blackboard specials of seasonal items include game and fresh fish and traditional meals of beef, chicken, and lamb.

---

4 Brandywine Valley

The Brandywine Valley is a great 1- or 2-day excursion into rolling country filled with Americana from colonial days through the Gilded Age. Most of the outstanding attractions are on the Delaware side, most of the historic inns and restaurants in Pennsylvania.

Many of the farms that kept the Revolutionary troops fed have survived to this day. There are 15 covered bridges and 100 antique stores in Chester County alone, with miles of country roads and horse trails between them. Spring and fall are particularly colorful, and don't forget Delaware's tax-free shopping.

Brandywine Valley is particularly rich in history. Without the defeat at Brandywine, Washington would never have ended up at Valley Forge, from which he emerged with a competent army. When the Du Pont de Nemours family fled post-Revolutionary France, they wound up owning powder mills on the Brandywine Creek. Every pioneer needed gunpowder and iron, and their business grew astronomically, expanding into chemicals and textiles. The Du Ponts controlled upper Delaware as a virtual fiefdom, building splendid estates and gardens. Most of these, along with the original mills, are open to visitors. Winterthur houses the finest collection of American decorative arts ever assembled, and artists like Pyle and Wyeth left rich collections now on public view.

Getting There

I-95 South from Philadelphia has various exits north of Wilmington marked for specific sites, most of which are off Exit 7 to Pa. 52 North. If you have time, Pa. 100 off this, linking West Chester to Wilmington, passes through picturesque pastureland, forest, and crops. For more information, call the **Brandywine Valley Tourist Information Center,** just outside the gates of **Longwood Gardens** at **215/388-2900** or toll free **800/343-3983.** For motorists on I-95,

Delaware maintains a visitors information center just south of Wilmington, between routes 272 and 896. It operates from 8am to 8pm.

Chadds Ford

Land where a Native American trail (now U.S. 1) forded the Brandywine Creek was purchased from William Penn by Francis Chadsey, an early Quaker immigrant. The present **Chadds Ford Inn,** at the junction of U.S. 1 and U.S. 100 (☎ **215/388-7361**) became one of the village's first requirements, a tavern. Taverns were important to small villages in the middle colonies; they served as mail depots, law courts, election hustings, and occasionally prisons. Before the Battle of Brandywine, Washington's officers stayed at the inn; afterward, British troops slaughtered the cattle before marching on the capital of Philadelphia. A small shopping area augments the premises.

The **Brandywine Battlefield State Park** (☎ **215/459-3342**) is a couple of miles east of Chadds Ford on Route 1. It has no monuments (since the guides say the actual battle was fought outside park borders), but Washington's and Lafayette's reconstructed headquarters mark the site. The park is open Tuesday to Saturday from 9am to 5pm; Sunday from noon to 5pm. The grounds, which are excellent for picnicking and hiking, are open from Memorial Day to Labor Day until 8pm.

WHAT TO SEE

★ **Longwood Gardens,** Rte. 1 just west of the junction of Pa. 52, Kennett Square, PA 19348. ☎ **215/388-6741.**

This is simply one of the world's great garden displays. Pierre S. Du Pont devoted his life to horticulture; he bought a 19th-century arboretum and created the ultimate estate garden on 1,000 acres. Some 300 of these are open to the public. You should plan a half day here.

A Visitor Center has a multimedia briefing of the estate's aim. Most people head to the left, toward the Main Fountain Garden, with special evening shows of fluid fireworks mid-June through August at 9:15pm on Tuesday, Thursday, and Saturday. Wrought-iron chairs and clipped trees and shrubs overlook the jets of water, which rise up to 130 feet. A topiary garden of closely pruned trees surrounds a 37-foot sundial.

If you prefer indoors, four acres of massive bronze and glass conservatories are among the finest and largest in the United States. Orangery displays are breathtaking. African violets, bonsai trees up to 400 years old, hibiscus, orchids, and tropical plants are the staples, but look for anything from Easter lilies to scarlet begonias. Subsections display desert plants, plants of economic utility, and roses, among others. The plants are exhibited only at their peak and are replaced with others from the extensive growing houses. A parquet-floor ballroom was later added, along with a 10,000-pipe organ, a magnificent instrument played during the year and on winter Sunday afternoons.

Ahead and to the right of the Visitor Center, more gardens and fountains await along with hints of Mr. Du Pont's residence and lifestyle. Two restaurants (one a cafeteria) are available for surprisingly good meals.

Admission: $10 adults, $2 children 6–14; children under 6 free.
Parking: Free.

Open: April–Oct, daily 9am–6pm (conservatories until 5pm); Nov–March, daily 9am–5pm.

★ **Brandywine River Museum,** Rtes. 1 and 100, Chadds Ford, PA 19317. ☎ **215/459-1900.**

Virtually across the road from the Brandywine Battlefield State Park, the museum showcases the Brandywine school and other American painters. A 19th-century gristmill has been restored and joined by a dramatic spiral of brick and glass, and the museum's paintings hang in beamed galleries with pine floors. A new wing contains a gallery devoted to paintings by Andrew Wyeth. Howard Pyle, a painter and illustrator of adventure tales in the late 19th century, established a school nearby; his students included N. C. Wyeth, Frank Schoonover, and Harvey Dunn. Three generations of Wyeths, from N. C., Carolyn, and Andrew, to Jamie, have stayed, and the museum is particularly strong in their works. Many of the museum's exhibits display the art of book and magazine illustration at its pretelevision zenith.

Admission: $4 adults, $2 children under 12.

Open: 9:30am–4:30pm daily. A self-service restaurant is open from 11am to 3pm.

★ **Winterthur Museum and Gardens,** Rte. 52, Winterthur, DE 19735. ☎ **302/888-4600** or toll free **800/448-3883. Directions:** 6 miles northwest of Wilmington on Rte. 52.

The later home of the Du Ponts now provides the setting for America's best native collection of decorative arts. Henry Francis Du Pont, a great-grandson of E. I. Du Pont, was a connoisseur of European antiques. But when he turned his attention to a simple Pennsylvania Dutch chest in 1923, he realized that no study had illustrated how American pieces are related to European ones and how the concepts of beauty and taste differed in the two continents. Du Pont collected furniture, then native decorative objects, then interior woodwork of entire homes built between 1640 and 1840. Finally, he added over 200 rooms to put them on display. Because the museum was first a private home, the rooms have a unique richness and intimacy.

Winterthur' provides a variety of tours. The Main Museum displays the bulk of the collection and includes complete interiors from every eastern seaboard colony. Two guided tours cover special items such as the famous Montmorenci Stair Hall, two Shaker Rooms, fine examples of Pennsylvania Dutch decorative arts, and the Du Pont dining room. The tours—reservations are required—cost $12.50 for adults and $6 for young adults; children under 12 are not admitted.

In spring the extensive Winterthur Gardens explode with an abundance of cherry and crabapple blossoms, rhododendrons, Virginia bluebells, and azaleas. The lush, carefully planned gardens are well worth viewing any season. Admission to the gardens is $4 for adults and $2.50 for students, seniors, and children. Garden tram rides through the grounds are available when weather permits. There is a superb gift shop and a Garden Pavilion Restaurant seating 350.

Admission: The general-admission ticket available year-round includes a "Two Centuries Tour," a guided tour of chronologically displayed exhibits from the 17th century through the Empire period. The cost is $9 for adults, $7.50 for senior citizens, and $6.50 students over 12; children 12 and under are free. Reservations are not required.

Open: Tues–Sat 9:30am–5pm, Sun noon–5pm: **Closed:** Mon and major holidays.

★ **Hagley Museum**, Rte. 141, Wilmington, DE 19807.
☎ **302/658-2400.**

Directions: Pa. 52 to the junction of Del. 100 and Del. 141, then follow directions on 141.

The northern part of Delaware saw early skirmishes among the Swedes, Dutch, and English, and the Revolution was never far away. Since the early 1800s this has been Du Pont country, and the Hagley Museum shows how and when they got their start. It's a wonderful illustration of early American industrialism and manufacturing.

Hagley has four parts: an exhibit hall with introductory film, the museum building, the reconstructed grounds, and the Upper Residence. The museum building covers the harnessing of the Brandywine River, originally for flour mills; the Du Ponts, who made their first fortune in gunpowder, needed waterpower and willow charcoal—both were here, and the raw materials a barge ride away. E. Irénée Du Pont, the founder, had experience in France with gunpowder and lived at the Upper Residence (despite explosions, which happened every decade or so) to supervise the delicate production process.

Jitneys traverse the tour of the powder yard, but it's just as easy to walk between private family roads on the Upper Residence and the burbling Brandywine. A restored New Century Power House (1880) generates electricity here. The machine shop explains the production of black gunpowder; other buildings include the blacksmith shop, the schoolhouse for workers' children, and a foreman's home. None of the dormitories that housed the workers, symbolically under the presence of the Du Ponts at all times, survived. Next to the electrical generator, a waterwheel, steam engine, and water turbine show improvements in power through the decades.

The wisteria-covered residence of the Du Ponts was renovated by a member of the fourth generation, Mrs. Louis Crowninshield, who lived there until her death in 1958. The first floor reflects her taste for integrating French elegance with country vigor.

Admission: $8 adults, $6.50 seniors, $3 students; children under 6 free.

Open: Mar–Dec, daily 9:30am–4:30pm; Jan–Mar Sat–Sun 9:30am–4:30pm. Upper Eleutherian Mills Residence opens seasonally in spring and fall.

WHERE TO STAY

$ **Abbey Green Motor Lodge,** 1036 Wilmington Pike (Rte. 202), West Chester, PA 19382. ☎ **215/692-3310.** 18 rms. AC TV TEL

Rates: $42–55 single or double. AE, DC, MC, V. **Parking:** Free.

An excellent budget choice, close by the battlefield site at scenic routes 52 and 100. The family-run motel is designed in a courtyard set back from the road with its own picnic tables, gazebo, and outdoor fireplace. All rooms have double beds and a refrigerator, and six units have individual fireplaces.

★ **Brandywine River Hotel,** Rtes. 1 and 100, P.O. Box 1058, Chadds Ford, PA 19317-1058. ☎ **215/388-1200.** Fax 215/388-1200, ext. 301. 40 rms, 4 suites. AC TV TEL

Rates: $119 single; $125 double, including continental breakfast. AE, DC, MC, V. **Parking:** Free.

This 1988 hotel blends into a hillside in the heart of Brandywine Valley, with a facade of brick and cedar shingle, steps away from Chadds Ford Inn restaurant. The lobby has a huge open stone fireplace and friendly service, and guest rooms are decorated with Queen Anne cherry-wood furnishings, brass fixtures, chintz fabrics, and local paintings. Breakfast is served in an attractive "hospitality room" with a fireplace.

$ **Meadow Spring Farm,** 201 E. Street Rd., Kennett Square, PA 19348. ☎ **215/444-3903.** 6 rms, 3 with bath. $10 per child in parents' room. AC TV

Rates: $55–75 single or double, including full country breakfast. No credit cards. Two-night minimum on weekends. **Parking:** Free.

Anne Hicks operates this working 1936 farmhouse, complete with 250 cows, sheep, and poultry. Rooms come with Amish quilts, and common areas display family antiques and dolls. Families are welcome.

Facilities: Outdoor pool, hot tub in solarium, game room, pond.

You might also try **Guesthouses B&B,** R.D. 9, West Chester, PA 19380 (☎ **215/692-4575;** open noon to 4pm); they have dozens of charming rooms at rates from $31. Two weeks' notice is required.

WHERE TO DINE

Of the many inns and restaurants connected to them, try the **Chadds Ford Inn,** routes 1 and 100, Chadds Ford (☎ **215/388-7361**), with its Wyeth paintings; **Dilworthtown Inn,** Old Wilmington Pike and Brinton's Bridge Road, Dilworthtown (☎ **215/399-1390**), for homegrown vegetables and game birds amid 11 fireplaces; and **Longwood Inn,** 815 E. Baltimore Pike (Route 1), Kennett Square (☎ **215/444-3515**), showing off this area's position as a mushroom capital of the world.

Index

Now Save Money On All Your Travels By Joining
FROMMER'S™ TRAVEL BOOK CLUB
The World's Best Travel Guides At
Membership Prices!

Frommer's Travel Book Club is your ticket to successful travel! Open up a world of travel informationand simplify your travel planning when you join ranks with thousands of value-conscious travelers who are members of the *Frommer's Travel Book Club*. Join today and you'll be entitled to all the privileges that come from belonging to the club that offers you travel guides for less to more than 100 destinations worldwide. **Annual membership is only $25.00 (U.S.) or $35.00 (Canada/Foreign).**

The Advantages of Membership:

1. Your choice of **three free** books (any **two** *Frommer's Comprehensive Guides, Frommer's $-A-Day Guides, Frommer's Walking Tours* or *Frommer's Family Guides*—plus **one** *Frommer's City Guide, Frommer's City $-A-Day Guide* or *Frommer's Touring Guide*).
2. Your own subscription to the **TRIPS & TRAVEL** quarterly newsletter.
3. You're entitled to a **30% discount** on your order of any additional books offered by the club.
4. You're offered (at a small additional fee) our **Domestic Trip-Routing Kits.**

Our **Trips & Travel** quarterly newsletter offers practical information on the best buys in travel, the "hottest" vacation spots, the latest travel trends, world-class events and much, much more.

Our **Domestic Trip-Routing Kits** are available for any North American destination. We'll send you a detailed map highlighting the best route to take to your destination—you can request direct or scenic routes.

Here's all you have to do to join:

Send in your membership fee of $25.00 ($35.00 Canada/Foreign) with your name and address on the form below along with your selections as part of your membership package to the address listed below. Remember to check off your three free books.

If you would like to order additional books, please select the books you would like and send a check for the total amount (please add sales tax in the states noted below), plus $2.00 per book for shipping and handling ($3.00 Canada/Foreign) to the address listed below.

FROMMER'S TRAVEL BOOK CLUB
P.O. Box 473
Mt. Morris, IL 61054-0473.
(815) 734-1104

[ ] **YES!** I want to take advantage of this opportunity to join Frommer's Travel Book Club.

[ ] My check is enclosed. Dollar amount enclosed   *
(all payments in U.S. funds only)

Name _____

Address _____

City _____ State _____ Zip _____

All orders must be prepaid.

To ensure that all orders are processed efficiently, please apply sales tax in the following areas: CA, CT, FL, IL, IN, NJ, NY, PA, TN, WA and CANADA.

*With membership, shipping & handling will be paid by Frommer's Travel Book Club for the three free books you select as part of your membership. Please add $2.00 per book for shipping & handling for any additional books purchased ($3.00 Canada/Foreign).

Allow 4-6 weeks for delivery. Prices of books, membership fee, and publication dates are subject to change without notice. Orders are subject to acceptance and availability.

Please send me the books checked below:

FROMMER'S COMPREHENSIVE GUIDES

(Guides listing facilities from budget to deluxe,
with emphasis on the medium-priced)

	Retail Price	Code		Retail Price	Code
☐ Acapulco/Ixtapa/Taxco, 2nd Edition	$13.95	C157	☐ Jamaica/Barbados, 2nd Edition	$15.00	C149
☐ Alaska '94-'95	$17.00	C131	☐ Japan '94-'95	$19.00	C144
☐ Arizona '95 (Avail. 3/95)	$14.95	C166	☐ Maui, 1st Edition	$13.95	C153
☐ Australia '94-'95	$18.00	C147	☐ Nepal, 2nd Edition	$18.00	C126
☐ Austria, 6th Edition	$16.95	C162	☐ New England '95	$16.95	C165
☐ Bahamas '94-'95	$17.00	C121	☐ New Mexico, 3rd Edition (Avail. 3/95)	$14.95	C167
☐ Belgium/Holland/ Luxembourg '93-'94	$18.00	C106	☐ New York State, 4th Edition	$19.00	C133
☐ Bermuda '94-'95	$15.00	C122	☐ Northwest, 5th Edition	$17.00	C140
☐ Brazil, 3rd Edition	$20.00	C111	☐ Portugal '94-'95	$17.00	C141
☐ California '95	$16.95	C164	☐ Puerto Rico '95-'96	$14.00	C151
☐ Canada '94-'95	$19.00	C145	☐ Puerto Vallarta/ Manzanillo/ Guadalajara '94-'95	$14.00	C028
☐ Caribbean '95	$18.00	C148	☐ Scandinavia, 16th Edition (Avail. 3/95)	$19.95	C169
☐ Carolinas/Georgia, 2nd Edition	$17.00	C128	☐ Scotland '94-'95	$17.00	C146
☐ Colorado, 2nd Edition	$16.00	C143	☐ South Pacific '94-'95	$20.00	C138
☐ Costa Rica '95	$13.95	C161	☐ Spain, 16th Edition	$16.95	C163
☐ Cruises '95-'96	$19.00	C150	☐ Switzerland/ Liechtenstein '94-'95	$19.00	C139
☐ Delaware/Maryland '94-'95	$15.00	C136	☐ Thailand, 2nd Edition	$17.95	C154
☐ England '95	$17.95	C159	☐ U.S.A., 4th Edition	$18.95	C156
☐ Florida '95	$18.00	C152	☐ Virgin Islands '94-'95	$13.00	C127
☐ France '94-'95	$20.00	C132	☐ Virginia '94-'95	$14.00	C142
☐ Germany '95	$18.95	C158	☐ Yucatan, 2nd Edition	$13.95	C155
☐ Ireland, 1st Edition (Avail. 3/95)	$16.95	C168			
☐ Italy '95	$18.95	C160			

FROMMER'S $-A-DAY GUIDES

(Guides to low-cost tourist accommodations and facilities)

	Retail Price	Code		Retail Price	Code
☐ Australia on $45 '95-'96	$18.00	D122	☐ Israel on $45, 15th Edition	$16.95	D130
☐ Costa Rica/Guatemala/ Belize on $35, 3rd Edition	$15.95	D126	☐ Mexico on $45 '95	$16.95	D125
☐ Eastern Europe on $30, 5th Edition	$16.95	D129	☐ New York on $70 '94-'95	$16.00	D121
☐ England on $60 '95	$17.95	D128	☐ New Zealand on $45 '93-'94	$18.00	D103
☐ Europe on $50 '95	$17.95	D127	☐ South America on $40, 16th Edition	$18.95	D123
☐ Greece on $45 '93-'94	$19.00	D100	☐ Washington, D.C. on $50 '94-'95	$17.00	D120
☐ Hawaii on $75 '95	$16.95	D124			
☐ Ireland on $45 '94-'95	$17.00	D118			